WITNESS TO NEPTUNE'S INFERNO

The Pacific War Diary of Lieutenant Commander
Lloyd M. Mustin, USS *Atlanta* (CL 51)

Presented by
DAVID F. WINKLER

CASEMATE
Pennsylvania & Yorkshire

Published in the United States of America and Great Britain in 2024 by
CASEMATE PUBLISHERS
1950 Lawrence Road, Havertown, PA 19083, USA
and
47 Church Street, Barnsley, S70 2AS, UK

Hardback Edition: ISBN 978-1-63624-407-5
Digital Edition: ISBN 978-1-63624-408-2

A CIP record for this book is available from the British Library

Printed and bound in the United Kingdom by CPI Group (UK) Ltd, Croydon, CR0 4YY

Typeset in India by Lapiz Digital Services, Chennai.

For a complete list of Casemate titles, please contact:

CASEMATE PUBLISHERS (US)
Telephone (610) 853-9131
Fax (610) 853-9146
Email: casemate@casematepublishers.com
www.casematepublishers.com

CASEMATE PUBLISHERS (UK)
Telephone (0)1226 734350
Email: casemate@casemateuk.com
www.casemateuk.com

Front cover: USS *Atlanta* conducting a high-speed run during Navy acceptance trials prior to commissioning. (Archives Branch, Naval History and Heritage Command, Washington, DC; NH 51382)

Back cover: The charred hull of the *Yamazuki Maru*.

Contents

Introduction

Following World War I, many American citizens blamed the naval arms race between Great Britain and Germany as having been a cause of the cataclysmic conflict and sought to contain further naval spending by the United States. Hearing these pacifist calls and desiring to trim the budget, President Warren Harding hosted a naval arms conference in Washington between 1921 and 1922. The resulting understanding between the five post-World War I naval powers of the United States, United Kingdom, Japan, France, and Italy led to a moratorium on new capital ship construction and the imposition of tonnage restrictions on the fleets of the five signatory nations.

Advocates for sea power, such as Capt. Dudley W. Knox, had opposed the building restrictions and were concerned about the anti-naval sentiments that had led to the conference. Recognizing the public relations value of American naval history to educate the public on the importance of maintaining a strong Navy, Knox published "Our Vanishing Naval History" in the January 1926 Naval Institute *Proceedings*, to alert readers that many primary source records needed for telling the Navy's story were packed away in the nation's attics and closets. To encourage the recovery of these historical resources, Knox argued for the creation of what would become the Naval Historical Foundation two months later in Washington, D.C.

The Foundation attained such success in answering Knox's clarion call as to fill a warehouse at Fort Washington, Maryland, with primary source records by the conclusion of World War II. Concerned about long-term preservation and accessibility to researchers, the Foundation's post-war president, retired Fleet Adm. Ernest J. King, arranged for the collection to be hosted by the Library of Congress Manuscript Division. Over the next half-century the Foundation would continue to collect and add to the Manuscript Division collection. In 1998, the Foundation's president, retired Adm. James L. Holloway III, ceded the whole collection to the Library of Congress for perpetuity. At that time Holloway had initiated another history collection effort. With a $20,000 grant provided by Ambassador William H. G. Fitzgerald, the Foundation hired yours truly, a graduate student, to conduct oral history work. That graduate student would attain his Ph.D. at American University and publish his dissertation on the Incidents at Sea Agreement (IncSea) between the United States and the Soviet Union. During the research for that dissertation,

I interviewed Vice Adm. Henry C. Mustin, who headed the Policy and Plans Division (OP-06) within the Office of the Chief of Naval Operations (OPNAV) during the mid-1980s and headed the American delegation during annual IncSea meetings with the Soviet Navy during a contentious period that included the Soviet shoot-down of Korean Airline Flight 007.

As the guy hired to set up an oral history program in 1996, I recruited volunteers to conduct and transcribe interviews with individuals that had been recommended to the Foundation as good candidates. Based on my dissertation research and time on active duty as a surface warfare officer, I knew we wanted to capture the rest of the "Hank" Mustin story. Happily, the admiral was agreeable to host me and my volunteer partner, retired Capt. Bill Peerenboom, for a series of interviews covering a remarkable career that included riverine warfare in Vietnam and implementation of the Navy's Maritime Strategy of the 1980s. Chock full of informative nuggets, the interview has been repeatedly cited and quoted in numerous articles and books on U.S. naval strategy in the late Cold War as well as contributing material incorporated into John Fass Morton's *Mustin—A Naval Family of the 20th Century*. The interview remained posted for viewing at the Naval Historical Foundation's www.navyhistory.org website.

At the conclusion of one of our interview sessions, Vice Admiral Mustin pulled out a standard government-issue olive-green canvas-covered notebook and explained it was a diary kept by his father, Lloyd M. Mustin, from the time he had served as assistant gun boss in the light cruiser USS *Atlanta*. "Do you think this is something anyone would have an interest in?" he asked. Taking the diary back to the office, I quickly grasped the significance of the handwritten narrative of the war in the Pacific over the first 10 months of 1942. Hundreds of naval memoirs and oral histories have been written and recorded in the decades following World War II, and most are very good. However, they all were written or recorded with the benefit of hindsight. Knowing the outcome has a certain influence in the telling of the story. In contrast, Lloyd Mustin's diary offered a real-time perspective of a mid-grade officer who was unaware of what the next day may bring.

Though Lloyd's penmanship was better than mine, my first course of action was to have the diary typed out into a Word document that could be shared with the family. The executive director of the Foundation, the late Capt. Ken Coskey, supported the idea. Chief Yeoman Frank Arre, who was assigned to the Naval Historical Center (now the Naval History and Heritage Command) to be sub-assigned to the Foundation as a flag writer for former Chief of Naval Operations Admiral Holloway, proved up for the task. Digital copies of the diary were shared with the family, which included the aforementioned John Fass Morton, who found it useful for his 2003 book that was published just prior to the commissioning of the destroyer USS *Mustin* (DDG 89).

Besides members of the Mustin family, I shared copies of the diary with some of the junior officers of the *Atlanta* wardroom whom I interviewed to attain backstory material. Ed Corboy was trained as a journalist and would publish a series of articles about the "*Mighty A's*" exploits in the *Chicago Tribune*. Another "JO," Robert Graff, was also generous with his time. Both lent insights to the formation of *Atlanta's* wardroom and crew in the weeks before Lloyd scribed his first diary entry. Graff subsequently sat down with James D. Hornfischer, who was gathering primary source material for his forthcoming *Neptune's Inferno: The U.S. Navy at Guadalcanal*. Not only did Hornfischer depart the interview with some good quotes from Graff, but he also copied the Mustin Diary and a self-published memoir written by Electrician's Mate William McKinney that Graff had earlier shared with me. Hornfischer quoted both sources in his outstanding book.

As the staff historian for the Naval Historical Foundation, as well as a commander in a Navy Reserve History Unit repeatedly recalled back to active duty to document American combat operations in Iraq and Afghanistan, more immediate priorities caused me to defer work on this project. Thus, when I learned of the passing of Vice Admiral Mustin on April 11, 2016, I was heartbroken, not only because of the loss of a great naval leader whom I visited on many occasions subsequent to our series of interviews, but because I felt I let him down by not getting this to press so that I could present him a copy of the finished product.

With that I redoubled efforts to build on the narrative that not only discussed Lloyd Mustin and his views on the ongoing conflict in the South Pacific, but also the operation of *Atlanta*, as that light cruiser approached that fateful Friday the 13th in November 1942. I approached the aforementioned James Hornfischer, as not only did he author several well-received works on U.S. Navy combat operations during World War II, but he served as a literary agent and helped several other aspiring authors get published. Hornfischer was most gracious in reviewing the manuscript I sent that topped over 200,000 words, and he kindly explained it was not ready for prime time, observing I was too ambitious in trying to cover all of this ocean in one manuscript. Subsequently, it was back to the drawing board. But again, I had to defer working on this project as I was selected to be the 2019–20 Class of '57 Chair of Naval Heritage at the U.S. Naval Academy followed by selection as the Charles Lindbergh Chair of Aerospace History at the Smithsonian Air and Space Museum during the pandemic years of 2020–21. Sadly, with Jim's untimely passing in 2021, he did not have the opportunity to review this more focused manuscript. In naming this *Witness to Neptune's Inferno*, I pay homage to Jim and his outstanding book that I heavily cite in this manuscript.

In addition to the tragic loss of life and widespread illness caused by COVID-19, the shutdown of the economy had negative consequences to the non-profit sector— especially those that relied on public gatherings to raise funding to sustain operations. Such was the case with the Naval Historical Foundation that held a congressionally approved memorandum of agreement with the Navy to lease the National Museum of the U.S. Navy for private receptions and its own income-generating events. Faced with what they saw as a financial "death spiral," the leadership of that organization opted to disestablish the organization and transfer remaining assets and some programming to the U.S. Naval Institute, despite the vigorous opposition of several members of the organization who attended a special membership meeting held in Washington on the 81st anniversary of the Japanese bombing of Pearl Harbor.

On the bright side, the disestablishment of the Naval Historical Foundation, at the close of 2022, has enabled this former staff historian the opportunity to complete this project that furthers the historical narrative of one of America's great naval families: the Mustins. Perhaps John Fass Morton was a bit premature in titling his 2003 book *Mustin: A Naval Family of the 20th Century*, as Vice Adm. Hank Mustin's youngest son John also achieved that rank on August 7, 2020, when he was named Chief of Navy Reserve. With the following generation of Mustins already in uniform and climbing through the ranks, this is clearly a naval family for both the 20th and 21st centuries.

I thank the team at Casemate for agreeing to publish and market this work. Thank you copy-editor Julie Frederick for your helpful wordsmithing. Of course, a final thanks goes out to my wife Mary and daughters Xepher and Carolyn for their support over the years.

CHAPTER I

The Naval Battle for Guadalcanal: The First Night

In 1999, Chief of Naval Operations, Adm. Jay Johnson, sent a message to all Navy commands directing an annual commemorative event to recognize the "courage and tenacity of Sailors who fought a vicious air and sea battle against overwhelming odds" to turn back the Japanese attempt to capture the islands at Midway in early June 1942. At many locations across the United States and overseas, this event would take the form of a "Dining In," a formal black-tie dinner with specific protocols for serving the meal and toasting afterwards. The intent was to replicate the long-standing "Trafalgar Night" tradition of the Royal Navy, where British sailors come together to celebrate Adm. Horatio Nelson's fabled victory over a combined French–Spanish fleet in 1805.[1]

Many have called Midway the U.S. Navy's "Trafalgar." Indeed, the Central Pacific sea battle that occurred from June 4 to 6, 1942, is one of the American armed forces' greatest triumphs. The destruction of four of the Imperial Japanese Navy's vaunted aircraft carriers that had launched aircraft a mere six months earlier against Pearl Harbor proved to be a stunning setback for the empire. However, the victory was no "Trafalgar" in that, unlike the French and the Spanish, the Japanese remained a very potent sea power. And unlike the British, who could exploit their victory to establish a blockade around the continent to squeeze Napoleon and his allies, the Americans had to focus on fighting a naval battle on another ocean, a battle that was not going well in mid-1942 as German U-boats were claiming hundreds of thousands of tons of vital shipping.

With the German Army advancing deep into the Soviet Union and pushing across North Africa toward the Middle East, the United States had to pursue a "Europe first" strategy. However, when the Japanese began construction to build an airstrip on Guadalcanal, an island on the southeastern end of a Southwest Pacific chain known as the Solomons, the United States had to act, as a Japanese airbase on that island would threaten shipping lanes between the United States and Australia. So on August 7, U.S. Marines stormed ashore and captured the nearly completed airstrip and named it Henderson Field, to honor a Marine flier who gave his life at Midway.

However, the Japanese refused to go quietly. Understanding the strategic importance of the island, they used the cover of darkness to repeatedly land reinforcements on the island. These troops, backed by Japanese naval bombardments and air attacks, launched repeated assaults against the Leathernecks to drive them off the island. The U.S. Navy attempted to interdict the Japanese reinforcement and bombardment missions with mixed success. From early August through to December there would be a series of vicious naval engagements contesting control of Guadalcanal that, if considered as one elongated sea battle, made Midway look like a mere skirmish. The waters between Guadalcanal and the adjacent island of Tulagi became known as Ironbottom Sound, for good reason.

The climax of Imperial Japan's effort to dislodge the American garrison from Guadalcanal occurred in mid-November 1942. Intercepts of Japanese radio transmissions and reports from coast watchers posted in southern Bougainville and the northern tip of that island warned of a massing of enough shipping to attempt the landing of an entire division on Guadalcanal. To support such a landing operation, Fleet Adm. Isoroku Yamamoto brought in units of the Combined Fleet. Vice Adm. William F. Halsey Jr., as the newly installed Commander South Pacific Area and South Pacific Forces, appreciated the consequences of Japanese reinforcements and countered the move with his own operation to place additional Marines and Army soldiers onto the island. Arriving at "Cactus," the code name for Guadalcanal, on November 8, Halsey met with Marine Maj. Gen. Alexander Vandegrift to assess the situation on the island and would not catch any rest that night thanks to a barrage from a Japanese destroyer. The sleep-deprived American commander may have taken some comfort in the knowledge that two convoys with American reinforcements were or would soon be en route.[2]

Halsey placed Rear Adm. Richmond K. Turner in tactical command of the American reinforcement operation to be conducted between November 11 and 12. Turner, designated as Commander Task Force 67, departed from Noumea, New Caledonia, during the afternoon of November 8 embarked on the transport *McCawley*. Three other transports, the heavy cruiser *Portland*, the light cruiser *Juneau*, and three destroyers, departed Noumea with *McCawley* to rendezvous early on November 11, southeast of San Cristobal Island with a group of warships coming from Espiritu Santo, New Hebrides. While en route, Turner's group would be joined by the destroyer *Shaw*. The Espiritu Santo group, having departed on the morning of November 10, was commanded by Rear Adm. Daniel J. Callaghan. Embarked on the heavy cruiser *San Francisco*, Callaghan also had tactical command of the heavy cruiser *Pensacola*, the light cruiser *Helena*, and six destroyers. However, he would have to send back the heavy cruiser along with two destroyers for use as part of another task force being formed by Halsey at Noumea. Another group, led by Rear Adm. Norman Scott, on board the light cruiser *Atlanta*, had four destroyers and three cargo ships depart Espiritu Santo on the morning of November 9 and got a head start.[3]

Despite efforts to evade enemy submarines and land-based patrol planes, a large Japanese floatplane spotted the Scott group early on November 10. Anticipating that Yamamoto would send a heavy naval force down from Rabaul to challenge the American reinforcement effort, Halsey deployed 24 submarines around the Solomon Islands. He then ordered a second task force to depart from Noumea consisting of the aircraft carrier *Enterprise*, battleships *South Dakota* and *Washington*, two cruisers, and eight destroyers to provide additional cover for the landing effort. However, with *Enterprise* still recovering from blows inflicted during an earlier engagement, the surface combatants sortied alone.[4]

Meanwhile, Scott's group with its three cargo vessels arrived at Guadalcanal early on November 11. Turner emphasized that a speedy unloading of the vessels would be critical to free up the combatant ships to assume defensive positions against oncoming enemy air and surface forces. At 0905, unloading operations were disrupted as a radio report from Guadalcanal told of incoming enemy bombers and fighters. Scott placed the three cargo ships in a column formation behind the *Atlanta* and his four destroyers on the flanks, all steaming on a northerly heading.

At 0938, *Atlanta* began to put up a barrage of steel, cutting down several of the attackers. Marine fighters from Henderson Field contributed to the spirited defense and accounted for several additional Japanese aircraft. Several of the enemy planes were able to drop their bombs, slightly damaging the cargo ships with near misses. One ship, the *Zeilin*, would need to return to Espiritu Santo that night to repair a flooded cargo hold. Cargo offloading continued, despite the distraction of another air attack nearly two hours later that focused on installations ashore.[5]

Later that evening, combatant vessels under Callaghan's command reached the vicinity in advance of Turner's transports. Callaghan's and Scott's ships joined together overnight to patrol waters adjacent to Guadalcanal. Early on the 12th, Turner's four transports arrived and started putting troops and additional equipment ashore, and the two remaining cargo ships from Scott's group resumed emptying their holds.

The reinforcement operation did not go unnoticed. A Japanese shore battery fired on Scott's cargo ships, and American shore and shipboard counterbattery activity soon forced the Japanese gun crew to cease fire.

In the early afternoon of the 12th, a coast watcher posted up the chain on the island of Buin radioed the approach of a flotilla of Japanese Betty bombers escorted by Zero fighters. Marine and Army fighters and pursuit aircraft from Henderson Field rose to meet the airborne foe, and Turner formed two columns with his transport and cargo ships and correctly positioned his air defense ships to give his gunners good target angles on the low-flying twin-engine bombers. The Japanese aircraft split into two groups to cross-bracket the Americans with air-dropped torpedoes, but Turner foiled the tactic by turning his ships perpendicular to one of the approaching groups. The Japanese pilots, seeing broadsides of American steel hulls ahead, swooped in low for the attack. The Americans savaged the oncoming Japanese bombers, dropping one after another into adjacent waters, and then turned hard left to allow those torpedoes that were dropped to run harmlessly on a parallel track. Fighters from Henderson Field ripped into the second group of bombers, forcing them to attack prematurely into withering antiaircraft fire. Again Turner's forces evaded dropped torpedoes streaming under the surface. Only one bomber escaped. In contrast, Turner's forces survived relatively unscathed. Friendly antiaircraft fire aimed at the bombers skimming just above the surface hit the destroyer *Buchanan*, and a damaged Japanese bomber crashed into *San Francisco*, killing 30 sailors and injuring more.[6]

Meanwhile, American scout planes had spotted elements of the Imperial Japanese Navy approaching from several bearings. One morning sighting placed two battleships or cruisers, a cruiser, and six destroyers some 335 miles to the north. Another pilot reported five destroyers coming in from the northwest. With no transports in company, Turner concluded that Admiral Yamamoto was setting the stage for a night bombardment. Indeed, the battleships *Hiei* and *Kirishima*, light cruiser *Nagara*, and 14 destroyers were to rendezvous and form a raiding party under the command of Vice Adm. Hiroaki Abe. Steaming past Savo Island into Ironbottom Sound, the Japanese gunships intended to rain tons of high explosives down on the Americans ashore and crater Henderson Field inoperable. With the shore-based U.S. air menace eliminated, 11 transports loaded with some 40,000 troops and supplies would be able to discharge their cargoes unmolested, tipping the balance ashore decidedly in Japan's favor.[7]

Safely escorting the unloaded transport vessels out of harm's way, Turner had little choice but to order his outgunned cruisers and destroyers to prevent a crushing bombardment on the American soldiers and Marines ashore. Unfortunately for Turner, the two American battlewagons en route with their escorts still had much distance to cover.

Turner, still embarked on *McCawley*, would not see action that night. Instead, he counted on his two subordinates, Callaghan and Scott, to carry the fight to the enemy. Callaghan, still embarked on *San Francisco*, had overall tactical command. The bridge of *Frisco* was familiar territory for "Uncle Dan" Callaghan, as he was dubbed by his sailors. Only six months earlier he paced the same deck plates as the ship's skipper. A graduate of the Naval Academy Class of 1911, his career path took him on duty on board several cruisers and battleships. Prior to the war, he had served as President Roosevelt's naval aide on a shore tour.[8]

To approach the restricted waters off the north side of Guadalcanal, Callaghan ordered his ships into a tactical formation known as "B-1" or "Baker-One"—simply a long column. The destroyers *Cushing*, *Laffey*, *Sterett*, and *O'Bannon* led the way, followed by *Atlanta* with Scott embarked, and then *San Francisco*, *Portland*, *Helena*, and *Juneau*. Four more destroyers brought up the rear. Samuel Eliot Morison later criticized Callaghan's formation as "it prevented the rear destroyers from making an initial torpedo attack." In addition, his two destroyers with the latest SG radar were also amongst those in the rear. Callaghan would never have the chance to defend his decision as he would not survive the battle.[9]

The converging Japanese forces had rendezvoused at mid-afternoon and proceeded at high speed toward the objective, not anticipating major opposition. Abe's two battleships, *Hiei* and *Kirishima*, steamed parallel, with *Nagara* and six destroyers positioned to screen the two capital ships. To thwart anticipated torpedo boat attacks, the Japanese commander placed two groups of destroyers ahead on the flanks.

For the Americans approaching from the southeast, the seas were calm as a slight breeze blew from the southeast. With the moon having gone over the horizon, the opposing forces closed, illuminated only by stars peeking through the low-lying clouds. Flashes of distant lightning from squalls in the area portended the coming battle. Of note, one of those squalls nearly prevented the coming carnage as the Japanese force hit a torrent of rain northwest of Savo Island. Abe actually reversed course, thinking the weather could impede his mission; however, reports from his countrymen stationed on Guadalcanal assured him the climatic situation was temporary, so the admiral again proceeded on track.

Within the turrets and below decks on the Japanese ships, gun crews hauled up high-explosive shells from the magazines in preparation for a massive shore bombardment. For the early morning bombardment mission, the powder bags contained a mixture that generated heavy smoke with each discharge, concealing the muzzle flash that would illuminate the ships for American counterbattery fire. This "flashless" powder would prove advantageous that night. In adjacent engineering spaces, the tropical humidity made keeping the boilers fired all the more unbearable as sweat-drenched Japanese sailors responded to the engine orders. Topside, Japanese lookouts scanned the horizons for enemy ships.[10]

Unlike the Japanese, the Americans knew there were opposing ships in the vicinity. As Callaghan's column steamed on a westerly heading parallel to the American-held beaches past Lunga Point on the northern side of the island, lookouts could spot what appeared to be lighted beacons on the Japanese-held shoreline—an ominous warning. Lookouts also reported an unidentified aircraft flying above.[11]

Hence it was the Americans who would be first to detect the opposition. After 0100, a radar operator on the *Helena* started getting returns on his scope. By 0124, *Helena* sent a message that she had plotted three groupings of ships to the northwest, with the first two groupings at a range of about 14 miles appearing to screen a main grouping at 16 miles. The time it took *Helena* to transmit this information to Rear Admiral Callaghan on *San Francisco* ate up six precious minutes, in which one grouping of Japanese ships passed ahead from left to right of his advancing column. Meanwhile, Callaghan had ordered the column to a course of 310 degrees true to continue to run parallel to the island's coastline, which now angled up to the northwest. The course change also steered Callaghan's column directly at the oncoming Japanese as the two forces closed at a speed of 40 knots. At 0130, *Helena* sent out another report placing the enemy ships some 7 miles off the *Helena*'s port bow coming in on a course of 105 degrees true at 23 knots. Reacting, at 0137 Callaghan ordered a course change away from Guadalcanal, and *Cushing* shifted due north heading, with the remainder of the formation following in her wake. With crews at General Quarters, several of the American ships were tracking the Japanese with their fire-control radars awaiting the orders to fire.[12]

On the bridge of the *Hiei*, Vice Admiral Abe, not having radar, remained clueless about any surface ship opposition, let alone that a column of American destroyers and cruisers were in the process of crossing in front of his formation. Little did he realize, his three destroyers steaming ahead on his left flank had already crossed ahead of the oncoming Americans. Meanwhile, the destroyers *Yudachi* and *Harusame*, which had been ahead on Abe's right flank, had come left to steam directly ahead of the main body.

At 0141, Callaghan was seeking follow-up radar reports when lookouts on *Cushing* sighted one of the leading Japanese destroyers crossing ahead from port to starboard. *Cushing*'s skipper, Lt. Cdr. Edward N. Parker, ordered a hard left rudder to unmask his torpedo batteries and avoid collision. Cdr. Thomas M. Stokes, commander of Destroyer Division TEN, embarked on Parker's ship, radioed back the sighting report as the *Cushing* healed over to starboard. The lead ship's sudden turn threw Callaghan's column into disarray. The repeated rudder orders had compressed the American column, and many of the USN skippers became more concerned about avoiding collisions with other ships in the formation than in engaging the enemy. *Atlanta* turned left to avoid hitting the *O'Bannon*, which in turn maneuvered to miss the *Sterett*. The formation attempted to follow in the lead ship's wake. Stokes sought permission to "let them have a couple of fish," but once permission was granted, the targets had disappeared. After *Cushing* failed to launch any torpedoes, the column again turned north in an uneven procession. *Atlanta*, with a wider turning radius, veered off to the left side of the column.[13]

Steaming off the starboard quarter of Abe's flagship, Cdr. Terauchi Masamichi, in command of the destroyer *Inazuma*, heard the radio alert warning of the enemy's close proximity. Peering out ahead with his binoculars, Masamichi began picking out the looming silhouettes of the fast-moving American combatants. The Americans lost the element of surprise.[14]

In the mist of the confusion, *O'Bannon*'s radar operator spotted Abe's left flank force of three destroyers crossing ahead at a range of 4½ miles and some additional ships coming in at 7 miles. The Americans were clearly outnumbered and heavily outgunned and being flanked on both sides. Callaghan gave the order at 0145, "Stand by to open fire!"

Japanese searchlights clicked on from the port and starboard sides of the broken American column. A beam, most likely from the *Akatsuki*, which was steaming ahead of Masamichi's destroyer, caught the port bridge wing of *Atlanta*. The American cruiser didn't wait for orders. Salvos of armor-piercing 5-inch shells smacked into the offending destroyer, which had closed to within a mile. Masamichi watched his compatriot ahead take a debilitating pummeling, along with the *Nagara*, which took hits along the length of the ship from *Atlanta*'s forward twin-mounts. However, *Atlanta*'s muzzle flashes quickly made her a prime target for gunners and torpedomen on *Inazuma* and other warships with the Japanese main body. Shells ripped into the "*Mighty A*." One shell claimed Rear Admiral Scott and killed several other watch standers on the bridge. Capt. Samuel Jenkins survived the exploding shell with merely a wound to the leg. The real crippling blow came when a torpedo detonated beneath her keel, lifting the 6,000+ ton ship from the water. Reacting to the gunfire coming in from different directions, Rear Admiral Callaghan ordered, "Odd ships fire to starboard, even to port."

Samuel Elliot Morison described what transpired over the next 34 minutes as a melee, as "Japanese and American ships mingled like minnows in a bucket."[15] Both Japanese and Americans ashore looked out at one of the most furious sea fights ever fought. This phase of what would be dubbed "The Naval Battle of Guadalcanal" would be concluded with bloodied Japanese forces retreating to the northwest. It is impossible to fully reconstruct the battle, given the numerous course changes, conflicting reports, and varying claims. However, a rundown of the status of the 13 American ships at 0230 gives a sobering appreciation of the lethality of the action.

At about that time, the commander of the leading destroyer, *Cushing*, gave the order to abandon ship as fires, caused by hits from approximately 20 enemy projectiles, raged out of control. About 70 men were lost. As the lead ship, and therefore odd numbered, Parker had trained his guns to port and dished out rounds against an enemy destroyer before receiving hits amidships, severing power lines. Slowing but still heading north, the skipper looked to port to see the oncoming silhouette of Abe's flagship. He brought the ship right to unmask his aft torpedo tubes, and *Cushing*'s torpedomen put six fish in the water against the behemoth. Although none of the torpedoes hit, the wakes probably influenced the *Hiei*'s skipper to reverse course. Shortly thereafter, a light beam spotted *Cushing*, and again, shells ripped into the lead ship.[16]

At 0230, *Laffey* had already passed beneath the waves. Having nearly been rammed by *Hiei*, Lt. Cdr. William E. Hank, the skipper, had fired a spread of torpedoes, only to see them bounce off the Japanese battleship for not being able to arm at such close range. *Laffey* brought her 5-incher and machine guns to bear on *Hiei*'s bridge and let loose several volleys. Safely encased in an armored pill-box, Abe remained unscathed, but the explosions and impacting steel clearly inhibited his ability to comprehend the tactical picture. Stung by *Laffey*'s incoming shells, the

Japanese battleship fired broadsides that ripped into *Laffey*'s own bridge and other sections of the ship. Hit by a torpedo fired from another Japanese ship, the doomed destroyer was then riddled by shellfire from other enemy warships. As the order to abandon ship was given, an explosion ripped through the ship. She quickly sank, taking many of the crew, including Hank, down with her.

Sterett had first dueled with a Japanese cruiser and then took hits from the battleship *Hiei* and managed to survive to fight another day. At 0230, *Sterett*, with her aft guns and starboard torpedo tubes out of action, began to withdraw. A damaged steering gear and an ongoing firefighting effort aft kept her from overtaking the remaining American ships. The last ship of the leading four destroyers, *O'Bannon*, survived with minimal damage caused by the exploding debris from a Japanese capital ship.

Atlanta lay adrift to the south, having been put out of action early in the battle, not before inflicting serious damage on the enemy. In addition to being pierced by enemy shells and torpedoes, the light cruiser was hit by friendly fire emanating from the heavy cruiser *San Francisco*. Loss of life was heavy, with Rear Admiral Scott among those killed. Meanwhile, *San Francisco*, having been hit by an aircraft the previous day, withstood salvos from an enemy cruiser and battleship. The third salvo from the *Hiei* proved fatal to Rear Admiral Callaghan and several others on the navigation bridge of the heavy cruiser. When a shell ripped into the alternate command station, Battle Two, the ship temporarily lost communications and ship control. Additional gunfire from the Japanese BB and other ships knocked out all but one of the port gun mounts. In summary, the cruiser had absorbed 45 enemy shells, and damage control teams worked to contain 22 separate blazes. Fortunately, none of the shell hits occurred below the waterline. Besides Rear Admiral Callaghan and the ship's skipper, Capt. Cassin Young, some 75 sailors were killed.

Having taken a torpedo hit on the starboard quarter early in the battle, *Portland* was handicapped with the loss of her two inboard propellers, a disabled number three turret, and a rudder jammed in the right 5-degrees position. Consequently, the heavy cruiser steamed in a circle throughout the battle, inflicting damage on Japanese warships when they came into range. At 0230, *Portland* was still slowly circling amid the burning wrecks of American and Japanese warships. Following *Portland* into battle, *Helena* only suffered slight damage to her superstructure. *Atlanta*'s sister ship, the light cruiser *Juneau*, suffered a torpedo hit on the port side. Progressive flooding caused a severe list, forcing Capt. Lyman K. Swenson to withdraw from the fight to focus on saving his ship.

Of the four remaining destroyers, only two would survive to fight again. Following in the wake of the *Juneau*, *Aaron Ward* would be one of the two. However, this ship would return only after extensive repairs could be made, for at the conclusion of the engagement, she had lost steering control and had flooding in her forward engine room as a result of nine direct shell hits. *Barton*'s demise was tragically quick. The senior surviving officer wrote afterwards:

After about 7 minutes of continued fire, the *Barton* had stopped to avoid a collision with an unidentified friendly ship ahead when one torpedo, evidently from the enemy column to the right, struck the forward fire room on the starboard side. A few seconds later a second torpedo struck the forward engine room and the ship broke in two and sank in approximately 10 seconds.[17]

Few of the sailors inside the ship escaped. Unfortunately, the tragedy was compounded for those who managed to leap off the sinking hulk into the water, as another destroyer sped over them and then depth charges exploded in the waters below. Over two-thirds of the crew perished as a result of the fight.

Monssen fought well for about 30 minutes before enemy destroyers flooded her with spotlights. Thirty-seven shells ripped into the hull and superstructure, turning the ship into a flaming incinerator. Shortly after 0230, the order would be given to the surviving crewmen to abandon ship. The last ship in the American column, the destroyer *Fletcher*, had a charmed life that evening, escaping relatively unscathed.

During the action, the Americans lost two destroyers, and two more destroyers would eventually succumb to inflicted wounds. Eventually, the Americans would also give up on efforts to salvage *Atlanta*. Incredibly, the severity of the damage could have been far worse had the Japanese had armor-piercing versus high-explosive shells in their ammo hoppers.

As indicated by the earlier narrative, neither did the Japanese escape unscathed. The battleship *Hiei* had her superstructure plastered by over fifty shells and suffered steering and communications difficulties. American gunfire had also accounted for the sinking of the destroyer *Akatsuki*. *Yudachi* suffered an explosion at 0220 and burned dead in the water 5 miles south of Savo Island. The crippled battleship and destroyer would not last to see another sunset. The Americans also inflicted minor to moderate damage on the destroyers *Ikazuchi*, *Murasame*, and *Amatsukaze*. All three escaped.

The severely damaged American flotilla would receive one more staggering blow. At dawn, the slightly damaged cruiser *Helena*, and the crippled cruisers *San Francisco* and *Juneau*, were in a formation steaming southeasterly away from Guadalcanal and the bloodied waters north of Lunga Point. The unscathed *Fletcher* and damaged *Sterett* steamed ahead on the flanks to screen for enemy submarines. On the *Sterett*, Lt. Charles Raymond Calhoun had fixed himself a sandwich in the galley and stopped in the wardroom where several of *Sterett*'s wounded lay receiving care. He recalled that an unidentified plane sighting spurred the exhausted crew to General Quarters. Calhoun rushed to his battle station at an aft gun director. From his perch he peered out through a set of binoculars at *Helena*, *San Francisco*, and *Juneau*. As he scanned the light cruiser *Juneau*, he could not discern any damage from the torpedo hit sustained hours earlier.

Calhoun lowered his binoculars and continued to peer at *Juneau*, not realizing that the Japanese submarine *I-26* had just fired a spread of torpedoes. One of those torpedoes sped on a collision course with the ship that Calhoun was gazing at. He recalled:

> Without the slightest warning, she exploded—disintegrated—in a tremendously violent blast. I watched with horror as whole 5-inch gun barrels flew hundreds of feet into the air. Huge pieces of the ship's superstructure were hurled sky high in lazy parabolic curves. A gigantic column of black and gray smoke went up for thousands of feet. Yellow and orange flames flashed at the center of the explosion for the first few seconds, but soon there was only an immense cloud of smoke, which seemed to hang motionless for minutes.

Calhoun peered out with his binoculars, but as the smoke rose he could see nothing. "Not a stick, or a spar, or a boat, or a life buoy; nor was a single man visible."[18]

Back off Lunga Point, *Juneau*'s sister ship, *Atlanta*, struggled to stay afloat. On board Captain Jenkins made a difficult decision. With no salvage facilities in the vicinity, his ship listing heavy to port, and more enemy forces expected that evening, he ordered his ship to be scuttled. The evacuation of the ship was orderly. The wounded were taken off, and then uninjured crewmen lowered themselves onto small craft sent out from Guadalcanal. One of those survivors was the assistant gunnery officer, Lt. Cdr. Lloyd M. Mustin. Having time, he ventured back to his stateroom to collect some personal items. Included among his possessions was a diary that he had kept since the *Mighty A* had been placed in commission 11 months earlier.

CHAPTER 2

Lloyd M. Mustin

Born at the Philadelphia Navy Yard on July 30, 1911, Lloyd M. Mustin came into a distinguished family that had accomplished much in many fields, including naval. He would build on that naval tradition by rising through the ranks to retire as a vice admiral in 1971. Before passing away in 1999, he witnessed his first son Henry achieve that same rank. His grandson John would also earn his third star when he took command of the Navy Reserve in August 2020.

The Mustin line had French Huguenot and English roots. In 1795, George Mustin, his wife Mary Elizabeth, and six children came to Philadelphia from Devonport, England. In Philadelphia, they had three more children. Lloyd traced his lineage to one of these three, a John Mustin, who fathered John Jr., who in turn fathered Lloyd's grandfather Thomas Jones Mustin.

Thomas would marry Ida Croskey who would bear him two sons. The first, Henry Croskey Mustin, came into the world on February 6, 1874. Henry grew to love his father, a man of vigor who delved into the Philadelphia textile industry. Tragically, the father died of pneumonia contracted when he took off his winter garments to warm 14-year-old Henry and his younger brother John when the three were stranded on a train in the middle of a January blizzard. Within three years Ida married William S. Lloyd, who built on the textile business, and more significantly, served as a devoted stepfather to the two boys. Henry and his brother John were well cared for, and Henry eventually paid homage to the man by naming his first son for him.[1]

Lloyd's naval heritage came from his well-known father and also from his mother's lineage. Corinne Montague—the socialite who would eventually fall for a young naval officer stationed at the Washington Navy Yard—traced her ancestry to the Sinclair family of Scottish nobility. Arthur Sinclair IV was born around 1787 at Norfolk and was the first of Lloyd Mustin's forebears to serve in the U.S. Navy, serving as a midshipman with Thomas Truxtun on *Constellation* during her 1799 triumph over *L'Insurgente* in the Quasi-War with France. By the time the War of 1812 came about, the now Lieutenant Sinclair received command of *Argus* and captured several

British merchantmen. He finished the war on the Great Lakes, leading naval forces to several victories over the British.[2]

After the war, Sinclair returned to Norfolk, where he commanded the Navy Yard at Gosport and established "The Nautical School," an institution that would serve as a predecessor to the U.S. Naval Academy. Sinclair married the only daughter of a Richard Kennon of the Continental Army, and Sally Kennon would deliver five children of which three were boys who also would serve in the Navy. The eldest boy, another Arthur, served in the Mexican–American War, participated in Commodore Matthew C. Perry's expedition to Japan in the early 1850s, and commanded *Vandalia* during an adventurous cruise in the South Pacific in 1859.[3]

Arthur Sinclair V signed on with the Confederacy where he served on the ram *Mississippi* at New Orleans and later operated blockade runners. He vanished while embarked on the *Lelia*, lost in a storm on her maiden voyage from England.

His first son, Arthur Sinclair VI, also served the South, surviving engagements in both *Merrimack* (CSS *Virginia*) and *Alabama*. He would also father several children of whom the fourth, Lehia Sinclair, would become Lloyd's grandmother. She married Walter Powhatan Montague of Baltimore and they would produce four children; the last, Corinne, would grow up to marry Henry.[4]

It was Henry who started the Mustin naval dynasty with his entry into the Naval Academy in 1892. A natural athlete who earned the nickname "Rum," Henry was a four-letter man as a fencer, rower, track star, and football quarterback. He graduated in 1896 as a Passed Midshipmen and received orders to the armored cruiser *New York*. In the wake of the *Maine* explosion, Henry was assigned to support Capt. William T. Sampson's Court of Inquiry that had been convened to look into the tragic explosion. Henry's duties included surveying the wreck and drafting drawings of the remaining hulk for the Court's evaluation.[5]

Again embarked in *New York* at the start of the Spanish–American War, he witnessed the demise of the Spanish flotilla during the battle of Santiago. Now an ensign, he eventually received orders to join the Asiatic Fleet in Manila. To get to the Philippines, he embarked as a division officer on the collier *Scindia* and made the long trip around South America and westward in company with the battleships *Oregon* and *Iowa*. *Scindia* broke down and had to be towed to Honolulu. Facing the prospect of heading to San Francisco for major repairs, Henry swapped jobs with an officer on the water-distilling ship *Iris*, which arrived at Manila on March 18, 1899. By this time the Philippine insurrection was challenging the American forces in the region and Henry longed to get into the action. By August he was reassigned to the flagship *Oregon*, which supported gunboats that were engaged in interdiction work. On the night of September 25, Henry swam ashore with *Oregon* crewmembers to successfully capture the insurgent steamboat *Taaleno*. Once in American hands, Henry worked feverishly to make the boat seaworthy. Henry would not command her, though. Instead, he received command of the gunboat *Semar* and found himself supporting numerous Army operations to put down the insurrection of Filipinos within the thousands of islands in the archipelago. In one operation, Henry grounded his small craft to enable his gunners to fire point-blank into enemy positions that threatened an Army landing. By year's end, Army forces, supported by *Semar* and other naval units, seemed to be closing in on elusive insurgent leader Emilio Aguinaldo.[6]

However, Henry's gunboat days were numbered. In March, he reported for duty on the new flagship, the armored cruiser *Brooklyn*. There he met Lt. William S. Sims, who would influence his career. After a few months in *Brooklyn*, Henry was transferred to the two-masted schooner *Isle de Cuba*, and the young naval officer again found himself supporting Army operations ashore into 1901. Finally, after two years of action in the Philippines, Henry received orders to the homeward-bound *Newark*.[7]

In September 1901, now Lt. (jg) Henry Mustin reported for duty with torpedo boats at the Norfolk Navy Yard, but he fell ill and needed two months to recuperate. Reassigned to the Naval Academy, he familiarized himself with the *Holland*, the Navy's first submarine then stationed there.[8] At the end of July 1902, he reported to the battleship *Kearsarge*, the flagship of the North Atlantic Squadron. Within months he qualified as a turret officer. During *Kearsarge's* deployment to Europe in 1903, Henry had the opportunity to visit the Royal Navy's Gunnery School at Whale Island where he witnessed the latest British advances in telescopic sights. Looking at the British design work, Henry felt confident that he could build a better mousetrap. Returning to the East Coast, Henry suddenly felt cursed to receive orders as executive officer of the supply ship *Culgoa*.[9]

However, lying within the steel confines of *Culgoa* were machine shops. The inventive Henry was soon putting the machinery to good use, designing and building gun sights, first for the *Kearsarge*, then for the battleship *Missouri*. His creativity led to more designs and to patents as he supported efforts made by Sims and others to improve gunnery. After deploying to the Caribbean in June 1905, he reported for duty at the Washington Navy Yard, home of the Naval Gun Factory. Inside the M Street walls, Henry tinkered with optics and producing better gun-sight telescopes.[10]

Although Henry patented many of his designs, he could not claim royalties for his cleverness, as the Navy claimed he invented it while on duty. Ironically, such rules did not apply for foreign navies, and Henry earned cash and honors for his design from the British and the Germans, two of America's potential foes on the high seas.

While on duty at the Washington Navy Yard, Henry received his promotion to full lieutenant. More significantly, he met Corinne Montague late in the summer of 1906. So began a courtship that would be interrupted when Henry received orders back to *Brooklyn*. The Philadelphia-ported armored cruiser promptly steamed down to Cuba for two months and then returned for placement in reserve. Henry managed to get orders back to the nation's capital, where he could continue the courtship. He proposed to Corinne on March 3, 1907. Seventeen days later, he reported as the ordnance officer to the commissioning crew of the battleship *Kansas*.[11]

One officer in Henry's new wardroom would eventually rise to serve as an operational commander for his first son. His name: Ens. William F. Halsey. Once placed into commission, *Kansas* would partake in numerous exercises and participate in the review of ships that was part of the Jamestown Exhibition. Meanwhile, Henry was buoyed by positive reports from *Missouri* about the four Mark XI telescopes of his design that were undergoing evaluation.[12]

The prospect of a world cruise did not thrill Henry, who thought the time spent traversing the globe could be better spent on local fleet exercises. He also faced the prospect of being away from his bride-to-be! Consequently, Corinne and Henry exchanged wedding vows in Baltimore on October 29, 1907, and honeymooned in New York, where the *Kansas* and six other battleships were being fitted out to go to sea.[13]

The New York-based ships departed for Norfolk in early December, where they met up with the other naval vessels that would make the epochal voyage. On December 16, "The Great White Fleet" departed on a course to South America. For the next four months, the 16 battleships, escorts, and auxiliaries worked their way down to the Straits of Magellan and then up the West Coast of South and Central America, making festive port visits along the way. Henry took advantage of what limited opportunities there were to improve the effectiveness of his green gun crews.[14]

Upon arriving in San Diego in April 1908, the lieutenant was pleased to see Corinne, who had arrived via train from the East Coast. For nearly the next three months, the fleet prepared for its trans-Pacific journey, and Henry took time off to spend a second honeymoon with his new bride touring California. With the fleet finally leaving San Francisco on July 7 for Honolulu, Corinne chose not to be left behind, booking passage with nine other wives on a Japanese passenger ship bound for Hawaii. After spending time with her husband on the beaches of Waikiki, she headed on to Sydney to wait for the fleet that would arrive after a port call to Auckland, New Zealand.

The wives who followed their husbands and embarked with the fleet became known as "the Geese," and after a pleasant stay in Australia, they headed north to Yokohama where they waited the better part of a month as the American warships pulled into Manila and endured a typhoon en route from the Philippines. With the backdrop of a warm welcome extended by the hosting Japanese, Corinne and Henry once again reunited. They cherished their time together, as months would pass before they would meet again. In November, the fleet conducted battle exercises in the vicinity of the Philippines.

When *Kansas* arrived in Villefranche in mid-January 1909, Corinne once again met up with her husband, and the two joined with other couples for a trip to Paris.

Departing from the Riviera, *Kansas* passed through the Straits of Gibraltar with the rest of the Great White Fleet and arrived at Hampton Roads on February 22 to conduct a presidential review for President Theodore Roosevelt, who was finishing his second term in office. Again united with his beloved Corinne, the two would spend time together ashore as *Kansas* pulled into the Philadelphia Navy Yard for a badly needed overhaul.

During the summer, Henry received a promotion to lieutenant commander and spent quite a bit of time at sea as *Kansas* worked to regain her combat readiness. To his delight, he received orders ashore in October for duty at the Philadelphia Navy Yard, where he would continue his work on gunsights. By this time, the Royal Navy had commissioned the *Dreadnought*, an all-big-gun battle cruiser that rendered all navies obsolete overnight. The United States Navy began producing its own "dreadnoughts" with designs calling for main batteries containing 14- and even 16-inch caliber guns. Guns of such caliber could fire shells over the horizon, rendering deck-level gunsights useless. To fix the problem, the Navy commissioned its new battleships with large cage masts to serve as platforms for spotters. However, Henry saw the ultimate solution in aircraft hovering near the target reporting back results.[15]

In Philadelphia, his vision was reinforced through a friendship he had with Marshall Reid, a young man who had inherited a tidy sum and invested a bit of it to have Glenn Curtiss build him an aeroplane. Not only did the young lieutenant commander have opportunities to fly, but Corinne also flew in the aircraft, achieving some notoriety in the local papers. Henry and Reid attempted to establish a distance record by flying to Norfolk and back. Unfortunately, the engine blew as the two were puttering over a calm Delaware Bay. They safely landed, as the aircraft was equipped with a pontoon. Fog set in, precluding an immediate rescue. With the pontoon leaking, the two took turns sucking water and spitting over the side using rubber tubing they swiped from the fuel system. Staying afloat, the two were eventually rescued.[16]

Despite this unfortunate experience, the aviation bug had bit him and bit him good. "My father was hell-bent to get into naval aviation, which he thought was the next thing that he wanted to interest himself in, having straightened out naval gunnery," recalled his son Lloyd.[17]

Naval aviation was in its infancy, with a small naval air station having been established at Greenbury Point, across the Severn River from the Naval Academy. Unable to get orders to the unit, Henry received orders in December 1912 to be the first lieutenant on the battleship *Minnesota*. Saying farewell to Corinne and newborn son Lloyd, Henry deployed to the Caribbean where he met up with the Severn River aviators during fleet exercises and by April had soloed.[18]

Minnesota returned to Norfolk in early spring 1913, which enabled Henry to meet his second son, Henry Ashmead, shortly after Corinne delivered him.

Lloyd Montague Mustin's parents—Henry C. Mustin, who poses as Naval Aviator Number 11, and Corinne Montague. (Courtesy Archives Branch, Naval History and Heritage Command, Washington, D.C., NH 105934-A-KN and of the Mustin family)

The introduction was brief, as *Minnesota* deployed in response to violence in Mexico. The battleship returned that summer, allowing Henry to spend time with his wife and two sons. At the end of the year he received orders as executive officer and acting commanding officer of the battleship *Mississippi*, which was to serve as the training ship for the new Office of Naval Aeronautics. While the pre-Dreadnought battlewagon was deemed unsuitable for fleet use, the obsolescent *Mississippi* proved to be an ideal platform for a station ship. In January 1914, Henry used his battleship and a collier to transport the Annapolis-based naval air squadron down to Pensacola, Florida.[19]

Recognizing the clear weather advantages of the Gulf Coast, the Navy decided to reopen an old naval station located at Pensacola to serve as a naval aviation training facility. As commanding officer of *Mississippi*, Henry would oversee the process. Docked at the station's pier, the battlewagon provided berthing, messing, electricity, and other services to a facility that had been shut down three years earlier. All hands pitched in to make the old naval station operational. Aircraft arrived, as did the students who would learn to fly them.[20]

Meanwhile, Pensacola's location proved fortuitous as the ongoing unrest in Mexico escalated in the spring of 1914. President Wilson ordered naval forces to land ashore at Vera Cruz, and the Navy seized the opportunity to take some of its aircraft from Pensacola to perform scout work. Henry loaded floatplanes onto *Mississippi* and rushed across the Gulf of Mexico. On April 25, Henry launched the first naval aircraft to support combat operations. That morning a floatplane went aloft to locate a reported mine. Over the next two months, aircraft based from *Mississippi* and the

Lt. Cdr. Mustin is seated just to the left of the fuselage of a Curtiss "AB" type airplane, probably at Pensacola, Florida, circa late 1914. Some notable individuals sitting along with Mustin on that first row include (left to right) Lt. (jg) Robert G. Saufley, USN; Lt. (jg) Patrick N. L. Bellinger, USN; and Lt. Kenneth Whitling, USN. To his right are Lt. Albert C. Read, USN; Lt. Earle F. Johnson, USN; 1st Lt. Alfred A. Cunningham, USMC; 2nd Lt. Francis T. Evans, USMC; and Lt. (jg) Walter A. Haas, USN. Standing left to right behind Mustin are Lt. (jg) Robert R. Paunack, USN; Lt. (jg) Earl W. Spencer, USN; Lt. (jg) Harold T. Bartlett, USN; Lt. (jg) Walter A. Edwards, USN; Lt. Clarence K. Bronson, USN; Lt. Joseph P. Norfleet, USN; Lt. (jg) Edward O. McDonnell, USN; and Ens. Harold W. Scofield, USN. (Archives Branch, Naval History and Heritage Command, Washington, D.C.; NH 95805 (1))

cruiser *Birmingham* would serve as eyes for troops ashore. Henry, the visionary, could already see an offensive role for the aircraft.[21]

However, his tour as commanding officer of *Mississippi* came to an end when the American government sold the ship to Greece. Deprived of his command, he received orders to *North Carolina*, a ship destined to replace *Mississippi* at Pensacola. But with war breaking out in Europe, the armored cruiser was diverted to France on a relief mission to pick up stranded Americans. Once in France, Henry and other embarked naval aviators headed off into the hinterland to learn about French aviation advances. The *North Carolina* then entered the Mediterranean to look after American interests in the eastern Mediterranean. Henry was not pleased, feeling strongly that his talents were being wasted. Finally, at the end of the year, he received orders to return to Washington and then back to Pensacola to reassume command of the Naval Aeronautic Station.[22]

Settled in with his wife and two sons, Henry welcomed new classes of young officers arriving to take flight training. As the senior Henry often entertained, the elder son was introduced to some of the men who would form the backbone of naval aviation well into World War II. Men like George Murray and Marc A. "Pete" Mitscher eventually achieved flag rank and commanded carrier task forces in the Pacific during that conflict. Murray's career would be of exceptional significance to Lloyd, as he eventually became his stepfather.

Henry understood the next step in the evolution of naval aviation was the installation of a reliable catapult on ships to launch aircraft. On November 5, 1915, he personally demonstrated the concept when he was launched off by a catapult erected on the fantail on the *North Carolina*. Although buoyed by success, Henry quickly grasped the complexity of aviation operations off a conventional warship, which limited the potential for naval aviation. A ship dedicated to air operations would be the next step in the evolution of naval aviation. Appearing before the General Board in Washington in the summer of 1916, Henry called for the design and construction of a ship capable of launching and landing torpedo planes, spotter aircraft, and fighters.

Meanwhile, Corinne invited her 20-year-old cousin Bessie Wallis Warfield down from Baltimore to help entertain and raise the boys. She caught the attention of one of the aviator trainees, Earl Winfield Spencer, and a month later he would propose. Two divorces and over two decades later, after King Edward VIII of the United Kingdom abdicated his throne in order to marry her, Bessie Wallis would become the Duchess of Windsor.[23]

For Corinne's husband, the prospects of continuing his career as a naval officer began to wilt as he was passed over for selection to captain. A combination of circumstances had caused him to fall in disfavor in Washington. Stripped of his aviator wings, he subsequently received orders to be executive officer of *North Dakota*, an obsolete battleship homeported in Philadelphia. With the outbreak of World War I and its focus on convoy operations and anti-submarine warfare, Henry felt he had reached a dead end. However, when Navy Secretary Josephus Daniels solicited war-winning ideas in a message sent out to all commands, Henry responded with a scheme to launch aircraft off sea sleds that could motor at high speeds off the German coast, enabling close-range attacks of German U-boat facilities.[24]

The plan caught the attention of senior officials on both sides of the Atlantic. Henry would be recalled to Washington, but before he detached from *North Dakota*, he performed a heroic feat in a storm off Cape Hatteras after a swell had swept three sailors overboard. Two of the sailors were lost, but Henry managed to maneuver the ship so that he could dive in with a line attached to his waist to swim toward the drowning seaman. He later made light of the rescue, but the effort had put enormous strain on his body and would affect his health.[25]

Reporting to the Bureau of Construction and Repair at the Washington Navy Yard, Henry oversaw the design of the speed boats that would carry the aircraft and the acquisition of the planes themselves. If all went to plan, Henry envisioned

Caproni plane on sea sled, November 15, 1918. (Archives Branch, Naval History and Heritage Command, Washington, D.C.; NH 112975)

a force of hundreds of sea sleds would be in position to launch attacks against the Kaiser's undersea boat assets by mid-1919. In November, the project had come far enough along to allow for a sea trail. Although the initial test was scored a failure, a follow-on test in March 1919 validated the concept. However, with the end of the war in November 1918, a concept and test flight would be as far as the project would go.[26]

While the project didn't affect the course of the war, many took note of Henry's performance, and he finally earned the right to pin on eagles. Now, Capt. Henry Mustin would continue his advocacy for an aircraft carrier. Eventually, funds were made available to convert the collier *Jupiter* into the *Langley*.[27]

Henry again received command at sea, this time of *Aroostook*, a newly converted aircraft tender based in San Diego. Pete Mitscher embarked with him as senior squadron commander and commander of air forces assigned to the fleet at San Diego. Ensconced on the West Coast, Henry hoped to continue to sell the value of naval aviation in spotting for surface ship gunnery. With Mitscher aloft in an F-5L Curtiss JN "Jenny" observation plane providing feedback, the battleship *Mississippi*, commanded by Capt. William Moffett, scored higher in its gunnery drills than the other West Coast BBs combined![28]

In early 1921, Henry demonstrated the long range and versatility of flying boats with a trip down to Panama and back, a feat that got his comrades and him dubbed "the Columbuses of the air." Due to the pioneering work conducted by Henry and his peers, the Navy began to embrace naval aviation. Ironically, some of the battleship admirals, who once scoffed at the flying contraptions, became their chief proponents when the Army's Brig. Gen. Billy Mitchell made noises about unifying military aviation into a new air force service. To demonstrate that the Navy took its aviation seriously, the Bureau of Aeronautics was created in July 1921 with Moffett at the rudder. Moffett selected Henry to be his assistant chief.[29]

When the Washington Naval Conference adjourned after the signing of a treaty that limited further battleship construction and limited American fortifications in the Western Pacific, it became clear to Henry that naval aviation would become critical in a hypothetical war against Japan. After his vigorous campaigning, Congress authorized funds to convert two battle cruisers slated for scrapping under the treaty to become the carriers *Saratoga* and *Lexington*. Going before the Navy General Board, Henry argued for three more carriers, envisioning these ships operating as part of task force formations that could send aircraft to lash out at enemy ships and land masses.[30]

Given the austerity of the budget, Henry's vision fell on deaf ears. In the interim, *Langley* had joined the fleet and presented the Navy with opportunities to operate aircraft with the fleet. For Henry it must have been frustrating. Perhaps the stress of the job compounded the physical strain on his body caused by the rescue he made while on *North Dakota*. In January 1923 he was admitted to the Washington Naval Hospital, where doctors determined he had an aortic aneurysm—a ballooned artery that rubbed against his ribs. In March 1923 he began experiencing chest pains and updated his will to include his third son, who had been born in 1917. He would check in and out of naval hospitals in Washington and Newport, Rhode Island, as his condition worsened. On August 23, 1923, he died.[31]

Henry C. Mustin's death left Corinne widowed as the mother of three boys. The eldest, Lloyd, had just turned 12. Although still a young lad, Lloyd's father had left an impression on him, and he would learn to further appreciate the contributions his father made to the naval service as his life moved forward. Furthermore, he would inherit the tight association of relationships that his father had built with those officers who proved themselves to be pioneers in the early days of naval aviation and would later turn out to be some of the key Navy leaders during World War II.

Growing up the son of a naval officer, Lloyd and his two younger brothers had nomadic childhoods as they and their mom followed Dad to his various duty stations and occasionally attended boarding schools. At summer camps, Lloyd learned to pitch tents, a skill that would come in handy two decades later at a place called Guadalcanal. With the death of his father, Lloyd was eventually taken in by his uncle John Burton, who lived in Philadelphia.[32]

Meanwhile, Corinne stayed with a cousin at Gunston Farm on Maryland's eastern shore, where her two younger sons were attending a boarding school. From there she could catch ferries over to Annapolis to visit with family friends, including Lt. Cdr. George Murray, who had established a course in aeronautics at the Naval Academy. He had suffered the loss of his spouse a few years earlier. Murray was obviously attracted to Corinne but also cared much for the three sons of his mentor. In the fall of 1925, they announced their engagement.[33]

Here Lieutenant Commander Mustin visits with his two elder sons—Henry Ashmead and Lloyd Montague. (John Fass Morton collection)

A year later, they all attended a dedication ceremony in Philadelphia of Mustin Field, an airstrip co-located with the Naval Aircraft Factory. Lloyd and his brothers were impressed with all the speeches and presentations honoring their father, including a plaque from his Naval Academy classmates, and flyovers and other aerobatic demonstrations. However, despite his father's naval background, Lloyd was not initially committed to following in his wake. However, living in Philadelphia, he occasionally visited the inner basin of the navy yard and scampered around the ships in mothballs, including the *Olympia* of Manila Bay fame. Standing on the bridge where Commodore Dewey once said "You may fire when ready, Gridley" suddenly made him realize that he had a calling.[34]

Encouraged by his stepdad, the junior Mustin attended Columbia Preparatory School in Washington, D.C., to ready himself for the Naval Academy exams. He did well enough to earn a presidential appointment to go to the prestigious campus in Annapolis. Arriving in June 1928, Lloyd Mustin was still a month shy of his 17th birthday. Competing in the class standings with arriving plebes who in some cases were four years older with civilian college backgrounds, Lloyd realized he would have to work hard to succeed academically.[35]

In athletics, the young plebe made his mark early, scoring wins at swim meets competing in the 50- and 100-yard freestyle competitions. Although he struggled with chemistry, Lloyd survived his first year. Departing Annapolis in June 1929, he spent his youngster summer cruise on the battleship *Arkansas*, which took him and many of his classmates on a tour of Southern Europe and England. While underway, Lloyd performed numerous chores normally associated with enlisted sailors. His battle station was in turret six, the far aft turret where he loaded powder bags into the breech.[36]

Returning to Annapolis in September, the 18-year-old midshipman began to break away from his peers academically, scoring high grades in mechanical engineering and in ordnance courses. Dubbed by his fellow middies as "Mustie" and "Mustang," he continued to make waves in the pool, setting a Naval Academy 440-yard freestyle record in a competition against Dartmouth. Unfortunately, he began to have trouble with his eyesight, and when doctors determined he had astigmatism, his dreams of following in his father's footsteps as a naval aviator were dashed, all the more depressing given that summer featured aviation orientation.[37]

His junior year swimming exploits attracted the attention of Emily Morton, the sister of one of Lloyd's swim team buddies. By May, the two were going steady. With Emily, Lloyd found he was dating a girl coming from another family with a strong naval heritage. Emily's father had attended the academy a year apart from Lloyd's Dad and served with the senior Mustin on several occasions. Sadly, like his father, Emily's dad died in 1924 at a relatively young age. Her mother's father happened to be Thomas Benton Howard, a hydrographer who rose in ranks to become one of the Navy's first four-star admirals.

In the summer of 1931, Lloyd once again found himself on the decks of *Arkansas*, this time as a first-class midshipman on a North Atlantic cruise to Europe. There he was able to meet up with his mother to sightsee in Denmark and Scotland. As a gun-crew captain on a 5-inch mount, Lloyd's performance earned him a letter of commendation.[38]

During his senior year, Lloyd continued to pursue his relationship with Emily. He continued to excel in the pool and in the classroom. Upon graduation, he was ranked 18th of 423 midshipmen. Unlike other classmates, his prospects for immediate marriage were not promising. Since Emily was still only 17, her mother would not give her consent. After intense discussions between family members, Emily's mother changed her mind. With permission granted, the couple quickly married at St. Anne's church in Annapolis on June 8, 1932. Now an ensign, Lloyd Mustin prepared to take his bride across the country to Long Beach where the Asiatic Fleet-bound cruiser *Augusta* was ported.

Conventional wisdom said battleships were the place to be for a junior officer; however, Lloyd had spent two midshipmen cruises on the *Arkansas* and realized that ensigns could easily get lost within the junior wardroom. A cruiser, in contrast, featured a smaller wardroom and offered greater responsibilities. In addition, *Augusta,* as a heavy cruiser with 8-inch batteries, was designed to engage battleships.[39]

Throughout the remainder of 1932 and into 1933, the cruiser operated from the West Coast as the flagship of the Scouting Force. In early 1933, *Augusta* participated in Fleet Problem XXI off Hawaii. Lloyd rotated through different departments on the ship, first working in communications and then moving into the auxiliaries division. Returning to Long Beach, the cruiser was at anchor on March 10 when a strong earthquake hit Southern California. Looking out from the forecastle, Lloyd could see fires erupting ashore. His pregnant wife Emily felt the jolt that made their apartment uninhabitable.

That summer, *Augusta* underwent an overhaul at the Puget Sound Navy Yard. Moving up there to be with her husband, Emily gave birth to a son on August 31. The couple agreed to honor Lloyd's father by naming the boy Henry Croskey. The young ensign had just over a month and a half to enjoy fatherhood as the cruiser departed for Shanghai on October 20. The separation would be temporary. Meanwhile, prior to getting underway, a change of command ceremony placed Capt. Chester W. Nimitz as commanding officer. Nimitz immediately impressed the young ensign. He believed in training junior officers and holding them accountable. Under the watchful eye of Nimitz, Lloyd found himself frequently at the conn as the officer of the deck, maneuvering the heavy cruiser in a great variety of exercises. Lloyd would later insist his junior officers learn ship-handling skills when he was entrusted with a ship command, and his son Henry would follow his father's example.[40]

Arriving at Shanghai on November 9, Captain Nimitz welcomed Adm. Frank B. Upham, who broke his flag as Commander in Chief, Asiatic Fleet, in *Augusta,* enabling the former flagship *Houston* to depart for the States. To Lloyd's delight, his wife and son had already arrived on the steamer *President Cleveland.* Much as Corinne had followed the first Henry Croskey Mustin to Asia, Emily had made the trip with the second Henry Croskey tucked in a crib. The new Asiatic Fleet flagship made its way to Manila for the holidays. Emily and son followed on a passenger liner. After wintering in the Philippine capital, *Augusta* again returned to the China coast as did Emily and son. Besides having his crew perform the standard flagship duties, Nimitz insisted that all hands work on their small arms marksmanship and get involved in athletics competitions. Lloyd excelled at swim meets.

By May, Nimitz had Lloyd performing the duties of the assistant navigator, and he performed much of the navigational work to get the ship to the northern port of Tsingtao. During that Chinese port visit, Fleet Adm. Togo Heihachiro, the victor over the Russians at Tsushima in 1905, died. Captain Nimitz had met the legendary Japanese naval officer decades earlier and had great admiration for him. *Augusta* was Yokohama-bound to pay respects, arriving on June 4. While Upham, Nimitz, and senior officers from various navies honored the deceased hero, Lloyd had

Lloyd and his bride, Emily Morton Mustin, in China following their marriage. (Morton collection)

a chance to look over some Japanese Navy hardware, and he came away impressed by the quality of the ships and the men who crewed them.[41]

Nimitz steamed his ship back to Tsingtao, which would serve as the host port for the Asiatic Fleet summer exercises. *Augusta* scored well, earning a battle efficiency trophy. During the summer Emily and her husband and son spent time exploring the country's interior, including a visit to Beijing. During October and November, the Asiatic Fleet flagship headed down under for a visit to Australia, calling on Sydney, Melbourne, Fremantle, and Perth. Following port calls in the Dutch East Indies, she would return to Manila in time for Christmas.[42]

As the ship entered 1935, Lloyd helped implement new damage control standards that were being instituted fleet wide. His experience would come in handy later in his career. Again, as winter turned to spring, the flagship returned to China, where a relief awaited Captain Nimitz. Before he left, he had advised his junior officers to seek destroyer duty. With his orders taking him to the Bureau of Navigation, which handled personnel detailing, Nimitz would be in a position to see that his officers' wishes were granted.[43]

The summer schedule and routine mimicked that of the year before. In the fall, Bangkok was the destination, with Adm. Orin G. Murfin having relieved Upham as the Asiatic Fleet commander. Returning to Manila in November, Lloyd and his wife and son spent their last winter together in the Philippines before he would be detached in April 1936 with orders to a *Mahan*-class destroyer under construction. Lloyd would be the plank-owner assistant gunnery officer, also filling the torpedo and communications officer billets in *Lamson*. Before reporting to Bath, Maine, as a member of the pre-commissioning crew, the Navy routed him through the Naval Gun Factory in Washington, D.C. and the torpedo school at Goat Island off Newport, Rhode Island. His time in the nation's capital was dedicated to learning about the Navy's new 5-inch/38-caliber gun that would see service into the 1990s. He had a particular interest in range-finding.

Joining *Lamson* early in the summer of 1936, Lloyd witnessed the builders' trials and began to familiarize himself with the ship and his shipmates. The ship then steamed down to Boston to be commissioned in October and remain at the naval shipyard for an extended fitting-out period to correct some structural problems.

After the Navy declared the ship fit for sea duty, she steamed down to Brazil and Argentina for her shakedown cruise. *Lamson* then returned to Norfolk, where additional tweaks were made.

With the exception of his time at sea, Lloyd had been able to spend a good bit of time with his wife and son. However, in early June the three were once again separated as Emily watched *Lamson* pull away from a Norfolk pier destined for San Diego via the Panama Canal. When *Lamson* arrived on the West Coast at the end of June, she was in port for only a few days when orders came to deploy to the South Pacific. *Lamson* deployed two other destroyers with *Lexington* to search for the missing Amelia Earhart. This time when he returned, Emily and baby Henry were there to greet him as Emily had driven across the country to set up a new homestead in Southern California.[44]

During the next few months, the new destroyer spent much time plying the waters off Southern California to conduct various exercises with other fleet units. In fleet competitions, *Lamson* excelled in her antiaircraft gunnery and in communications—two feathers in Lloyd's cap, as he also had taken on the duties as the communications officer. The news from the beach was also good, as Emily gave birth to a second child in May 1937. She had promised to name the child for her uncle Doug who died the previous December. That the baby was a girl made no difference. Douglas Howard Mustin would be Henry's little sister.[45]

A month after the birth of his second child, the Mustin family again trekked across the country as Lloyd returned to the banks of the Severn with orders to spend two years at the Naval Postgraduate School, which was then co-located at the Naval Academy in Annapolis, to study ordnance engineering. At the time, the school offered a sub-specialty in fire control that would require the student to spend his second year at the Massachusetts Institute of Technology. Lloyd and three others—Horacio "Rivits" Rivero, Ed Hopper, and Corky Ward—opted for this study regimen and together would become known as the "Four Horsemen." However, before Lloyd traded the banks of the Severn for the Charles, he traveled down to Newport News to witness the christening of a new *Sims*-class destroyer named *Mustin* for his father. Emily served as the ship's sponsor and had the honor of smashing the traditional bottle of bubbly against the newly fabricated steel hull.[46]

By the time he reached MIT in the fall of 1939, the world was changing around the freshly promoted Lt. Lloyd Mustin. Germany had marched into Poland and President Franklin D. Roosevelt had established a neutrality patrol. As the situation in Europe deteriorated, Lloyd and his fellow "Horsemen" studied in the Electrical Engineering department and learned about servomechanisms, "the mechanical means to amplify low-power command signals to control the motion of heavy equipment."[47] The four officers sought naval applications for this new technology. While Ward and Hooper decided to develop a servomechanism for the 16-inch guns on the new battleship *North Carolina*, Mustin and Rivero sought an application for antiaircraft guns to enable them to track close-in passes by enemy aircraft. Their thesis, "A Servo-Mechanism for a Rate Follow-Up System," did contribute to the development of what would become known as the Mark 14 and 15 gunsights—tracking systems that would be mass produced and supplied to multiple ship types and classes.[48]

Upon finishing their work at MIT, the four officers were sent to Bausch and Lomb, in Rochester, New York, to the Washington Naval Gun Factory, the Bureau of Ordnance, and to the Dahlgren Proving Ground, to share their technical knowledge with the naval manufacturers, research and development people, and testers. While at the Bureau, Lloyd learned of another new technology—radar. While at Dahlgren, Lloyd worked on improving the effectiveness of a variety of short-range weapons against attacking aircraft. At the time, the Naval Gun Factory was fielding the 1.1-inch machine gun for testing and eventual deployment. Lloyd found the weapon to be unreliable. Typically, it would fire a few rounds and then freeze up. The Bureau's response was to make Lloyd the project officer for the gun, with authority extending back to the production line at the Naval Gun Factory. Lloyd found that the specifications for the gun's parts were too tight. By loosening up the tolerances, the gun was not only easier to produce, but also more reliable. While the gun did well at the Dahlgren Proving Ground, it was not as successful in its service with the fleet.[49]

Another gun that Lloyd became reacquainted with at Dahlgren was the 5-inch 38 that had been designed at the Naval Gun Factory at the Washington Navy Yard. During testing there was a troubling reoccurrence of breech closure failures. Lloyd recalled the innovative solution they came up with to increase the necessary tension to close the breech once the shell was loaded:

> We would put the gun level at which point the bottom of the breech plug is easily accessible, and from the bottom of that breech plug we would suspend a 5 inch 38 [drill] projectile. The drill projectile weighs the same as the regular one—55 pounds. We would tension the spring until the breech closed lifting that extra 55 pounds with it.[50]

Whereas the 1.1-inch machine gun saw limited distribution, the 5-inch 38 proliferated. "We had the anti-aircraft defenses of Moscow including U.S. Navy 5 inch 38 guns," Lloyd recalled. The twin-mount configuration would be included in the armaments of all new battleships and refits of the older ones, cruisers, *Essex*-class aircraft carriers, and eventually in destroyers.[51]

With his experience at sea followed by his post-graduate education and follow-on tours, Lt. Lloyd M. Mustin was one of the most knowledgeable naval officers in the world in the field of shooting aircraft out of the sky. Thus his selection to be the assistant gunnery officer of the Navy's first antiaircraft light cruiser, *Atlanta*, represented a wise choice by the Navy's detailers. With Lloyd embarked, the gunnery department would have a leader who would be able to train the crews to fire effectively the 5-inch 38-caliber guns and 1.1-inch machine gun systems that he understood inside out.[52]

CHAPTER 3

The Construction and Commissioning of USS *Atlanta*

23 December, 1941

Atlanta underway from Fed. S.B.&D.D. Co. [Federal Shipbuilding & Drydock Company] yard, Kearny, New Jersey, for N. [Navy] Yard, New York, for commissioning, about 0600. Arrived about 1000, set ship-keeping watch.

24 December, 1941

Commissioned, about 1000. Margaret Mitchell (Mrs. John R. Marsh), the sponsor, among those present. Lots of publicity—"An Xmas present for the Axis", etc.

- - - - -

I was detached duty Naval Gun Factory, Washington, D.C., on 16 Aug. 1941 to report SupShips Kearny for duty CFO *Atlanta*. Reported 25 Aug., the day before a 19-day C.I.O. [Congress of Industrial Organizations] strike was ended by the Navy taking over the plant. Acting as Assistant Gunnery Officer. Ship launched Saturday, 6 Sept. Em & Peggy Handy drove up the previous day to attend; launching party at Coca-Cola plant; lots of bubbly.

After war began, stood security watches at the shipyard. A great farce; no real measure of security possible under the provisions made. No arms issued anyone.

The "delivery" was a farce. We were no more completed, from a satisfactory operating point of view, then about 95%, Gunnery, 80%.

***

Driving along the northbound lanes of the New Jersey Turnpike approaching the Pulaski Skyway, a glance off to the right reveals a heavily industrialized area at the confluence of the Passaic and Hackensack Rivers. Known as Kearny Point, the property covers the remnants of the former Federal Shipbuilding and Dry Dock Company and the site of a unique chapter in the history of industrial–labor relations within the United States. A product of America's industrial mobilization for World War I, the United States Steel subsidiary shared the long-standing corporate ethos on the non-recognition of workers' rights to form labor unions. During the Depression, when shipbuilding contracts were few and jobs were scarce, union organizers made little headway, as workers were happy to have a job at any wage.[1]

Yet over time, as the Federal Government invested its dollars into shipbuilding to jump start the economy and strengthen the nation's maritime capabilities in an increasingly dangerous world, the management–worker dynamic changed to a point where the Federal Government had to intervene. However, unlike past interventions where the state acted on behalf of corporate interests, at Federal Shipbuilding the seizure seemed to favor labor. From the standpoint of the Secretary of the Navy, Frank Knox, a Republican serving in President Roosevelt's Cabinet, his objective in taking over the yard was to enable work to continue on warships that would prove vital for the nation's defense.

As Federal Shipbuilding's workforce grew in the late 1930s, the new workers were bullied by the shop foremen—so called "Snappers"—loyal to the yard's management team, led by Lynn H. Korndorff, whose 6-foot-6-inch stature was physically intimidating. The Snappers overlooked unsafe conditions, resulting in frequent debilitating injuries—sometimes even death—among the workers assigned to the different shops.

Union organizer Mike Smith's background as Scotch-Irish Roman Catholic allayed fears of Communist allegiances, and on February 26, 1937, he gathered over 500 Federal Shipbuilding workers at the Ukrainian Hall in Jersey City to hear the Industrial Union of Marine and Shipbuilding Workers of America (IUMSWA) President John Green deliver a fiery speech to promote union membership. Building on the momentum of the Jersey City rally, Smith obtained the critical mass needed to charter a local. At a March 15 meeting, over 1,000 workers met to elect officers and chartered Local 16 of the IUMSWA. The following month, claiming 80 percent of the Federal Shipbuilding workforce as members, Local 16's leaders approached management about contract negotiations.

Willing to meet with leaders of the upstart union, President Korndorff listened to the list of demands, including recognition of Local 16 as the sole bargaining agent for the workers.[2] Korndorff would not yield until after the workforce walked out on strike on May 18. After three days, Korndorff agreed to allow Local 16 to be the exclusive bargaining agent. He refused to allow Federal Shipbuilding to be a total union shop or boost worker salaries, but the union welcomed the establishment of a minimum wage and formal grievance procedures.[3] Local 16 proceeded over the next few years to attempt to force Federal Shipbuilding to mandate union membership as a condition for employment at the yard—a demand that Korndorff considered ludicrous.[4]

Meanwhile, having won the contract to build the first two of a new class of light cruisers, on April 22, 1940, a keel was laid down at Federal Shipbuilding's Building Way Number 8, and within days, steel ribs began to shape the outline of a hull that would become *Atlanta*.[5]

Events overseas may have tempered the hostile management–union relations, with Germany having invaded and conquered much of Poland the previous autumn. Then, on May 10, 1940, Hitler's armies turned west to march into Holland, Luxembourg, and Belgium. The rapid capitulation of these countries exposed the northern flank of the Maginot Line as German armor supported by the Luftwaffe poured into northern France. Within three weeks, the Germans had trapped over 330,000 Allied soldiers at the French port of Dunkirk. With the extraction of much of that ground force—thanks to the efforts of the British Admiralty to press every available vessel along the channel coast into ferry service—the remaining French forces could only offer feeble resistance to the Nazi onslaught. On June 14, German troops marched into Paris. France formally surrendered eight days later, leaving Britain and her empire alone to stand up against Hitler.[6]

Although America remained neutral, President Roosevelt understood that the fall of Britain would have devastating consequences. While not a belligerent, America's actions could hardly be considered neutral. When the British lost 11 destroyers in a period of 10 days due to hostile actions in July 1940, the President arranged for a trade of 50 obsolescent destroyers for American basing rights at British installations in the western Atlantic. As the magnitude of the German aerial assault in what would become known as "The Battle of Britain" became apparent, Roosevelt declared a state of emergency on September 8, 1940, clearing the way for the creation of the Office of Production Management to coordinate armaments production and overseas export.

Following his electoral victory in November, Roosevelt pushed through the Lend-Lease Act, a bill that would enable the United States to sell armaments to any anti-Axis nation in exchange for direct or indirect payments deemed acceptable. After some heated debate in the House and Senate, the bill was passed and signed into law in March 1941. With the establishment of "Neutrality Patrols" in the western Atlantic to protect cargo ships carrying materials overseas against the German maritime threat, neutral America could hardly be called non-belligerent either.[7]

Over in Asia, neutral America favored China in its struggle to contain Imperial Japanese expansion. During the summer of 1940, President Roosevelt initiated bans on a growing list of materials to Japan while American arms found their way to China. Servicemen in the armed forces "volunteered" to travel to China to advise and fly with the Chinese Air Force, with units such as the Flying Tigers. In May 1941,

Roosevelt decided to forward deploy the main elements of the Pacific Fleet at the naval base at Pearl Harbor, Hawaii.[8]

With ongoing hostilities in both Europe and Asia, Congress repeatedly increased appropriations to increase military spending. Three days after the Germans marched into Paris, Congressman Carl Vinson introduced a bill calling for a 24 percent expansion of the fleet. The legislation moved quickly, and by the time the President signed "The Two Ocean Navy Bill" in mid-July, the expansion goal was increased to 70 percent.[9]

For the Federal Shipbuilding and Dry Dock Company, the legislation meant new contracts to build additional destroyers, cruisers, troop transports, and cargo ships. With a sense of urgency, construction accelerated on the destroyers and cruisers currently under contract. With work on *Atlanta* ahead of schedule, plans progressed for the ship's christening and launching ceremony. On May 2, 1941, Capt. A. T. Bidwell, an assistant of Adm. Chester W. Nimitz at the Bureau of Navigation, wrote to Mayor Roy LeCraw of Atlanta to seek a nominee to serve as the ship's sponsor. Nimitz welcomed LeCraw's nomination of Mrs. John Marsh, better known as Margaret Mitchell, author of *Gone with the Wind*, to be the sponsor of the ship. However, he declined the mayor's suggestion that the ship be christened with a large bottle of Coca-Cola.[10]

With Operation *Barbarossa*, the German invasion of the Soviet Union, the scale of the overseas conflict dramatically increased. On the day following the June 22, 1941 attack, Local 16 pledged to refrain from strikes for the next two years. This pledge would be incorporated into an Atlantic Coast Standards Agreement approved by both the company and the union, with the support of Secretary of the Navy Knox, the Maritime Commission's Emory S. Land, and the Office of Production Management.

However, in late July the prospects for long-term labor peace quickly faded following a ruling by the Federal Defense Mediation Board on Local 16's demands for a closed shop and the reclassification of some of the jobs within the shipyard. The Board recommended that Federal Shipbuilding adopt a modified union shop with grievance boards to be convened to address the reclassification issues. While the decision failed to convert the Kearny shipyard into a closed shop, company management was now forced to fire union members who allowed their dues to lapse. The ruling, if instituted, assured Local 16 retention of its current strength as it sought to recruit new non-members. Korndorff saw the ruling as unwarranted, as it dictated Union say on whom he could retain as employees. Why should he become the enforcer of union membership?

With inaction on Federal Shipbuilding's part, 6,000 members of Local 16 packed into Newark's Mosque Theater on the evening of Sunday, August 3, and voted with their leadership to call a strike. Union leaders met with company officials the next day but failed to sway Korndorff to implement the Defense Mediation Board ruling.

With that, the 124-member executive board of Local 16 met and voted unanimously to call a strike. When the 3,000 workers left to go home after the final shift on August 6, 250 picketers appeared at the yard's front gate facing U.S. Highway 1. Overall, the job action affected 16,000 workers.[11]

Korndorff, flying to Washington on the afternoon of the strike's first day, did not receive a sympathetic reception from Sidney Hillman at the Office of Management and Production and officials at the Maritime Commission. Spurning an offer from the union to provide workers to allow the planned August 9 launching of *Atlanta* to occur also proved to be a public relations setback for the embattled shipyard president, who declared that the event would have to be delayed indefinitely.[12]

With Korndorff unyielding, speculation rose about presidential intervention. In New Jersey, Local 16 called for the Navy to take over the yard. However, the President was not in Washington, as newspapers reported he was taking an "Atlantic cruise." With the situation deteriorating further in Europe as Soviet armies retreated deeper into Russia, President Roosevelt, embarked on the cruiser *Augusta*, arrived at Argentia Bay, Newfoundland. There he met with Winston Churchill, who arrived on the battleship *Prince of Wales*, for four days of talks that would lead to the draft of the Atlantic Charter, which called for the defeat of the Axis and provided the framework for the post-war United Nations. The strike in Kearny would have to wait.[13]

Although he felt on principle he was on solid ground, the meetings in Washington shook Korndorff's confidence about the ultimate outcome. Believing President Roosevelt would act against Federal Shipbuilding, Korndorff took preemptive action, sending a telegram to Secretary Knox offering the plant to the government, citing the national defense as being of far greater importance than the welfare of the company.[14] On August 12, Korndorff met with Knox to discuss his telegram. After two meetings, Knox informed reporters that "no decision has yet been reached" regarding government control of the shipyard.[15] His legal advisor, Adlai Stevenson, rushed to Maine to meet the presidential party disembarking from *Augusta* at Portland with a draft presidential executive order directing government seizure. President Roosevelt held off until his return to Washington on August 19, to allow him to directly appeal to Green and Korndorff to reopen talks. Neither party budged.[16]

Finally, on August 23, President Roosevelt signed the executive order authorizing the Navy's seizure of the shipyard, blaming the company's management for failing to abide by the Mediation Board's recommendation. Yet the press release announcing the seizure failed to state whether the Navy would operate the plant in accordance with the Mediation Board's decision.[17]

With both the union and company leadership pledging cooperation with the government, troops from Fort Dix were consequently not called upon to seize the yard. Instead, the Navy sent Rear Adm. Harold G. Bowen to New Jersey to assume responsibility for the yard's operation.[18]

A graduate of the U.S. Naval Academy's Class of 1905, Bowen served on numerous combatants and staffs, serving mainly in engineering officer billets. During the 1920s and 30s, the Navy assigned him to duties of growing responsibility at Navy shipyards. In 1935, he was promoted to rear admiral and assumed the duties as the Chief of the Bureau of Engineering. Under his tenure, new construction warships, such as *Atlanta*, were being powered by high-pressure boilers and high-speed reduction turbines.

Well acquainted with Bowen's abilities, Secretary Knox saw him as the right man for the job. As director of the Naval Research Laboratory over the previous two years, Bowen oversaw atomic research and radar development and held a collateral duty as technical aide to the Secretary of the Navy.[19]

As Bowen's train traversed the terrain after departing Union Station on the morning of August 24, the rear admiral huddled with his staff: "We had these discussions all the way up from Washington, anticipating as we did trouble with the strikers and expecting no trouble with management."[20] Much to their collective surprise, when they arrived at the yard in a station wagon, Union picketers waving American flags stood clear to allow Bowen direct access into the yard. In contrast, it was Korndorff who refused to yield, thinking the seizure of his yard was still negotiable. It took the late arrival of Under Secretary James Forrestal to convince the corporate executive that the Navy intended to begin operating the shipyard immediately and his presence was no longer needed nor desired.[21]

Given the adversarial relationship with Korndorff, Local 16's Executive Committee welcomed the change at the top, even though Bowen refrained from implementing the Defense Mediation Board's recommendations. With the union voting to end their job action, the picketers joyfully tore up their signs. Steps were taken to reopen the yard on Monday morning to ready the various shops to welcome the returning workforce on the following day. With welding torches and rivet guns in hand, work again went ahead to complete *Atlanta*, *Juneau*, other contracted destroyers, and merchant ships.[22]

Arriving as preparations resumed to ready *Atlanta* for launching, Lloyd Mustin recalled his first impressions of the new cruiser in Building Way Number 8:

> She was the first of a new class of cruiser that had appeared in the first big naval building increment authorized in the late '30's. There were six of them authorized. They turned out to be 6,000 tons. They had sonar equipment and depth charges like a destroyer. They had torpedo tubes like a destroyer which none of our post-World War I cruisers any longer had.[23]

Lloyd recalled the reasoning for putting torpedoes on *Atlanta* was to give the ship a punch that everyone would have to respect. He lamented that the main armament of 5-inch 38-caliber guns didn't command that respect. Cruisers of the *Atlanta*-class "were designed with, as they eventually came out, a total of eight 5 inch 38 twin mounts, three on the centerline forward, three on the centerline aft and one on either broadside." Lloyd didn't think this gun arrangement was too useful "but we made it work."[24]

He remembered having first being introduced to this class during an indoctrination lecture at Naval Postgraduate School in 1938:

> I recall rather distinctly that these ships were identified at that stage of their design having five twin mounts. They were going to have three mounts forward and two mounts aft, sort of a 5 inch counterpart of that class of 6" light cruiser [*Brooklyn*-class] that we had built starting in the mid-'30's. Somewhere along the line as the design developed, they found that instead of five twin mounts, they could arrange and provide for six and that both forward and aft they all could be superfiring. That is, the second mount from the bow would be higher than the first one so that it could fire above it and the third one would still be higher so it could fire above the second. Then, somewhere along the line they decided that they could carry two additional mounts, one on either broadside, that brought the ships up to a total of eight. This arrangement differed from the *Brooklyn*-class, which had its third turret at deck level with a reduced field of fire.[25]

Atlanta's design created a vessel unmatched in its ability to fire an antiaircraft broadside. With her heavy antiaircraft armament and electronic capabilities, the designers estimated berthing would have to accommodate 26 officers and 523 enlisted, as well as an additional 58 men if the ship were to serve as a flagship for a destroyer flotilla. *Atlanta*, when completed, would hold 35 officers and 638 enlisted. To take on the additional bodies, the mess deck was reduced and the crew had to eat in shifts.[26]

Although the workers went back to work, the strike had impeded the progress of the ship's construction in more ways than just time lost. Taking in the sight of the hull that would someday serve as his future home, the future assistant gunnery officer gazed at *Atlanta*'s recently delivered gun mounts that had been left exposed to the hot summer humidity and thunderstorms. "There was a lot of rust in critical areas, things of a sort the shipyard didn't even know how to cure. I could see we were eventually going to have to do it ourselves and eventually we did."[27]

Lloyd's arrival preceded that of both the prospective commanding and executive officers, so instead he checked in with the Supervisor of Ships, the Navy's representative at the normally civilian-run shipyard, charged with overseeing the proper execution of the shipbuilding contract. With the Navy having actually taken charge of Federal Shipbuilding, the incumbent must have been reassessing his job description. Arriving around the same time, Lt. Cdr. Norman W. Sears, a graduate from the Naval Academy's Class of 1925, assumed duties as the pre-commissioning commanding officer. Seven years senior to Mustin, Sears would eventually assume duties as *Atlanta*'s first lieutenant responsible for deck operations as well as the damage control assistant. For the two weeks following Lloyd's arrival, the small naval contingent worked within the Navy-operated yard to prepare for the launching of the cruiser. Beginning at 0400, on September 6, workers methodically pulled away the remaining keel blocks and supports, called bents, from the hull.

Margaret Mitchell of *Gone with the Wind* christens *Atlanta* at Federal Shipbuilding, setting in motion the launching of the new light cruiser into the Hackensack River. (Archives Branch, Naval History and Heritage Command, Washington, D.C.; 19-N-27282) (Archives Branch, Naval History and Heritage Command, Washington, D.C.; 19-N-27284)

By mid-morning, arriving VIPs could see that only two cradles, fashioned out of 200 tons of yellow pine timber, kept the 542-foot-long ship upright in place. Launching attendees joining Margaret Mitchell included New Jersey's Governor Charles and Mrs. Edison, Under Secretary of the Navy James V. Forrestal, Rear Adm. Edward J. Marquart of the New York Navy Yard, and Rear Adm. Bowen. As Lloyd noted, his wife Emily and friend Peggy Handy made the trip up from Maryland to witness Mitchell grasp the bottle of champagne and crack it squarely against the ship's bow, spattering the suds over the hard steel.

The cruiser then began a slow descent down the ways, picking up speed as she backed into the murky waters of the Hackensack. As the stern splashed into the river, horns sounded. Four tugs quickly approached the free-floating hull to rein in the ship and tow her to a berth in the finishing basin to continue the installation of weapons and other equipment.[28]

Meanwhile, the launching party capitalized on another Atlanta connection as the local Coca-Cola bottling plant, located across from the yard, hosted a lunchtime reception where Lieutenant Commander Sears accepted a silver punch bowl presented on behalf of the citizens of Atlanta.[29]

With the exception of the staff officers, all of Lloyd's fellow senior officers in *Atlanta's* wardroom were Annapolis grads with similar experiences at sea. With the future cruiser moored in the finishing basin, riveters and welders continued work on the ship's interior and exterior. *Atlanta's* growing Navy contingent stepped over electrical cables, acetylene hoses, and pneumatic gear that snaked over the decks as they sanded out rust and helped install various equipment. That the work continued at a rapid pace could be in part credited to the leadership of Rear Admiral Bowen. That the union did not return to the picket lines in light of the Navy's reluctance to also implement the Defense Mediation Board's decision is a tribute to Bowen's initiatives to drastically reduce the high death rate through initiating safety indoctrination for new employees and bringing in outside consultants to review construction hazards. By employing a management-by-walking-around leadership style, Bowen nipped potential problems and established a respectful relationship with the union leadership and the workers. Bowen would later write: "Korndorff recognized the union, but didn't meet it socially, while I met the union socially but did not recognize it."[30]

Shortly after the launch the prospective executive officer Cdr. Campbell "Dallas" Emory relieved Sears as the senior officer present, enabling Sears to double-check hatch fittings, fire pumps, and damage-control communication circuits. Also embarked, Lt. Cdr. Arthur E. Loeser and his Assistant Lt. John "Jack" T. Wulff were busy readying what would become their engineering plants. The communications officer, Lt. Paul T. Smith, and supply officer, Lt. D. C. T. Grubbs, had also reported aboard as did Lloyd Mustin's immediate boss—the gunnery officer, Lt. Cdr. W. Richardson David "Bill" Nickelson.

Also arriving on September 22 were the ship's first two officers with reserve commissions, both having graduated from the Naval Midshipmen School at Northwestern University, having entered the Navy through the V-7 program that had been established a year earlier—Ens. G. (George) Bowdain Craighill, Jr. and Ens. Edward D. Corboy. As the two new officers reported to the two-story building that housed the offices of the pre-commissioning crew, Corboy glanced at the light cruiser: "The sunlight striking her mighty turrets was a stirring sight … it was inspiring to know that the ship bearing those turrets was to be the fastest and most graceful cruiser in any navy." Introduced to the assistant gunnery officer, the two young men each received a hearty handshake and were invited along for a mini-tour of the guns and fire-control equipment. Lloyd showed off the armaments with the same pride with which "a mother would introduce her children."[31]

On two occasions *Atlanta* departed down Newark Bay for short cruises. On October 28–29, the cruiser-to-be headed out to the Atlantic escorted by the destroyer *Dahlgren* (DD 187) to undergo builder's trials.[32] Following tweaks to numerous mechanical and electrical systems, on November 21, the vessel crossed the Hudson River for the East River. After passage under the Brooklyn Bridge, *Atlanta* entered a drydock at the New York Navy Yard. Passing her hull inspection, the nearly completed cruiser left on the afternoon of November 23 for an overnight journey to Rockland, Maine. Picking up her acceptance trial riding late next morning, *Atlanta* steamed into Casco Bay to initiate a series of full-power runs of four-hour segments, astern runs of one-hour duration, full-ahead to full-back "crashes," and then running tests to standardize shaft turns for 12 knots on up to full ahead. On her best run

Atlanta produced about 80,000 SHP (shaft horsepower) and attained 34 knots. While en route to Boston on November 27, she cruised at 30 knots and 25 knots. After delivering her trial riders to the Charlestown Navy Yard, *Atlanta* returned to Kearny after a pitstop at the New York Navy Yard.

As the calendar turned to the fateful month of December, the man slated to command this sleek new warship finally arrived. Following five months of coursework at the Naval War College, Samuel Powell Jenkins reported aboard as the prospective commanding officer of a ship slated to join a peacetime Navy. That status changed during his first weekend on board. With much of the crew on liberty over in New York City, news of the attack on Pearl Harbor was gleaned from radio reports and newsboys hawking late editions on streetcorners. With the shocking news, sailors made their way back to Kearny. The following morning, many of these pre-commissioning crew members crammed into the ship's office with Captain Jenkins to listen to President Roosevelt exclaim "December 7, 1941, a date which will live in infamy" and call for Congress to declare war against Japan—a sobering thought for these men who were about to place a warship in commission. Shocked by the Japanese attack, Rear Admiral Bowen expressed dismay when he heard that Army radar had detected the attack but the information was not acted on. As the director of the Naval Research Laboratory, he had worked hard to get radar in the field, and the outcome at Pearl Harbor made many feel their efforts were for naught. Still in command at the Naval Research Laboratory, Bowen yearned to focus more of his attention on researching and developing the technology that could win the war.[33]

Fortunately for Bowen, the attack extracted a commitment from Local 16 IUMSWA to: "pledge our wholehearted cooperation to the President and the Government of the United States, in the crusade for the preservation of democracy in a world which is being harried and destroyed by the 'mad dogs' of the Axis." The union local also resolved to "pledge ourselves to land every effort to increase our production of the vital defense vessels so necessary for the extermination of the menace which at this moment threatens the security and freedom of the democratic peoples of the world."[34]

For three months, the Navy had walked on a tightrope in operating a shipyard and dealing with the union, and with the union's patriotic commitment, Bowen saw an opportunity to get the Navy out from under the responsibility for running Federal Shipbuilding. With the Local 16 resolution in hand, Bowen suggested to the Navy secretary that the time was ripe to return the shipyard "while the going was good." Knox readily agreed. On January 5, 1942, President Roosevelt signed an executive order relinquishing control of Federal Shipbuilding and Drydock Company.[35]

Unfortunately for Bowen, his successful handling of Federal Shipbuilding thwarted going back to work full-time at the Naval Research Laboratory. As the proven fixer, the Navy would tap him on seven more occasions during the war to seize and operate industrial facilities to assure war production.[36]

However, as reflected in his autobiography, he did take pride that the ships built at Federal Shipbuilding would contribute to the eventual victory at sea. As Bowen moved on to stateside duties, one of those ships, the *Atlanta*, prepared to play her part to attain victory with a young officer embarked who would record his observations on that conflict in a diary.

Meanwhile, the headlines in the newspapers continued to be bad. America's declaration of war against Japan brought that nation's Axis partners into the conflict with America, and with the battleships of the Pacific Fleet lying in the mud of Pearl Harbor, there was very little the United States could do to blunt the Japanese thrust into the Philippines, Hong Kong, Singapore, and the Dutch East Indies. Indeed, there was concern that America's West Coast could be subject to attack. Meanwhile, in the Atlantic, Nazi submarines were off America's coastline sinking thousands of tons of American and Allied shipping.

Thus, a sense of urgency existed to get *Atlanta* to sea. The Navy needed combatants to restore its order of battle, and Americans were looking for any good news to pin their hopes on. However, for Lloyd Mustin and his shipmates, the Bureau of Ships' decision to accept early delivery of the light cruiser would prove to be a source for future frustrations.

Departing Kearny at daybreak on December 23, *Atlanta* steamed down Newark Bay and made a left turn to pass under the Bayonne Bridge, the world's longest arch span, across Upper New York Harbor Bay past the eyes of the Statue of Liberty and up the East River, passing under the suspended spans of the Brooklyn and Manhattan Bridges before arriving at pier G, berth 12, at the Brooklyn Navy Yard.

With weather forecasters calling for rain on Christmas Eve, a tarpaulin was stretched across the ship's quarterdeck and stern section to protect the VIPs from the inclement weather. By 1100, the official party was seated on the quarterdeck, looking down at seated guests on the pier and the ship's crew, which had grown to over 200, which was standing in formation.

Rear Adm. Adolphus Andrews, Commandant of the Third Naval District, and Rear Admiral Marquart were piped aboard as the crew and guests had been assembled on the fantail. When the commissioning party reached the stern, they saw that the officers were lined up in ranks amidships facing forward, and the enlisted crew stood in ranks to port and starboard. Guests sat under a canvas that had been raised over the stern. The officers wore their long blue coats over their service dress blue uniforms, while the enlisted kept warm under peacoats and donned blue flattop hats.[37]

Capt. Harold V. McKittrick, the captain of the yard, read the commissioning orders and turned to Captain Jenkins. Jenkins ordered his men to face the ship's stern and called his crew to attention as a two-man detail unfurled the national ensign. After the playing of the national anthem, Jenkins read his orders from the chief of the Bureau of Navigation dated October 15, 1941, assigning him as

Atlanta is commissioned on Christmas Eve, 1941. Following the ceremony Margaret Mitchell presents Capt. Samuel Jenkins a silver punch bowl as a gift from the city for which the ship was named. (Archives Branch, Naval History and Heritage Command, Washington, D.C.; NH 57450) (Archives Branch, Naval History and Heritage Command, Washington, D.C.; NH 57449)

commanding officer. Jenkins looked out to his assembled crew and distinguished guests and stated: "It's an honor indeed to be the captain of the first major warship to join the Navy since Pearl Harbor."[38] Jenkins then ordered the setting of the first watch. The chief bo'sun's mate stepped forward with his pipe, piped the call, and the bluejackets broke ranks and assumed positions by their stations. On the quarterdeck, Lt. Cdr. James S. Smith assumed duties as the first officer of the deck in port. Admiral Andrews gave a blustery speech, stating "this is a fighting ship" and extolled the crew: "your job from this day forward is to use its guns to blast and smash the enemies of this country."[39]

Miss Mitchell again was on hand to address the crew of the ship named for her city. She told the sailors, "We know that when the time comes you will give a wonderful account of yourselves." Because of Mitchell's star power, the City of Atlanta commissioned a portrait of the author for the ship in lieu of the standard silver set. The famed author also presented Captain Jenkins a large silver punch bowl. As the ceremony proceeded, the skies cleared, and at the conclusion, America's newest warship basked in sunlight.[40]

Following the ceremony, the crew and their families and friends were served lunch on the ship's mess decks, while the officers were served a meal in the wardroom. After 1600 the officers left the ship for a more elaborate reception in Manhattan at the St. Regis Hotel that was underwritten by Cola-Cola.[41]

Yet despite all the pomp, Lloyd Mustin saw much work needed to be completed if *Atlanta* was to effectively contribute to the war effort.

CHAPTER 4

The Fitting Out and Workups of USS *Atlanta*

8 Feb 1942

Left N. Yd. N. Y. for "shakedown." Lay in Gravesend Bay 8th–10th, taking on ammunition and cleaning ship. Then down to Chesapeake Bay for target practices. Fired about 700 rounds of 5", in AA [antiaircraft] and surface practices; also lots of machine gun stuff.

Then went to Casco Bay, Me. for anti-sub practice. Not much accomplished, uneventful in general.

14 March 1942

Arrived N. Yd. N. Y. again for final trials, etc. Came down from Casco via Cape Cod Canal and Hell Gate. Much sub activity in Atlantic coastal waters, which the Capt decides it's damn well for us amateurs to stay clear of. Had had trouble through all practices, due to lousy installation work. Circuits grounded, phones dead, gear broken. No tools, spares, drawings, etc.

29 March 1942

All final trials complete, and underway for sea. Lots of work items remain undone, and some original installation work uncomplete. Still have only 2 1".1 gun directors, instead of 4, and 1 SC Radar. But lots of ships have zero of either.

No way has been found to get the 5" twins (enclosed) onto close-range AA targets. They can't pick them up, being too blind.

Em came to N.Y. 25th thru 28th. Very swell for a goodbye. Ship is going to Pacific Fleet, which I know but which still cannot tell; when home next, there's no knowing. A sort of 2nd honeymoon, using a windfall check from the Germantown Trust Co.

Went to Gravesend Bay, again, to top off with ammunition and to await orders. We have been definitely assigned to CruDiv 10, Atlantic Fleet, all along, so the Pacific stuff will surprise the troops.

***

During *Atlanta*'s first three months in commission, Lloyd Mustin's entries into his little green log book were few, likely due to trips to Washington and a busy in-port schedule that involved the continuous tweaking of the ship's sensors with her gun platforms.

Though entries in Lloyd's log were thin, the entries in *Atlanta*'s official deck log were voluminous. Tradition has it the deck log entry for the first watch of the new year be in rhyme. One stanza of *Atlanta*'s entry read:

> To comfort our ship, ere she goes forth;
> Be it Tropic Clime or the frozen north;
> To blast our foes from their evil thrones;
> We receive from the dock steam, juice, water, and telephones.

Throughout January the crew worked "high speed, early and late" to address the many deficiencies noted by Lloyd in his diary entry.[1] On January 9 shore connections and lines were disconnected to allow for *Atlanta* to be transferred into Dry Dock No. 4. For the next 11 days, the light cruiser would sit on keel blocks as yard workers and ship's company tackled issues within the engineering plant, interior communications, and electronics. During the drydocking Lloyd traveled to Washington, where presumably he visited the Naval Research Laboratory and Naval Gun Factory. At the Naval Research Laboratory, one of *Atlanta*'s newly assigned officers, Lt. (jg) J. A. Wallace, was spending the first month of 1942 learning all he could on the latest radar technology.[2]

As the officer having the challenge of installing and calibrating the ship's radar systems, Lloyd would welcome Wallace's help. Lloyd took pride that the *Atlanta* was the first cruiser to get the Mark 37 fire-control radar system. *Atlanta* would have two of these directors. The Mark 37 had first appeared on the *Sims*-class destroyers and was being placed on the new construction battleships *North Carolina* and *Washington*. He described it as "an enclosed turret-like structure that sat on top of a cylindrical barbette, and this structure really carried only the optics, the pointer's and trainer's telescopes, and a third telescope for the director-officer plus the range finder, which was a stereoscopic range finder."[3]

In contrast to previous gun director systems that had the fire-solution computing mechanisms collocated at the director, the Mark 1 computer was situated below decks in a plotting room. Designers calculated that the previous Mark 33 system that incorporated the computer in the topside enclosure had too much weight, and with the addition of radar antennas, there was a potential of putting top-heavy ships to sea. As designed, the two towering barbette-mounted gun directors located just aft of the bridge and the second stack made for a recognizable feature of the class.

Lloyd noted that when the radar components were built, they could not be fitted within the barbette, and as with the computer, they also were placed below. Since the void wasn't filled, it provided a perfect lookout perch, featuring protection from the weather, and with the barbette's 1.5-inch-thick plating, flying shrapnel.[4]

Indeed, the *Atlanta* did receive fire-control radar for its gun batteries—the FD. In Navy nomenclature, F stood for "Fire Control" and D meant the fourth model. Again, *Atlanta* seemed chosen for special attention, as the Bureau of Ordnance allocated two of the first eight sets of this model to the light cruiser. Other sets were placed on the battleships *North Carolina* and *Washington*. For Lloyd, the arrival of these new devices caused some trepidation. For the past three years he had become one of the Navy's foremost experts on gunnery. "These radars included some features that were absolutely, of course, quite new to me compared to the bed spring things that I had seen at the Naval Research Laboratory in that introductory indoctrination in 1940."[5]

After installing the antennas on the Mark 37 directors and additional equipment below, training commenced. No schools existed, so Lloyd employed "seat of the pants, trial and error" training to include tracking subway cars rolling across the nearby Manhattan and Williamsburg Bridges across the East River. In addition, *Atlanta* was one of the first ships to receive the new SC air search radar. Lloyd recalled the radar operated at 200 megacycles, versus 400 megacycles for the FD. The antenna was a flat array placed on the masthead, and the transmitter and modulator were installed on the bridge level in back of the charthouse, perhaps 80 feet below the antenna.[6]

As the diary noted, on February 8 at 0912, personnel at pier C, berth 3 cast away the final lines, which were pulled aboard by *Atlanta*'s deckhands as tugs pulled the light cruiser out into the East River. With a pilot providing speed and rudder directions, *Atlanta* passed under the Manhattan and Brooklyn Bridges. After a pilot boat extracted the pilot as the ship passed the Statue of Liberty, Captain Jenkins took the conn and guided *Atlanta* through the Verrazano Narrows and turned the ship to port and coasted toward an anchorage spot in Gravesend Bay on the Brooklyn waterfront just northwest of Coney Island. The ship's anchor settled in the mud below at 1012.[7] At 1250 a barge came alongside. Working parties worked well into the night and through the next day to haul aboard 5-inch shells, powder cartridges, and smaller caliber ammunition onto the ship. While much of the ammo found its way into the forward and aft magazines deep below, sailors placed 20mm and 1.1-inch ammo in small ready service rooms dubbed "Clipping Rooms" adjacent to those gun mounts.

On the afternoon of February 10, tugs came to remove the barge, and at 1459 the anchor cleared the Gravesend Bay floor and "Underway, Shift Colors" was announced as Captain Jenkins took the conn. As *Atlanta*'s shafts began to turn, the now-armed cruiser passed through open netting through the narrows and steamed by the Ambrose Lightship. As the cruiser cleared Ambrose Channel, Jenkins ordered General Quarters, and the crew remained at their battle stations for 42 minutes as "manned and ready" reports slowly filtered to the bridge. With the present threat of U-boats, Jenkins ordered the speed increased to full, and a zigzag plan was implemented as the ship proceeded on an overnight journey to Norfolk. As the cruiser sped down the Jersey coast, a blimp based out of Lakehurst patrolled overhead, keeping a lookout for U-boats. As the sun set, the blimp veered off, and *Atlanta* continued through choppy seas under darkened ship conditions.[8]

With the waves bobbing the light cruiser along, many of the new sailors felt woozy. The next morning at 0630 General Quarters was sounded, a practice that would continue in coming months at dawn and sunset when the light cruiser was most vulnerable to being attacked by enemy submarines. After securing from GQ at 0742, *Atlanta* proceeded on, picking up a pilot as the ship held the Cape Henry lighthouse abeam to port. Under the pilot's guidance, *Atlanta* turned up the Thimble Shoal Channel, into the Chesapeake Bay, and up into Hampton Roads, where she dropped her hook at assigned anchorage berth 21 at 1411. That afternoon a small boat came alongside transporting two physicists and a radio engineer from the Naval Research Laboratory.[9]

Atlanta spent much of the following day running back and forth 17 times over a degaussing range that had recently been placed off Cape Charles. German magnetic mines exploited a natural occurrence, as ships' hulls became magnetized over time as they steamed over the Earth's magnetic fields. Embarked Naval Research Laboratory technicians evaluated the readings of underwater sensor measurements that gauged

Atlanta conducting a high-speed run during Navy acceptance trials prior to commissioning. (Archives Branch, Naval History and Heritage Command, Washington, D.C.; NH 51382)

the light cruiser's magnetic footprint. Upon concluding the degaussing runs at 1730, Captain Jenkins turned north into Chesapeake Bay and dropped anchor at 1847 off Nassawadox Creek along the eastern shore.[10]

Underway the next day at 0748, *Atlanta* once again plied in protected waters, buffeted by bitterly cold winds blowing across the Chesapeake. For Lloyd Mustin, February 13 would mark a milestone, as he stood the first of many, many watches as the officer of the deck underway. During his 8–12 watch, *Atlanta* steamed in what seemed to be endless circles. The navigator, Lieutenant Commander Smith, and his quartermasters took readings off the gyro and the magnetic compasses to determine the deviation on the latter in the wake of the degaussing. In addition, tests were conducted to calibrate *Atlanta*'s radio detection finding gear. Once the maneuvers were completed, the light cruiser turned up the Potomac River and arrived and anchored that afternoon off Mattawoman Creek adjacent to the Indian Head Naval Powder Factory, presumably to drop off the Naval Research Laboratory physicists.[11]

On Valentine's Day, *Atlanta* returned to Hampton Roads. For the following two days *Atlanta* would get underway for the primary purpose of calibrating the radio detection finding gear. Reception of wavelengths of 485 kilocycles was followed by 380 kilocycles and so on. Meanwhile, the first lieutenant, Lieutenant Commander Sears, assisted by Lieutenant Perkins, ran the crew through an exhausting series of damage control drills simulating fire, flooding, and collision. In addition to practicing firefighting, shoring bulkheads, and dewatering spaces, the ship's sick bay staff gave first aid lectures and trained the crew to set splints, apply bandages, and administer morphine.

Having anchored overnight in the Chesapeake on the evening of February 16, it was now time for *Atlanta*'s gunnery department to swing into action. Recently promoted Lt. Cdr. Bill Nickelson, assisted by Lloyd Mustin and the division officers, worked on calibrating the guns and radars and training the men. Gunnery was labor intensive. The green gun crews slowly went through the motions of loading and actually firing the guns for the first time. The eight 5-inch 38 mounts each had a crew of 13. Working together, the crew could fire a salvo every four seconds. However, for that to happen, men in the upper handling rooms below the gun mounts had to keep the electro-hydraulic hoists moving, with shells coming from the magazines below. However, before you could run, you needed to crawl and walk. On the afternoon of February 17, each of the 5-inch 38 twin mounts systematically fired test shots. A total of 64 rounds broke down to four rounds per barrel. Besides breaking in the virgin gun crews, the test shots determined if gunfire could cause inadvertent structural damage or affect interior communications. Lloyd expressed frustration about many of the phone circuits going dead.[12]

After another night of anchorage in the Chesapeake Bay, *Atlanta* got underway at 0749 on February 18 and reported for duty to the Commander in Chief, Atlantic Fleet. That day the smaller 1.1-inch were broken in, and on the following day the

20mm guns fired for the first time, expending some 480 rounds. Having spent two nights anchored off Nassawadox Creek, *Atlanta* got underway at 0754 on February 21, and within an hour Captain Jenkins had the ship at General Quarters. Included in this morning's series of drills was transfer of ship control to Battle II, the backup bridge that the ship's designers placed just aft of the second Mark 37 gun director. From Battle II, Commander Emory was able to take control of the rudder and transmit orders to the engine rooms to adjust speed.[13]

Finally, having operated around Chesapeake Bay for a week, *Atlanta* again made the trek up Thimble Shoal Channel to anchor at berth 25. Among the notable ships in port that day was the carrier *Hornet*. Following the dispatch of a contingent of shore patrol, Captain Jenkins authorized liberty for his crew.[14]

After the short respite, at 0916 on Sunday morning the first lieutenant reported the anchor had cleared the bottom, and Captain Jenkins once again took the conn and aimed his ship toward Thimble Shoal Channel. Turning up into Chesapeake Bay, the light cruiser anchored off Tangier Island that evening in anticipation of a week of intensive training. Underway the next morning, the crew went to General Quarters for 1 hour and 12 minutes to conduct on-station training before breaking for the midday meal. At 1202, the crew again went to General Quarters, and throughout the afternoon 5-inch rounds were systematically fired, starting with Mount One, all the way forward to Mount Eight back on the stern where Seaman Dunaway patiently waited for his chance to load shells. Overall, 127 rounds were expended. During the exercise, Bill Nickelson's and Lloyd Mustin's gun crews had to deal with two hang-fire incidents on the left barrels of Mount One and Seven as a shell failed to fire. In both cases the crews were able to extract the shells and toss them over the side.[15]

After anchoring again off Tangier Island, *Atlanta* again raised her hook just before 0800 on February 24, and with the crew at GQ an hour later, Bill Nickelson's and Lloyd Mustin's 5-inch 38 gun crews engaged in their first antiaircraft training as a plane towed a target sleeve that was tracked from the forward and aft gun directors. On the first pass, the light cruiser fired four shells at the sleeve. The exercise abruptly ended on the second pass after six shots when the sleeve parted and came fluttering down into the bay. To give the 1.1-inch and 20mm gun crews something to shoot at, balloons were released into the wind to enable them to fly in the path of the smaller caliber AA guns. Lloyd recalled that most of the balloons got away.

Such became the routine for the rest of the week. As Lloyd indicated in his diary, the *Atlanta* expended approximately 700 rounds of 5-inch ammunition in AA and surface modes first at stationary targets and then at moving targets.

What challenged Lloyd and his shipmates was getting the ordnance on target using the fire-control radar. The FD radar was quite primitive, and it required teamwork to operate. The "trainer" had the job of sweeping the antenna across the horizon toward targets that were reported by lookouts or the long-range search radar:

> By changing the phase of feeding the antenna successive pulses of energy went out in lobes which were deliberately displaced off the electromagnetic axis of the antenna. The successive lobes scanned for different quadrants and the trainer saw the target pips. Instead of a single target pip he was shown two pips. One came from the lobes that were displaced to the right and the other came from the lobes that were displaced to the left. Of course, if the target were off the central axis of the antenna one lobe would give a stronger echo than the other and the way he got his alignment on the target was to equalize the size of the two pips.[16]

With the trainer determining the approach axis, the "pointer" controlled the elevation, and "got the same sort of thing for the lobes that were displaced above and displaced below. He lined up on the target in elevation by matching the size of the two pips."

Once the approach axis and vertical angle was determined, a radar range operator took charge. Lloyd recalled:

> He was in the back of the director right alongside of the range finder operator where in the original design space had thoughtfully been left for an additional man. No explanation, just a space. But the upshot of the whole thing was that the optical range finder operator and the radar range finder operator were shoulder-to-shoulder back there. On visible targets you could cross check with the optical range finder.[17]

That the radar range operator and the Mark 37 optical range finder worked in tandem was critical to the air defense operation. While the FD radar operators could track a target, they had no ability to determine if the target was friend or foe. Assuming it was daylight and the skies were clear, the optical range finder had the benefit of a tremendously high-quality, high-capability optical instrument. Lloyd recounted, "The radar fellow could tell you more accurately than the optical guy what the range was to the target, but the optical guy could tell you what the target was … he was seeing the actual thing, and this helped in discriminating occasionally between friendly and enemy."[18] During those cold mornings over the Chesapeake that February, the pilots of the aircraft towing the target sleeves were counting on the optical range finders to keep them alive.

Four decades later, Lloyd reflected that the FD had many shortcomings:

> It was primitive indeed. I think Bell Telephone Laboratories designed it for the Navy, and Western Electric built it. It was a relatively low frequency thing, about 400 megacycles, which is a relatively low radar frequency. Therefore, the wave length, of course, varies inversely with frequency so it had a relatively long wave length, and thus it was not capable of very high orders of discrimination between the two targets at nearly the same range and things of that sort.[19]

Lloyd recalled that "this was a fairly cumbersome way of doing things, but it worked. It took a lot of training of your crew to enable them to perform this sort of awkward function and do it in the split seconds that you have available."[20] Lloyd also made the following observations about the SC air search radar:

> The feed from the transmitter to the antenna was by co-axial cable and it just wouldn't work. It just wouldn't work. It didn't have the power to feed that antenna through that length of transmission line and get enough power out into the air to get an echo back from a target and back down the wave guide and give you a usable signal down in the radar room.[21]

Lloyd expressed frustration about the lack of capability to detect aircraft at the ranges needed to adequately prepare for fleet defense. Furthermore, though the radar was not intended to detect ships, Lloyd figured it should be able to pick out vessels located inside of visual range—a capability that would be useful at night or in inclement weather.

For Lloyd, the arrival of Ensign Wallace just prior to *Atlanta* departing for her shakedown cruise was cause for hope. A graduate of a three-month course at MIT and follow-on orientation at the Naval Research Laboratory, the newly trained arrival had studied the technical and practical maintenance aspects of the radars that were being installed out in the fleet. However, "Our young radar officer did his best to tune and re-tune and sharpen everything up to absolute performance to the best of our ability to get it to perform, and it wouldn't perform." A continuing dialogue with the Naval Research Laboratory in Washington ensued. "Some modifications appeared eventually. Before too many months, literally preamplifiers and other things to multiply many fold the output power and to improve many fold the receiver sensitivity and all of these things made it capable of picking up aircraft at useful ranges." Lloyd finally expressed satisfaction that *Atlanta* could acquire aircraft at 50 and 60 miles out and could pick up ships at 15 or 20 miles distant.[22]

On February 27, following early gunnery drills, the sailors of *Atlanta* were treated to the spectacle of America's two newest battleships as the light cruiser passed *North Carolina* steaming by to port and *Washington* which passed to starboard.[23]

Crewmembers experienced a short weekend off Norfolk with limited liberty time as the cruiser once again raised her hook for a midday Sunday to engage in power runs. As *Atlanta* approached her designed speed there was excessive vibration within the stern.[24]

On March 3, Captain Jenkins took the conn as *Atlanta* got underway after sunset in the Chesapeake to spot targets at night, a skill the Japanese had demonstrated over the previous week in the battle of the Java Sea and the battle of Sundra Strait where the Imperial Japanese Navy twice triumphed over a combined flotilla of Australian, British, Dutch, and American warships. With the loss of the heavy cruiser *Houston* along with the Australian cruiser *Perth* early on the morning of March 1, the pre-war American Asiatic fleet had been effectively eliminated.[25]

After an overnight anchorage in Chesapeake Bay, Commander Emory took the conn on Wednesday morning as *Atlanta* got underway; after gunnery exercises and a brief rendezvous with *North Carolina*, the light cruiser made one final run up Thimble Shoal Channel. After a temporary anchorage, *Atlanta* was allowed to berth port side to pier 7 to take on some additional ammunition and supplies. For those who were authorized liberty that evening, the in-port berth spared them the boat ride. On March 6, *Atlanta* departed Hampton Roads estuary. Clearing the entrance to Chesapeake Bay, the ship turned on a northeasterly course into the North Atlantic headed to Portland, Maine.[26]

As *Atlanta* passed east of Cape Cod, she found herself heading into high winds and heavy seas. Green water broke over the bow, and the weight of the sea pounding down on the deck caused the ship to shudder. For crewmembers spoiled by three weeks of steaming in the protected waters of the Chesapeake, the 25-degree rolls tossed loose gear and weakened the stomachs even of Old Salts. With the bridge of the ship well up on the superstructure, the officer of the deck, which rotated between Lieutenants Perkins, Smith, Mustin, and Wulff, and their respective watch teams, had a heck of a ride.[27]

Unlike the trip to Norfolk, there was liberty most evenings, with half the crew being allowed to go ashore. For the enlisted, Portland didn't offer much. Many of the bars were crowded with sailors from other ships, including the carrier *Wasp*. No doubt the weather was a factor in Lloyd's comment about not getting much accomplished at Casco Bay. On March 13, *Atlanta* cleared Casco Bay and conducted some gunnery and engineering "crashback" drills to see how fast the Black Gang—a term that hung on from the days of coal—could get the ship's screws to reverse their spin. The light cruiser took a coastal course down to Boston for a brief stop and then out into Massachusetts Bay and down through the Cape Cod Canal, passing under the raised railroad lift bridge at 1838. Clearing the canal, the cruiser turned right and headed into the Long Island Sound for a nighttime transit. After passing under the Bronx–Whitestone Bridge at 0731 the next morning, the ship passed through Hell's Gate and traversed the waters of the East River to return to the Brooklyn Navy Yard and tie up at pier G, berth 13. Across from *Atlanta* floated her sister ship, *Juneau*.[28]

Once back at the Brooklyn Navy Yard, workers poured aboard to correct additional deficiencies unveiled during the shakedown and make necessary alterations. Life rafts were redistributed around the ship, strapped to the sides of gun mounts and other exterior bulkheads. Workers installed additional scuppers on the bridge wings to allow for better drainage to prevent lookouts from having to stand in pools of water during and following rainstorms.

The ship received additional armament. K-Guns, capable of firing 300-pound depth charges abeam, were installed on the stern to augment the two racks containing 600-pound depth-charge barrels designed to roll off the fantail. Also back aft, an additional 1.1-inch gun was positioned to protect the ship from enemy aircraft sneaking in from directly astern.[29]

Technicians worked to improve the SC radar, and the Mark 37 gun directors were modified to incorporate a "sluing sight." Lloyd described the sight in these terms:

> ... very crude open sight mounted outside of the shield of the director in a position so that the director officer by standing up in his position with his head and shoulders out of the hatch above him could use this sight as an alignment device. It was connected into the director's power drives in such a way that in whatever direction you moved the sight you caused the director to move that way and at very high rates if necessary. It gave him a means for looking around with the wide field of view of the eye, seeing a target and quickly getting the director around and on to that target.[30]

Atlanta was one of the first ships to receive the modifications as Lloyd recalled receiving a telephone call from the Bureau asking if he would have an interest in having the modification installed. "I seized the opportunity."[31]

As the ship underwent alterations, the rumor mill churned out dope on *Atlanta*'s future assignments. Many crewmembers, based on their experience in Maine and the distribution of cold-weather gear, assumed that the cruiser would join the war against the Nazis, escorting convoys across the Atlantic fending off attacks from Luftwaffe bombers and Kriegsmarine U-boats and surface combatants. Lloyd Mustin was one of the few on board who knew the ship's ultimate destination.[32]

Knowing what lay ahead, Captain Jenkins granted leave and liberty to allow crewmembers to spend time with their families. As Lloyd noted in his diary, "Em" (short for Emily) visited for three days for what would be a "second honeymoon." Still, work continued on readying the ship for sea, and from March 24 through March 26, the light cruiser once again found herself high and dry in drydock number 4. During the drydocking, yard workers removed the two huge three-bladed monstrosities and installed two smaller four-bladed variants. Though the smaller screws could only get the light cruiser up over 30 knots, the high-speed vibration was drastically reduced.[33]

Returned to pier G, *Atlanta* took on fuel on March 28. As Lloyd wrote in his diary, the ship pulled away the next morning from the pier for the last time as the announcement "Underway, Shift Colors" was made at 0803. However, the cruiser loitered in New York waters at Gravesend Bay for a few more days to load additional ammo, and run a degaussing range. For many of the wives, the pain of watching the ship depart Brooklyn was rubbed in by seeing the ship off Coney Island for three days thereafter before being gone for good.[34]

CHAPTER 5

En Route to Hawaii

5 April 1942

Finally underway from Gravesend Bay for Panama, there to report to CinCPac [Commander in Chief, Pacific] and get further orders. We always seem to get underway on Sundays.

We are now, of course, considered as full-fledged members of the fleet, just over 3 months after commissioning, which itself was 2 months ahead of schedule. Boy, what a mess! Tools for Gunnery Dept., 50% on hand, spares, 30%. Instructions & drawings, 70%, but the new and troublesome stuff is what has its drawings, etc., missing.

Intended complement, 21 officers (though the greatest boob would know quite a few more required), accommodations provided for 27. 34 on board, 4 double rooms having been made into 2 bunkrooms, 17 regular, 17 reserve. 13 in Gunnery, 6 of whom are reserve Ensigns (3 have previous sea duty, however). Original crew complement 540; 670 on board. Mess compartments filled with crew's bunks; lots of them jury-rigging hammocks. A draft of 125 men, 10 days in the Navy was received one day in filling up.

8 April 1942

Arrived Pacific end of canal 1800. Many barrage balloons, much AA stuff visible, signs of much more, invisible. Blackout every night, curfew, etc. Bent a prop, probably on a lock safety chain, just as we were clearing the last lock, and docked with one engine. Have to stay awhile for a check-up. Many sub alarms enroute; 1 sighted. No attacks.

12 April

(Sunday again) Underway. We were docked in the Balboa dock to have the prop straightened. Also found the bilge keels bent, I think by the knuckle-headed pilot putting her on a shoal trying to get around and into the slip at the dock entrance. About 30% of the supposedly red-hot new type plastic anti-fouling paint had fallen off the bottom, too, perhaps on account of being painted on in freezing weather in the N.Y. Yard's great rush to "get us out." Nothing was done about this; we undocked with nothing on the bottom but rust, in the large areas involved.

We were to have a sleeve target, for a little AA practice. Being Sunday, though, such was considered "not practicable" by ComUtWing [Commander Utility Wing].

Enroute Pearl Harbor, via Clipperton Island, which we are to reconnoiter for signs of possible use by Japs.

17 April

Arrived off Clipperton Island, a low atoll, with one big rock. Uninhabited since the last war. We came in all loaded for bear, ready to bombard areas, using the rock, etc., as aiming points for offset shooting, with grids all laid out, etc. Or anything else—air, surface, or sub. An undercurrent of excitement—the Japs might have been there, fueling subs, etc.

Found a schooner lying off "Skidbladnir" of San Pedro, Cal., fishing for sharks for their livers. Capt., Mate & one hand had landed on island, for curiosity, leaving cook & 1 hand. Blow made up, she dragged & they had her underway. Unable to get the men off island on account of the surf. Decided they could make out okay and left.

***

After getting underway from Gravesend on April 3 at 1024, Captain Jenkins called his crew to General Quarters for a half hour as the ship passed the Ambrose Lightship and turned onto a southeasterly heading toward Florida and the Caribbean. Once out into the Atlantic, Captain Jenkins spoke to the crew using the 1MC general announcing system. The crew learned that *Atlanta*'s destination was the Panama Canal and that the ship expected to arrive there in a few days. Jenkins also promised his crew that throughout their service together, he would brief them on upcoming operations as they left port. In addition, he emphasized that the cruiser was steaming unescorted through submarine-infested waters so the crew needed to remain alert.[1]

As indicated by Lloyd Mustin's muster report, Captain Jenkins had a good size audience. *Atlanta* was not short on crew, steaming with a full wartime complement of 670.

In contrast, a ship of comparable size in today's Navy is operated by a crew one third in size. The difference in the size, of course, was that every function on *Atlanta* was more labor intensive, from working the gun mounts, to operating the radars, to firing the boilers that drove the light cruiser's engines.

As Lloyd notes, there was a split in the wardroom between regular and reserve officers. All of the senior line officers—the captain, executive officer, and department heads, except for the medical and supply officers—were graduates of the Naval Academy. Most of the junior ensigns such as Corboy were graduates of the V-7 officer training program that had been initiated in 1940.

Despite implementing a zigzag scheme as a countermeasure to U-boat torpedo attack, *Atlanta* made rapid progress down the East Coast. Wary of that threat, Captain Jenkins would have his crew at their General Quarters stations at dawn and at sunset when lighting conditions made the ship most vulnerable to submarine attack. This routine would continue into the Pacific. Suspecting that the approaches to the Panama Canal on the morning of April 8 could be U-boat infested, Captain Jenkins again sent the crew to their battle stations.[2]

Atlanta got head-of-the-line privileges as the pilot, Capt. F. A. Dear, of the canal's Marine Division, came aboard and met Captain Jenkins on the bridge. Passing the city of Colón off the port beam, the cruiser steamed to the entrance of the canal to make—due do Panama's geographic position—a west to east passage to the Pacific. Ashore Army soldiers stared at the sleek new ship as she slid by and *Atlanta*'s sailors stared back. At midday the light cruiser made its way up through the three steps of the Gatun Locks for a total lift of 85 feet. As lines were cast ashore to guide the ship into each 1,000-foot-long lock, the word was passed to shift colors and a signalman hauled down the national ensign from the main mast while others raised a national ensign on the fantail and the jack up the staff on the bow.

The passage through Gatun Lake allowed fresh water to flush out the ship's condensers, fire main, and toilet-flushing systems. Once across the lake, *Atlanta* passed through the Gaillard Cut, the 8-mile excavation at the continental divide, and then descended via the Pedro Miguel Lock followed by a pair of locks at the Miraflores complex. The near perfect transit was then marred at approximately 1814 by a sudden vibration on the port shaft after the cruiser had cleared the west Miraflores Locks. The port engine was immediately secured, and *Atlanta* continued along using starboard shaft with the helmsman adjusting her rudders to compensate. Arriving at Balboa, *Atlanta* tied up at the fueling dock to take on 224,764 gallons of black oil, and early the next morning, a Panama Canal diver descended below. Returning to the surface, the diver reported to Captain Jenkins that one blade on the port propeller "was bent back at a distance of 4 feet from hub cap for a length of about 8 inches." Captain Jenkins asked for and immediately received permission to dry dock his ship to repair the blade.[3]

The unexpected delay in the trip to Pearl Harbor proved to be a boon to the crew in the form of liberty.

On Saturday April 11, *Atlanta* eased into the 1,076-foot-long graving dock that the Navy had built soon after the completion of the canal. As the water drained, to Lloyd's dismay, the drydocking exposed vast areas of the underside where the paint coating had fallen away. However, with the rush to repair the blade and return to sea, there would be no opportunity to remove the rust and apply a new coat.[4]

With the repair made, water flowed into the dry dock and *Atlanta* again floated. The boilermen lit the burners and the ship slowly began to build up steam to get underway. Departing for Pearl Harbor on Sunday morning, April 12, in accordance with orders issued by the Commander in Chief, Pacific Fleet, Lloyd had hoped to obtain the services of some tow planes to get some target practice, but the aircraft were not operating on the Sunday Sabbath. The lack of tow plane services did not deter Captain Jenkins from calling his crew to General Quarters to continue the process of breaking in the new arrivals.[5]

Years later, Lloyd recalled that the Navy's carriers had been conducting token raids against Japanese-held islands:

> I think there were probably two strategic purposes, one of which was to give the country something to take as reassurance that the war wasn't going entirely as the Japanese chose to have it go. The other was hopefully to slow the Japanese down a little bit in some of the apparent feeling of complete freedom to range at will over the whole world.

The enemy had earned American respect for their ability to use sea power to strike across vast expanses of ocean. As stunning as the attack on Pearl Harbor was, Lloyd remembered being impressed about reports of Imperial Japanese Navy operations against British installations in the Indian Ocean. His recollections affirmed his diary notes that there was a concern that the Japanese fleet could be operating *east* of Oahu: "I can tell you we resented bitterly the inadequacy of that little SA radar up at the mast head. We had a crow's nest up there. We kept a lookout aloft at the masthead 24 hours a day, and this was no foolishness."[6]

En route to Hawaii, *Atlanta* received orders to check out Clipperton Island, located in the eastern Pacific Ocean approximately 1,000 miles west of Balboa. Lloyd described it as "a single solitary rock sticking out of the ocean."[7] He believed it had once hosted a guano mining operation. Claimed by the French, the island was suspected of serving as a Japanese refueling station for submarines that could operate against the Panama Canal.

Lloyd recalled that Captain Jenkins timed the approach of the island to coincide with daybreak, so that *Atlanta*'s guns could be unleashed on an unsuspecting submarine or merchantman. The crew stood poised at General Quarters. "As this gray dawn broke, lo and behold, sure enough here right close aboard the Island was a ship and behaving in a very suspicious way." Lloyd looked out and saw a beautiful white painted schooner, but the sails were not rigged. Captain Jenkins ordered Lieutenants Perkins and Smith to lead a boarding party. Armed with sub-machine guns and other weapons, the boarding party stepped into the motor whaleboat and were lowered over the side.

"The boarding party got aboard the schooner, and, lo and behold, then things were even more suspicious." Lloyd recalled Perkins interrogated the cook who said that *Skidbladnir* was a shark fishing schooner. "They fished for shark for the shark livers commercially."

Perkins discovered that "they had found themselves in the vicinity of Clipperton Island, and looking through binoculars they could see the remains of this guano mining industry, a few overturned carts, and some little narrow gauged railroad tracks, and so on." The cook told the lieutenant that the captain and first mate and another crewmember had taken a boat ashore to look around the island. Unfortunately, while the crew explored the remains of the guano mines, the wind caused the *Skidbladnir* to drag her anchor off the narrow shoal into deep water. "Here she was, the anchor just dangling down touching nothing." Meanwhile, the surf kicked up by the sudden gusts trapped the skipper and his fellow shark hunters ashore as they helplessly looked out at their schooner drifting away.

Fortunately, Perkins, with his New England background, knew something about sailing and instructed the boarding party sailors on what needed to be accomplished. Once the anchor was hauled in, Perkins got the *Skidbladnir* underway with her sails, and *Atlanta*'s sailors nudged the shark schooner close enough to the island to drop the anchor to get a firm hold. Lloyd remembered they "wished them well and went on our way, an incident of the war that I am sure appears in absolutely no history books whatsoever and probably never will."[8]

In contrast, a few hours after *Atlanta*'s Clipperton Island adventure, on the other side of the date line, the carrier *Hornet* launched Army B-25 bombers against Tokyo and other Japanese targets. Led by Col. Jimmy Doolittle, the raid caused minor damage to the intended targets and could hardly claim to have avenged Pearl Harbor, but the strike boosted American morale and served as a psychological blow to make the Japanese realize the homeland was not invulnerable. Just as the Japanese had exploited the mobility of naval forces to project power over vast distances, the Americans were determined to let their Pacific opponent know that two could play the game.

Along with *Hornet, Enterprise* made the North Pacific crossing to provide air cover for the American Task Force. With B-25s strapped down on her deck, *Hornet* was extremely vulnerable. Lloyd had a personal connection with the mission in that his stepfather George Murray commanded *Big E*.[9]

CHAPTER 6

Arrival Pearl Harbor

25 April 1942

Arrived Pearl Harbor. Except at Clipperton, saw nothing from Panama until morning of arrival, picked up by plane (JRS) [a Sikorsky amphibious aircraft] on patrol.

California just floated into dock shortly before; she is a mess. Three torpedo hits, none of which penetrated A/T [anti-torpedo] protection, yet she sank by flooding through manholes, etc., which had been opened for Admiral's inspection. Due to the flooding, will be some time before she is ready.

West Virginia still on the bottom, ready for pumping out. Five torpedoes, none through A/T stuff except 2 close together; sinking the result of same story as *California* (also same for all the BB's, at time of the 7 Dec. attack.) Also a bad bomb hit, plus fire.

Arizona a mess. Looked just like the pictures that were released. Bad bomb and torpedo hits, terrible oil fire and turret magazine explosion forward.

Oklahoma upside down; turned over almost 150°. Publicity releases say she'll be salvaged. Since she wasn't much good before hand, I can't see how it'll be worth it, if it is done.

Utah also upside down. No pretense she'll be salvaged.

Downes & Cassin afloat. They were in drydock during attack, with *Pennsylvania*. Few hits, many near misses; their oil burned in the dock. Hulls all warped and wrinkled, back of one broken by subsequent floodings & unfloodings of the dock during later alarms as she remained partly buoyant. They are to leave for West Coast shortly under own power—glad I'm not going in them. More publicity stuff.

Many stories still current about 7 Dec.

Blackout every night, 1800 liberty for crew, no boats to run after dark, curfew ashore at 2100.

Task Force 16 arrived few hours before us, from the raid on Tokyo, etc. *Enterprise, Hornet, Northampton, Vincennes, Nashville*, some 1500-ton DD's of the *Monssen* class, 1 big tanker of *Neosho* type. Nobody saying nothing at no time, to nobody. But all looking well satisfied. Saw George.

30 April '42

Task Force 16 out again. Had lunch with George day before, aboard his ship (*Enterprise*). We are to join this task force, but are having material troubles that we will stay in to correct.

The Northern Pump Company hydraulic gear for our 5" fuze-setting shell hoists was found on the burn during some practice firings on the way out. No drawings available, of course. Local repair forces all stumped. Man being flown out from the states—Mr. W. Cody, of the N. P. Co.

Also some engineering trouble. Condenser tubes starting to go. One salted up on way out. Six knots very embarrassing in sub waters.

6 May '42

Went out to fire some practices, both AA & surface. Did very satisfactorily, except machine guns still try to spot their tracers onto long-range target, hence are way low and behind. Hear this is common in the real stuff too. Hoists seem all okay. We go to sea at about 8,300 tons, which isn't bad for a 6,000-ton canoe.

More stories on Pearl Harbor: that 1,500 bodies are believed to be still in the damaged battleships. On these, still blacked out nights, with nothing stirring except the faint voices of the guns' crews on watch, the ghosts of some of those dead men stir. And ask: Why? (to be answered by Senator Wheeler, etc.)

One of the Jap 2-man subs is on display at the sub base. It is nearly undamaged; was found on North side of the island with both crew members dead inside.

The [U.S.] sub crews come in from cruises to the Japanese coast that last 90 days. A terrific figure. They get fuel at Midway, going (& coming, if needed), but not stores, food, etc. Stay out as long as there's a shoe to eat. One is in that got quite a depth charging. She came all the way home on the surface.

8 May '42

Sailing orders. Battle of the Coral Sea dope filling the papers. We get report Task Force 1 (all the BB's) arrived safe in San Pedro! Christ—What a place for them to be fighting the war! Task Force 17 (*Lexington* & *Yorktown*, with their cruisers, etc.) and Task Force 47(?) (subs) must have carried the load. *Lexington* reported two torpedo hits; slowed to 20. The *Neosho* was on her way there with fuel escorted by *Sims* (DD 409). Dive-bombers got both, leaving TF 17 on the spot for fuel. TF 16 was fueling in the Hebrides when it all broke—maybe they'll get in some licks.

We were going to proceed alone to join TF 16. Now, however, will take a convoy. *Ranier*, big ex-C3, ammunition ship, and *Kaskaskia*, *Neosho*-class tanker. *Dale* (DD 353) to accompany. Then changed to *McCall* (DD 400).

***

Lloyd Mustin's description of the devastation wrought by the Japanese attack of December 7 is comparable to that of many others who arrived in Oahu during that time, including his shipmates. Once the *Atlanta* navigated through the minefields shielding the channel entrance, Ed Corboy wrote, "all hands strained their eyes for a sight of what the Japs had done to us in their sneak air raid of Dec. 7." They first noticed the blackened hangars at Hickam Air Field. "Then came the litter of masts and turrets on the beach to our port side." *Atlanta* then steamed past the hulks of the destroyers *Cassin* and *Downes*. "Their steel sides, ripped by the infernos that had gutted them, seemed to cry to us for vengeance."

As the cruiser slid forward, the crew noted the oil-soaked shorelines and then battleship row appeared off the port bow. Corboy wrote, "The USS *Oklahoma* lay on her side. At her stern was the *West Virginia* still sitting on the bottom, but ready for raising."[1] That all the damaged ships still flew their national ensigns left a deep lasting impression on all.

Yet already, Navy engineers were making tremendous strides in getting the damaged warships back into action.

Of the warships damaged, *Arizona* and *Utah* were not salvaged. Lloyd was also correct about the *Oklahoma*. To right the ship, an enormous series of pulley rigs were constructed on Ford Island and the hull was slowly turned back over. However, engineers determined that the effort to put the old battleship back into service at that stage of the war was not worth the cost, and after the war the Navy would sell the hull for scrap. *Oklahoma* never did face the cutters' torches though. While being towed to the West Coast, a storm swamped the hull, causing the carcass of the old battlewagon to plunge to the bottom of the Pacific.

The same could almost be said of *Downes* and *Cassin*. Badly battered, the hulks of the two destroyers were towed back to the West Coast, and new ships, built on the original plans, were built around the intact engineering plants. To say that the Navy salvaged these two destroyers is a stretch, but as Lloyd noted, "Publicity." As for Lloyd's observation on the *California* which had entered Dry Dock Number 2 on April 9, the damage had been caused by two torpedoes, a direct bomb hit, and some near misses.[2]

With the Doolittle raid task force arriving at Pearl Harbor, Lloyd later recalled wasting no time trying to extract some lessons learned. Looking over the *Nashville*, he noted the fifteen 6-inch 47 rapid-fire guns, spaced within the five triple turrets, were without paint:

> There she was with paint burned off all her guns. Obviously, they had gotten pretty hot firing a lot of rounds in a hurry. So I went over there to find out what the problem was. The problem was that this little Japanese picket boat took very radical evasive action. She just steamed in circles, and so forth, and, of course, there is no prediction out of any of our computers of then and now, that is our gun computers, of the future position of somebody who is not steaming in a straight line. She just plowed the water up and all over the place before she figured out how to sink that little fellow.[3]

In contrast to peacetime gunnery drills where the target steamed fairly predictably and steadily, the *Nashville*'s recent experience taught Lloyd that the only way to counter such evasive tactics would be to close on the enemy so as to shorten the flight time of the projectile to the target. "Then you just shoot right at him."[4]

Besides visiting *Nashville*, the diary noted a stop at *Enterprise* to visit George. George, of course is George Murray, the commanding officer—Lloyd's stepfather and mentor. Born on July 6, 1889, in Boston of Scotch-Irish stock, George Dominic Murray's naval career followed in the wake of Lloyd's father Henry. A member of the Class of 1911, Murray graduated 15 years after the senior Mustin. He served on two ships before receiving orders to Pensacola for flight training at the recently established Naval Aeronautic Station, then commanded by Cdr. Henry Mustin. He would be designated as Naval Aviator #22. During his time at Pensacola, George joined Henry for a quick deployment to Mexico to support General Pershing's campaign against Pancho Villa—a campaign in which Henry earned the distinction of being the first American aviator to be shot at from the ground.

The aviators socialized, and George must have been acquainted with Henry's young wife Corinne and her four-year-old son Lloyd. Among the social events was George's own marriage to Margaret C. Connolly of Boston. As America's entry into World War I approached, George Murray returned to New England to serve as an inspector at the Gallaudet Aeroplane Company in Norwich, Connecticut. During the final months of World War I, he stayed stateside as the first commanding officer of Naval Air Station Anacostia, Washington, D.C.

While serving as executive officer at Naval Air Station San Diego, tragedy struck when his wife passed away, a victim of the influenza epidemic. In late 1921, he joined the aircraft tender *Aroostook* and later commanded Spotting Squadron Five. He returned to the East Coast to serve as the chief inspector at the Philadelphia Naval Aircraft Factory. With the sad death of his mentor in 1923, the widower exchanged letters with the widow. The correspondence continued as George deployed to the Asiatic Fleet in command of the newly formed Torpedo Squadron 20.

Upon returning to Annapolis in June 1925 to serve a six-month stint as an aviation indoctrination officer, the couple married and George took on the responsibility of raising Lloyd and his two younger brothers. The newly formed family had two years together as George performed staff duties in Washington. In 1927, George departed for tours with the Battle Fleet in the Pacific. A year later Lloyd began his plebe year at the Naval Academy.

As Lloyd Mustin progressed through his four years at Annapolis, his stepfather found himself serving as the assistant naval attaché to American embassies in London, Paris, Berlin, and the Hague and serving as a technical advisor for the forthcoming Disarmament Conference in Geneva.

With Lloyd commissioned and serving on the cruiser *Augusta*, George returned to the States in the summer of 1933 for a two-year tour as the air operations boss on the carrier *Saratoga*. After a tour ashore at Pensacola, he returned to "*Sara*" for a year tour as executive officer, and then he commanded *Langley*, shortly after America's first flattop had been converted to be a seaplane tender.

After a Washington tour at the Bureau of Aeronautics, Capt. George Murray assumed command of *Enterprise* on March 21, 1941. Fate spared Murray and the "*Big E*" as a storm delayed the carrier's planned December 6 arrival from Wake Island to Pearl Harbor.[5]

In early February 1942, aircraft from *Enterprise* soon saw action over the Marshall and Gilbert Islands, striking a blow against the Japanese defenders. *Enterprise* planes then lashed out against Japanese soldiers who had recently captured Wake Island, and in March the naval aviators struck at Marcus Island. As noted, *Enterprise* then provided air cover for the Doolittle raid launched from *Hornet*.

Throughout this period, the feisty Vice Adm. William "Bull" Halsey and his staff were embarked to command and oversee the task force's operations against the Japanese. The crewmen of *Enterprise* admired the warrior in Halsey, but perhaps they appreciated the talents of George Murray even more. The saying went, "the Admiral will get us in, and the Captain will get us out."[6]

Anxious to deploy with *Enterprise*, Captain Jenkins must have found the mechanical and engineering problems as detailed by Lloyd frustrating. However, while many of the crew were itching to get after the Japanese, it is hard to imagine that many were overly upset about the prospect of extra liberty in what they perceived to be a tropical paradise.

On May 6, *Atlanta* departed Pearl Harbor in the morning for waters off the islands of Maui and Kahoolawe to test the improved accuracy of the guns. The crews of the 5-inch, 20mm, and 1.1-inch guns would take turns firing at sleeve targets towed by aircraft. Finally, a radio-controlled drone appeared, and the

5-inch 38 batteries successfully engaged it, knocking the craft out of the sky. The high-caliber marksmanship instilled confidence in the crew, which took to calling the ship "*Mighty A.*"[7]

Regarding the comment about Senator Wheeler, Lloyd took a sarcastic poke at Senator Burton Kendall Wheeler, a Democratic senator in Montana. Wheeler, along with such senators as William E. Borah of Idaho and Gerald P. Nye of North Dakota, had been in the vanguard of Americans who had espoused a policy of isolationism before the war. Wheeler had been a harsh critic of President Roosevelt's foreign policy. Speaking out against the Lend-Lease Act in January 1941, Wheeler exclaimed:

> Never before has the Congress of the United States been asked by any president to violate international law. Never before has this nation resorted to duplicity in the conduct of its foreign affairs. Never before has the United States given to one man the power to strip this nation of its defenses. Never before has a Congress coldly and flatly been asked to abdicate.[8]

Looking out at the destruction wrought by the Japanese attack, Lloyd obviously had contempt for those who had maintained an "America First" agenda prior to the war.[9]

The observation of the two-man submarine is also noteworthy. There were five Type-A midget submarines that were assigned to participate in the attack on Pearl Harbor. Four of the five have been located. The submarine Lloyd refers to was probably the one launched by the Japanese submarine *I-24* late on December 6. Driven away from the mouth of Pearl Harbor by depth charges on the morning of December 7, the midget submarine drifted around Oahu. The next day, with its battery power depleted, the two-man boat was caught on a reef. Setting a demolition fuse to destroy the boat, the two crewmen left the boat. Ens. Kazuo Sekamaki made it ashore and was captured. The body of his partner, Petty Officer Kiyashi Inagaki, washed ashore a few hours later. Since the detonator failed to go off, the submarine remained intact and was placed on display at Pearl Harbor before being sent stateside, where it was displayed in conjunction with War Bond drives. Eventually, the submarine would be placed on display at the National Museum of the Pacific War at Fredericksburg, Texas.

Less likely, Lloyd could have been looking at the hulk of a second midget submarine that was pulled off the bottom of Pearl Harbor by the fleet landing shortly after the attack. Destroyed by depth charges, the hulk contained the remains of the two crewmen. This midget sub was subsequently placed back into Pearl Harbor, and a new pier was built over it. Two additional midget submarines were located after World War II outside of the opening to the harbor. In 1960, a Navy diver discovered the third submarine in Kashi Lagoon in 75 feet of water. The mystery behind this discovery was that no human remains were found. Then in 2002 submersibles operated by the Hawaii Undersea Research Laboratory found the two-man boat that had been attacked and sunk by *Ward* in the early morning hours before the air attack. The location of the fifth submarine also remains a mystery. Photographic evidence has suggested it may have gotten off a torpedo attack against *West Virginia* and *Oklahoma*.[10]

In addition to *Enterprise*'s forays against the Japanese, Lloyd astutely observed how the submarine force was taking the fight into enemy waters. When the war began, the United States had 73 submarines in the Pacific and Asiatic theaters. By April 1, American submarine skippers claimed 300,000 tons of Japanese shipping. The tallies would only improve as more boats, skippered by aggressive young officers, would reach the Western Pacific. The submarine he saw was probably *Thresher*, which had returned from a shortened war patrol on April 29. Having departed Pearl on March 23 on her second war patrol, *Thresher* provided meteorological data from Japanese coastal waters to support the Doolittle raid and then attempted to attack Japanese shipping. After missing a merchant ship with a spread of three torpedoes early on April 10, *Thresher* sunk the freighter *Sado Maru* later that day. Alerted, Japanese naval forces rushed to the scene and the Americans endured a vicious depth-charge attack. Ironically, the boat suffered greater damage when a rogue wave hit the conning tower and saltwater flooded into the interior. The boat then returned to Pearl.[11]

On May 8, he notes the battle of the Coral Sea. The four-day battle that began on May 4, 1942, was, and remains, the largest naval battle ever fought close to Australia. Although a Japanese invasion of Australia itself may have been seen as an overreach by Japanese strategic planners, the Japanese objective to capture Port Moresby on New Guinea and Tulagi in the Solomon Islands would have put American–Australian sea lanes as well as a swath of northeastern Australia within reach of Japanese aircraft. With her sea lanes across the Indian Ocean up into the Atlantic also threatened by Axis sea power, Australia might have been forced to withdraw from the war effort.

What distinguished the battle from past fleet engagements was that the opposing fleets never came within visual range. Starting with the *Yorktown*'s raid on Japanese naval forces supporting landings on Tulagi on May 4, the contest became a maneuver at sea in which timing was key, as opposing air flotillas searched out enemy surface forces. In the maneuver-at-sea chess game, the Allied task force, led by Rear Adm. Frank J. Fletcher, had the upper hand on the morning of May 7 as he had placed his carriers between the enemy invasion force and the enemy's carrier strike forces. And to ensure Japanese transports would not slip through during the forthcoming air battle, Fletcher dispatched Rear Adm. John G. Crace, RN, with a blocking force consisting of the following to operate south off New Guinea: Royal Australian Navy cruisers *Australia* and *Hobart*, cruiser *Chicago*, and three American destroyers. Lloyd's uncertain reference to a Task Force 47 (submarines) likely referred to Capt. Waldo Christie's Task Group 42.1 based in Brisbane, Australia. Christie commanded two divisions of submarines—a total of 11 obsolete S-boats that would not factor in the battle.

That morning, the Americans suffered their first ship losses when aircraft from the Japanese fleet carrier aircraft attacked the destroyer *Sims* and oiler *Neosho*. After evading two waves of bomb-dropping Japanese planes, the two ships received multiple hits, and in the case of *Neosho*, a direct hit from a crashing bomber. With two of her

Lexington's demise represented a loss of 25 percent of American carrier airpower in the Pacific, and *Yorktown* also sustained crippling blows. (Archives Branch, Naval History and Heritage Command, Washington, D.C.; NH 57455)

three bomb hits landing within the engine room amidships, the destroyer buckled and quickly passed beneath the waves, while *Neosho* would engage in a long losing struggle to remain afloat.

Meanwhile, American naval aviators from *Lexington* and *Yorktown* had located the Japanese invasion force, which was escorted by the light carrier *Shoho*. The quote "Scratch one flattop" subsequently entered the Navy lexicon. That afternoon, the fog of war was exacerbated by bad weather. One flight of Japanese aircraft flew nearby Fletcher's carriers without seeing the American flattops. American fighters, vectored by radar, shot down nine of the attackers. Such were the hazy conditions that some confused Japanese pilots nearly landed on the American flight decks, thinking them their own!

Recognizing the vulnerability of their invasion force to further American air attack as well as the blocking force, the Japanese turned back their transports, effectively handing the Allies a strategic victory.

This left the two opposing carrier forces to trade blows the following morning. On the morning of May 8 both sides launched air strikes aimed at the other's carriers. With *Zuikaku* hidden by a squall, *Shokaku* received three bomb hits from *Lexington* and *Yorktown* bombers, eliminating her capability to launch aircraft. Repairs for *Shokaku* and the need to replace aircraft and pilots lost from *Zuikaku* forced the Japanese to remove these carriers from forthcoming operations.

Overall, however, the Japanese had the better day. At least three torpedoes and perhaps two or three bombs dropped by Japanese naval aviators hit their mark against *Lexington*, while the nimble *Yorktown* turned approximately a dozen bomb releases into near misses. Finally, one bomb did puncture the smaller carrier's flight deck and detonated above a fireroom. *Lexington* fell victim later in the day to massive internal explosions. However, Japanese claims of sending *Yorktown* to the deep proved premature. Samuel Eliot Morison declared it a "tactical victory for the Japanese, but a strategic victory for the United States." He further described it as "the first purely carrier-to-carrier naval battle in which all losses were inflicted by air action …"[12]

CHAPTER 7

Underway for New Caledonia

10 May '42

Underway for Noumea, New Caledonia, with our group of 4. We are Task Group 16.19. *Ranier* has 4,000 tons of ammunition aboard—boy, there really must be some fleet base down here someplace, to handle that! *McCall* and *Atlanta* screening on bows, the train in column. Zigzagging as always, but this knucklehead got hold of a British zigzag plan book someplace, so we do it that way. And change a dozen times a day, one plan to another. Zero time for them is whenever executed, which makes a hell of a mess. (The *Ranier* skipper is O.T.C.—these ideas are his.)

13 May

Sorta wild. A sub contact, which proved false. Right in the middle of that, a plane reported sighted, and General Quarters sounded. 10 minutes after securing, another plane & more G.Q. . A real one, who wouldn't approach—turned tail. Could have been Jap, or perhaps an Army job from Palmyra Island, which was off to the east. All hands plenty keyed up at the possibility this was a shadower. Then another sub contact, also false. By sunset General Quarters, everyone had had a fill. *McCall* also had one false sub contact.

14 May, 1942

Started auspiciously with G.Q. 0330, when a plane (unidentified) was heard to pass overhead. Then the regular dawn G.Q. at 0515. At 0630 a sub contact (false), on my watch. First I've had—it was on the quarter, and I couldn't have done much anyway.

Crossed the line today λ [Longitude] 167–35–00 W. My 5th official Southbound crossing, of which I have quite a few additional unofficial. 600 pollywogs onboard. 2 more sub contacts, both of which proved false.

Everyone is somewhat keyed up. Naturally. The Japs outnumber us to beat hell in this ocean, and we're up against a tough Navy that doesn't keep its BB's home. With no air scouts, and tied down to these 2 beefboats, the *McCall*'s and our 5" guns seem like pretty small potatoes, to what we can easily run into. And with every day we get nearer to where they are, loaded for bear.

15 May

Busy forenoon watch today. Sighted a plane, just at end of a drill, of which I'd been forewarned, to see how well reports got through. It got through fine then, alright, only I thought it was still the drill. Turned out to be a PBY, on Easterly course, lat. about 07–45 S, long. about 171–30 W. Just at secure from that G.Q., *McCall* had a sub contact. Turned out false. Then another "air contact" by us—birds! About 1600 passed *Sabine* (*Neosho*-type tanker) and *Gwin* (DD) Northbound. *Sabine* high and light—more oil expended into fighting ships, for chasing Japs.

16 May

Orders changed during night. Fueled from *Kaskaskia* this morning, 140,000 gallons. Then she, *Ranier* & *McCall* left headed South, while we went S.W. Fueled at about L. 10 S, λ 175 W, 249 miles N.W. of Samoan group. They are going to "Bleacher" which is Tongatabu, and we to "Acorn" to rendezvous with T. F. 16. "Acorn" is just a spot on the chart, north of Fiji, apparently. T. F. 16 with most of T. F. 17 amalgamated, is en route back to Hawaiian area.

18 May 1942

Crossed 180th Meridian, so the 17th didn't exist. The morning press carries stories of strong Jap forces moving South. Our intelligence reports agree. Maybe we won't go home direct after all. Sighted a B-24 on parallel course, headed for Noumea probably.

19 May 1942

Joined TF 16 at dawn today. Stuck us with CruDiv 5 (*Northampton*, *Pensacola*), 060° from axis. Treating us just like any other cruiser, which seems to me to be a darn poor utilization of our special characteristics. Dope on Coral Sea action says Jap land-based planes played an important part, ours played none—even to letting the damaged carrier *Shokaku* get away. The good old "U.S. Air Force," as the Army boys love to call themselves, is up to its old tricks. Probably busy reading about how beautiful they are in one of MacArthur's communiqués.

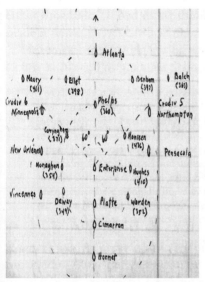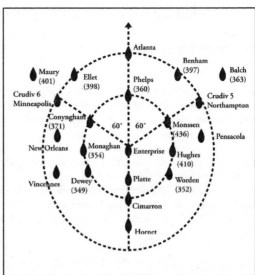

Lloyd Mustin's illustration of the formation 7-V extracted from his diary, re-drawn for clarity.

Enterprise & *Yorktown*, CruDivs 5 & 6, 2 tankers, and about 3 DesDivs seems to be the composition of T.F. 16 now.

20 May

Had 2 of these, [two May 20ths on] account of re-crossing the date line. On the second one, *Enterprise* SBD flew into the water about a mile ahead of the carrier, after a dawn take-off. Plane went right on down; no trace of pilot or passenger. During the morning went to G.Q. three times, on air contacts, radar contacts, etc. Third time, saw three PBY's on parallel course, passing about 15 miles abeam. Course 58° T [true]; probably enroute Pearl Harbor from somewhere down under. We are passing along just about the reverse of our Southward track.

OTC has decided we aren't just another cruiser, after all. We are now all by ourselves in position 2000, dead ahead of the carrier (4,000 yards). Task Force 16 cruising disp. [disposition] 7V, in which we are [see plot above]:

Every station unit but us has some DD's around to worry the subs a little.

21 May

Half-masted colors 15 minutes today during funeral on *Hornet* of a man who walked into a plane's prop.

At sunset, after the evening scouting flight returned, *Hornet* reported on voice radio: "One SBD, which departed to search sector 300–315, now ½ hour overdue. Cannot pick up by radar." It never came back; no search was started. Perhaps Canton Island will be asked to have a PBY take a look.

22 May

0830 recrossed equator, northbound, on course 022°, long. 168°—30 West.

23 May

A simulated torpedo attack on our force today by *Enterprise* planes. It was a beauty—we will look like hell if the Japs ever get off as good a one. Ships are supposed to screen the carriers in order to get in between and knock the planes off as they come in, as *Minneapolis* and *Phelps* did when Japs came in on *Lexington* in Coral Sea (getting six between them). But attack was finished before we got our helm over. They'll have to station us closer if our 16 5"- 38's are to help them any in such a case.

New information concerns Jap offensive against Alaskan area. Perhaps we'll see some cold weather. Also a pending grab by them against Midway again. Hope it won't be more "Too little and too late" in both places, but with the forces we have at Pearl Harbor & westward, I don't see how it can be helped.

25 May

Another carrier plane lost. No rescues.

Simulated air attacks on the force by our own planes have continued, all hands getting steadily better at repelling. Today dive-bombing and torpedo combined. Really beautiful work. Our D.B. technique is new—they come corkscrewing down, instead of the straight dive. Would make a very tough gun target. Our location within the formation is continually experimented with.

***

At last *Atlanta* deployed for a two-week span. In his entry for May 10, Lt. Lloyd Mustin discussed departing Pearl Harbor as a group of four. For the morning departure the destroyer *McCall* led the way out the channel followed by *Atlanta*. Following the two combatants came the ammunition ship *Rainier* (which Lloyd misspelled in his diary entry), and the oiler *Kaskaskia*. Once on the open seas, Captain Jenkins announced to the crew that they were en route to Noumea, New Caledonia. There, *Rainier* and *Kaskaskia* would offload tons of ammunition and many gallons of petroleum products to build up a base that would be critical in sustaining the Allied effort in the Southwest Pacific.

Captain Jenkins also warned the crew that they would be passing within range of Japanese airfields in the Gilbert and Marshall Islands, so the possibility of fending off an air attack was real. To further prepare the foursome for such an attack, tow planes dragging target sleeves flew out that first day to provide target practice. *Atlanta* scored a direct hit on the tow plane's first pass, eliminating the sleeve that had been in trail. The *McCall* and gun crews on the two logistics ships took their turns firing at other sleeves.[1]

While not as glamorous or sleek looking as the new battleships, cruisers, and destroyers sliding down the building ways, the American effort in the Pacific simply could not be sustainable without the ammo ships, oilers, and other logistics ships that were authorized for construction by Congress in the 1930s.

The Tampa Shipbuilding Company built the ammo ship as a C2-T cargo ship under a Maritime Commission contract. She was launched on March 1, 1941, with the name *Rainbow*, but that name changed when the Navy acquired the ship for conversion to an ammunition auxiliary on April 16, 1941. The Navy's first two ammunition ships commissioned after World War I were named *Pyro* and *Nitro*. With the commissioning of *Lassen* in May 1941, another Tampa Bay Shipbuilding Company product, the Navy began a custom of naming these vessels for volcanoes, hence *Rainier*.

Commissioned at Norfolk on December 21, 1941, the ship had a mere three-day lead on *Atlanta* with regards to time in service, and the 13,876-ton ammo ship passed into the Pacific in early 1942 and already made two runs from the mainland to Pearl Harbor.[2]

During World War II, most combatants received their ammo in port, or as illustrated by *Atlanta*, by barge when the ship was moored. Thus advance bases became very strategic locations that enabled ships to replenish expended ordnance. Ships such as *Rainier* did have the ability to replenish ships at sea, and later in the war this capability would be used to sustain the huge task forces that would eventually bring the war directly to Japan's home islands.

However, so long as ships did not engage in combat or conduct extensive target practice, the magazines stayed full. Fuel, in contrast, was a constantly diminishing commodity. Since the Navy switched from sail to steam, a major headache had always been keeping the bunkers full. An example of this logistical nightmare was the 1907–08 world cruise of the Great White Fleet. To keep the battleships steaming on their westward journey around the globe, the Navy had to charter 49 foreign colliers to meet with the warships at ports along the way. Occasional late deliveries highlighted the fleet's vulnerability to being dependent on foreign shipping. In 1908, Congress responded by appropriating funds to build two fleet colliers and purchase three merchant colliers.

As with ammunition replenishment, the idea was to use these ships to coal ships at anchor or pier side. However, in 1913, the collier *Cyclops* demonstrated it was possible to refuel at sea using a stern to forecastle arrangement with the pre-dreadnought battleship *South Carolina*.

The slow, laborious, and inefficient process was made unnecessary by the introduction of a new propellant—black oil.

In the years leading up to America's entry into World War I, the U.S. Navy began converting many of its ships and constructed new vessels to burn the liquid fuel. The need for "fuel ships" or "oilers" became immediately apparent, and *Kanawha* and *Maumee* were commissioned in 1915 and 1916 respectively, starting a tradition of naming oilers for rivers.

With America's entry into World War I, a flotilla of destroyers, under the command of Cdr. Joseph Taussig, steamed across the Atlantic to augment the British Grand Fleet. Recently constructed, these tin cans had enough capacity in their fuel tanks to make the trip without refueling. However, the Navy's older destroyers did not have the "legs" to make it across. To get them over, the Navy stationed *Maumee* at mid-ocean. On board the oiler, the executive officer, Lt. Chester W. Nimitz, teamed with Lt. (jg.) Glenn B. Davis, Chief Boatswain Michael Higgins, and Lt. Fred M. Perkins from the Destroyer Force to devise a means of "towing" the receiving ship alongside by use of a 10-inch hawser and two 6-inch breast lines. Using this "broadside" method, the *Maumee* would then pump fuel through two 3-inch hoses.

The system worked! By July 5, 1917, *Maumee* had completed 34 "UnReps" (Underway Replenishments), clearly demonstrating the viability of a system that would enhance the Navy's mobility for many years to come. *Maumee*'s skipper, Lt. Cdr. Henry C. Dinger, observed that if excellent seamanship skills were employed, it might even be possible to dispense with the towing hawser. Further experimentation during the inter-war period proved him correct.[3]

With the Navy's new construction programs of the 1930s, the fleet desperately needed oilers to keep the new ships moving on the high seas. *Kaskaskia* was built for the Esso Oil Company by Newport News Shipbuilding and Drydock Company and launched on September 29, 1939. The Navy acquired the ship on October 22, 1940, and placed her in commission a week later. Assigned to the Pacific Fleet, she was located at San Francisco during the attack on Pearl Harbor and had made numerous important fuel deliveries to Pago Pago and other locations in the weeks prior to this mission.[4]

As demonstrated by its nonstop solo journey from Panama to Pearl Harbor, *Atlanta* had some very long legs. However, a prudent skipper took every opportunity available to top off his tanks given the vulnerability of his floating gas station. Refueling at sea provided opportunities for officers to hone their ship-handling skills as the *Atlanta* approached the *Kaskaskia* from astern and pulled up alongside. As the fuel flowed from the oiler, the two ships surged forward at about 12 knots, with the *Kaskaskia* trying to maintain a set course, and the conning officer on the *Atlanta* shouting slight course and speed change adjustments to the helm and lee helmsmen.

It was the vulnerability of the two logistics ships and their vital cargoes that earned *Atlanta* an escort mission. Besides being able to fire shells into the air, the light cruiser was valued for her anti-submarine warfare abilities, being equipped with a primitive sonar and armed with depth charges.

To perform the escort service, the Pacific Fleet paired *Atlanta* with *McCall*, a destroyer of the *Benham* class that was built at the Union Plant of Bethlehem Shipbuilding at San Francisco. Commissioned on June 22, 1938, the DD was a Pacific Fleet veteran by the time *Atlanta* came on the scene, having screened the *Enterprise* during raids conducted earlier in the year against Japanese positions in the Marshall and Gilbert Islands.

For the mission, Capt. William W. Meek in *Rainier* was the Officer in Tactical Command (OTC), having the responsibility of setting the group's course, speed, and defensive formation. A graduate of the Naval Academy's Class of 1913, two years ahead of Jenkins, it could be inferred that Meek had an earlier date of rank and was senior to Jenkins, and thus command of TG 16.19 was his. With four ships, Meek deployed a "Y" pattern, with *Atlanta* and *McCall* positioned ahead off the bow of his ship to starboard and port. The oiler followed in his wake. This formation enabled the two ships to use their sonar to best effect.

What annoyed Lieutenant Mustin was Meek's continual changing of the zigzag plan and his decision to make zero time the time of execution. It is easy to understand his frustration given that the Navy had very workable zigzag procedures that conformed to "Zulu" time or Greenwich Mean Time. The standard procedure would be for the OTC to order his group, "Standby to Execute Plan C." On board various ships, deck officers would pull out the tactical publication for zigzag plans and would go to Plan C. They would see a 24-hour set of changes off the base course starting at midnight Zulu time (which would be sometime during the daytime in the Pacific, depending on the ship's location). For example, at 0000Z the pub [publication] would specify come right 15 degrees off of base course, at 0015Z come left 20 degrees off of base course, at 0035Z come right 5 degrees off of base course, at 0045Z steer 15 degrees right of base course, and so on. So to execute a zigzag plan, the officer of the deck simply had to look up at the Zulu clock and look up that time segment in the zigzag plan and be ready to come to that course when the OTC sent the "Execute" signal.

The *Rainier* OTC complicated the lives of the watch standers of the four ships, as they had to plot out the course time changes based on whatever the start time was. This could introduce an element of error if someone calculated an incorrect turn time. Just a few minutes off could send ships on a collision course. To this added complexity the OTC decided to frequently change the zigzag plan!

Obviously, Lloyd preferred to keep the execution of the zigzag plan simple and for good reason—the crew needed to focus on being ready to defend the ship on a moment's notice. There was the submarine threat, which was the reason for the zigzag plan—to complicate an enemy sub skipper's targeting for firing his torpedo spread. But as the plane sightings indicated, there was a threat from the air, and no one could be certain regarding the location of enemy surface units. With this being *Atlanta*'s first wartime assignment, the crew became a bit edgy. One lookout mistook a seagull for an enemy aircraft, sending the crew to battle stations. Shortly thereafter, Lt. Jack Broughton held additional lookout training.

Lloyd made brief mention of the crossing of the equator—his fifth "official" time. He also made note that there were 600 polliwogs on board. Despite the heightened state of alert caused by reported aircraft and sub sightings, *Atlanta* went ahead with crossing of the line ceremonies.[5] As Lloyd noted, the crew was awakened early as they rushed to General Quarters before dawn when lookouts heard an unidentified aircraft overhead. The crew then hardly had a chance to go back to sleep when they were sent back to their battle stations at daybreak as Captain Jenkins had them do every day at sea. Securing from General Quarters, the crew then meandered to the mess decks to grab some chow. Breakfast was interrupted at 0630 as Lieutenant Mustin, standing watch as officer of the deck, reacted to the report of a submarine contact by again sending the crew to their battle stations. Once they determined they had a false contact, at about 0845, all hands shifted into pirate uniforms. Many of the crew fashioned their attire, taking advantage of Engineering Department ragbags that contained many colorful scraps of cloth. At 0900 the deck log recorded the arrival of Neptunus Rex and his royal entourage. During the personnel inspection, one of King Neptune's followers smeared a grease graphite concoction over the face and hair of each polliwog. Another member of the party carried a pair of scissors and gave impromptu haircuts. Stripped down to their waist and lined up barefoot, the polliwogs ran through a gauntlet of about a dozen shellbacks wielding rope or canvas-covered water-soaked truncheons. Once through the gauntlet, the polliwog faced his highness himself. A fire hose kept the deck moist to enhance the effects of electric shocks being dispensed by one shellback to the polliwog as the King gazed down to consider the man's credentials and the ultimate punishment he should suffer. Finally, the last step consisted of the polliwog crawling through a canvas chute, approximately 30 feet in length with about a 3-foot-wide diameter. As the polliwog approached the chute, King Neptune's electrician once again zapped him, driving him down on to the deck and into the chute.

Next the polliwogs were called up before the King and forced to drink a vile concoction and receive additional verbal abuse. Finally, the King declared an end to hostilities and certified all of the former polliwogs as shellbacks. Each new shellback was issued a diploma—an important document to retain to offer proof of having endured the ritual at some future date.

On May 16, following a morning refueling from the oiler, *Atlanta* bid farewell to *Rainier*, *Kaskaskia*, and *McCall* and headed west to join up with fleet units returning to Pearl Harbor. Following two days of independent steaming, Lloyd had the 4 to 8 watch on the morning of May 19. Calling the crew for the early morning precautionary GQ at 0540, those having topside battle stations were treated to the spectacle of Task Force 16, commanded by Vice Admiral Halsey embarked in *Enterprise*, coming over the horizon.[6] As noted earlier, *Enterprise*, commanded by Mustin's stepdad, *Hornet*, and their escorts had departed Pearl Harbor on April 30 to reinforce naval forces arrayed against a Japanese invasion force aimed at capturing Port Moresby, New Guinea. Had not *Atlanta* needed downtime to repair engineering problems and straighten out other mechanical hiccups, the cruiser would have joined up for what eventually became a long training cruise.

However, sending the two carriers to the Southwest Pacific was a prudent move. American naval intelligence had begun putting the pieces together on the Japanese operation as early as March 25, with radio interceptions that discussed a geographic designation of "RZQ" and an operation codenamed "MO." By mid-April, reports of Japanese carriers withdrawing from operations in the Indian Ocean and the movement of other units to the Southwest Pacific, including the new light carrier *Shoho*, further tipped the Japanese hand.

By the time Doolittle's bombs were dropping on Japan, Nimitz had confidence in his intelligence about Japan's next move and ordered Rear Adm. Frank Jack Fletcher to take Task Force 17 built around *Yorktown* and *Lexington* to the Coral Sea between New Guinea and the northeast coast of Australia. As the end of April approached, American–Australian codebreakers based in Melbourne had a firm handle on the details of the upcoming Japanese operation. Quickly turning Halsey's ships around after their strike against Japan, Nimitz understood time and distance precluded Task Force 16 from being on scene during the initial Japanese movement into the Coral Sea. However, in a prolonged struggle, Halsey could have been the cavalry coming to the rescue!

With the withdrawal of the Japanese from the Coral Sea, Nimitz summoned his Southwestern Pacific forces back to Hawaii. Having withdrawn to the south and then to the east, Fletcher divided his forces on May 11, sending cruisers and destroyers that had formerly screened *Lexington* up to Noumea for an overnight stopover to offload the hundreds of survivors they had rescued from that ill-fated ship. From there on the morning of May 13, the cruisers *Minneapolis* and *New Orleans*, accompanied by the destroyers *Monaghan*, *Phelps*, and *Worden*, steamed north and on the following day met up with Task Force 16 located off Efate in the New Hebrides. Fletcher had his other ships stay with the wounded *Yorktown* as she made her northeastern trek or steam independently to Pearl Harbor.

Missing from the formation were battleships, a fact that Lloyd lamented in an entry on May 14, writing: "The Japs outnumber us to beat hell in this ocean, and we're up against a tough Navy that doesn't keep its BB's home." Not all of the U.S. Navy's dreadnoughts had been put out of action at Pearl Harbor. A potent force of modernized World War I era battleships based on the West Coast was available to Nimitz. By April, sufficient repairs had been made on the December 7 veterans *Pennsylvania*, *Tennessee*, and *Maryland* to put them out to sea. *Colorado* had been in overhaul at Puget Sound Navy Yard when the Japanese attacked and was ready for service at the end of March 1942. The Navy also transferred the battlewagons *New Mexico*, *Mississippi*, and *Idaho* from the Atlantic to the Pacific via the Panama Canal.

Yet Nimitz, to Lloyd Mustin's consternation, held these heavy gunships in reserve thousands of miles from the contested waters of the Pacific. Barely able to manage over 20 knots, these venerable warships could not keep up with Nimitz's carriers that were criss-crossing the Pacific. Their boilers also guzzled oil, and Nimitz's inventory of oilers was limited. Finally, the BBs were vulnerable to air attack. While many argued that British and Japanese successes at Taranto and Pearl Harbor, respectively, marked the end of an era where the battleship was the queen of the seas, others initially were not convinced. Since these warships could not maneuver to defend themselves, they were, in effect, "sucker punched." However, late in the morning of December 10, east of the Malay Peninsula, Japanese shore-based aircraft swarmed upon the British battleship *Prince of Wales*, battle cruiser *Repulse*, and escorting destroyers.

Without defending aircraft to thwart the attackers, the two capital ships received multiple hits from torpedoes and bombs and rolled over to sink in the early afternoon. Tacticians came away with the lesson that battleships needed air cover to operate, and Nimitz had little to spare. The old battleships would not remain on the sidelines for long. Their 14- and 16-inch guns would play a key role in shore bombardment in the upcoming Pacific island-hopping campaigns. In addition, after being backfitted with 5-inch 38 mounts, plus an array of 40mm and 20mm antiaircraft artillery, these warships would more than hold their own against kamikaze and other attacking Japanese aircraft.[7]

Lloyd was displeased with the commander of the cruiser screen around the *Enterprise* and *Hornet*, Rear Adm. Raymond A. Spruance, who was embarked on *Northampton*. Assigned to Cruiser Division 5, Lloyd's ship took station at a relative bearing of 60 degrees off the bow of *Enterprise* at a distance of 4,000 yards. Astern of *Atlanta* steamed the cruisers *Northampton* and *Pensacola*. Over on *Enterprise's* opposite flank, Cruiser Division 6, consisting of Coral Sea veterans *Minneapolis* and *New Orleans* along with *Vincennes*, mirrored the stations of CruDiv 5. Four destroyers, spaced about 2,000 yards apart in a line abreast led the formation. Following *Enterprise* were the oilers *Platte* and *Cimarron* and finally the *Hornet*. With *Hornet* some miles distant off *Atlanta's* port quarter, it's understandable how Lloyd mistook her for her sister ship *Yorktown*. Lloyd probably would have preferred to see *Atlanta* placed in the van, to take better advantage of the ship's radar, sonar, and AA capabilities. Within a few days he got his wish. On May 20, Spruance placed *Atlanta* 4,000 yards ahead of *Enterprise* with *Phelps* positioned between the two ships.

As Lloyd's diary attests, the 3,000-mile trek back up to Pearl Harbor was not uneventful. Operating aircraft as sea is a dangerous endeavor even in peacetime. Lloyd mentioned two incidents involving *Hornet*. On May 21, he mentioned the loss of a man in *Hornet* who had walked into a prop—unfortunately not an uncommon tragedy. Later that day, *Hornet* lost a scout plane due to reasons unknown.[8]

The next day *Atlanta* and the task force, steaming on a course of 022 degrees, crossed the equator at a longitude of 168 degrees–30 West.

In his diary entries of May 23 and 25, Lloyd goes into detail about simulated raids conducted by the air groups on *Enterprise* and *Hornet*. Of the two, the air group on *Enterprise* was more experienced, since *Hornet's* air group was ashore during the April Doolittle raid. The practice attacks trained both the aviators and the defenders below. Although the gun crews could not expend ordnance, they gained experience in tracking and slewing the AA batteries onto the targets.

Lloyd wrote glowingly of the new dive-bombing techniques being employed by the bombing squadrons. By combining well-developed techniques and technology, the U.S. Navy had the most capable dive-bombing capability in the world. Navy pilots first demonstrated this tactic in an October 22, 1926 raid against battleships and cruisers steaming off of Long Beach, California. With lookouts scanning the horizons, the sudden descent of Curtiss F6C-1 Hawk biplanes from 12,000 feet surprised the big gunship crews.

Slow and aerobatic, biplanes were ideal platforms for vertical diving and bomb dropping. However, with the development of such sleek monoplane fighters as the Japanese Zero, the biplane became obsolete as a combat aircraft, and many questioned the future of dive-bombing.

The problem was new monoplane dive-bomber prototypes descended at such speed, that the pilot had to release the bomb at a much higher altitude to be able to pull himself out of the dive. The higher release point obviously decreased accuracy. Designer Edward H. Heinemann found a partial solution to the problem by installing split flaps on the wings to create an "air brake." Unfortunately, the flaps caused severe fluttering when the prototype aircraft descended. A fellow engineer suggested perforating the flaps with 3-inch holes. It worked! The alteration was incorporated into what became the Douglas Aircraft Company's SBD-2 "Dauntless."[9]

When confronted with a well-coordinated air assault supported by fighter aircraft, the prospects for the defender were bleak. Unfortunately, the lack of such a coordinated attack would cost many of these aircrews their lives in the upcoming battle that Mustin was getting indications of.

On the day before their return to Pearl Harbor, Lloyd notes how the position of his ship was constantly undergoing adjustment. Clearly, with a major engagement coming at Midway, others in the chain of command were thinking about the air defense problem and how to best use *Mighty A*.

CHAPTER 8

Layover

26 May

Pensacola lost a man overboard, an hour out of Pearl Harbor. We were in column astern, and picked him up. I went in the boat. We hadn't had him out of the water long when the first shark appeared. But the OTC has something to say about us stopping there in submarine waters. We know the Jap subs prowl here.

Noted that the "*Haruna*," which the Army Air Corps boys loudly advertise as having been sunk by them (Colin Kelly and all that) is undergoing repair in Japan. Christ—she got clean away from them, just as the *Shokaku* and *Zuikaku* managed to limp safely out from under their noses after our carriers had banged them up in the Coral Sea. Those blowhards ought to get up a balloon corps.

Arrived back in Pearl Harbor about 1200; moored in berth F-8. A distinguished row. Reading from right to left it goes: *Atlanta*, the remains of the *Arizona*, the still-sunken *West Virginia*, and the upside down *Oklahoma*.

P.S.—The OTC did have his say about our stopping. And the S.O.B. we fished out had jumped on purpose! Slightly nuts.

We clearly will not be here for long.

27 May '42

Saw George get his Navy Cross today, on the deck of his ship, presented by Adm. Nimitz. It was for doings during the raid on the Marshalls. The Admiral remembered me; we had a talk on old times in the *Augusta*, etc. Sortie is tomorrow, with trouble expected early.

Heard the dope on the *Lexington*. She was lost, alright—no admissions yet, of course. It must all be heavily sugarcoated for the public. The Japs got 5 aerial torpedoes into her, which only slowed her to 25 knots. But her fire mains must have been cut up—a dive-bomb hit as she was withdrawing started a fire that couldn't be controlled. It spread and raged for hours, and finally in night they had to abandon her. Probably 1,000 lost. God—the old *Lex* gone, and not by battle damage, but that damn fire. The *Phelps* had to sink her—five more torpedoes, to turn the trick.

***

"Man Overboard!" It's a constant fear of sailors everywhere to somehow get swept over the side and to see your vessel pass on over the horizon knowing that it will be only a matter of hours before you succumb to the elements, unless you are first located by sharks. By catching a glimpse of a befallen sailor, alert aft lookouts have saved many lives over the years. There are risks involved in recovery operations, especially in wartime. Of note, it was a man overboard incident involving Lloyd's father that allegedly contributed to his eventual demise. In this case, the man overboard incident took place a mere 50 miles from Oahu at about noon in relatively calm seas. Reacting instinctively, Captain Jenkins maneuvered *Atlanta* in position to drop a small boat in the water, with Lloyd serving as the boat officer. After pulling the

Atlanta at Pearl Harbor in May 1942. (Archives Branch, Naval History and Heritage Command, Washington, D.C.; NH 97806)

sailor into the boat, Lloyd learned the sailor had intentionally jumped over the side. Later Jenkins received a rebuke from the officer in tactical command, Vice Admiral Halsey, for taking such a risk to perform a job better suited for destroyers during wartime. Years later, Lloyd came to his commanding officer's defense, pointing out that there were no destroyers in the vicinity at the time.[1]

Lloyd also expressed a continuing contempt for Army Air Force propaganda. On December 10, 1941, Cpt. Colin Purdie Kelly, Jr. lifted off in his B-17 Flying Fortress from Clark Field in the Philippines to seek a reported Japanese aircraft carrier. Failing to find an enemy flattop, he attacked a Japanese amphibious force, dropping three bombs, damaging a light cruiser and destroyer. On the return to Clark, Kelly's plane was jumped by Japanese A6M Zero fighters. With the fuselage in flames, Kelly ordered his crew to bail out as he attempted to reach Clark. However, the plane exploded, resulting in the loss of Kelly and one crewmember. Kelly was subsequently lionized, receiving the Distinguished Flying Cross (posthumous) and U.S. Junior Chamber of Commerce Distinguished Service Award. Streets, parks, and schools would be named for him. Meaning no disrespect towards Kelly, Lloyd must have felt the Army Air Force had exploited his death for publicity purposes.[2]

Toward the end of the day, a harbor oiler came alongside. With hoses connected, the oiler's pumps began to pump black oil into the cruiser's depleted fuel tanks. Clearly, as Lloyd indicated, they would not remain at Pearl Harbor for long.[3] At Pearl Harbor a team of cryptologists, under the leadership of Cdr. Joseph Rochefort, had made successful inroads to breaking the Japanese code and was providing Admiral Nimitz with timely information about Japanese ship movements and dispositions.

Japanese messages had named "AF" as the next objective. But what was AF? Nimitz's codebreakers had confidence that AF stood for Midway. Washington was not convinced. To confirm the hypothesis, Midway broadcasted a clear transmission saying its water distillation plant was out of operation. Soon afterwards, a radio intercept team in Melbourne intercepted a Japanese message stating that AF was low on fresh water.[4] With the target confirmed, Nimitz rushed additional reinforcements to the small island group 1,000 miles to the northwest of Oahu. Once refueled, the ships of Task Force 16 would be ready to steam. But would it be too little, too late, as Lloyd had feared in his diary entry of May 23?

With four Japanese fleet carriers forming but one of the several Japanese ship formations approaching Midway, the Americans needed additional carriers to improve odds of success. *Saratoga* would soon be en route from the West Coast but would not arrive in time. Having the battered *Yorktown* available would help. But *Yorktown* had yet to return from the Coral Sea, and reportedly her damage would require weeks of repair.

On May 27, Captain Jenkins granted liberty to the third of the crew that had missed a turn during the previous time. Lloyd was among those who departed the ship on that sunny day. Instead of heading into Honolulu, he steered himself over to berth F-2 at Ford Island where *Enterprise* was tied alongside, taking on fuel, stores, and ammunition for the upcoming fight. At 1345 Officers' Call was sounded. Seven minutes later the band struck up ruffles and flourishes, and Admiral Nimitz arrived to present the awards. Lloyd looked on as the Pacific Fleet Commander presented his stepfather with a Navy Cross "for distinguished service in the line of his profession as Commanding Officer of USS *Enterprise*." The accompanying citation noted his courage and resourcefulness that saved the ship from serious damage on February 1, 1942, while "his ship was under heavy bombing attack in enemy waters." Nimitz continued down the rank, bestowing recognition on a number of officers and enlisted sailors who had served the nation with distinction during the first six months of the war. At the end of the line stood a heavy-set barrel-chested African American mess attendant. For his actions while assigned on *West Virginia* on December 7, Admiral Nimitz presented Dorie Miller a Navy Cross, the highest honor ever presented to a Black sailor up until that time.[5]

Adm. Chester W. Nimitz presenting Dorie Miller with a Navy Cross. Captain Murray is in the line of officers in the background. (Archives Branch, Naval History and Heritage Command, Washington, D.C.; NH 62656)

That Nimitz recognized and spoke with Lloyd, whom he first met when Lloyd was an ensign assigned to the gunnery department on the cruiser *Augusta*, is no surprise. Part of Admiral Nimitz's mystique was his ability to memorize names and faces—not only of the officers who served under him but also of their wives and children.

After the ceremony, Lloyd joined with George to call on Capt. Marc A. "Pete" Mitscher over on *Hornet* which was at berth F-10-S. The two men had long been friends with Mitscher, who graduated the Naval Academy a year ahead of Murray. The reason for the call, however, was business. With the Japanese attack on Midway only days away, the two men conferred on tactics. Lloyd observed that both men were skeptical about the ability of antiaircraft guns to fight off determined air attacks, but both had learned, based on recent actions in the Coral Sea, that even with an effective combat air patrol, some enemy aircraft would get through.

The two men discussed how gun crews needed to train harder to acquire targets and speed up the delivery of ammunition on the target. However, the discussion then focused on the tactics in current use to evade bomb damage, which consisted of ships wildly maneuvering at 25 knots to evade the falling bombs and torpedoes dropped from above.

The problem with this evasive strategy was that ships in the formation became widely dispersed. "No unit was in any position to help support another unit. A good intelligent attacker could then pick off his targets one by one at his leisure."[6]

The two captains examined the problem and determined that some tactical integrity needed to be maintained by the ships in the Task Force formation so that the gun crews from the various ships could be mutually supportive in their gunfire. Lloyd recalled: "They broached the thought that 'let's not do it that way. Let us consider whether we can't maintain some kind of tactical integrity while in this violent evasive maneuver phase.'"[7]

As the two captains talked and the young lieutenant listened with great interest, a fourth man entered *Hornet*'s captain's cabin. Rear Adm. Raymond Spruance, the commander of the cruiser destroyer screen around the carriers, suddenly found himself in command of Task Force 16 due to the skin rash that afflicted Vice Admiral Halsey. Experiencing severe discomfort, the task force commander had checked himself into the Pearl Harbor Naval Hospital on the previous day. When Admiral Nimitz visited Halsey, he saw immediately he was in no shape to have command during the forthcoming battle. At Halsey's recommendation, Nimitz named Spruance to command the task force built around *Hornet* and *Enterprise*.[8]

When Murray and Mitscher pitched their new approach, the new boss responded favorably. Under previous doctrine, two carriers operating aircraft together in close proximity would be steaming parallel into the wind, with the rest of the ships in a circular screen around the two. "When they came under attack, the two carriers would separate, each from the other, but predesignated ships from the circular screen would go with carrier A, and other predesignated ships would go with carrier B and would stay with her by matching her evasive maneuvers."[9]

Lloyd credited that conversation for initiating a change in the defensive doctrine now calling on ships in the formation to turn with the high-value ship so that the full gun power of the task force could be used against the attackers.

Meeting Spruance was not an inspirational moment for Lieutenant Mustin. Congratulating Spruance on his new assignment, Lloyd anticipated a Halsey-like pronouncement declaring, "We are going to go after them and we are going to get them." Instead, he recalled Spruance meekly responded, stating something like "Well I hope I can do all right." It suggested anything but confidence.

However, Spruance may still have been surprised by the suddenness of being given responsibility for Task Force 16. Understanding that Halsey's affliction was going to take him out of the fight, Spruance fully expected Nimitz to assign one of the more senior naval aviators present at Pearl Harbor to lead the *Hornet–Enterprise* task force.

Also, as historian Gordon W. Prange pointed out, Spruance was the antithesis of Halsey's personality. "Halsey appealed to the imagination and emotions; Spruance spoke to the mind and the intellect. Halsey often wrapped his thoughts in picturesque, exciting words; Spruance expressed himself in economical pointed language."[10] In responding to Lieutenant Mustin, the admiral, understanding the forces arrayed against him, was speaking with candor.

Spruance departed. He had an appointment to meet with Admiral Nimitz and Rear Admiral Fletcher who had just returned from the Coral Sea on the battered *Yorktown* as the award ceremony on *Enterprise* had concluded. Nimitz had summoned the commander of Task Force 17, which had once included the carrier *Lexington*, to his office to get a debriefing on that costly victory. Now with the details on Coral Sea clear in his mind, Nimitz sat down with his two task force commanders for a frank discussion of what they were up against and the measures needed to inflict a blow against the enemy.[11]

With Task Force 16 replenished, Nimitz directed Spruance to depart the next day to a point northeast of Midway. Fletcher would follow as soon as *Yorktown* was repaired and refloated.

Meanwhile, the details of the recent battle that the carrier had fought in had spread to the ships of Task Force 16. In contrast to the scuttlebutt that Lloyd jotted down, the Japanese had scored two bomb hits and two torpedo strikes on "*Lady Lex*." As Lloyd lamented, *Lexington* had not been lost because of damage inflicted by the enemy, but because of the inability of the crew to combat two explosions caused by leaking vapors from aviation fuel tanks that racked the ship. An image of smoke billowing out from the vessel with hundreds of sailors lowering themselves on lines let down from the forward flight deck on the port side would become one of the more iconic photographs of the war at sea. Eventually the giant carrier had to be put down with torpedoes from one of her escorting destroyers.[12]

The next morning Captain Jenkins set the Sea and Anchor detail as Task Force 16 departed to engage in a certain battle.

CHAPTER 9

En Route Midway

1 June 1942

The force that sortied was about as before, with only a few DD's changed, and one less of them. But Adm. Spruance (CCD5) [Commander, Cruiser Division Five] is OTC; Halsey is in hospital with his very annoying skin infection.

The Japs are reported to have two *Haruna* class BB's (ex-CC's), 5 or 6 CV's, about eight CA's, 20 DD's, and 40 troop transports and auxiliaries, heading for this grab on Midway.

Yesterday (31st) we all fueled out of tankers. *Cimarron* for us (80,000 gallons), then they shoved off to return to P.H. [Pearl Harbor]. Waved "Good luck" as they shoved—and 3 DD's went along to get them there. We are now the *Enterprise* (flag) and *Hornet*, CV's; *Minneapolis*, *New Orleans*, *Vincennes*, *Northampton* & *Pensacola*, CA's; us, and 8 DD's, mostly of the *Dewey* class. A fine match for this Jap outfit.

And all this while our BB's are in San Francisco, reportedly. I can't understand the school of strategy that for any reason could keep them there under the present circumstances.

Anyway, there'll be some land-based aircraft on our side, plus TF 17 (*Yorktown* with whatever CA's are in Pearl Harbor, and DD's as are available), plus maybe TF 8. TF 8 being the *Saratoga*, repairs completed, plus our sister *San Diego*, newly arrived on West Coast, plus some other stuff. They leave San Diego 3 June, at best speed. Hope to Christ those Army saps bomb the right fleet.

Today we arrived at our spot, 300 miles N. by E. from Midway, and started just cruising in this area. We hope to jump them after they've gotten started on Midway, a surprise from the flank. Weather poor; rainy with fog and low clouds during the clearer parts; damp and chilly.

It can start anytime now—unless it's all a big fake on their part, to draw us off from down South. Seems just a touch too pat to be the McCoy.

The Capt. addressed the crew over the General Announcing system, giving them an idea of what's up. A certain keying-up, at least, is in evidence. Everyone has looked to his life jacket, his gun, helmet, knife, and gas mask; ammunition all up; last minute checks made. Now we cruise, and wait.

2 June

Today, as yesterday, the Radio Direction Finder was able to get bearings on Jap transmissions. 270 KCS, voice, strength 5. Probably submarines, and undoubtedly close. We have some subs patrolling off Midway ourselves.

These Jap subs are in an area we have traversed—hard to believe we are undetected (though the fifth column in Oahu should have made that of small moment anyhow).

TF 17 joined up. *Yorktown, Portland, Indianapolis*, 5 DD's of the *Sims* class. They are to operate in visual touch with us, for the time being.

3 June

This, by the schedule, was the day things were to start, and they did. First, a report of a raid on Dutch Harbor. Then a second, and a third. Then word that Jap main body had been sighted by a patrol plane, 700 mi. W. of Midway.

Which makes dawn tomorrow the witching hour.

More RDF bearings on their subs—seems to be all around our area.

Add 2 BB's of the *Ise* class to expected Jap force; also, parachute troops, special landing equipment of all types, marines and special amphibious army units. Looks like a full-dress affair.

A false alarm G.Q. this morning, on an air contact that proved to be *Yorktown* planes, was answered with some alacrity!

***

Although the Americans had cracked a bit of the Japanese naval ciphers by early spring, it was not until much later in May that Nimitz had a full appreciation of what he had contended with at Midway. When he met with Spruance and Fletcher on the afternoon of the 27th, Nimitz asked his intelligence officer, Capt. Edwin T. Layton, about the composition of the approaching enemy forces.

Layton detailed a Japanese striking force, a support force, and an occupation force converging on the island. He identified the striking force as centered around the carriers *Kaga, Akagi, Soryu*, and *Hiryu*, with two battleships, two heavy cruisers, and twelve destroyers serving as escorts. The support force contained two additional battleships, four heavy cruisers, a light cruiser, a small aircraft carrier, and ten more destroyers. He then described the occupation force as containing numerous troopships and support vessels, escorted by even more cruisers and destroyers. Finally, Layton projected that the Japanese would deploy their submarines as a warning shield between Hawaii and Midway. Predicting that the initial Japanese air strike was set for the morning of June 4, Layton further projected that the incoming aircraft would come in from a bearing of 325 degrees from the atoll.[1]

The force Lloyd cited in his June 1 entry reflects the briefing that Layton gave to Nimitz and the task force commanders. Adm. Chuichi Nagumo's First Carrier Striking Force coming in from the northwest had many of the ship types mentioned, including the *Haruna* and sister *Kirishima*, two British-designed battle cruisers built prior to World War I. Extensive refitting during the 1930s added armor and firepower at the cost of speed and earned them the battleship designation.[2]

The original Japanese plan had called for the six aircraft carriers that had conducted the Pearl Harbor strike to perform an encore performance at Midway. However, *Shokaku* was damaged at the battle of the Coral Sea, and in that engagement *Zuikaku* lost 40 percent of her aircrews.[3] Thus, the two veteran carriers had to remain in home waters for repair and personnel replenishment. *Nagumo* steamed with the remaining four December 7 veterans.

What Layton and subsequently Lloyd Mustin missed was the "Main Body" consisting of the super battleship *Yamato*, battleships *Nagato* and *Mutsu*, a light cruiser, a light carrier, and nine additional destroyers. At the time, the Americans were unaware of the existence of the recently commissioned *Yamato*, a behemoth that nearly displaced 70,000 tons fully loaded and boasted a main battery of nine 18-inch 45-caliber rifles mounted in three triple turrets. In contrast, America's two newest battleships, *North Carolina* and *Washington*, displaced 41,000 tons fully loaded with a main battery of nine 16-inch 50-caliber guns.[4]

From the bridge of his super battleship, Adm. Isoroku Yamamoto oversaw the complex Japanese operation, which also included the planned capture and occupation of the Alaskan islands of Kiska and Attu. Though the plan called for the seizure of islands near Alaska and in the mid-Pacific, his actual objective was the destruction of the American fleet. Understanding America's industrial capacity, he had few illusions about Japan's ultimate fate unless the U.S. Pacific Fleet could be eliminated as a fighting force.

Up on the signal bridge, *Atlanta*'s signalmen copied down the Morse code dit-dots coming across the ways articulating Spruance's intent to attack Japanese forces from their flank. If Spruance had disappointed Lloyd with his lack of feistiness when they met in *Hornet*, the words the admiral penned for the conclusion of his message—"THE SUCCESSFUL CONCLUSION OF THE OPERATION NOW COMMENCING WILL BE OF GREAT VALUE TO OUR COUNTRY"—probably did little to change the senior lieutenant's mind.[5]

Lloyd correctly identified the cruisers attached to Task Force 16, but he missed counting one of the destroyers in the screen. Still, even with the extra destroyer, the Americans were woefully outgunned. Spruance did have an advantage of having some competent leaders in his operational chain of command. For the overall command of the two carriers, Spruance had Captain Murray wear the hat as Commander Task Group 16.5. Operating the cruiser screen as Commander Task Group 16.2 fell on Rear Adm. Thomas C. Kinkaid. Capt. Alexander R. Early ran the destroyer screen as Commander Task Group 16.4.[6]

During the transit up, Captain Jenkins relentlessly conducted gunnery and damage control drills to hone the crew's ability to fight as a team. On May 31, the oilers *Cimarron* and *Platte* topped off the task force. As Lloyd noted, *Atlanta* received a gulp of 80,000 gallons from *Cimarron*. With their mission complete, the oilers returned to Pearl and Task Force 16 pressed ahead, arriving northeast of Midway on June 1. Decades later in his oral history, Lloyd was struck by how the calm ocean "seemed to be endlessly dotted with those familiar blown glass fishing floats the Japanese used." Lloyd remembered that *Atlanta* dodged the floats, for there was a concern that there could be mines attached below them.[7]

The "Fifth Column" remark Lloyd wrote reflected an attitude held at the time that Japanese immigrants living in Hawaii had collaborated closely with Tokyo to coordinate the Pearl Harbor attack and were continuing to report on the movements of American naval forces. On the West Coast of the United States such beliefs led to the internment of thousands of Japanese Americans. With the eventual surrender of Japan, no evidence could be found to substantiate the concerns.

The weather remained overcast on June 2 as Task Force 16 changed course frequently throughout the day. At 1633 a lookout spotted Task Force 17 on the eastern horizon.[8] The late afternoon rendezvous with Task Force 17 which centered on *Yorktown* represented the result of one of the greatest quick repair jobs in naval history. After suffering two bomb hits and a near miss on May 8 during the battle of the Coral Sea, the American flattop limped into Pearl Harbor on May 27 trailing oil. Many crewmembers anticipated that the ship would return to the West Coast for three months of repair. Rear Admiral Fletcher thought it would take at least two weeks to make the carrier seaworthy.

However, when she entered Drydock #1 early on May 28, hundreds of yard workers swarmed on to the ship. Sparks flew as workers patched holes, repaired piping, and shored up bulkheads. Working around the clock, the craftsmen had the ship ready for sea in two days. The timing could not have cut it much closer. As part of Yamamoto's elaborate plan, a screen of Japanese submarines was to take picket stations between Midway and Hawaii. Their mission was to report any U.S. Navy ship movements toward Midway once the Japanese attack began and to inflict damage on any such reinforcements. Departing on the morning of May 30, Task Force 17 managed to transit the waters between Pearl Harbor and Midway just before the Japanese picket submarines arrived at their stations. Fortunately for the Americans, the radio transmissions that *Atlanta* picked up were negative sighting reports. The Americans arrived undetected.[9]

Upon arrival, Fletcher assumed tactical command of the two task forces and directed Spruance to operate Task Force 16 about 10 miles southward to enable line-of-sight communications to be maintained. At 1924, *Atlanta*'s log indicated that Task Force 16 was heading west at a speed of 14 knots. As for attack plans, Fletcher ordered that *Enterprise* and *Hornet* be ready to launch their air groups on short notice. *Yorktown*, and the accompanying cruisers, would have the responsibility of launching scout planes to seek out the enemy, which *Yorktown* promptly did the following morning of June 3.

As *Yorktown*'s scouts headed out on the assigned vectors, *Atlanta* steamed on a northwesterly heading as the guide ship in an 11-Victor disposition that placed the light cruiser and her antiaircraft armament at the center of the task force with the two carriers stationed off her port and starboard beams. At 0920, *Atlanta*'s lookouts must have spotted the returning *Yorktown* scouts. Unable to discern the country of origin, the ship set General Quarters, sending Lloyd to his "ConAft" [control aft] station aft near Battle II. Over the next four days, Lloyd would spend much time ruminating in his upper deck observation post where he could see some 20 miles over the horizon.[10] After some tense minutes, with many pairs of binoculars studying the aircraft, the aircraft were determined to be friendly. Throughout the day the two task forces stayed in the general vicinity northeast of Midway.[11] One aspect of the pending battle proved fortuitous to Lloyd. Figuring he would be spending much time at GQ, Lloyd convinced the senior watch officer to take him off the officer of the deck watch bill.

Lloyd's comments about the Japanese air attack on Dutch Harbor in the Aleutians and the sighting of Japanese ships west of Midway reassured many that their intelligence was good, which instilled confidence. Lloyd's Dutch Harbor observation was accurate, as aircraft from the Japanese carriers *Ryujo* and *Junyo* swooped down on that Aleutian installation to preempt resistance to the forthcoming landings on Attu and Kiska.

However, Lloyd's comment about the reported sighting of the Japanese main body proved to be accurate only in that the Americans were not privy to the existence of Yamamoto's battleship group. At nearly half past nine, Ens. Jack Reid, piloting a PBY Catalina flying boat, spotted a formation of ships some 700 miles from Midway bearing 262 degrees. The heavy warships spotted were not those of Yamamoto but those of Vice Adm. Nobutake Kondo, which were escorting the invasion force. Nine B-17 bombers lifted off from Midway later in the day to drop bombs on Kondo's ships from 8,000 to 12,000 feet.[12]

Reports received by Task Force 16 and *Atlanta* must have buoyed morale. Army Flying Fortresses claimed to have hit two battleships and scored a near miss.

However, the Americans were not finished the day. Cdr. Logan C. Ramsey and Cdr. Cyril T. Sinard concocted a farfetched scheme to arm patrol planes—PBYs with torpedoes for a night attack against the approaching Japanese invasion force.

Four of the radar-equipped twin-engine Catalina flying boats lifted off at 2115, and lumbered westward with torpedoes rigged under their wings. At about 0130, the planes slowly moved in on an unsuspecting Japanese transport group. Of the torpedoes dropped, one scored a hit on the oiler *Akebuno Maru*. Although 23 Japanese sailors were either killed or wounded, the oiler licked her wounds and resumed her spot in the advancing formation.[13]

Members of the wardroom "groused a bit because the battleships were not included in the junket"—a view clearly shared by Lloyd. No doubt this view was held by the battleship sailors themselves. Though the American Pacific Fleet battle line had been decimated during the attack of December 7, repair work on the West Coast had readied *Pennsylvania* and *Maryland* to rejoin the war effort, along with *Colorado*, which had been at Puget Sound when the Japanese had attacked. By then, *Idaho*, *Mississippi*, and *New Mexico* had joined the Pacific Fleet from the Atlantic. On the West Coast, Adm. William S. Pye deployed Rear Adm. Walter S. Anderson with the *Maryland* and *Colorado* along with three destroyers on May 31 to search for a Japanese aircraft carrier reportedly prowling 650 miles to the northwest of San Francisco. Once the battle of Midway was well underway, Pye himself headed out with four additional battleships, the light carrier *Long Island*, and five more destroyers to rendezvous with Anderson in Pacific waters thousands of miles to the east of the action.[14]

That the battleships were not operating at the tip of the spear en route to Midway came down to a question of fuel. It could be argued that the loss of the fleet oiler *Neosho* at the battle of the Coral Sea was near as fatal a blow as the loss of *Lady Lex*. With only seven tankers assigned to the Pacific Fleet, Nimitz's logisticians had to make difficult decisions. The West Coast battleships and their escorts were capable of burning 300,000 barrels of fuel a month—equal to the entire storage capacity of the Pacific Fleet at that time. In addition, not only did the old battleships consume mass quantities of black oil, but they could not keep pace with the carriers.[15]

As the American air defenders at Midway lashed out at the approaching enemy, a weather front provided cover for Nagumo's First Carrier Striking Force. The question the American commanders pondered was, would this force appear on the fourth at its projected location?

CHAPTER 10

Midway: The Pivotal Day

4 June

Dawn G.Q., as usual, but apparently the Jap had not shown much of his hand, since yesterday's report—at least not enough for us to show ours. Did hear that B-17's had followed up yesterday's contact with a bombing attack—"some damage" on not very well identified ships. Then eight (I think it was) PBY's went out with torpedoes for a night attack, reported "completed." No damage information to us. It was a bright moonlight night, crystal clear. Anyhow, after seeing the sun safely up at 0630 (we are on +10 time), we secured from GQ and went back to condition watches.

About 0830 got word attack on Midway by carrier aircraft had started. Went to GQ headed West 30 knots, launched all aircraft. TF 17 not a part of TF 16, but in sight usually distant about 10 miles. Visibility exceptional, sky clear, few scattered clouds.

Midway reports eight planes downed by their AA, some damage to Jap striking force composed of 2 BB's, 4 CV's, 4 CA's, done by Midway planes. This force apparently close to Midway, but 250 miles from us.

Our aircraft got there by about 1100 and got in combined attack. Of the three carriers, VTBrons [V=Fighter; T=Torpedo; B=Bomber Squadrons] (about 3x18=54 planes), 12 survived to land on Midway. Japs machine-gunned parachuting pilots, also men in the water in their rubber boats (positive reports of survivors). *Kaga* and *Akagi* identified among the carriers. SBD's got in their dive-bombing attack also—losses must have been bad, but hard to estimate. I believe we had 6x18=108, about, in the attack, with only 70 or so in sight next day. Zero fighters were bad medicine.

However, the Japs appeared completely caught napping, and both BB's, all CV's, several CA's were reported badly hurt. Midway had sent frantic "help" calls by radio on the first attack, to make it look like we weren't loaded for bear. A TBD pilot later rescued reported seeing *Kaga* or *Akagi* go down, and later seeing Jap cruisers shelling and sinking a smaller CV (*Soryu* class?) which was dead in the water. Other Japs burning.

This force is a pretty sight, tearing West at 30 knots, clear weather, sunny, with calm sea.

About 1400 carrier planes began arriving back; we turned to 090° for landing. Every time a group appeared, turn to 090; as soon as aboard, turn around again and go West. TF 17 got farther and farther separated from us, and our two carriers also got separated. We stayed with *Hornet*. About 1430 Japs appeared; they'd followed our planes back. Got to TF 17 first, and worked out on *Yorktown*. We could see them perfectly at 23 miles though the ships were hull down and out of our gun range. Much gunfire; one down, a flaming comet. But they got 2 torpedoes and 3 dive-bomb hits, with what looked like about a 30-plane attack. Black smoke billowed from the Y—we could see it still, 80 miles away. All available fighters from TF 16 helped.

We took off another bombing mission. (The 3rd—Number 2 all came back with bombs on, just after attack on the Y. Must have missed objective.) It got back to their carriers and made an unopposed attack. Reported no air opposition, 2 BB's, 2 CA's, 4 CV's badly damaged and burning. Landed them aboard before dark.

PT boats from Midway ordered out after dark to see what they could do. No results reported.

A force of Jap cruisers & DD's is reported headed for us, distance 100 miles. They apparently are separate from the "Striking Force"—perhaps an "Escort Force." The "Transport Group" hasn't been seen by our planes; other reports indicate it perhaps 200 miles due West Midway.

To my agonized amazement, we run away all night—course about 120, averaged, for several hundred miles total ground covered since plane recovery. I can't see why, with radars thick in our outfit, and everyone with 30 knots plus, that we have anything to fear in moving the other way to take favorable position for further action, especially since the Jap air strength now seems done for.

About 2200 secured from G.Q.—what a day. (Toward afternoon, low scattered clouds had come in to about 5/10—helped the attack on *Yorktown*.)

***

It is worth noting Lloyd indicated that the Task Force was now operating on +10 time. During the previous three days, Spruance's ships had operated on +11 time, as

Midway is only 7 degrees from the International Date Line. The resetting occurred at 2200 on June 2 as clocks throughout the task force were pushed ahead to 2300. Most likely Rear Admiral Fletcher's Task Force 17 had been operating on a +10 time, and for command and control purposes, Rear Admiral Spruance conformed to minimize confusion.[1]

Using local time as a baseline, Lloyd secured from General Quarters just after 0430. As Atlanta's crew left their battle stations to have breakfast, patrol aircraft winging out from Midway and Yorktown had yet to spot Vice Adm. Chuichi Nagumo's First Carrier Striking Fleet. More significantly, the Japanese remained oblivious to the existence of Task Force 16 and 17.[2]

Yet as a precaution, concurrent with his launch of air strikes at sunrise to soften up Midway's defenses, Nagumo ordered seven aircraft to fan out from north to east to south to assure the commander that there were no American forces lurking over the horizon. Given subsequent events, strategists would be harsh on the vice admiral for not sending out two search sorties. Had he launched a spread of aircraft in the early pre-dawn hours, perhaps one of the planes would have spotted the silhouettes of the American warships as the sun came up over the horizon. As it was, the reconnaissance aircraft lifted off along with other aircraft that were destined to strike Midway. Scout planes from the Kaga, Akagi, and battleship Haruna lifted off at 0430, with two from the cruiser Chikuma being catapulted shortly thereafter. The cruiser Tone had some difficulty getting her floatplanes aloft with Scout Plane #4 departing at approximately 0500 on an easterly course of 100 degrees. As the scout planes fanned out, a strike force of 108 aircraft had formed up and began heading in a southeasterly vector toward Midway.[3]

As noted, simultaneous to 0430 Japanese carrier launches, 10 dive-bombers fanned out from Rear Admiral Fletcher's flagship in a westward search pattern. Eleven Catalina PBY aircraft from Midway also joined the search. Fletcher, as the overall officer in tactical command of the two task forces, had assumed responsibility for scouting, directing Spruance to have Hornet and Enterprise ready to launch attacks once the Japanese were sighted. Meanwhile, a force of Oahu-based B-17s was en route to drop additional bomb loads on the spotted invasion force.[4]

Lloyd's diary entry of Midway coming under attack at 0830 coincides with subsequent histories that place the arrival of the Japanese air armada at 0630. His report of eight enemy aircraft lost during the spirited defense of Midway was in line with initial Japanese and apparently some American estimates. Post-analysis of the air battle upped the Japanese losses to about a dozen aircraft downed by American air and ground defenses. What he failed to mention was the cost of American lives and aircraft. Alerted by PBYs and radar, pilots of the Midway-based Marine Fighter Squadron (VMF-221) climbed into the cockpits of 20 Brewster F2A-3 "Buffalos" and quickly roared into the sky, joined by Navy aviators in six Grumman F4F-3 "Wildcats."

In repeated dogfights against the Japanese Zeros, the skilled American fliers found themselves outmaneuvered by the famed enemy fighter planes. Fourteen of the pilots would not return, and most of the rest bailed out of or returned with aircraft so shot up as to be not flyable. One pilot counted 72 bullet and cannon holes in his plane. But the Marine and Navy pilots' ferocity rattled the attackers into thinking they were twice the number, and the fierce ground fire and excellent camouflage of targets also caused the bombers to be off the mark. The Japanese air commander would call back for the need for a second attack.[5]

Looking back at Midway, many of the Japanese participants blamed the defeat on "Victory Disease"—an arrogant overconfidence that led to several blunders, such as the inadequate reconnaissance plan on the morning of June 4. However, the Americans must be credited with contributing to this overconfidence by executing a brilliant operational deception plan using the airwaves. With the Pearl Harbor to Midway section of the trans-Pacific cable intact, Admiral Nimitz used this communications pipeline to coordinate the American buildup. Meanwhile, the airwaves carried routine administrative messages designed to reinforce the appearance that the Americans were oblivious to Japanese moves. Assuming that the Japanese radio operators intercepted Midway's radio pleas for help, it could have only reassured Yamamoto and Nagumo that their operation was proceeding as planned.

If Nagumo did receive such a snippet of intelligence, he had little chance to ponder over it. His air strike on Midway failed to catch the American land-based attack planes on the ground. As previously noted, B-17s had lifted off early to attack the invasion force, and one of the PBYs that had departed just prior to the Flying Fortresses spotted Nagumo's force at about 0520 at 180 miles to the northwest. Twenty-five minutes later, another flying boat spotted two flights of Japanese aircraft heading southeasterly and radioed in clear English: "Many planes heading Midway bearing 320 degrees, distance 150."[6]

Alerted, the Americans put everything they had left on the ground that could fly and drop ordnance on ships. The result became a polyglot of different models of Army and Navy aircraft winging their way toward the approaching Japanese carriers. Six new Navy TBF Avenger torpedo planes joined with a Marine squadron of older SB2U Vindicator torpedo planes and SBD Dauntless dive-bombers, four Army B-26s, and the remaining B-17 bombers. At about 0710, minutes after Nagumo was appraised for the need of a second strike on Midway, the TBFs and the B-26s made their attack runs on his carriers. Dodging a swarm of defending Zeros and blistering AA fire, the Americans pressed their torpedo runs. As reflected by Lloyd's diary, the attackers claimed hits. Yet the Japanese evaded the fish dropped by the Americans and knocked down several of the attackers. What unnerved Nagumo was a valiant attempt by a crippled B-26 to crash into the bridge of his flagship *Akagi*. Fear turned to relief as the twin-engine American light bomber veered off at the last moment and crashed into the sea.

With the skies temporarily free of American intruders and no apparent American carrier task forces in the region as confirmed by all scout planes except the tardy #4 off *Tone*, Nagumo ordered the arming of his remaining aircraft with bombs for a second strike.

As Japanese deck crews on *Kaga* and *Akagi* switched ordnance, at about 0728 a report filtered in from scout plane #4: "Sight what appears to be 10 enemy surface ships in position 10 degrees distance 240 miles from Midway, Course 150 degrees, speed over 20 knots."[7] More than the unexpected presence of enemy warships, what must have disturbed Nagumo was the dearth of information on the presence of American carriers. Yet as the First Striking Fleet commander awaited specifics about enemy ship types from *Tone*'s scout plane, his ship skippers skillfully dodged a hail of bombs while his Zeros and antiaircraft gun crews tore into the attacking aircraft. Of the successive waves of dive-bombers, Army B-17s, and then torpedo planes, only the Army bombers left the scene with the number of planes that arrived. All three groups claimed hits on enemy carriers and battleships. Indeed, a post-war Marine Corps history of the battle maintained that Marine Corps SBDs had landed two 500-pound bombs on *Akagi*, citing post-war interrogations of the Japanese carrier's captain. At this stage, the Americans believed they had sunk at least one or two cargo ships and damaged perhaps 10 more. In reality, the only hit scored had been made on an oiler during the night attack by the PBY.[8]

Lloyd reflected these claims in his diary, and his belief in these claims would no doubt contribute to his later harsh judgments on Rear Admiral Spruance. Later, in his oral history, Lloyd questioned the command relationship that Nimitz had imposed between the senior Rear Admiral Fletcher commanding Task Force 17 and the junior Rear Admiral Spruance heading Task Force 16:

> Apparently there was some sort of overall command responsibilities vested in Fletcher by Nimitz. Nimitz, of course, was in overall command of the operation which included forces additional to those in the two carrier task forces, but between the two carrier task forces, Fletcher, as the senior of the two, was supposed to have some sort of command responsibility over these two task forces. But it was never made apparent to us on the scene. No tactical command influencing what we did in Task Force 16 appeared to come from Task Force 17. Of course they would have come from voice radio to all that heard them.[9]

However, as Lloyd noted, on the morning of the 4th, the two task forces were steaming, separated by about 10 miles. At this distance, there was an alternative to radio communications. At 0607, using flashing light, a *Yorktown* signalman blinked a message to *Enterprise* from Fletcher, directing Spruance to take a southwesterly heading to close on Nagumo's force and to launch as soon as the enemy's location had been pinpointed.[10]

Spruance hardly needed prompting. Although he had intended to continue closing on the Japanese carrier force and launch his strikes at 0900, he had heard the "Many planes heading Midway" transmission of the enemy air raid. Then came a sighting report at 0603 of two Japanese carriers and battleships 180 miles to the northwest of Midway. Sightings of Nagumo's ships caused him to expedite his plan. As the staff that Spruance inherited from Halsey plotted the positions on a navigation chart, Spruance reached for a maneuvering board that he liked to carry with him. Looking down at the square pad, he marked Midway Island at the center and then plotted the distance and bearing of the two opposing forces relative to the Midway. Using his thumb and index finger as measuring dividers, he quickly determined that Nagumo's carriers lay 175 miles to the west, within striking range, albeit the maximum striking range of his torpedo planes. If he could get his planes airborne, he understood he might be able to catch the Japanese at the end of the recovery phase from the Midway strike—when they would be most vulnerable.[11]

Initially Task Force 16 sped west; however, since the light winds were coming from the east, the two carriers had to reverse course to a southeasterly heading to launch their aircraft. Hence his two carriers, along with *Atlanta* and the rest of the escorting cruisers and destroyers, turned into the wind and at 0700 the first plane lifted off from *Hornet*. Six minutes later the *Enterprise* launched her aircraft.

Atlanta's war diary recorded: "Japanese ships reported to southwest. Cleared ship for action and went to General Quarters. Maneuvered at various courses at high speed throughout the day as antiaircraft screen for HORNET while her air group made repeated attacks."[12]

As Lloyd related in an earlier diary entry, it was extremely difficult to defend against the mock coordinated attacks that the *Enterprise* and *Hornet* air groups staged against the task force en route to Hawaii. However, to stage such an attack, the air groups have to depart en masse, which requires aircraft flying off the decks to form up and circle the carrier in a holding pattern. This wastes fuel. Today's Navy solves this problem by launching tanker aircraft to perform in-flight refueling of the loitering aircraft. Back then, with no in-flight refueling capability, the Navy launched aircraft that had the greatest range and fuel capacity first.

As noted earlier, at 0728 *Tone*'s scout plane #4 reported back to Nagumo the presence of Spruance's task force. In the clear skies to the west, *Tone*'s plane was visible to Spruance's lookouts. Knowing his presence had been exposed and realizing the distance between him and the enemy widened with each passing moment due to his southwesterly heading, Spruance gave the order at 0745 to send the circling dive-bombers on their way to catch the Japanese before they could react.[13]

Once the launch was complete, scattered groups of 116 fighters, bombers, and torpedo planes were en route to what was intended to be a coordinated attack. Fletcher, meanwhile, held back on launching his planes until 0838 to allow for the recovery of his scout planes and to affirm that all the enemy's carriers had been located.[14]

On the *Akagi*, Nagumo pondered the reports received from *Tone*'s scout plane. He considered launching the aircraft he had on deck to immediately go after the Americans; however, such an action meant possibly sacrificing pilots on returning aircraft from Midway who would have to ditch their aircraft due to low fuel and no flight decks to land on. Nagumo decided to land the Midway raiders. Once these aircraft were on board, at 0917 he turned his force to the northeast, close on the direction of the U.S. Navy's two task forces. The destroyer *Arashi* stayed behind to prosecute attacks on the American submarine *Nautilus*, which had been vainly firing torpedoes at Nagumo's fleet in the midst of the morning's air attacks from Midway.[15]

By this time, American aircraft from 11 squadrons embarked on the three carriers were heading toward a spot of ocean where the Japanese carrier force was projected to be heading. After watching the American aircraft head westward over the horizon, a period of intense waiting began for the crew of *Atlanta*. In the radio room officers and enlisted sailors stood by speakers waiting for transmissions from the three air groups. Topside, lookouts watched Wildcat fighters on combat air patrol circle the two task forces and kept an eye out for enemy aircraft.

Nagumo's sharp turn to the northeast threw off many of the attackers. Arriving at the interception point, *Hornet*'s dive-bombers, bomb-laden scout planes, and fighters continued on and then returned home without sighting the enemy. The bombers and scout planes had enough fuel to return to *Hornet* or land on Midway. The fighters did not have enough fuel and had to ditch. Fighters from *Enterprise* did find the enemy carriers, but their timing did not coincide with an attack, while a half dozen *Yorktown* fighters did mix it up with defending Zeros. All three torpedo squadrons found Nagumo's force and drove home attacks, first VT-8 from *Hornet*, then VT-6 from *Enterprise*, and finally VT-3 from *Yorktown*. Lumbering along in their sluggish TBD Devastators, the American pilots were easy targets for the defending Zeros and antiaircraft gunners. Some of the pilots did get their fish into the ocean, but the Japanese carrier skippers skillfully maneuvered their vessels to avoid the underwater missiles. Only four of the 41 torpedo planes launched off of American flight decks would return. VT-8 was completely decimated, with one survivor, Ens. George Gay, in the water among the Japanese fleet. As Lloyd Mustin opined, the Zero fighters were bad medicine.[16]

However, the sacrifice of the torpedo crews was not in vain as they drew the Zero pilots to a low altitude, allowing dive-bombing and scouting squadrons from *Enterprise* and *Yorktown* to arrive overhead unmolested. *Enterprise* planes pierced *Kaga* with four bombs and holed *Akagi* with two more. The *Yorktown*-based dive-bombers scored three hits on *Soryu*. With fueled and armed aircraft on deck and piles of ammunition awaiting return to the magazines, the three ships quickly became burning infernos. By 1030, the Japanese were well on their way to losing half of the carrier force that attacked Pearl Harbor six months previous.[17]

On the *Atlanta* the noon meal was served to the crew at their General Quarters stations, and as the sailors chowed down on pea soup and ham sandwiches, radio transmissions from both American and Japanese circuits gave a boost to morale. However, the joviality was disrupted as eyes turned south to witness the air attack on *Yorktown* just beyond the horizon. Soon a black pillar of smoke appeared.

The fourth Japanese carrier, *Hiryu*, escaped attention from the Americans and at 1050 launched a counterattack. As Lloyd noted, the distance between the two task forces had lengthened and the Japanese came across *Yorktown* and Task Force 17 at about noon. Forewarned by radar, both Spruance and Fletcher sent up fighters to engage the raiders. The Japanese lost several aircraft to the aggressive American combat air patrol and the withering flak put up by *Yorktown* and her escorts. However, three bombs found their intended target, puncturing holes aft of *Yorktown*'s starboard island, amidships, and forward.[18]

Although hardly glamorous, damage control has been kept on par with gunnery and other combat skills bred into American sailors. While not everyone had been trained to fire a 5-inch gun, everyone understood how to handle a fire hose and shore up bulkheads to maintain flooding boundaries. Such was the case with *Yorktown* on June 4, 1942. Sailors quickly reacted to douse the flames. Down in the engineering spaces, repairs were quickly made and fires relit. Within two hours "*Y*" was building up speed to 19 knots and the ships of Task Force 17 were steaming to catch up with Spruance's forces.

Yorktown hit by three bombs from *Hiryu* aircraft on June 4, 1942. (Archives Branch, Naval History and Heritage Command, Washington, D.C.; NH 94451)

Watching *Yorktown*'s recovery from an increasing distance, Lloyd realized the carrier that had withstood two multiple bombings within a period of 27 days was especially vulnerable. He later recalled that he had been tempted to go up to the bridge to suggest to Captain Jenkins that he request *Atlanta* to be chopped to Task Force 17 to provide additional flak cover for the damaged carrier. He then reminded himself that his primary duty was to remain in charge of the aft mounts and that others were handling the problem. Indeed, Spruance did detach the heavy cruisers *Pensacola* and *Vincennes* plus destroyers *Benham* and *Balch* to aid Fletcher's screening force. In retrospect, if *Atlanta*, with its superior AA capability, had been sent to guard *Yorktown*, the carrier might have survived. Perhaps Spruance had considered sending the light cruiser but then thought about its lack of combat experience. *Atlanta* still had not fired a shot in anger.[19]

Meanwhile, the surviving aircraft from the morning attacks on Nagumo's force returned to the flight decks of the Task Force 16 carriers. On board *Enterprise*, Spruance pondered his next move. As the smoke rising from *Yorktown* attested, the remaining Japanese carrier was still a threat. Yet while he had an approximate location based on a 1000 sighting report, the surviving Japanese carrier could have moved to anywhere within a 75-plus-mile radius of that position. In contrast to his morning decision to quickly launch an uncoordinated attack that yielded devastating blows but also cost dearly in planes and aircrew losses, Spruance decided to wait until he had pinpointed *Hiryu*'s whereabouts.

Spruance's decision to hold off raised the ire of the chief of staff, Capt. Miles R. Browning, who urged an immediate launch. By 1430, *Hornet* and *Enterprise* had recovered their aircraft along with planes from the stricken *Yorktown*, and were prepared to launch another strike. However, Spruance kept the planes waiting on the two flight decks. Browning must have become exasperated when a second wave of planes from *Hiryu* approached from the northwest.[20]

Atlanta and the other ships of Task Force 16 received a reprieve as the second wave of aircraft from *Hiryu* decided to go after *Yorktown*. Two of the attackers were able to place torpedoes against the damaged carrier's hull.

With the onrush of water causing the ship to list to 26 degrees, the carrier's skipper, Capt. Elliott Buckmaster, ordered the crew to abandon ship. Four destroyers closed in to pick up some 3,000 sailors.[21]

Revenge would be swift. As *Hiryu*'s second attack pressed in on *Yorktown*, Spruance received an updated position report on the remnants of Nagumo's force from one of *Yorktown*'s scout planes. *Enterprise* turned into the wind and *Hornet* soon followed. A pick-up group of 24 dive bombers from *Big E*'s scouting and bombing squadrons and survivors from *Yorktown*'s bombing squadron lifted off and turned toward the reported *Hiryu* position with 15 aircraft from *Hornet* following minutes behind. Just past 1700, the group assailed the Japanese, with four of the aircraft landing bombs on the bow of the *Hiryu*. Within minutes, the last of Nagumo's carriers was ablaze from the forecastle to the stern. When *Hornet*'s aircraft arrived, they diverted their bomb drops onto the escorting battleships and cruisers which nimbly evaded the lethal falling iron.[22]

And the decision of what to do next was Spruance's to make. Earlier in the afternoon, after the Task Force 16 commander launched his air attack against *Hiryu*, he sent a message to Fletcher, informing him of this action and requesting further instructions. The senior admiral, having transferred his flag from *Yorktown* to the cruiser *Astoria*, deferred to Spruance, responding, "Negative, will conform to your movements."[23] Fletcher, realizing he had limited command and control facilities on *Astoria*, passed tactical command of both task forces to Spruance, who had a much better picture of the situation embarked in *Enterprise*.

While Spruance must have been elated with the reports about the fate of *Hiryu*, he also noted that Nagumo's escorting battleships and cruisers remained unscathed. In addition, Vice Adm. Nobutake Kondo's Main Body Invasion Force with its bevy of battleships and cruisers was steaming a mere hundred miles to the west of the Americans. Conceivably, if he continued westward at a 25-knot pace and the Japanese pursued an eastward track at the same speed, the two forces could meet up in less than two hours. Even with his advantage in radar, the prospect of a night engagement against Japanese battleships was out of the question. In addition, Nimitz's instructions for his mission to protect Midway remained forefront in his mind, and there was a chance Admiral Yamamoto might order the amphibious assault to go forward anyway.

Consequently, Spruance ordered the two task forces to the east until midnight. At that time they would turn north for an hour and then proceed west so that they would be positioned to defend Midway in the morning against further Japanese assaults.[24]

With his overwhelming firepower, Yamamoto aimed to engage Spruance in an all-out night fight. Having lost confidence in Nagumo, he ordered all the First Carrier Striking Fleet's major surface combatants—less those conducting recovery operations with the burning carriers—to fall in under Vice Admiral Kondo. Kondo issued orders to his warships to prepare for a night engagement.[25]

In addition to the hoped-for engagement with the American naval forces, Yamamoto still had four cruisers and two destroyers heading for Midway to conduct a pre-dawn bombardment that had been planned as a preliminary to the invasion. Unfortunately for the Japanese commander, the time of the year afforded his fleet few hours of darkness in which to hide. With no sign of Spruance's forces, at 0020 Yamamoto terminated the bombardment. At 0255, with sunrise due in less than two hours, the Japanese commander issued orders to cancel the Midway operation and withdraw to the northwest for a June 7 refueling rendezvous. On *Atlanta*, awake and napping crewmembers had yet to realize that victory had been won.

CHAPTER 11

Midway: Final Blows

5 June

Reveille 0430—pouring, blinding rain, and us some 150 miles E. of Midway. The Admiral seemed able to face 1,000 yd. visibility by day, though, and off we go W at 30 kts. Enemy forces reported 50 miles West of Midway. About 0900 secured from morning G.Q., since nothing appears imminent, and people are half-asleep on their feet.

In afternoon, weather good, Army B 17's are out; report 2 BB's, 4 CV's, 2 CA's burning; air opposition zero, bombing enemy at will. Still nothing sunk, however, except according to that survivor's story.

By 1800 we take off a bomber flight. *Yorktown's* planes landed in *Hornet* and *Enterprise*, but we total only 67 SBD's, no TBD's. It made attack with no air opposition; reported further damage. Enemy is now withdrawing at best speed; we keep damaging but not <u>sinking</u>! God, now it is easy to see why our BB's should be here. Instead of going in for a decision, we keep way out of sight and pick with dive-bombers. B 17's also got in an attack.

Our planes get lost on coming back often—have to land in the water when their wheels won't go down, from damage I suppose. The DD's stop for the crews, but the planes go down like stones.

6 June

The third day of the doings and things still pretty well fogged up. I suppose it'll be called the "Battle of Midway." As far as I know (for some reason, the Exec wants to keep his officers in ignorance), it has been like this.

6 June [Second Log Entry]

Another day starting with Tojo lost, on account of us keeping so god damned far out. This super caution cannot be explained to me as anything but wastage of glorious opportunity. At least we should and could easily do contact scouting by one or more radar ships—but no, day dawns with us 250 miles from the enemy, and a scouting flight has to go out first, to find him. Then we run like hell that way and fuel oil doesn't last forever.

One BB & CA, plus some other unspecified ships are found. Evidently the Japs are scattering. *Yorktown* appears to have gotten safely off to Pearl Harbor, leaving us to carry on the fight. But now on the third day the enemy, who was lined up for the kill, has had plenty of time to do a hell of a lot of scattering. God—a radar directed night torpedo attack by our DD's would polish off these cripples in jig time—not to mention what five 8" cruisers could do to their "burning" carriers and cruisers. But instead, we stay 150 miles away.

3 TBDs have been assembled from the spares. They and the SBDs work on the one BB & CA all day, in relays. The damage is evidently heavy—but the ships are afloat!!! And while we pick away here, the others are hauling ass for Tokyo, unmolested and repairing their damages, and getting ready to take advantage of what they've learned in another try.

In the afternoon comes word of possible air attack from Wake, 700 mi. South. Christ—with fighters galore, fast ships, and deadly AA batteries for that kind of work, we turn N.E.; BB & CA to South of us. It kills me!

Reported that B 17's are coming out after "some cruisers." Perhaps the "Escort Force." Hope some damage can be done, but have small hopes. That force appears unmolested, so far, and will probably get a lot of the other damaged ships, or their survivors, home.

Army is reported to have failed to deliver an effective attack in Alaska in the 48 hours since the Dutch Harbor diversion, and our forces there request our help to keep Japs from getting away.

Saratoga & her force due in Pearl Harbor today and probably out again immediately—hope the enemy won't have completed his withdrawal before she gets here to at least stop one other unit beside the one we're still working on.

Our fighters and dive-bombers work on the light ships with machine guns—when we have good 8" and 5" rifles gathering rust here in an intact, undamaged, and damned respectable cruiser and destroyer striking force. Someone has, by now, damn near completed the fluffing of a chance to strike a blow that would have a decisive effect on the whole naval war in both the Pacific and Indian Oceans (hence for the whole allied cause.)

At least, in one of the raids of the afternoon, today, the *Hornet* group was able to report that they'd sunk a converted carrier. Since the Japs are probably building these by the dozen out of their big merchantmen, it doesn't seem as though that's awfully important—nor could it have required much sinking, which is probably why she sank.

The BB our outfit has been working on is of the *Haruna* class, the CL a *Mogami*. BB dead in the water all day; CL 10 knots, as of last report.

7 June 1942

We are now withdrawing—did so all night—leaving the BB, CV, and several DD's still afloat. This to my mind can find no excuse in any book. The DD's, at least, and probably the CL, will get back—and then it won't be long before their dive-bombers will be using our technique, which will be plenty tough. I believe the Jap CinC of the Second Fleet was in this BB as OTC—what a catch he'd have been.

Our yesterday morning's search found, besides the above group, a cruiser group. The Army worked on it with B 17's. Announced two hits with 1,500-pound bombs on a damaged *Mogami*, which sank in 16 seconds. (Photos showed, instead, USS *Nautilus*!!)

I believe some subs are on their way out to dispatch the crippled BB—at least, God dammit, they ought to be a sub, by the way, put 3 fish into a *Soryu* class CV that had been damaged in the 4 June affray (the *Nautilus* did the job).

On her way limping home, the *Yorktown* evidently ran into trouble with Jap subs. She took 3 more fish, and one of her DD's (*Hammann*—412, I understand) was sunk. Sister ship of the *Sims*—also of the *Mustin*, which I hope is still doing OK. Some 2,300 of her crew have been taken off for landing, and the salvage force from Pearl Harbor had taken over. She has a 17° list, but will be saved if nothing further comes up.

Word of continued trouble in the Alaskan area comes in. 2 CV's, 4 CA's, some DD's, of the enemy are there, raising hell in the fog. We rendezvous to fuel tomorrow, then may have a little job to do up north.

Tonight CTF 16 put out a long message to TF 16, summing up the action. Christ, it now appears that there is some uncertainty as to whether we had a BB or a CA that we were working on for so long. 3 CV's are claimed and the 4th seems quite likely, but they had 12 to start the war, with many big merchantmen in process of being converted—seems like a pretty undecisive blow. All in all, it sums up to me to be a horrible muffing of a glorious opportunity the likes of which may not recur this war. It could have been a Salamis; it was a bush-league brush. All because of CTF 16's horrible failure to seek a decision with his cruisers and destroyers, all concentrated and intact, against scattered small groups of the enemy, badly hurt, each one of which would have been snuffed out with consummate ease. I can't see how this bozo can fail to be relieved of his command when the story gets to the Navy Department. King, I don't believe will take this sort of muffing, fluffing, indecision, and failure.

***

Vice Adm. Takeo Kurita, embarked in *Kumano*, which led *Suzuya*, *Mikuma*, and *Mogami*, sped ahead of his two escorting destroyers toward Midway on the evening of June 4 and during the pre-dawn hours of June 5. Admiral Yamamoto's recall order did not reach Kurita until past 0200, when he was within 90 miles of Midway. Clearly, had Kurita continued, he would not have been able to arrive off Midway under the cover of darkness, given the early arrival of dawn. Without Nagumo's carriers to provide air cover, Kurita's ships would have had to fend off Midway-based aircraft as well as air attacks from *Hornet* and *Enterprise*.

The approach of the Japanese cruiser force had not gone undetected. The submarine *Tambor* radioed having sited the four cruisers and observed their reversal of course. Suddenly, a lookout on *Kumano* spotted *Tambor*. The flagship sent a flashing signal to the ships astern to turn left 45 degrees to avoid an anticipated torpedo spread. However, in the darkness, the last ship in line, *Mogami*, did not react fast enough and forged ahead into a turning *Mikuma*. The impact of the collision caused a fire and crushed *Mogami*'s bow back some 40 feet and punctured a fuel tank on *Mikuma*.[1]

After assessing the situation, Kurita left his two destroyers to protect the two crippled cruisers that could still forge ahead, albeit at a slower speed of advance. As daylight arrived, Spruance, having heard *Tambor*'s report, had turned toward Midway to preempt the possibility of a Japanese surface bombardment of the island.

Reacting to *Tambor*'s report, a flight of B-17s lifted off from Midway at dawn but could not find the wounded prey. They were followed by a dozen Midway-based Dauntlesses and Vindicators that did press an attack through withering antiaircraft fire. No hits were scored, except by Cpt. Richard Fleming, USMC, who crashed his damaged torpedo plane into the aft turret of *Mikuma*. Eight B-17s followed, with one bomber killing two *Mogami* sailors with a near miss.[2]

Reports of the two ships that filtered back to Task Force 16 and Lloyd Mustin in *Atlanta* had identified the Japanese ships as a cruiser and a battleship, an interesting observation considering the two ships were sisters, both built in the past decade and displaced roughly 12,000 tons. Historian Gordon Prange speculated that the damaged bow on *Mogami* probably pushed out a much wider bow wave that contributed to the deception. Only after pictures were developed after a completed photo-reconnaissance mission late on June 6 was Spruance able to assess what these two ships were.[3]

Fortunately for the two Japanese cruisers under duress, Spruance elected not to conduct flight operations that morning due to poor weather conditions. *Atlanta*'s deck log and war diary noted that visibility was reduced to 1 mile. According to *Atlanta*'s log, after steaming east and then an hour south during the night, the task force turned west at 0400 and adjusted to 230 degrees at 0631. At that time the speed increased to 20 knots. At 0719, the speed increased to 25 knots as Spruance acted on inaccurate reports which stated that the two Japanese carriers were burning but afloat. At 1000, *Atlanta*'s deck recorded that the skies had cleared and the carriers were launching aircraft. In contrast to the 67 aircraft that Lloyd reported lifting off on the afternoon aircraft launch, 58 dive-bombers flew off the flight decks of the two carriers. The sortie's search for the burning carriers yielded nothing because *Hiryu* had passed beneath the surface earlier in the day. The flight did come upon the destroyer *Tanikaze*, which had been dispatched to assure *Hiryu* was gone and not recoverable to the Americans. Thinking this was a cruiser, the American dive-bombers swooped down on the Japanese tin can, which evaded all bombs and even shot down one of the attackers.[4] Lloyd Mustin's diary again reflected incorrect reports about bomb damage.

In his diary Lloyd referred to the number of aircraft that were forced to ditch for a variety of reasons. Now, with darkness setting in and the returning dive-bombers still in the air, Spruance ordered the ships to turn on their navigation lights and the carriers to illuminate their flight decks to facilitate aircraft recovery. On *Atlanta*, with the carriers looming in light nearby, the lookouts strained even harder to spot periscopes or torpedo wakes. Although risk was involved in lighting up the task force, Spruance was painfully aware that without his aircraft, he would have been defanged, helpless to continue the battle should the Japanese choose to resume the invasion. Fortunately, all but one of the dive-bombers were landed on his two flight decks.[5]

By dusk, Spruance had determined that Kondo's battleships and cruisers, fleeing into a heavy weather front, might have been able to evade his carrier aircraft, so he decided to turn from the northwest to the west with the hope of capturing *Mikuma* and *Mogami* before they too could slither away. *Mikuma*'s trailing oil slick gave away her position to an early morning *Enterprise* scout plane. During the morning, *Hornet* dive-bombers delivered blows on the two cruisers. However, as Lloyd noted in his diary, they didn't seem to make much headway in sinking the unfortunate Japanese ships. The problem, Spruance realized, was that the bombs being dropped were not armor piercing and thus were merely mangling topside superstructure, not affecting the vessel's overall watertight integrity.

With the next wave of aircraft, this time from *Enterprise*, came three Devastator torpedo planes that had been patched together. The plan was for the dive-bombers to neutralize *Mogami*'s and *Mikuma*'s antiaircraft batteries and then have the torpedo planes puncture holes below their waterlines with their air-dropped fish. The *Enterprise* dive-bombers scored more hits but failed to suppress the antiaircraft fire, so the second phase of the attack was not carried out.

Hornet launched a third wave of dive-bombers against the two stricken ships. *Mogami* survived five bomb hits and eventually would be escorted to Truk.

Commenting decades later, Lloyd noted, "They beat her up terribly and left her dead in the water." Conjuring up another iconic World War II image, he described:

> … a picture from the port quarter, and here torpedoes hanging part way out of the tubes obviously jarred out by the shock of bomb hits, fallen down with the nose of the torpedo in the water, turret guns this way and that way, smoke rising here and there where it shouldn't be coming from, men in the water alongside. Of course, everyone claimed they sunk her, but they didn't. We broke off action and the Japs got her underway and got her back to Japan. She fought a lot of the rest of the war. It was a pity.[6]

However, hits on *Mikuma* set off munitions that proved fatal. The captain ordered the ship abandoned, and *Mogami* and the two escorting destroyers picked up many of the survivors. She passed beneath the waves that evening.

Fortunately for the Americans, it was Raymond A. Spruance, not Lloyd M. Mustin, in command of Task Force 16. Lloyd, with his aggressive tact, would have played into Admiral Yamamoto's hands. Although the collision of *Mogami* and *Mikuma* was tragic, Yamamoto saw the two ships as a potential lure to engage Spruance. As his two cruisers fended off air attacks on June 6, he hoped that their westward advance could draw the following Americans within range of land-based bombers on Wake Atoll. In addition, he dispatched two cruisers and a destroyer squadron to come to their rescue should Spruance surge some of his warships ahead to polish off the damaged cruisers as Lloyd advocated. Also, these cruisers broadcasted fake messages to make the Americans think there were more targets worth going after in the vicinity of Wake airspace. Anticipating that Spruance would take his bait, Yamamoto wheeled his escaping force of capital ships to the south through the evening of June 6.[7]

As Task Force 16 steamed toward the sunset on June 6 with *Atlanta* in the center of the formation serving as the guide, only four destroyers remained to screen the six cruisers and two carriers. Spruance's umbrella of surface warships had lightened as he had detached some to help guard a heavily listing *Yorktown*. Spruance reassessed his situation. Concerned that he could be heading within range of Japanese airpower based at Wake, aware that his ships were running low on fuel, and realizing that his aircrews and sailors were being pushed beyond physical exhaustion, the task force commander reversed course. Years later, Lloyd recalled:

> Too much of that [Japanese] force survived simply because our own force just ran out of steam. One by one we dropped off the destroyers. They ran out of fuel. The last one we had was the *Conyngham*. She was of the *Mahan*-class … [a] very long-legged class that we had been building back there in '37 and '38.[8]

As reflected in his anguished final paragraph of his entry of June 7, Lloyd felt an opportunity had been lost. Yet for Spruance to continue the pursuit, given the number of ships remaining in Task Force 16, would have been foolhardy.

Submarines also concerned Spruance. The Japanese had deployed to support the invasion and planned a decisive battle with the American fleet. Occasionally, during the engagement, a lookout would spot a periscope and the task force would react with an emergency turn to disrupt any torpedo targeting.

Well to the east of Spruance, an abandoned *Yorktown* listed with the ships of Task Force 17 under Rear Admiral Fletcher in the vicinity. A minesweeper took the damaged carrier in tow on June 5 but could not make much headway. On the morning of June 6, a salvage party stepped off the destroyer *Hammann* that had pulled alongside, and sailors scampered about to put out the remaining fire, ease the list, and prevent additional flooding. Led by Captain Buckmaster, the sailors made exceptional progress by the early afternoon, when a spread of torpedoes came in from the starboard beam. One torpedo missed. Two passed under the keel of *Hammann* and exploded against *Yorktown*. The fourth torpedo hit *Hammann* amidships and broke the destroyer in two, sending her under with many hands in less than four minutes.[9]

Three of the escorting destroyers proceeded to hunt *Yorktown*'s assassin, which happened to be the Japanese submarine *I-168*, while two other destroyers picked up survivors. Escaping with his salvage party to the destroyer *Benham*, Buckmaster still hoped there was a chance that he could save his ship in the morning. However, during the evening, seas continued to pour into the chambers opened by the two torpedoes. At 0600 on June 7, *Yorktown* began her plunge to the bottom of the Pacific to await discovery decades later.[10]

Later that day, Spruance sent a message to Task Force 16. Lloyd kept a copy in his diary.

BEGIN MESSAGE:

FROM: COMMANDER TASK FORCE SIXTEEN
TO: TASK FORCE SIXTEEN.

YESTERDAYS ATTACKS BY ENTERPRISE HORNET AND YORKTOWN BOMBERS ON DEFEATED AND FLEEING ENEMY COMPLETED AN AIR ACTION COVERING THREE FULL DAYS X ESTIMATE OF ENEMY LOSSES AS RESULT OF ACTION BY TASK FORCES 16 AND 17 ON THURSDAY THREE CVS SUNK ONE CV ON FIRE AND BADLY DAMAGED ONE BB OR LARGE ARMOURED SHIP AND ONE CA DAMAGED X OF THREE CVS SUNK ONE WAS AKAGI ONE WAS OF HIRYU CLASS ONE PROBABLY KAGA X DAMAGED CV PROBABLY ONE OF HIRYU CLASS WAS LAST SIGHTED BY VP FORENOON FRIDAY ON NORTHWESTERLY COURSE BURNING X OUR ATTACK GROUPS FAILED TO SIGHT HER ON TWO HUNDRED FIFTY MILE FLIGHT LATE FRIDAY AFTERNOON X SHE MAY HAVE ESCAPED OR SHE MAY HAVE BEEN ABANDONED AND SUNK X OUR ATTACK GROUP SIGHTED ONLY TWO SMALL SHIPS PROBABLY DDS X YESTERDAY SATURDAY OUR SEARCH PICKED UP TWO SMALL ENEMY FORCES BOUND FOR HOME X FIRST WAS 2 CAS 2 DDS HEADED SW BOMBED DURING FORENOON WITH HITS REPORTED ON BOTH CAS X SECOND GROUP WAS 2 CAS 3 DDS

HEADED WEST X OF THESE ONE CA OF MOGAMI CLASS WAS WRECKED AND ABANDONED OTHER SMALL CA RECEIVED BOMB HITS ONE DD SUNK OTHERS STRAFFED BY VF X OUR CARRIER AIR GROUPS HAVE DONE A MAGNIFICENT JOB IN SPITE OF HEAVY LOSSES SUFFERED ON THURSDAY FORENOON IN THE INITIAL ATTACK WHICH DECIDED THE FATE OF THE BATTLE OF MIDWAY X THEIR FOLLOW UP BLOWS ON OUR RETREATING ENEMY WERE CARRIED OUT WITH GREAT DETERMINATION X THE JAPS STATE OF MORALE AT THE END OF THE BATTLE WAS INDICATED BY ABANDONING TO THEIR FATE THE CREW OF THE MOGAMI CLASS CRUISER WHEN THE OTHER SHIPS OF THAT GROUP LEFT WITHOUT EFFECTING RESCUE OF PERSONNEL X THE PERFORMANCE OF OUR SHIPS DURING THIS PERIOD LEAVES NOTHING TO BE DESIRED X TASK FORCES 16 AND 17 HAVE AGAIN HELPED TO MAKE HISTORY X WELL DONE TO ALL HANDS.

END MESSAGE

CHAPTER 12

Midway Postmortem

10 June 1942

On the 8th we rendezvoused with *Cimarron* and *Guadalupe* (*Neosho* class tankers, both) for fueling in a spot about 200 mi. due north of Midway, having come 350-odd miles (by eye—guessing from a look at the chart), about 075° from our farthest west. When we finally got both tankers together some of our ships were pretty low—one DD said 1,500 gallons oil on hand. We had sent 2 to help *Yorktown*, then had to detach 2 for fueling, so we were down to 4. Then we ambled along at 12–15 kts through submarine infested waters—2 carriers & 6 cruisers supposedly screened by the 4 DD's. This guy must be trying to use the force for sub bait.

Christ, this ship at least has a QC [sonar] and depth charges—we could form part of the AS protection. But no, jug-head hasn't any more learned to take advantage of our special characteristics there than he has of our special AA battery.

Took all of the 8th & 9th to fuel, and at about 1800/ 9th took off in 060°, 20 kts, to rendezvous with Task Force 17, to get our replacement planes from the *Saratoga*. Understand she has TBF's for us, to replace our deathtrap TBD's. The crime of it all is that apparently these TBF's had been available all along on the Atlantic coast, sitting in some god-damned storehouse—evidently all it took to get them was to report that we had no more VTB's.

Heard that the *Yorktown* was lost after all; also one sub. The "Battle of Midway" looks all the more horrible as time goes by.

This morning we met the *Sara*, with *San Diego*, *Portland*, *Astoria*, about 4 DD's of *Sims* class (TF 17). Fog and rain have prevented the plane transfer, so we've spent the day on 180° at low speed (into the wind) waiting for favorable conditions. Meanwhile, what will happen if some stray Jap sub chances along will be just too GOD DAMN bad. *Kaskaskia* is with TF 17; she is to go with us.

I have decided that I will try, next time I see George to persuade him of the advantages that can be gotten by specially disposing the *Atlanta* to take advantage of her characteristics. I thought the tactical handling of the carrier groups at the "Battle of Midway" was ghastly, absolutely the direct cause of the *Yorktown*'s loss, and certain, if repeated, to lose us one carrier the next time, one the next and so on. It looked like a perfect duplication of the events leading up to the tragedy of the *Lexington*. If I can get my ideas across to George, perhaps he can get them into the ear of the Task Force Commander. These aviators have too much on their minds to know anything about sound AS procedure, or AA stuff either.

We keep getting more dope on Jap fleet movements, and it keeps looking worse. However, the good laugh of the day was to read the Tokyo version of Midway, at long last released.

11 June 1942

Orders received this AM for TF 16 return to P.H., arriving PM of 13th. The last few days have been barren of reports from Aleutian area, indicating that Japs have withdrawn—it was a feint after all. Force they had up there was apparently *Hosho, Ryujo, Kasuga* (CV's), two *Atago*'s, plus light forces.

Saratoga had given us our planes this AM. A classic of the dear old USA's war effort in fact, as distinguished from the pap & pollyanna now scattered around the newsprints: To replace all losses of both carriers we got: 5 TBD's (lovely deathtraps) and 29 SBD's. Jesus H. God!

Wonder what toll the Jap subs will exact en route home. They were loaded into the Hawaiian chain to support the Midway grab.

***

As Spruance's aircraft worked over *Mikuma* and *Mogami*, the carrier *Saratoga*, escorted by *Atlanta*'s sister ship *San Diego* and four destroyers, arrived at Pearl Harbor. Refueled and replenished, *Saratoga* headed out the next day with an additional destroyer plus the oiler *Kaskaskia* in company. Nimitz had a simple mission for the veteran carrier—to fly off aircraft to *Enterprise* and *Hornet*, to enable those two battle-seasoned carriers to further pursue operations against the Japanese.[1]

Lloyd Mustin laments the diminished destroyer screen for the task force and rightly admonishes the task force commander, Spruance, for not adroitly employing *Atlanta* to best advantage. Once he heard about the loss of *Yorktown* he also criticizes the tactical handling of the carriers. On this he could not criticize Spruance since Fletcher initially was the on-scene tactical commander, and it was Nimitz as the overall commander who ordered his forces to operate as two separate task forces. In this case the Pacific Fleet commander cannot be faulted. Going into what clearly presented itself as the most crucial battle of the war to date, Nimitz had two task forces that had been operating together in different areas of the Pacific in the months prior. Each task force had matured and had grown accustomed to working together. The task force commanders had an understanding of the strengths and weaknesses of each of the ships, ship commanders, and crews that served under them. Nimitz only had to reflect on the disastrous battle of the Java Sea to see the results of throwing ships together as a pick-up squad to confront the enemy.

The other factor Lloyd overlooked was that the arrival of *Yorktown* on scene was a fortuitous bonus given the damage she received at Coral Sea. Given the tenuous availability of CV 5, Spruance understood he might have to go it alone.

To Fletcher's credit, he did intend to have the two task forces operate within visual range. Unfortunately, wind conditions were such that maneuvers for flight operations pulled the two forces apart.

Whereas Nimitz's task force organization leaves little room for criticism, Yamamoto's complex scheme using separate strike forces to converge on Midway from different directions, as well as sending two light carriers and supporting forces on a feint to the Aleutians, justifiably earned him harsh criticism from historians and other analysts. The addition of *Yamato* and the other battleships and escorts of Yamamoto's Main Body to Nagumo's screen could have provided the extra defensive firepower to thwart the American air attacks.[2]

As witnessed by what happened to both sides in the battle, clearly there was merit in Lloyd Mustin's critique. For the Americans, later in the war they would employ large multi-carrier formations protected by a coordinated combat air patrol and rings of battleships, cruisers, and destroyers bristling with antiaircraft guns to ward off Japanese attackers. Such was the effectiveness of the American air defense at the battle of the Philippine Sea, dubbed the "Great Marianas Turkey Shoot," that the Japanese then resorted to desperation tactics in the form of the kamikaze.

Spruance discreetly blamed the performance of *Hornet*'s air group for the loss of *Yorktown* since her dive-bombing and scouting squadrons were no-shows on the initial attack on Nagumo's carriers. Spruance speculated in his endorsement of Captain Mitscher's battle report that had *Hornet*'s SBDs turned to the north like their *Yorktown* and *Enterprise* comrades, they might have taken out *Hiryu* on the initial attack. However, since weather conditions temporarily hid *Hiryu* from view of *Yorktown*'s and *Enterprise*'s dive-bombers, it could hardly be assumed that *Hornet*'s planes would have discovered her. Spruance's critique was overly harsh.[3]

Adm. Raymond A. "Jug head" Spruance has fared better in the writings of historians than in the estimation of Lloyd Mustin. Naval historian Samuel E. Morison rated Spruance's performance as superb, emerging from the battle as "one of the greatest fighting and thinking admirals in American naval history."[4]

Having crossed the International Date Line late on June 5, Spruance's carriers completed their combat operations the next day. While doing so, the destroyers *Worden* and *Maury* departed the formation to seek fuel from one of the fleet oilers operating from Pearl Harbor. Entries in *Atlanta*'s war diary tracked the egress of Task Force 16 back across the date line. As Lloyd observed, one of the destroyers was practically running on fumes. To conserve black oil, Spruance slowed the speed of advance to 15 knots as the formation headed east on a course of 085 degrees true on June 7. Thus, the spotting of *Cimarron* early on June 8 was a welcome sighting. The task force formed a disposition around the fuel ship allowing the thirstiest ships to get their bunkers replenished. Upon learning that the oiler *Guadalupe* and two escorting destroyers were to the west, the task force commander sent *Atlanta* to corral the floating gas station and her attendants. Along the way the light cruiser came across the *Worden* and *Maury*. With enemy submarines still a threat, Captain Jenkins directed the two tin cans to form a screen.

At mid-morning, lookouts spotted the oiler along with the destroyers *Ralph Talbot* and *Blue*. The six ships then formed up and proceeded on a course of 149 degrees true to the southeast, meeting up with Task Force 16 at 1400. For the rest of the afternoon, the various screening ships took turns fueling from one or the other of the two oilers.[5]

The next morning fueling resumed. By the early afternoon, with the task force positioned back to the northeast of Midway, *Atlanta* took her turn alongside *Cimarron*. The light cruiser came alongside to what appeared to be a floating milk carton. Lloyd recalled: "When we came alongside of her to fuel, her bow was out of the water to where her keel was showing." He went on: "to fuel us she had to give us fuel out of her own bunkers as distinguished from her cargo fuel … that gave us enough to get back safely to Pearl Harbor."[6]

With the two oilers barely holding enough oil to make it back to Pearl on their own, Spruance detached them along with the destroyers *Hughes*, *Phelps*, and *Blue* to return to Oahu. The task force commander then ordered the ships to steam on a northeasterly heading in cruising formation 10-Victor.[7]

On the morning of June 10, Task Force 16 met up with *Saratoga* and her escorts. Inclement weather forced the delay of aircraft, as *Atlanta*'s log read: "Maneuvered at various courses and speeds attempting to get out of fog and rain." There would be no flight operations that day as *Spruance* turned the formation south at a speed of 12 knots. Lloyd expressed frustration with the slow southerly heading. However, Spruance deliberately pointed the force into a southerly heading into the wind hoping for a sudden break in the weather that would allow for flight operations. The problem for Spruance was he did not want to advance south too quickly as he needed to turn around and head north in view of pending orders to challenge Japanese forces that had moved against the Aleutians. Obviously, the slow speed of the formation made it vulnerable to Japanese submarines; however, the inclement conditions also served to hide the Americans.

Toward the end of the day, Lloyd wrote he was humored by the Japanese media claims about the outcome of the battle. The press declared Midway a grand victory. The celebratory "Battleship March" was played prior to radio bulletins that provided updates on the victory. In the June 11 edition (June 10 at Midway) of *Japanese Times and Advertiser* the lead article featured the caption "NAVY SCORES ANOTHER EPOCHAL VICTORY" over a painting of Japanese aircraft bombing a helpless American flattop. The lead sentence of the article read: "Blasting all American hopes of conducting guerilla warfare on Japan by means of aircraft from aircraft carriers, the mighty Imperial Navy has sunk two more of these monster warships." Clearly this sentence was designed to assuage lingering concerns about the Doolittle raid. To their credit, in contrast to wildly exaggerated past claims, the boasting of the sinking of two American carriers, a cruiser, and a submarine may not have been an over-exaggeration, being that Japanese pilots who attacked the *Yorktown* in subsequent waves thought they had attacked two different carriers and the *Nautilus* had received a solid depth-charging as she operated in the vicinity of the Japanese carrier forces. To claim the *Hammann* as a cruiser was a bit of a stretch; however, several of Spruance's pilots had made the same claims about Japanese destroyers they had dropped bombs on.

What must have amused Lloyd and his shipmates was the lack of acknowledge-ment of losses. Indeed, the extent of the losses was not even made known within the circles of the Imperial Navy. Sailors returning to Japan were restricted from going ashore. The debacle was kept from the Japanese public through the end of the war. Not all in the Japanese military hierarchy felt comfortable with this policy, Rear Adm. Ryunosuke Kusaka, Nagumo's chief of staff, had recommended that the true facts be made known to the Japanese nation. His recommendation was ignored.[8]

What must have stunned and disgusted Lloyd and his shipmates were the American media's initial reports of the battle. Thanks to the return of the Army B-17s to Hawaii, well before the return of Fletcher's and Spruance's forces, an Army interpretation of the battle was first to hit the presses. On June 9, 1942, the *New York Times* editorialized that the "main damage to the Japanese fleet off Midway was inflicted by our land-based airplanes." Three days later, the *Honolulu Advertiser* reported claims made by Army pilots that they hit three carriers, either a battleship or a cruiser, a cruiser, a destroyer, and a large transport. Spruance, for one, was incensed with the inaccurate claims made by the Army. Once he returned to Hawaii, he would take steps to assure the Navy received its proper credit; however, it wouldn't be until after the war, after interviewing Japanese veterans of the battle and reviewing Japanese records, that the truth would come out on how little Army airpower contributed to the final victory. In the meantime, Lloyd's low esteem of Army aviation certainly was knocked down a few more pegs.[9]

At daybreak on June 11, the weather had cleared and naval aviators in succession flew off *Saratoga* and landed either on *Enterprise* or *Hornet*. Spruance then turned his task force on a due north heading toward the Aleutians, as Captain Jenkins suspected he would. However, before the ships could travel three hours along that track, Admiral Nimitz issued orders to Spruance to return to Pearl Harbor. *Atlanta's* 1025 war diary entry read: "Force ordered to return to Pearl Harbor." Apparently, the Pacific Fleet commander sniffed that Yamamoto still hoped to smash Task Force 16 and he felt no obligation to provide him with the opportunity.

Throughout the rest of June 11 through June 13, the task force continued on a southeasterly heading. The anticipated victorious arrival probably contributed to slow step-ups of speed that were noted in *Atlanta's* log over that time span. Entering the harbor, Lloyd remembered: "We steamed in with the biggest U.S. Ensigns in the ship at both mastheads."[10]

Whether Lloyd had an opportunity to confer with his stepfather on the issue of carrier task force formations is not noted in later passages. If Murray did get Mustin's two cents he would have the opportunity to employ it himself. Soon Murray would have an opportunity to command his own task force in the upcoming Solomons campaign.

CHAPTER 13

Back at Pearl

14 June 1942

Arrived P.H. yesterday. Mountains of mail—two postcard ads for me. Very discouraging. Funny how everyone in the ship hangs on the expectation of mail deliveries as though it was their next breath from way under water.

Wee Vee [*West Virginia*] now up and into dry-dock. *California* out, apparently being readied for trip to coast.

21 June

Went out with *San Diego* for target practice. Fired MG's first—about 1,500 rounds 1".1, some 20mm, and the BAR's. Plane dropped sleeve on deck: 2 .30 caliber holes! These MG's are still lousy—they can't seem to learn. Then a sleeve five-inch run at 15,000 ft—fair. Only one run when many had been intended because of towing plane trouble. Got off 58 rds [rounds]; plane said sleeve was cut off aft of mouth ring. Then a long-range surface practice at a high-speed target towed by *Boggs*. Forward group opened at 15,500 yds closing—looked poor to me. After group opened at 10–12,000, during turn away and run out. Got many straddles. Had radar range on sled all the way, for after group. On way in, fired four spreads of star shells, as illumination practice, and to clean the copper out of the guns. Supposed to dry-dock Wednesday to get our bottom cleaned. It's foul.

24 June

Wednesday—no docking. *Northampton* went in instead.

26 June

Went out last night with *S.D.* [*San Diego*] again for drone AA firing. Simulated torpedo-plane attack. We got ours in 42 secs, they got theirs in its second run. The shooting looked fair, anyhow (ours).

8 July

To sea again for target practice. This time with TF 16 (reorganized) plus *San Francisco*. Quite a program of firing. Day long range, light Battle Shore Bombardment, High Altitude Drone firing, Torpedo Drone firing, High Altitude and Torpedo sleeve runs, machine guns, and some tactics.

George has gone to CinCPac's staff—no longer has the *Enterprise*.

TF 16 now includes *Enterprise, Portland, Chester, Louisville, Atlanta, Balch, Benham, Ellet, Manny Monssen, Gwin, Grayson. Chester* & *Louisville* on West Coast however.

11 July

Back in again. Things went fair. TF 16, now under Admiral Kinkaid and Cru TF 16, Admiral Tisdale, ain't what they used to be. Bunch of amateurs. *Portland* & *S.F.* [*San Francisco*] the worst. Wasted the max. of time to accomplish the minimum of gunnery training, of which all hands used plenty. The machine guns are grossly neglected—you only hear of them after some ship is sunk they could have saved, when everyone agrees that they missed low & behind. Seems they're supposed to learn by intuition judging from the training provisions.

What should stand into Pearl Harbor but the *North Carolina*! A damn good shot in the arm to me, because I read it as meaning that now at last we're going to play for <u>keeps</u> around here.

Have had several looks at the *Wee Vee*, in dock, this trip. Her underwater protection certainly seems more than adequate—wonderful, seems best like it. That she sank even from the beating she got, certainly looks bad. If she'd been in a decent condition of watertight closure she'd never have gone. The story still persists that all those ships were wide open, and boy it must be true.

***

On the afternoon of June 13, Task Force 16 returned to Pearl Harbor. *Atlanta* moored back at C-6 port side tied to *San Diego*, her Quincy-built sister ship. Throughout the war Lloyd corresponded with his mother and wife.[1] Obviously he was disappointed with what little was awaiting him upon arrival, given the backlog of over two weeks of mail. Lloyd's observation on the crew's expectations for mail was dead on. The giddiness felt at the passing of the word "Mail Call" is similar to that of a child hearing "you can open your presents now" on Christmas.

For Lloyd, his diary omits an important milestone in his career—a promotion! ALNAV 119 dated June 15, 1942, not only announced his promotion to lieutenant commander, but the promotion of fellow OODs [officers of the deck] Smith and

Wulff. Two days later another ALNAV announced that the ship's senior medical officer Lieutenant Commander Gardner had risen in rank along with 10 of the ensigns. No doubt given the number of promotions and the location, the opportunity presented itself for a traditional Wetting Down party where the promoted officers host a party for their fellow officers and the captain closes with congratulatory remarks for those promoted.[2]

Lloyd Mustin has a passion for gunnery, and his diary amply reflects this as he comments on the amount of intense training that *Atlanta* underwent during this period. After a week in port, *Atlanta* got underway on June 21 with her sister ship at 0730 and spent the morning firing ammunition before securing the guns and returning to Pearl Harbor in the early afternoon. After three more days in port, *Atlanta* and *San Diego* departed in the late afternoon of June 25 accompanied by the destroyers *Benham* and *Ellet*. During the following morning, *San Diego* took the opportunity to shoot at a drone aircraft and then returned to port. Crewmembers took note that *San Diego* couldn't hit her target. During the afternoon *Atlanta* took her turn.[3] While Lloyd took some pride in the effectiveness of the main 5-inch 38 batteries, he is critical of the performance of the smaller caliber weapon crews, especially the machine guns.

As Lloyd indicated, *Atlanta* was due to enter the drydock to get her hull scraped and repainted. Her brief drydocking in Panama revealed that *Atlanta*'s protective coatings of paint had fallen away, exposing bare steel to rust and marine growth. Lloyd noted that where the coating had not fallen off, "there wasn't any significant amount of fouling on the bottom of the ship." Lloyd attributed the failure of large sections of the paint due to its application during very cold weather at the Brooklyn Navy Yard.[4]

On Wednesday July 1, *Atlanta* entered Pearl Harbor's drydock #2, and once the huge basin was near cleared of water, four-man teams, armed with scrapers and wire brushes, climbed over the side. Lowered to below the now-exposed waterline, the *Atlanta* crewmen worked their way down as shipyard painters worked over them to spray a coating of rust preventative. Between the gunk coming off the hull and the paint spraying down from above, the scrape teams were covered in grime at the end of the day.[5]

In the adjacent drydock #1 sat *West Virginia*. Refloated on May 17, the battleship had been eased into the huge drydock on June 9 while *Atlanta* was away with Task Force 16. The initial damage report of five torpedo hits had been revised to seven, once the inspectors were able to examine the damage closely. Besides having her portside caved in by several Japanese aerial torpedo hits, the *Wee Vee* had been hit by two bombs.

At the time of the attack, *West Virginia* was in condition "X-Ray," the minimum condition for watertight integrity, meaning many hatches and doors were open to let the crew move about the ship with ease. Had there been enough warning to allow the ship to call General Quarters and increase the watertight integrity to condition "Zed," it is possible the ship could have stayed afloat. However, what saved the ship from the fate of the *Oklahoma*, which rolled over, was the quick action of Lt. Claude V. Ricketts, who counter-flooded compartments on the starboard side, enabling the 33,000+ ton battleship to sink and rest on the harbor bottom.[6]

Late afternoon on July 2, drydock #2 again was flooded, and *Atlanta* moved out for a temporary berth latched to the starboard side of *California*. This battleship had preceded *West Virginia* in drydock #1 and now was ready to return to the States to undergo reconstruction.[7]

After a very long weekend, on Wednesday July 8, *Atlanta* shifted colors at 0802 and departed Pearl Harbor for training exercises with *Enterprise, San Francisco, Portland, San Diego*, and other ships from Task Force 16. After initial gunfire exercises with *San Francisco* and *Portland* in the early afternoon against targets towed by tugs, *Atlanta* refreshed her gun crews with AA practice for guns of all calibers at aerial targets. However, by knocking her airplane drawn target sleeve during its second pass, the AA exercise ended early.[8] As *Enterprise* conducted flight operations the next day, Captain Jenkins had his crew run through a number of damage control drills. On July 10, *Atlanta* and a group of destroyers detached to bombard the uninhabited island of Kahoolawe. Rejoining the task force, *Atlanta* then ended the day by guarding *Enterprise* against a night attack by two destroyers attempting to emulate Japanese tactics.[9]

The task force returned to Pearl Harbor on July 11, but not before *Portland, San Francisco*, and *Atlanta* steamed again in a column formation with guns aimed at

North Carolina as seen during the battleship's sea trials off the East Coast in 1941. The arrival of this big gun ship boosted Lieutenant Commander Mustin's morale. The ship is preserved today at Wilmington, North Carolina, as a memorial and museum. (Archives Branch, Naval History and Heritage Command, Washington, D.C.; NH 61327)

a tow target. Returning to C-6, *Atlanta* once again tied up alongside *San Diego* for one more stint in port. The next day, a Sunday, a fuel barge came alongside to enable the light cruiser to replenish her bunkers and stores for an imminent deployment back into combat. Given this situation, the arrival of *North Carolina* must have been a morale booster, as the crew had previously encountered the battleship in the waters of the Chesapeake. Because of the attention the ship received during her sea trials, she picked up the nickname "Showboat."[10]

Though sleek looking, the new battleship really wasn't much more powerful than the older battlewagons that had been sunk seven months earlier. The big difference was *North Carolina* had at least 7 knots of speed over her World War I vintage sisters and thus could keep up and serve within carrier task forces.[11] As Lloyd noted, her arrival signaled that the United States was getting ready to "play for keeps."

CHAPTER 14

Heading South

15 July 1942

Underway headed South. *North Carolina* has joined our TF; *Chester* & *Louisville* still absent. We are to pass to control of ComSoWesPac [Commander Southwest Pacific] mission, the support of amphibious operations in that area. I guess a grab at Rabaul. We are to proceed to Nukualofa Anchorage, Tongatabu (called "Bleacher" last time we were down this way) as our first stop and to fuel. Then more orders there, I suppose. CinCPac has put out a "Standard Carrier Task Force Cruising Instruction," which we now follow. It is identical in almost all respects with the old TF 16 stuff that started with Halsey.

The *N.C.* [*North Carolina*] seems to be treated in this outfit as just one more CA. Perhaps a slightly super CA—she gets 2 DD's for screen. We cruise like this:

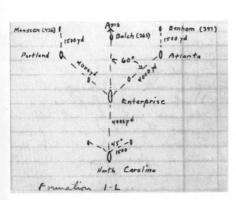

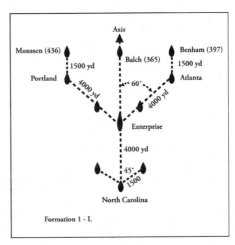

Lloyd Mustin's illustration of the formation 1-L extracted from his diary, re-drawn for clarity.

Seems unnecessary far from the carrier, for us to help her much. On "Prepare to repel air attack" we are to close to a 1,500-yard circle, as before.

19 July '42
Sunday—crossed the equator Southbound again—6th official time for me. λ [Longitude] 165–45 W. Our UP [United Press] correspondent Bob (R.C.) Miller, and 15 new recruits were the only pollywogs. War was again not allowed to interfere with official duties of the Royal Court of His Majesty.

Incidentally, this is our first cruise with a correspondent; there are also 2 in *Enterprise* and 1 in *N.C.*—they are certainly not all here because this will be a pleasant vacation cruise. Bob Miller seems a fine guy.

22 July
Sighted Tan Island [Tanna Island, Vanuatu] to stbd. Our first land, other than Hawaiian Archipelago since Clipperton Island. Tan is Easternmost of Samoan group.

23 July
A TBF went into the water this morning at launching of the dawn flight. Pilot lost; mech picked up. Second plane loss so far; first was an SBD which failed to return from the evening search flight—pilot's name Dexter.

During the last month in P. H., *Enterprise*'s arresting gear was strengthened and her VTBron equipped with new TBF's. They look plenty good—fast, powerful, maneuverable—range 2,000 miles, when equipped as scout. SBD's still are the dive-bombers. These are little honeys, undoubtedly, in my mind, the best single-engine dive-bombers in the air today. F4F-4's are our fighters still—they can dish out plenty, with 6 .50's, and can take it, with full armor, leak-proofing, etc, but they are heavy and climb poorly, so are crushingly outclassed there by all Jap VF types, which can also outmaneuver them easily.

Had a big session of air attacks on the formation today. Very useful practice and education for us. Lot of new aviators in *Enterprise*, all practicing up to show their stuff. They look O.K. too. There's been much more of this, this cruise, then on the previous ones. Then, they were old hands & didn't need the stuff, they figured. But we did.

24 July 1942
Arrived Nukualofa. TF fueled from *Mobilube* and *Kanawha*. Four loaded transports here to join us. *Wasp* & *San Juan*, plus others were to have met us here yesterday but have left. It looks like our boss forgot that this place is across the date line, so that it is really the 25th here—the way

we dawdled along on the way down looks as though he forgot about the day he was going to load—then he got here a day late. All just adds on to various other small things to make it look like this was a rather hastily thrown-together venture.

Arrived about 1030, having lain off the entrance for two hours, stopped, while the various entry arrangements were muddled over. Fortunately no subs were lying around (evidently). The anti-sub mentality is awful low—maybe the Japs deserve no greater respect on past performance, but the Krauts will wise them up, and it'll raise hell with us when we least expect it.

Underway again 1630, the others having preceded us out. Headed Westerly, of course, destination not yet announced.

26 July

25th didn't happen, Kinkaid having gotten in step with the rest of this part of the world on dates at midnight last night.

At dawn we are in formation with the train as follows: TF 16 as was, 4 AP's: *Jackson, Adams, Hayes, Crescent City*, 1 AK, 4 DMS's: *Trever, Zane, Southland* and *Hopkins*.

In the afternoon we rendezvous with the rest of our playmates for this little to do.

TF 44—HMAS *Australia, Canberra* and *Hobart, Chicago* & *Salt Lake City*, 12 transports (*Barnett*, etc.) full of Marines of the amphibious force, PacFlt (some Army too, I should guess), and about 6 DD.

TF 18—*Wasp, San Juan*, 2 *New Orleans* class, and about 6–8 DD's.

TF11—*Saratoga*, 3 *New Orleans* class, 6–8 DD's, and some tankers.

Quite a little get-together. Our transports & DMS's joined Task Force 44.

27 July

We now have only 4 DD's—3 went with TF 44, as did apparently, some of the CA's of the other TF's, and some of their DD's. They are going to practice landings in the Fiji's. The carrier forces will practice too, I guess: also fuel.

30 July

Still messing around just south of the Fiji's. TF 44 not in sight. We fueled yesterday (all TF 16). Eighty-five thousand gallons for us, from our old pal the *Cimarron*. Air operations in coordination with the landing exercise have been big yesterday & today. The carrier task forces just kill time cruising around in certain areas! Bait for a sub, it looks like to me—we are all a trifle touchy, I guess, on the way they regard subs around here.

My birthday today. As a present I am back on the O.O.D. watch list. Ever since between Pearl Harbor & Midway, someplace, I'd been standing watch in gun control. Where I'd a hell of a right rather be, I suppose—the OOD catches it all the time from the Skipper—he's very touchy about exaggerated accuracy of station keeping. Everyone has some hobby, I guess, and our skipper is more than welcome to this one, by gosh. He's certainly a hell of a fine Captain to be serving under, which everybody knows and appreciates. How lucky we are, compared to some ships we run across!

The business certainly ought to be getting underway before very long now. It is Tulagi.

Various of the Fiji group in sight, in all directions, at various times.

1 August

Rendezvoused with the transport group this afternoon. I believe we proceed westward now, with another fueling of sorts, before the business starts. There's certainly been plenty of fiddling around on this operation. CTF 16 touched a new low today in the botching of his tactical handling of his ships. Small reassurance to see this sort of amateur stuff and realize that it is what is taking us into a <u>tough</u> spot.

3 August

Passed South of Efate Is. this morning and into the Coral Sea. Rendezvoused with tanker & started fueling the DD's of all three TF's. They are now actually task units, task force 61 being the whole business, transports and all.

A fighter crashed into the water and burned all its gas. No trace of pilot.

4 August

Still fueling. We may get to fuel ourselves—we should. Now down to about ⅔ capacity, all burned in useless fiddling around.

5 August

Didn't get to fuel. We all are still moving generally West about 280°. Making about 8 kt good, keeping company with the transports. To go that slow the carrier groups steam faster, as a help against subs, but circle around and back and forth all over the place. We could be going to Brisbane, or Moresby, or Rabaul, etc., on this course, which is the idea, as far as confusing the Japs is concerned. We will turn and run North to Tulagi at the last moment. "D" Day has not yet been set, apparently, though it should come soon.

***

Although the Japanese had received a stunning blow at Midway, their navy remained largely intact and potent. Adm. Ernest J. King argued that the United States could not focus entirely on Europe and ignore Japan. Continuing Japanese operations helped to make his case.

Japanese activity in the Southwest Pacific was of particular concern to King. Just prior to the battle of Midway, Japanese engineers surveyed a site inland from Lunga Point on the north side of Guadalcanal with the intent to construct an airstrip. Located some 550 miles east of New Guinea toward the southeastern end of the Solomon Islands chain, Guadalcanal featured thick tropical forests, grassy ridges, steep ravines, and a volcanic peak that rose approximately 8,000 feet from the surrounding seas. An average annual rainfall of 165 inches fed the crocodile-infested streams and kept the humidity close to 100 percent on most days. Building an airfield and conducting flight operations in such an environment would prove a challenge, but Japanese planners realized that such an airfield would place their aircraft within range of the primary sea lane between the United States and Australia. Planes from this airfield could also threaten American bases at Espiritu Santo, Efate, and possibly New Caledonia.[1]

Throughout June, Japanese engineers concentrated on building a wharf. This activity did not go unobserved. Patrol aircraft and an Australian coast watcher posted on Guadalcanal kept Allied commanders alert. A report from a reconnaissance plane that flew over the island on July 4 provided enough detail to enable analysts to conclude an airfield was the ultimate goal of the construction effort. Radio intercepts the next day solidified this conclusion. A coast watcher report of the arrival of a dozen Japanese cargo ships on July 6 to offload heavy construction equipment confirmed suspicions.[2]

Even before the purpose of the construction activity became apparent, King targeted the Solomon Islands as the place to begin offensive operations against the Japanese Empire. Tulagi, a smaller island across from Guadalcanal, had been occupied by the Japanese in May for use as a seaplane base. On June 24, King directed Nimitz to capture Tulagi "and adjacent positions." A Joint Directive, issued on July 2 by the Joint Chiefs, affirmed King's desire to conduct offensive operations in the region and divided responsibilities geographically between General MacArthur and Admiral Nimitz, with the Guadalcanal area coming under Nimitz's purview. A day after the July 4 reconnaissance report gave him a sense of urgency, King specified Guadalcanal to be the adjacent position.[3]

Codenamed Operation *Watchtower*, the plan was to use regiments of the recently constituted 1st Marine Division. Many of the Marines, including their commander, Maj. Gen. Alexander A. Vandegrift, had recently arrived at Wellington, New Zealand. In late June Vandegrift met in Auckland with his operational commander, Vice Adm. Robert L. Ghormley, who had been named to lead the recently established South Pacific Command. Ghormley informed the Marine general of Nimitz's directive and that D-Day had been set for August 1.[4]

While Ghormley and Vandegrift met, a key individual who would be wedged between them in the chain of command was still on the West Coast. Having served as King's assistant chief of staff for planning, Rear Adm. Richmond K. Turner was tapped to serve as Commander, Amphibious Force South Pacific. Flying out to Pearl Harbor on July 4, he met with Nimitz over the next three days to discuss the upcoming operation. A major concern he had, shared by Vandegrift, was that the forces being assembled lacked training in amphibious warfare. Nimitz concurred and approved the training schedule. As updates on Japanese activity were being received on July 6, instructions went out from Pearl Harbor directing Ghormley to scout the Fiji Islands for a rehearsal site.

On July 9, three Marine officers flew from New Zealand to New Caledonia and then on to Suva, Fiji. While they were en route, Ghormley received the official operation order from Admiral Nimitz to seize the two Solomon islands.[5]

Arriving in Fiji, the Marine scout team worked with their British hosts to identify a suitable landing site. The mountainous Koro Island was a possibility. Although the team scouted this tropical island during a high tide that masked the surrounding coral reefs, they were not enamored with the place and recommended against staging a rehearsal there when they returned to New Zealand to brief Ghormley, Vandegrift, and the recently arrived Turner.

Turner was not to be deterred. Since no alternative sites were recommended, Turner insisted on a Koro rehearsal, even if it meant having to put off the invasion by a week. Constant downpours in New Zealand also complicated the situation as the efforts to load the transports were slowed.[6]

Meanwhile, on the morning of July 15, *Atlanta*, as part of Task Force 16, departed Pearl Harbor for her last time. Four days out of Hawaii, *Atlanta* crossed the equator once again. Unfortunately for Robert C. Miller—the United Press reporter embarked to cover the forthcoming campaign—and 15 other newly reported crew, over 600 shellbacks stood ready to run the pollywogs through the traditional rituals. For Miller, who would have a distinguished career as a war correspondent, retiring in 1987, the ordeal ended with a stay in the sick bay to recover from multiple bruises.[7]

As the task force headed south, across the Pacific at Wellington, New Zealand, Rear Admiral Turner embarked his staff in the transport *McCawley*. Turner would fly his two-star flag from the "Wacky Mac" for the next year. In addition to Turner and his staff, Marines of Vandegrift's 1st Marine Division boarded *McCawley* and other transports berthed at the New Zealand port with a departure date set for July 22.[8]

Lloyd lamented being placed back on the O.O.D. (officer of the deck) watch bill where he would come under the scrutiny of Captain Jenkins. Inside the pilothouse, Lloyd focused on keeping the ship assigned to its station.

On July 24, or rather July 25, *Atlanta* maneuvered through the narrow coral passage leading to Nukualofa, the port for the island of Tongatabu, a part of the Tongan or Friendly Islands. Located in the South Pacific just on the other side of the International Date Line, the island would serve as an idyllic respite for thousands of American sailors during the war. Looking ashore, Lloyd could see a small town with scattered houses and shops.[9]

Lloyd and his shipmates had expected to see *Wasp* and her escorts; however, the task force commander's staff had failed to account for the date line. The aircraft carrier had ventured far since an earlier meeting at Casco Bay in Maine. During the previous four months, *Wasp* had crossed the Atlantic to reinforce the British Home Fleet, entered the Mediterranean on two occasions to ferry aircraft to the British bastion at Malta, and then returned to the States for transfer to the Pacific Fleet. She had left San Diego for Tongatabu on July 1 as the flagship of Task Force 18, a formation centered on five troopships that were carrying additional Marines for the upcoming invasion of Tulagi and Guadalcanal. *Atlanta*'s reunion with the carrier would have to wait a day. However, the troopships were still present, awaiting the arrival of Task Force 16.

Once anchored in the harbor, *Atlanta* dropped her starboard motor whaleboat in the water to perform assorted chores. *Maury* came alongside the starboard side and took fuel from the light cruiser. In addition to fuel, the destroyer received freshly baked loaves of bread from *Atlanta*'s bakery. Later that day, it was *Atlanta*'s turn to replenish her bunkers, and she pulled alongside the tanker *Mobilube*.[10]

Just before sunset, the ships left Tongatabu. Past midday the next day, July 26, *Atlanta*'s lookout once again spotted masts on the horizon. Task Force 16 met with Task Force 18 centered on *Wasp*, Task Force 11 built around *Saratoga*, and Task Force 44 consisting of American and Australian cruisers and destroyers plus transports carrying regiments of the 1st Marine Division. At a point located some 400 miles south of the Fiji Islands, some 72 ships assembled for what many sailors dubbed "Operation *Shoestring*." The overall commander of this force embarked in *Saratoga* was Vice Adm. Frank Jack Fletcher, the veteran of the Coral Sea and Midway battles. Rear Adm. Leigh Noyes had command of the Air Support Force, which included the three carriers and escorts that included *North Carolina*, five heavy cruisers, *Atlanta*, 16 destroyers, and three oilers.[11]

Despite the hastily thrown together nature of the operation, the invasion force represented one of the largest gatherings of Allied sea power to date. To assure that everyone was on the same page, Fletcher called a meeting in his flagship that afternoon to discuss the rehearsal and following invasion. The meeting would prove controversial. Fletcher declared his carriers would only remain on station for the first two days of Operation *Watchtower* to provide air cover. Turner protested, arguing that it would take at least four days to offload his transports. Fletcher, not wanting to expose his forces to enemy air attack, could not be persuaded otherwise.[12]

With dissension within the leadership, the large formation proceeded to the Fiji Islands, where Turner's amphibious force and reinforcements by warships of the other three task forces was designated as Task Force 62 and broke off to conduct a practice amphibious invasion on Koro Island, codenamed Operation *Dovetail*. The remaining ships, including the carriers and *Atlanta*, were redesignated as Task Force 61.

On July 28, Turner's task force appeared off the northern coast of Koro Island to begin a four-day rehearsal that aimed to move Marines ashore on the first and third days and return them on the second and fourth days. As Lloyd noted, the carriers also rehearsed, sending up bombers to conduct mock raids to support the Marines ashore. On the third day, the aircraft were allowed to expend live ordnance. Likewise, cruisers and destroyers sitting off the three beaches that simulated landing sites at Guadalcanal, Tulagi, and the tiny island of Gavutu were allowed to fire live rounds on the third day.

The rehearsal did not go well. Coordination problems put the landings well behind schedule. Worse news came when it became apparent that the landing craft were approaching the beaches at low tide. Landing craft propellers began striking coral heads that lurked just below the surface. In some cases, the boats unloaded the Marines short of the beach, dumping them into deep water, while others discharged their human cargoes on the wrong beaches. Many others, when confronting the coral obstacles, returned to their embarkation points. Those Marines who made it ashore supplemented their rations with coconuts, tropical fruit, and in some cases, farm animals from abandoned local villages and then prepared to bivouac.

On July 29, boats were sent in to retrieve these Marines. In addition, throughout the day other Marines clambered down the sides of the transports to the landing craft for runs that would approach the beaches and return. As Turner watched the progress, he fumed at how slowly the transports were placing boats in the water and the sluggish boarding by the Marines. Meanwhile, repair crews worked to restore boats damaged the previous day.

The original plan for July 30 called for a repeat of July 28 except with the addition of live ordnance. With the botched landing attempts two days previous, Turner directed the landing craft to approach to just 2,000 yards off the beach to loiter and then return with the time of the H-Hour shifted back to 1030. The air portion of the bombardment was judged a success, with bombs hitting the correct targets at the correct time. Not everyone got the word about the shift back of H-Hour and not landing the Marines. At about 1000, Marines off the transport *Fuller* hit the beach.

Fortunately, lookouts on the destroyer *Ellet* spotted the Marines, and the tin can maneuvered to signal a landing craft that the H-Hour had been moved back and incoming ordnance from destroyers offshore would soon be straddling the beaches. A frantic recall returned most of the Marines to the boats, although some wound up stranded ashore to endure a bombardment and another night under tropical skies.

On July 31, these Marines were retrieved, and there were additional loading and offloading drills. In the late afternoon, the transports raised their anchors and headed out to join with the carrier force.[13]

On August 1, the day after Lloyd Mustin's birthday, the forces regrouped and headed west toward the Coral Sea. The group maintained a westerly heading to keep the Japanese guessing. On August 4, those crewmembers of *Atlanta* who had not been informed earlier, were told about the objective.

CHAPTER 15

Landings at Guadalcanal and Tulagi

6 Aug

190 miles from Tulagi, due South, at noon, on course north 15 kts. Rain, fog, & haze keep visibility low. Though it seems unbelievable, perhaps we are undiscovered still. Or perhaps the trap is waiting to be sprung. The *Cummings* (365) reported sinking a sub at Espiritu Santo last night. She was escorting the "*Pres. Tyler*," a transport—possibly one of ours which fell out due to breakdown—I don't know. Also got a report the *Tucker* (374) ran on one of our own mines over there, broke her back, and is in a wreck. There seems to have been confusion about who was to put what mines where, and when, and who was to get out the dope about it. Dawn tomorrow starts the show.

The axis of our disposition was rotated to 135° tonight evidently for the battle. That puts us 195° T from the carrier, which will be operating south of the islands. In other words we, the strongest AA unit with the carrier groups, are on the disengaged side, which is incidentally also, of course, on the side away from the sun. Jug-head though still hasn't seen the light, apparently.

7 August 1942

0530 G.Q., about 20 mi. S of W end of Guadalcanal. Prevailing wind ESE; carriers to operate in parallel lanes, order from Guadalcanal: *Ent.*, *Sara.*, *Wasp*, lanes running about 120° to 300°, five mi. apart, starting from where this is. Transports to go E. of Guadalcanal for Tulagi and N. coast of Guad., where Japs are building an airfield. Air operations started in the dark; saw 2 planes lost by take-off crashes. They exploded on hitting, making bright flashes in the dark. There is an extensive flight schedule for covering the occupation forces. First flights left about 0600 (sunrise), and were getting back at 0800.

Dope we got said Japs fully surprised. 18 planes destroyed on water, unopposed landing at Tulagi & Guadalcanal. Fighting developing ashore on Guad., I think, and there is opposition in other parts of the Tulagi area (Florida Island, the main one of a cluster). No air opposition, TBF's horizontal bombing, F4F's strafing, SBD's dive bombing, and the Marines working on land. Ships covered landings with shore bombardment—the 3 Aussie cruisers, 2 of *New Orleans* class, the *Chicago*, *San Juan* and many DD's were with the transport group.

During AM got report of departure Rabaul Jap H.B.'s [heavy bombers] & fighters. They arrived on schedule, but we saw none; they worked on transports. On fighter voice circuits we gathered they left in a hell of a hurry, jettisoning their bombs. One 250-pound hit on a DD (*Mugford*) killed 5; small material damage. 10 dive-bombers came 2 hours later; no results. Pretty successful day.

Only got 4 out of these attacks, which seems rather poor.

8 August 1942

0530 G. Q. again; Japs still holding out here and there, and air operations to be done for support. Received report 40 two-engine bombers on the way, sighted off Bougainville and due 1230–1300. We expect stepped up operations of this sort. They arrived on schedule, 40 two-engine, carrying fish, plus some 10 high level. 25 F4F's to oppose. I hate to think what they could do, but so far only heard of 1 hit (fish) in *Jarvis*' bow, bad, causing her to be beached, and 1 hit in *G.F. Elliot* (AP), which is seriously afire. 12 enemy downed for sure so far today, more possible. The AP afire amidships.

The carriers are up to their usual stuff, acting entirely independently, perhaps 10–15 miles apart at times. They thus each require complete, non-mutually supporting protection, both surface and fighter. Result is that the *North Carolina*, 5 heavy cruisers, us, and about 15 DD are rushing madly around just screening the 3 CV's, no outfit able to help another (just as when the *Yorktown* got hers at Midway). Also, only 25 VF (one carrier's complement) could be spared for the transports, because all the rest were over the carriers (100 miles or so from Tulagi). It's a wonder the Japs didn't make a killing in Tulagi (or on one isolated carrier, right before the eyes of the other two, per Midway).

Tonight received a contact report, 3 cruisers, 3 destroyers, position about 300 mi. away, headed this way. Also two seaplane tenders. These certainly wouldn't be coming unless other stuff was on the way. The Japs won't lose Tulagi lying down, as some of us had guessed. (The Exec had it all figured as a pushover. He is an excellent illustration of the kind of officer not to have in a fighting Navy).

Maybe it's just a coincidence, but the way these carriers operate seems chicken-hearted as hell to me. When the air report came in they all started SW and kept going. Ended the day down off San Cristobal, pretty god damn far from Tulagi for fighter support, if you ask me. I wonder when we will ever get the nerve up to really go after these bastards, seek them out to destroy them. Seems to me like this would have been a swell time to hunt these planes down and get every damn one. But you can't do that while running like hell in the other direction.

***

Though *Atlanta* would be assigned to screen the carriers during Operation *Watchtower*, Captain Jenkins received a copy of the invasion plan should unforeseen circumstances dictate the light cruiser detach to support Turner's landing force. Lloyd recalled: "I had worked like a dog on reading this amphibious Op Order before the landings occurred. To make a long story short, I never got finished—it was about 5 inches thick and it was minutely detailed in every particular. It practically told the individual boat coxswain when to put on left rudder and when to put on right."[1]

On his opening entry on August 6, Lloyd notes the destroyer *Cummings* and troopship *President Tyler*. *Cummings*, a *Dale*-class destroyer built in the mid-1930s, suffered minor damage from bomb fragments during the December 7 attack on Pearl Harbor. In the following months, the ship performed escort duty, initially shepherding convoys between San Francisco and Pearl Harbor. *Cummings* continued to perform this mission in the South Pacific during June and July. The *President Tyler* had been built in 1920 in the aftermath of World War I by the New York Shipbuilding Company at Camden, New Jersey. The merchant ship was acquired by the Navy from American President Lines in January 1942, and some 2,000 racks were installed to carry combat troops. In *Cummings*'s official history and in post-war historical narratives, no credit is given for a sub kill.[2]

Lloyd noted the loss of *Tucker*. Built in the mid-1930s, this *Mahan*-class destroyer was also located at Pearl Harbor on December 7. As with *Cummings*, this destroyer spent the first five months of the war on convoy duty between Hawaii and the West Coast before heading to the Southwest Pacific. *Tucker* left Auckland for the Fiji Islands on July 30. Arriving at Suva, *Tucker* picked up orders to escort the SS *Nira Luckenbach* to Espiritu Santo. To get to that base, the two ships departed on August 1, headed north of Efate, and aimed for the Segond Channel. Three days later, as *Tucker* navigated the channel, she passed over and detonated a mine that broke her keel and killed three sailors. *Nira Luckenbach*, the ship *Tucker* was protecting, provided lifeboats for the crew of the foundering destroyer. A tug arrived within hours to attempt to tow her to shallow water but the damage proved fatal. Early in the morning of August 5, 1942, *Tucker* settled in 10 fathoms of water. Sadly, it was later discovered that the minefield had been laid a day earlier by American minelayers. Unfortunately, news of the new minefield never reached the two ships.[3]

One of the planes that Lloyd observed crash on takeoff was an SBD off *Saratoga*. The two-man aircrew was never found. At 0622 *Atlanta's* deck log recorded: "Sighted Guadalcanal Island to the eastward."[4] Indeed, as a glimmer of light shone in the east, the dark silhouette of Guadalcanal became plainly visible on the northeastern horizon. With first light came the arrival of the aircraft over Guadalcanal and Tulagi, catching the Japanese by surprise. The Japanese seaplane squadron based at Gavutu—a tiny island in the protected waters on the southern side of Tulagi—was sunk in place. Those few Japanese pilots who hopped into their floatplanes were gunned down by swooping Wildcats before they could get airborne.

Atlanta would see no action that historic day, as the light cruiser with her strong antiaircraft gunnery was held back to accompany the aircraft carriers. Meanwhile, Turner's amphibious force had already maneuvered past Cape Esperance on the northwest end of the mountainous island and slowed to place landing craft in the water. At 0614, 8-inch shells from the heavy cruiser *Quincy* tore into the camp of the 13th Japanese Naval Construction unit. Made up mainly of Korean conscripts, the unit scattered into the jungles to escape the incoming salvos. Shells from the cruisers *Vincennes*, *Astoria*, and *Chicago* tore into jungle, ripping up trees and foliage.[5]

On the various transports, the word was passed to land the landing force. The first American amphibious assault since the Spanish–American War commenced. In contrast to the bungled landings at Kora Island a few days earlier, the embarkation of Marines and movement of landing craft ashore was textbook. Soon the first waves of Marines were landing about 4 miles east of Lunga Point on the north side of the island. With Navy aircraft and gunfire pinning down Japanese defenders at Lunga Point, boats shuttling in 11,000 Marines from 15 transport ships were not molested. Throughout the day, the Americans were able to increase the size of their footprint and bring supplies ashore. Instead of combating enemy troops, the Marines of the 1st Marine Regiment fought their way into the rainforest toward high grassy ground that was supposed to be a mere 2 miles from the beach. It turned out that objective was much further inland, and the Marines would spend an evening bivouac in the jungle, battling land crabs and malarial mosquitoes. Meanwhile, men of the 5th Marine Regiment cautiously surged westward toward the Lunga River delta. Imagining enemy troops in the thick undergrowth, some of the inexperienced leathernecks popped off rounds into the jungle.[6]

While the Marine infantry pushed inland, the logistical situation on the beaches became a nightmare as working parties slowly offloaded landing craft and stacked materials haphazardly across the beach front. The slow progress threatened Turner's timetable.

To the north on the smaller island of Tulagi, the element of surprise enabled Turner's landing craft to disembark Marines ashore unopposed except for a lone sniper. Aircraft off *Wasp* circled overhead to cover the landings. Offshore the heavy cruiser *Chicago*, accompanied by one of *Atlanta*'s sisters, the *San Juan*, and destroyers *Monssen* and *Buchanan* provided additional support. However, as the Marines advanced through the jungle toward the island's southern tip, they came upon some steep hills that concealed caves and the positions of Japanese Army machine gunners. With light fading and Marines not making much headway against enemy crossfire, the Marine commander chose to resume the attack at dawn. That night the enemy launched a vicious counterattack. In what would be the first of many hand-to-hand combat actions of the campaign, the Americans held their ground.[7]

A mere 3,000 yards east of Tulagi rose the twin islands of Tanambogo and Gavutu, connected by a 500-yard causeway. Electing to capture Gavutu first because of its higher topography, the Marine 1st Parachute Battalion encountered stiff resistance. Again, *Atlanta*'s sister *San Juan* came in to plaster Japanese defensive positions. Not having fully secured Gavutu, the Marines attempted to assault Tanambogo that evening, but the defenders broke up the attempted landing by small craft with concentrated bursts of small-arms fire. With reinforcements, the Marines gained control of the two islands the next day. Overall, the fight for Tulagi, Gavutu, and Tanambogo would claim 122 Americans. Some 863 Japanese sacrificed their lives defending these small islands for the Emperor.[8]

Vice Admiral Ghormley's opposite, Vice Adm. Gunichi Mikawa, had been caught by surprise. Responding to a frantic report from Tulagi, his initial reaction was to scramble two waves of aircraft from Rabaul. Coast watchers, perched on islands along what became known as "the slot," reported the incoming intruders, enabling Rear Admiral Turner to have his landing force get underway and place his combatants in a defensive perimeter. The first wave of aircraft consisted of 24 Betty bombers armed with 250kg anti-personnel bombs for a previously planned raid on New Guinea, escorted by 17 Zero fighters. For the Zero pilots, the round trip pushed close to the aircraft's range. They would have little fuel to expend in dogfights. They arrived at 1315.[9]

The attackers were initially met by eight Wildcats off *Saratoga*. Blue-painted fighters off *Enterprise* and *Wasp* also came to the defense of Turner's ships off Guadalcanal. SBDs conducting ground support missions also brought their weapons into the fray. A burst of fire from a Dauntless tail gunner severely wounded Lt. Saburo Sakai, one of Japan's leading aces. Blinded in the right eye and paralyzed on his left side, the wounded Japanese pilot, who had just shot down an American fighter and dive-bomber, nursed his crippled Zero back to Rabaul.[10]

Japanese pilots claimed nine Wildcats and a Dauntless in this initial air-to-air combat. However, the American defenders, along with gunners from the ships below, prevented the Bettys from making deliberate slow passes. Consequently, their payloads fell aimlessly into the sea.

The second wave consisted of nine Aichi D3A1 Type 99 "Val" dive-bombers that made the trek down from Rabaul and arrived at 1430. Without fighter escort, the Vals were easy game for the combat air patrol provided by *Enterprise*. Only one of the nine would make it back to its base. Overall, 14 of the enemy aircraft did not return that day. Only the destroyer *Mugford* sustained damage, with a bomb hitting the after deckhouse, taking out two 5-inch guns. More significantly, the blast killed 19 men and wounded 32 more.[11]

Ashore the next morning, the Marines resumed their forward movement. The 1st Marine Regiment, having not reached the grassy high ground, received orders to seize the airstrip. By late afternoon, they reached the dirt-surface strip and found it completely abandoned. Meanwhile, their compatriots with the 5th Marine Regiment had seized the construction camp that had been hastily abandoned a day earlier when the American bombs and shells started landing. As these Marines surged to the mouth of the Lunga River, they came upon a huge supply depot with trucks, a miniature railroad, equipment, an electric generator, and food, including bags of rice. Soon a captured ice-making machine hosted a sign "Tojo Ice Plant, Now under new management, J Genung, Sgt. USMC."[12]

During the first two days the approximately 2,000 Japanese construction laborers and accompanying 200 special naval landing force troops put up token resistance and withdrew into the jungle to the west bank of the Lunga River. Over on Tulagi, the Japanese resistance was broken, and their seaplane base on the tiny island of Gavutu and adjacent Tanambogo were in American hands.

In the air, the Japanese situation was not faring any better. As the Marines moved to seize the Guadalcanal airstrip, Mikawa sent aircraft airborne with the objective of attacking Ghormley's aircraft carriers. However, Mikawa's scout planes could not locate *Enterprise*, *Wasp*, or *Saratoga*, so 23 Betty bombers loaded with Type 91 aerial torpedoes, 9 Vals, and a fighter escort of Zeros diverted to hit the invasion fleet. Once again, Turner's forces were forewarned by a coast watcher. Turner entrusted command of his cruiser and destroyer forces to an Australian, Rear Adm. Victor A. C. Crutchley, who effectively deployed his gun platforms into a defensive screen. Wildcats roared off the decks of the carriers to intercept the enemy fliers. While the Japanese tactic of coming in low succeeded in evading radar, it made their twin-engine bombers easy fodder for diving Wildcats and gunners on the defending warships. Wildcats off *Enterprise* felled three of the twin-engine bombers that were classified as a Type One Land Attack Plane and derisively labeled by their crews as "Type One Lighters" for their propensity to explode into spectacular fireballs when their fuel tanks were hit. As the bombers came in low, gun crews were treated to repeated pyrotechnic displays as their ammunition tore into the cigar-shaped fuselages. *San Juan* alone accounted for five enemy aircraft losses. Japanese aircraft losses were heavy, with 17 of 26 aircraft falling to American gunfire. However, the destroyer *Jarvis* sustained a torpedo hit on her starboard bow, killing 15 sailors, and a Japanese pilot steered his flaming Betty into the transport *George F. Elliott*. Eventually, the blazing ship had to be abandoned and scuttled.[13]

Mikawa, not yet fully realizing the gravity of the situation facing the Japanese forces in the region, took additional measures beyond launching air raids. Initially, he sought to place a few additional Japanese forces on Guadalcanal. At Rabaul, 519 Japanese sailors boarded the vessels *Meiyo Maru* and *Soya*, which quickly departed on a southeasterly heading escorted by three small combatants. This initiative was stillborn. Finally understanding the scope of the American landing force, Mikawa recalled the small convoy. Just after the flotilla turned back after midnight early on the 8th, torpedoes from *S-38* slammed into *Meiyo Maru*, killing 373 of those embarked. The commander of that submarine, Lt. Cdr. Henry G. Munson, was a classmate of Lloyd's at the Naval Academy.[14]

Instead, Mikawa concentrated on marshalling his available surface combat power, ordering five cruisers and a destroyer in the region to make best speed to Rabaul to join with two cruisers that were already present. A scouting B-17 aircraft spotted these six ships just before they arrived at the Japanese base. Embarking on the cruiser *Chokai* late on the 7th, Mikawa eventually steamed with a force of seven cruisers and a destroyer en route to Guadalcanal.

The Japanese admiral understood he was heavily outgunned. In addition to the numerous cruisers and destroyers protecting Turner's troopships and cargo vessels, three American aircraft carriers stationed southwest of Guadalcanal provided an air threat. To have any chance at success, Mikawa realized he had to fight the enemy at night, as his sailors were experienced in this element in their use of torpedoes and gunfire. Darkness would also remove the American advantage in the skies.

If Mikawa had any notions of sneaking down the slot undetected, they were quickly squashed. As the ships cleared St. George channel that evening, they practically passed over *S-38*. Although the old American sub couldn't get a firing solution for a torpedo spread, she was able to send a contact report.[15]

Darkness protected Mikawa's force as they steamed along the northeastern side of Bougainville. However, for Mikawa to achieve his objective of engaging Turner's forces at night, he would have to advance toward Guadalcanal during the daylight hours of August 8, within plain view of scout planes. Given the B-17 and *S-38* sightings the previous day, Allied maritime patrol aircraft were alert to look for the Japanese, and at 1025, a Royal Australian Air Force Hudson came upon Mikawa's force. Antiaircraft fire kept the Aussie from getting a close look. From a distance, the Japanese force appeared to consist of three cruisers, three destroyers, and two seaplane tenders, which Lloyd correlates in his diary entry.[16]

That the Australians misidentified the makeup of the Japanese force was a mistake, but a mistake that could have been overcome if not for a second mistake: the failure to immediately report the sighting. Radio silence makes sense as a means to mask one's position. However, the pilot chose to maintain radio silence despite Mikawa having him in full view with his gunners trying to drop him from the sky.

Instead, the Australian aircrew noted the Japanese formation and continued on their planned search pattern, finally reporting the sighting when they returned to Milne Bay, New Guinea late that afternoon. By the time the report reached Turner at 1845, it was too late to send out additional reconnaissance missions. Had the sighting come in earlier, follow-on search planes could have spotted Mikawa much closer to Guadalcanal, noted his force included six cruisers, and called for air attacks.[17]

Mikawa had his own reconnaissance capability, and on August 8 five scout planes lifted off from his cruisers to search for American activity. Two of the planes flew over the American amphibious forces, and by noon Mikawa had an accurate picture of what he was facing. He then ordered his formation to increase speed to 24 knots as they passed between Bougainville and Choiseul. Late in the afternoon, the Japanese commander sent out Signal Order No. 25, directing his force to launch a torpedo attack on the ships anchored off Guadalcanal and then to speed across the channel to engage American forces at Tulagi.[18]

To compound the situation for the Americans, as Mikawa's force approached Guadalcanal, Lloyd in *Atlanta* was steaming away. As noted, nearly two weeks earlier, Vice Admiral Fletcher announced at a planning conference he would only provide air cover for the amphibious operation for the first two days, fearing air attack from Japanese land-based air forces. Though talked into staying a third day, the vice admiral decided to stick with his original intentions. All day on the 8th the three carriers operated independently of each other, much to Lloyd's consternation, with the escorting battleship *North Carolina*, cruisers, and destroyers split between the three floating airfields to fend off any enemy attacks. Instead of concentrating his afloat antiaircraft firepower to thwart any enemy air attackers, Fletcher chose to retain two thirds of his fighters for combat air patrol, only allowing approximately two dozen to fly cover for Turner's forces off Guadalcanal.

Having moved eastward, the carriers were now steaming off the northwestern cape of San Cristobal Island, the next island the Solomons chain, still within 120 miles of Savo, the small volcanic island that bisected the sound between Guadalcanal and Tulagi. When he recovered the last of his aircraft at 1807, Fletcher sent a message to Vice Admiral Ghormley recommending his withdrawal, citing the reduction of his fighter strength to 78 aircraft and the need to refuel as reasons. Not waiting for Ghormley to respond, Fletcher turned his force to the southeast.[19]

Samuel Elliot Morison observed that Fletcher had no indication of Japanese knowledge of his presence, since he had operated unmolested for nearly two days. Morison concluded: "... his force could have remained in the area with no more severe consequences than sunburn."[20] A post-war Naval War College study concluded that having experienced first-hand the damaging attacks on *Yorktown* at Coral Sea and Midway and the eventual loss of that famed ship at the latter battle, Fletcher sought to keep his carriers out of harm's way. The Naval War College study harshly criticized Fletcher for not consulting with Turner by radio.

As Fletcher's carriers and escort put distance between themselves and Guadalcanal, Turner's and Crutchley's staffs pondered the report of the three cruisers, three destroyers, and the two seaplane tenders. Clearly the Japanese were not going to attack at night with seaplane tenders. Looking at a chart of the Solomons, they noted the island of Santa Isabel, and its protected harbor of Rekata Bay. Located 155 miles from Savo, the location offered the enemy an ideal spot from which to launch harassing seaplane attacks. Gen. Douglas MacArthur's intelligence staff analyzed the Hudson sighting and came to the same conclusion. The message they sent to Turner at about 2000 reinforced the assessment that the Japanese surface force in the vicinity did not pose a pending danger.[21]

Still Turner ordered Crutchley to deploy his gunships to guard the approaches leading to the anchored transports. Crutchley sent his warships to patrol three defensive sectors: a southern sector blocking the passage between Savo Island and Cape Esperance on the northwest tip of Guadalcanal, a northern sector covering the waters between Savo Island and Tulagi, and an eastern sector covering the sea surface east of transports off Lunga Point.

As Lloyd wrote his final diary entry for the evening, Crutchley had tactical command of the force guarding the southern sector consisting of the Royal Australian Navy cruisers *Australia* and *Canberra* and the American heavy cruiser *Chicago* and the destroyers *Bagley* and *Patterson*. To the north, Capt. Frederick L. Riefkohl in *Vincennes* had tactical control of his cruiser and the cruisers *Astoria* and *Quincy*. The destroyers *Helm* and *Wilson* rounded up the northern force. Guarding the eastern sector, Rear Adm. Norman Scott had tactical control over the *San Juan*, a sister ship to *Atlanta*, the light cruiser HMAS *Hobart*, and the destroyers *Monssen* and *Buchanan*.

As an additional precaution, Crutchley sent out the destroyers *Blue* and *Ralph Talbot* to the west of Savo Island. Equipped with SC radar, the two ships were positioned to forewarn of any approaching enemy vessels.[22]

Crutchley's tactical command of the southern force proved temporary. Turner, infuriated at Fletcher's decision to withdraw, sought Crutchley's and General Vandegrift's counsel to discuss future operations. To get to Turner's flagship off Lunga Point, Crutchley broke his flagship, *Australia*, away from the southern sector and left Capt. Howard D. Bode in *Chicago* in command of the Allied naval forces between Guadalcanal and Savo.[23]

CHAPTER 16

Battle of Savo Island

9 August

Son-of-a-bitch-god-damn! Before this started, we were read a dispatch in which ComSoPac (Vice Ad. Ghormley) handed out some pap about "electrifying the world with news of a real offensive." Such manure. Some obsolete Jap cruisers and a couple of DD's with a few planes start to come our way and we run like rabbits. We are headed SE and have been all morning, leaving the transports, troops, and all their escorts to the mercy of Jap shore-based planes and all the ships they care to assemble. What an "offensive!" They're so god damn scared their lousy carriers will get hurt that the whole effective Pacific Fleet hauls ass at the mention of a few Jap planes.

Red-hot dope is that there's a Jap carrier been spotted in this area—said with bated breath! So instead of our 3 knocking her off, 3 of the world's largest run away from this reported 550' job.

Anyway, we are to fuel. Thanks to the previous bezeling of fueling arrangements, all hands are now pretty low. This may have something to do with our heading South. But I mistrust our future course, on the record. Perhaps we'll go back and wallop these apes—but perhaps not.

They are vulnerable as hell to attrition, I say, and we shouldn't fail to seize a chance to bust up any fleet unit, because it is irreplaceable. Also, this has got to be made into something big if it is to help Russia and by easing their natural fears of a Jap stab in the back—which I feel certain is one of the objectives. The Krauts are putting on what reads between the lines to be a damn effective and deadly drive into the Caucasus, and I know these yellow bastards are getting set to cash in from behind.

10 August

Rendezvoused with *Platte* and *Kaskaskia* at 1600—four hours late, as usual. At noon we were down to 145,000 gallons, which is kinda low for operating with a carrier. Mail is to go off by the tanker. Rendezvous is off Espiritu Santo of the New Hebrides group.

Took about 250,000 gallons in 1½ hours—TF 16 fueled first. Our fueling area—about due north of Noumea & west of Efate, is 540 miles from Tulagi.

11 August 1942

A dark, dark day, indeed. We got, this morning, a press release in which Adm. King says we've seized Tulagi and Guadalcanal, but admits the damage to the 8th, plus "one American cruiser sunk and two cruisers damaged"!! Jesus Christ, the stupid bastards running this show have really fixed us. The attack must have happened yesterday or the day before while we were busy running in the other direction with our vaunted power. This campaign to grab a practically undefended jungle dot in the water using the SoPac Amphibious Force with the support of almost the whole PacFlt, now looks like this from here:

First fumble: On 6 Aug., 22 days after leaving P. H., we start in for Tulagi partially empty of fuel because stupid planning cannot get us the necessary tankers in three weeks (at, of course, the very least) notice.

Second fumble: Though we are content to piddle from 3 to 6 August in the Coral Sea, timid planning will not shift the last planned fueling rendezvous closer than about 500 miles from the objective. All that extra oil, including the multiple daily air operations' requirements, is thrown away.

Third fumble: Our first blow wipes out their piddling 18 planes, and we land a crushingly superior force of troops at any and all selected beachheads, supported by ship and shore-bombardment capable of plowing the place under if necessary. Then this crushing force of troops is furnished daily, flight after flight of bomber supports, for which they can hardly even find jobs!! Yet the 3 CV's charge madly up and down the sea, in almost no wind, getting their 32 knot wind across the decks to take-off and land these repeated flights, all the while getting themselves, and their massive screens, more & more out of oil. There were enough Marines ashore to sew up the place without a plane in the air after the first day, especially with ship gun support.

Fourth fumble: A characteristic one, it seems: the method of reacting to the creation of an air threat to the carriers, which I have raved against before. Most aggravated here because 1) We had never been sighted. To think Rabaul bombers would fly 600 miles to our area, the location of which they didn't know, on the one-in-a-million chance of being able to attack us, when loaded transports are definitely located in harbor, and closer is completely fantastic. 2) At the time of arrival of their planes, known closely, there was on both days an extensive overcast, with low clouds, rain, etc., in our particular area, making our already extremely improbable detection practically <u>impossible</u>. 3) Even if, still, it should be thought necessary to provide the terrific protection, fighter and AA gun, that was reserved for the three independent carriers, the SBD's, with no bombs, could have helped give air protection. With 220 kts and 2 fixed .50's, they would give any Jap plane on a long-range mission, bomb loaded, a good tussle. In addition to which, by being vectored out to the approaching groups at long range, they could have helped locate targets for the F4F's even if they didn't do much good themselves as fighters. But no! They (and the TBF's too) were kept at their needless bombing of a handful of Japs hiding in the bushes.

<u>Fifth fumble</u>: With the transports and their escorts in Tulagi, attempting air support by F4F-4 from 120–180 miles away! Ridiculous and farcical.

<u>Sixth fumble</u>: With the transports and escorts still having a day or so to go before being ready to leave, to "withdraw" for fueling, leaving them without air protection against an increasingly stirred-up hornet's nest in Rabaul. One more day of operation, by at least a part of the carrier group (*Sara* had lots of oil) could certainly have been done. <u>Particularly</u> if the fueling rendezvous was properly close, instead of this timid 1,000 miles from Rabaul.

So now we have lost a cruiser. *San Juan, Vincennes, Chicago*, or another *New Orleans* class? A fine trade for a few planes knocked down. Son of a bitch!

It is clear in my mind, from the Coral Sea, Midway, and Tulagi campaigns, that we have no high commanders capable of playing ball in the same league with many of the Japs. Maybe we'll buy our way out of this war eventually by bringing in such a force that no brains and skill can prevail. Until we can do that, our prospects are zero. And any time we tangle in a battle of wits, of staff work, of ship-for-ship struggles, of thinking-on-our-feet, these little monkeys are going to make our doddering old fools look like specimens from some institution. What in Christ should be blamed for the top-rank fumbling, fuming, and fiddling around, I dunno. But I wish to God Wild Bill Halsey were back here to put a little fire, drive, and action into things. These other culls are so scared of a Jap they stop thinking the minute they hear one is around.

Christ—if we lose a cruiser taking Tulagi, what chance have we at Buka—let alone Lae, Salamaua, or Rabaul itself—not to mention getting on to Tokyo.

12 August '42

Boy, if yesterday was dark, I'd like to know what this is. The dope on what happened in Tulagi came in this morning, delayed—the Capt. showed it to me. The night of 8–9 August at about 0140 the Japs contacted our screens off Tulagi with CA's, DD's, PT's and SS's, with illumination by aircraft flares. *Vincennes*, *Astoria* and *Quincy*, with about 5 DD's, were NE of Savo Island; *Chicago* and *Canberra* were S, of Savo with several DD's and some DL's. *San Juan*, *Australia* & some DD's formed inner screens on the 2 AP groups anchored off Tulagi and Guadalcanal. The flares illuminated the outer screens from behind and in a 40 minute running engagement *Vincennes*, *Astoria*, *Quincy* and *Canberra* are <u>sunk</u>, *Chicago* torpedoed in the bow, and *Patterson* & *Ralph Talbot* damaged. One Jap sub believed sunk, other enemy damage unknown. <u>Jesus</u>, what a price to pay for Tulagi—and how tragically unnecessary. If our god damn carriers hadn't been so busy hauling ass for San Cristobal all afternoon the 8th, perhaps those three CA's, three DD's and two AV's could have been knocked off—either by air, or air-surface. The AV's undoubtedly brought the PT boat transports. But we are so busy beating our chests about Bulkeley in the Philippines, that we can't figure the other team can pull the same stuff. And the general idea that everything is to be done by aviation has blinded our jug-heads to the possibility of anyone's doing anything any other way, or to the need for providing against it.

The Marines in the Solomons have 30-days provisions, and "four units of fire" of ammunition, whatever that is—I hope to God they can hold out until we find someone with the guts and brains to go back there with this force and do the job up. Meanwhile, the Japs rule the area, thanks to our abject flight, and can land troops on many parts of the islands where the beaches cannot be defended—Florida Is., Guadalcanal, etc., with steadily growing air, sea and undersea support. I feel sorry for those poor damn Marines. Boy, have the Japs made fools out of our so-called leaders.

Completed fueling today. Three days of it. But haven't started anywhere yet—just steaming in circles, north of Noumea.

A floating mine was found and destroyed today by our force. One was reported off Hauru recently. Actually, no positive dope. It was not an adrift moored mine, possibly not armed when on the surface. Nobody expects the Japs to bother about the International Law that a floating mine should sink in a half-hour, though.

***

As previously noted, with the Japanese launching aerial attacks using torpedo-armed Bettys on the first two days of what was called Operation *Watchtower*, Fletcher reneged on his commitment to keep his carriers close to Guadalcanal for the first 72 hours. He also asked for tankers to be sent to refuel his carriers and escorts. Fletcher's decision, harshly criticized by such post-war naval history chroniclers as Samuel Elliot Morison, frustrated Lloyd Mustin as *Atlanta* cut through the South Pacific at 15 knots. In Morison's post-war operational history and in analysis conducted at the Naval War College, the noontime fuel status reports were reviewed and Morison opined that the fuel situation was not critical. However, Morison may not have accounted for the weather conditions. As Lloyd noted, calm winds forced the three carriers and their escorts to operate at flank speeds to maintain wind overdeck to operate aircraft. Keeping the carriers and escorts operating at high speeds consumed large quantities of black oil.[1]

Perhaps even Fletcher had second thoughts on his decision, for at 0100 early on August 9, Fletcher reversed the direction of his carriers in anticipation that Ghormley might override his desire to clear the area. Within an hour of the reversal of direction of Fletcher's carriers, hundreds of miles ahead disaster befell a combined force of American and Australian warships.[2]

It took Lloyd three days to uncover the truth about what happened around Savo Island in the early morning on August 9. He then makes some assessments of the situation, most of which stand the test of time. Seven years later the Naval War College would publish a 398-page strategical and tactical analysis of the debacle which summarized a list of 26 lessons learned. By that time, having access to the records of the Imperial Japanese Navy, the author of the study had a full grasp of the composition of the Japanese force—something Lloyd and his contemporaries lacked in the immediate aftermath of the battle.[3]

Otherwise, the report that Captain Jenkins shared with him gave a fairly accurate account of the magnitude of the Allied defeat. A number of circumstances conspired against the Americans and Australians that night. The failure of reconnaissance aircraft to make a timely report on the location of Mikawa's force was one contributor to Japanese success. Signals intelligence—decisive at Midway because Navy cryptologists had weeks of intercepted coded signals to work with—did not come into play because of the short-fuse nature of Mikawa's action. Mikawa's message to Japanese naval headquarters in Japan was intercepted, but it took the codebreakers another two weeks to discern the text.[4]

As Mikawa's force approached the channel between Savo and Guadalcanal, the crisscrossing picket destroyer *Blue* stood in the way. However, the destroyer had just turned and was steaming away from the path of the oncoming Japanese. Neither *Blue*'s stern lookout nor radar operators could not pick up the Japanese force. Lookouts on the picket ship on the northern approach, *Ralph Talbot*, did hear the drone of one of Mikawa's scout planes that he launched to confirm the Allied ship locations and provide illumination. Warnings from this destroyer went unheeded, and while other ship radars picked up the floatplane, many watch standers assumed the plane was friendly.[5]

Steaming in a column formation, Mikawa could see in the distance the burning hulk of the *George F. Elliott* as his warships came upon the Allied cruisers and destroyers in the southern sector. A heavy rain cloud south of Savo hid the oncoming silhouettes of the Japanese ships from eyesight and radar also failed to pick up the advancing foe. In contrast, the Japanese spotters were able to pick out the American and Australian warships. Mikawa's lookouts, using large mounted binoculars, spotted *Blue* as the American destroyer steamed on her sentry post using radar, having diminished capabilities thanks to the nearby landmass. Having slipped by that watchdog, the Japanese column of cruisers *Chokai, Aoba, Kako, Kinugasa, Furutaka, Tenryu, Yubari,* and the destroyer *Yunagi* closed on the American and Australian warships guarding the invasion area, and at 0133, Mikawa ordered an increase of speed to 30 knots and signaled "All Ships Attack." *Yunagi* failed to follow.[6]

With *Chicago* and *Canberra* 12,500 yards ahead and closing, at 0136 Mikawa gave the order for his ships to unleash their fish. Two minutes later the first salvos of Long Lance torpedoes went flying into the seas, aimed at the two cruisers and *Bagley*.

Minutes passed. With the torpedoes tracking toward their targets, the lookouts on the destroyer *Patterson* suddenly noticed one of the enemy cruisers and the destroyer radioed, "Warning—Warning: Strange Ships Entering Harbor." At about that time, the overhead Japanese floatplanes dropped flares over Turner's transports, making the two cruisers easy targets for Mikawa's gunners. On *Canberra*, two torpedoes and Japanese shells nearly arrived simultaneously. Caught flat-footed, the Australian crew rushed to their action stations and many were slaughtered en route as concentrated gunfire from five enemy warships scored between two and three dozen hits in a four-minute span. As the helmsman turned to unmask the main batteries, damage to the boiler rooms forced the ship to lose propulsion and power. A direct hit on the bridge killed Capt. Frank E. Getting and other senior officers. The Australian cruiser may have fired a few 4-inch rounds before succumbing. In less than five minutes, *Canberra* had been reduced to a listing floating bonfire.[7]

A Long Lance then found and knocked off a piece of *Chicago*'s starboard bow and a shell hit the base of the main mast. Recovering from the jolt, *Chicago*'s secondary battery gunners went after the light cruiser *Tenryu* and scored a hit that killed 23 Japanese sailors. Leaving the damaged American cruiser in his wake, Mikawa aimed his cruisers at the American warships guarding the northern sector. The disoriented commanding officer of the damaged American cruiser, Capt. Howard D. Bode, did not follow the Japanese. That a number of star shells fired by the heavy American cruiser failed to torch did little to help his situational awareness. However, unlike *Canberra* which lost electrical power to her radio room, *Chicago* could still transmit a warning to the American cruisers stationed to the north. She failed to do so.

Of the ships assigned to guard the waters south of Savo Island, the destroyer *Patterson*, after spotting the Japanese, engaged the enemy warships. While losing two after mounts to enemy fire, the destroyer fired on the *Tenryu* and *Yubari* and scored a hit of the heavy cruiser *Kinugasa* as Mikawa's formation turned to the northeast. A poorly executed column turn split the Japanese cruisers into two advancing groupings.[8]

At approximately 0145, watch standers on the cruisers *Vincennes*, *Quincy*, and destroyer *Wilson* began seeing the flares and noting gunfire to the southwest; however, a heavy cloud bank shrouded the extent of the carnage being inflicted on *Canberra* and *Chicago*. Then, at 0150, searchlights reached out from the south, illuminating not only *Vincennes* and *Quincy*, but also the heavy cruiser *Astoria*. With their prey exposed, Japanese gunners on *Chokai*, *Kako*, and *Aoba* methodically fired their armor-piercing rounds into the hulls of the American warships. Firing at *Astoria*, Mikawa's flagship failed to score hits, and the American heavy cruiser countered with her own 8-inch salvos. A quick ceasefire ordered by an awakened captain in *Astoria* sealed the cruiser's fate. Japanese shells from the three aforementioned cruisers and *Kinugasa* found their mark and began registering fatal blows.[9]

Photographed from a Japanese cruiser during the battle of Savo Island, USS *Quincy* (CA 39) is seen here burning, spotlighted by Japanese searchlights. *Quincy* would succumb to flooding. (Archives Branch, Naval History and Heritage Command, Washington, D.C.; NH 50346)

Quincy suffered a similar pummeling by shellfire. Illuminated by the cruiser *Aoba*, the cruiser found herself in the crossfire of the two advancing groupings, with *Furutaka* and *Tenryu* also scoring hits. Within moments the ship was a flaming pyre, but she kept fighting. Two torpedoes from *Tenryu* ruptured *Quincy's* portside, but the cruiser's heroic gun crews continued to return fire, with one round crashing into *Chokai*, just aft of Mikawa's perch on the bridge. However, another torpedo and additional shells sapped the life out of *Quincy*, which lost its way as seawater poured into her hull.[10]

Likewise, searchlights found *Vincennes*. As with *Quincy*, Japanese shells raked the superstructure. Shells from *Kako* ripped into *Vincennes's* aircraft hangar, setting the five stowed aircraft ablaze. A *Vincennes* shell damaged *Kinugasa's* steering gear and turned off her search light, but the American warship's flames provided ample illumination to attract a torpedo from *Chokai*, another from *Yubari*, and additional gunfire. By 0220, having set the three American heavy cruisers ablaze, Mikawa ordered his formation to a return to Rabaul via the north channel.[11]

Ralph Talbot blocked the path of the escaping Japanese flotilla and came in on the losing end of gun duels with the heavier armed Japanese. Fortunately, after absorbing four hits, the brave little destroyer was masked by a rain squall and would live to fight another day.[12]

Of the three cruisers of the northern group, Mikawa later observed that *Quincy* put up the most spirited defense. However, *Quincy* would be first to fall beneath the waves, sinking at about 0235. Such was the devastation absorbed by *Vincennes* that she would be second to go under just before 0300. *Canberra*, with her survivors picked off by *Blue* and *Patterson*, was finished off by a torpedo from *Ellet* at 0800. *Astoria's* crew made a valiant effort to keep the cruiser afloat. Surviving the night with the assistance of *Bagley*, *Astoria* would see her last sunrise. At 1100 a magazine exploded. By noon the captain and remaining crewmembers were pulled off, and 15 minutes later the ship turned over to port and sank in what would become known as Ironbottom Sound.[13]

In summary, the Allies lost four cruisers and sustained damage on a fifth cruiser and two destroyers. In addition to the damage sustained on Mikawa's flagship, two of his other cruisers suffered minor shell damage, and all of his ships had metal dented thanks to small-arms fire. Lloyd knew from experience that the defending ships should have better accounted themselves. During a night gunnery exercise embarked in *Augusta* back in 1937, the junior officer witnessed how the Asiatic Fleet flagship put shells on target by methodically firing "a three salvo ranging ladder in 500 yard increments by individual turrets."[14] Understanding that at night victory often goes to the side that engages first, as illustrated at Savo Island, Lloyd knew that opening fire as fast as humanly possible was crucial and that the fall of shot served as an effective rangefinder. Lloyd's shock and disgust was shared by others in the Navy hierarchy and by many of his countrymen when news of the setback reached the American people two months later.[15]

As in the aftermath of the attack on Pearl Harbor, an investigation was conducted. Retired Adm. Arthur J. Hepburn traveled throughout the theater in early 1943 to reconstruct what had happened off Savo Island. He credited "complete surprise" as the primary cause for the Japanese victory. Several factors allowed for the Japanese to achieve that surprise. They included inadequate readiness within the Allied ships to conduct a nighttime engagement, failure to recognize the danger portended by overhead enemy aircraft, overconfidence in radar detection capabilities, poor communications, and inadequate reconnaissance. Admiral Nimitz agreed with most of the conclusions of the Hepburn Report, adding faulty intelligence and the lack of a leadership in the form of a flag officer with the southern force as factors.

One paragraph from the Hepburn Report that mirrored Lloyd's initial reaction read, "As a contributory cause ... must be placed the withdrawal of the carrier groups on the evening before the battle. This was responsible for Admiral Turner's conference ... [and] for the fact that there was no force available to inflict damage on the withdrawing enemy."[16]

Because of the myriad of factors that led to the Japanese triumph, Adm. Ernest King felt it would be unfair to blame one officer for the debacle. Consequently, some officers such as Admirals Crutchley and Turner would distinguish themselves later in the war. For others, the burden of responsibility held during a battle that claimed over 1,000 Allied sailors would be overwhelming. In the case of Capt. Howard Bode of *Chicago*, he would take his own life.[17]

Lloyd was correct in lamenting the plight of the Marines left ashore on Guadalcanal, surmising that had Mikawa taken out the transports and their supplies, the Marines ashore could have been exposed to a fate similar to Bataan. Years later Lloyd reflected: "It's just a mercy, of course, that they didn't realize the full extent of the catastrophic defeat that they had imposed on our forces because they could have remained in there for some hours destroying transports at their leisure. It would have been like shooting fish in a mine barrel."[18]

Though Mikawa inflicted what many consider the worst combat defeat on American naval forces in history, the Naval War College study is highly critical of his lack of aggressiveness, calling into question Mikawa's military character:

> Whereas he was probably successful as a surface ship commander, he was lacking in that resolute spirit ever found in commanders of the first rank. In addition, he does not appear to have been a deep military thinker, nor does he appear to have had a proper appreciation of the relation between strategy and tactics and of the necessity for insuring that his tactical successes contributed fully to the aims of strategy. Had he had this appreciation, is there any doubt that he would have attacked the transports and cargo ships as his physical objective?[19]

However, as with Fletcher who had witnessed *Lexington* and *Yorktown* go under thanks to enemy air attack, Mikawa saw what American naval aviation had done to the *Mogami* and *Mikuma* at Midway and reasoned that if he had regrouped his flotilla to attack Turner's transports, his ships would suffer repeated carrier aircraft strikes as they retreated to the northwest in the morning light.

Ironically, as Mikawa's cruisers began their attacks earlier that morning, Fletcher's carriers were steaming on a course of 320 degrees in the direction of Savo Island as Fletcher awaited Ghormley's approval for him to withdraw. At 0330 Ghormley's approval set in motion rudder orders to reverse course within the hour. However, in that time, reports of the disaster at Savo began to reach the radio rooms of Fletcher's carriers and Capt. Forrest Sherman, commanding officer of *Wasp*, sought to close Savo to launch an air strike in the pre-dawn hours to catch Mikawa's fleeing ships. His request was not passed on to Fletcher, who was not fully appraised of the battle until sometime between 0500 and 0600. Urged to again turn to close on the scene of the battle, Fletcher opined that such a move would only play into Japanese hands.[20]

So Fletcher's carriers continued on a 140-degree track until the mid-afternoon and then turned further out of enemy aircraft range on an easterly heading, increasing speed to 18 knots. During the evening the formation turned south then southeast at 15 knots in anticipation of meeting up with the oilers *Platte* and *Kaskaskia* the next day. As Lloyd noted in his diary, the rendezvous came late in the day and other ships of Task Force 16 took turns at the floating gas stations as the formation steamed on a westerly heading.[21]

CHAPTER 17

Continuing Struggle

13 August

Cimarron & 6 DD's joined our happy group at noon. All hands were to top-off with oil from her. Again, apparently, she was late. There is certainly room for improvement in the staff work in this line. However, at 2100 voice radio word headed us for Tulagi at 20 kts, leaving *Cimarron* behind. Must be something hot up there. Judging from the way the Japs are pouring stuff into Rabaul, and from there out into the Solomons, the Tulagi–Guadalcanal garrison is in a tough spot.

Forty Jap DD's to Rabaul in one report alone—there is going to be a bitch of a night session up here, some dark night, with torpedoes in the water as thick as flies.

14 August

An operation order came out today creating a "Surface Attack Force," composed of us, the *Minneapolis, San Francisco, New Orleans, Portland, Salt Lake City,* and *North Carolina,* with 4 DD's. The rest of the DD's stay with the 3 CV's. Very cheering news to me, because it looks like a sign of a turn for the better in this matter of the use of surface power. Perhaps there'll be a little surface "Offensive Screening" to keep these bastards from being able to get all set, somewhere up towards Bougainville, before they whip down onto our stuff at the time of their own choosing (just what they did on the 8th).

From the stuff the Japs are putting in here, including AP's, landing equipment, etc., it looks like this time we'll have to stand and fight, or else sacrifice the Marines. Amazing that this ship has not yet fired a shot in anger! I guess we'll all have a little buck fever when we finally do.

To our sorrow, last night's Northward jaunt petered out and we resumed our general circling. Just keeping at sea, near the area where the forces of activity is going to be, and waiting for the Jap to show his head out of his hole.

More study of the "Surface Attack Group" shows it's just so much paper & words.

15 August
Rendezvoused with *Cimarron* after all and topped off the DD's of all three carrier groups. Got off mail via the tanker again.

18 August
More fueling planned; this time to top off the whole force (three carrier groups). A long job. Mail to go again! I'll be a fluent correspondent at this rate.

Big surprise—the tankers brought us out some mail from Noumea. Latest date 8 July. Even included a few magazines. The last surviving Wardroom ones had long since disappeared completely.

20 August
Time marches on, but not in circles the way we do. Japs keep needling Tulagi–Guadalcanal with small daily raids, surface, air, or both, no single one of which is large, but the cumulative effect of which probably will be. Especially if, as I expect, they keep getting men ashore on Florida or Guadalcanal.

This is figured as the earliest day on which a massive Jap concentration, including up to two Divs of sea-borne troops can have had a chance to unite its Truk & Rabaul detachments and get down here. We came North to not far S. of the E. tip of San Cristobal in the early afternoon, then withdrew.

The *Long Island*, with *Helena* and DD escort, flew some Marine F4F's off yesterday (I think) for Guadalcanal field. Have seen her once or twice, around here.

21 August
More enemy activity in Tulagi area reported. I don't get to see the real dope as it comes in, under our Exec's stupid policy with regard to keeping that stuff secret, other than the Dept. heads, the reserve Ensigns who are on the coding board, and their reserve Ensign chums to whom they blab are the only ones who get the news when new. The regular officers who could understand it, digest it, use it in following the situation as a preparation for command themselves, someday, are kept in the dark as far as he finds possible.

Anyway, CTF 61 (the big boss of the whole operation) appears to have been finally stung to action—tonight we are heading in and by dawn will be only some 80 mi. S. of Guad.

Stack made a D.C. [Depth Charge] attack tonight. No dope on how she made out.

Australia, Hobart, and 3 DD's from TF 41 (the transport group) joined us today. *San Juan* came out with the tankers (*Platte* & *Kaskaskia*) on the 18th & has been with us since. All these have been added to the "Surface Attack Group" organization when it is to be used—in the present organization, they are with others of the carrier groups than our own. I don't know how divided though *S.J.* [*San Juan*] has been with *Wasp.*

22 August

Kawanishi 97 4-engined flying boat shadower shot down 1105 today, 25 mi. W. of us by *Enterprise* fighters. I guess he got the word out before he was finished. We were about 80 mi. S. of Guadalcanal.

Got dope on Marine engagement with Japs landed on Guadalcanal from Truk by DD's. About 1,000 landed 19th, from 16 DD's, all of which escaped scott free, thanks to the lack of action of our force. Landed E. of Lunga & started W. Marines met 800; 30 are alive (prisoners).

Also got word of Marine raid on Little Makin, carried in *Argonaut* and *Narwhal.* Much destruction done, and withdrawal completed in time to see flights of Jap bombers (probably from Jaluit) arrive and plaster everything on the island with bombs.

We are rounding E. end of San Cristobal tonight to be about 50–60 mi. N.E. of Malaita tomorrow A.M. Subs active S. of islands. *Portland* dodged torpedo tonight and *Selfridge* making D.C. attack at some time in another part of the formation. 35 kt. wind, and a bad chop make A.S.[anti-submarine] operations tough—but should make it a little tough for the SS too.

Message in today from CinCPac telling the boys to destroy Jap ships and to run risks if necessary to do it. Boy—my own sentiments to a tee, and so carefully not done, so far, by these birds running these task forces. The dopes have all of a sudden awakened to the realization that, by gosh, the airplane is here to stay, and have so lost their heads about it that now they are afraid to think of anything else. We've got a terrific force of surface ships here now, but all they do is hang on to the carriers' apron strings.

***

In the wake of the Allied defeat in what became known as the battle of Savo Island, and Fletcher's decision to withdraw his carriers, the situation for the Marines ashore on Guadalcanal soured. Despite the precarious situation of his cargo and troopships, Turner ordered the unloading to continue on August 9. Turner ran into luck this day.

Samuel E. Morison speculates that, not knowing Fletcher had withdrawn his carriers, aircraft of the Japanese 25th Air Flotilla patrolled the seas south of Guadalcanal in search of these important targets. Little did they realize that they could have made up for Mikawa's grievous mistake made before dawn by going after Turner's transports and cargo ships, which were sitting ducks, having reduced air cover with a significant portion of its antiaircraft capability now resting beneath the surface in the waters off Savo Island. For their efforts, the Japanese claimed to have sunk an American cruiser. This ship probably was the damaged destroyer *Jarvis*. Detached the previous day, the destroyer was en route to Sydney to obtain repairs. She was lost with all hands.

San Juan, one of *Atlanta*'s Fall River sisters that remained in the vicinity of Guadalcanal, had not fought at Savo due to her assignment, along with the HMAS *Hobart*, to guard the eastern approaches to the landing area. Lloyd's counterpart in *San Juan*, Lt. Cdr. Horacio Rivera, lamented how the outcome of the battle could have been different given *San Juan*'s more capable search radar.[1]

After *Atlanta* secured from General Quarters mid-morning on August 9, she commenced what seemed to be an endless patrol as part of one of three forces assigned to guard some 600 miles of sea lanes between the newly established base at Espiritu Santo and Guadalcanal. One observer embarked in *Atlanta* echoed Lloyd's comments on the fuel replenishment process: "About once a week the three forces rendezvoused with a lone tanker. The forces combined while fueling operations proceeded. The tanker fueled ships on both sides of her, fueling them one after the other. In a day the three forces would be completely refueled, leaving the tanker sitting high in the water."[2] Lloyd's diary, affirmed by *Atlanta*'s war diary, recorded that the refueling occurred more frequently with hookups with *Cimarron* on August 13 and 15, and *Platte* and *Kaskaskia* on August 18 (*Atlanta* took fuel from the latter).[3]

On Guadalcanal, the Marines had set up a 5-mile defense line to protect their nearly completed airfield. The Americans used captured Japanese rice and other provisions to augment the supplies that had initially been landed. The Marines also pressed captured Japanese weapons and construction equipment into service. The Marines used six trucks, six steam-rollers, four generators, a narrow-gauge railway with locomotives and hopper cars, and other leftover items to grade and extend the runway that had been nearly finished by the enemy.[4]

In his diary entries of mid-August, Lloyd Mustin failed to note that three APDs arrived at Guadalcanal on August 15. The World War I vintage *Colhoun*, *Gregory*, and *McKean* had started their careers as flush-deck "4-Piper" destroyers. With a boiler room and two stacks removed, the tin cans took on a new appearance and a new mission. Even with a reduced steam-generation capacity, the sleek warships could still top 25 knots. Arriving off Guadalcanal on August 15, the three ships offloaded aviation gas, ammunition, and bombs. More significantly, the ships landed a 120-man "Cub" detachment who would have responsibility for operating aircraft from Henderson Field. Two days later, Major General Vandegrift informed Vice Admiral Ghormley that Henderson Field was ready for operations in dry weather.[5]

Of course, the Japanese were intent on disrupting the airfield's grand opening. Long-range bombers rained iron from the sky. Whereas Lloyd reported a force of 16 Japanese destroyers had evaded the Americans to land troops, in reality, on the night of August 18, six Japanese destroyers steamed undetected past the American positions ashore. As Lloyd noted, they landed nearly 1,000 soldiers in an attempt to flank the Marines whose defensive positions were oriented toward the western side of the island. Afterwards, three of the destroyers steamed past the American foothold on the morning of August 19 and unleashed a daylight bombardment of Marines on Tulagi and Guadalcanal. Overhead, Army B-17s flying from Espiritu Santo came to the rescue and loosed racks of bombs on the enemy tin cans, with one bomb hitting an aft gun mount on *Hagikaze*.[6]

Meanwhile, Marines ashore became aware of the recent insertion of fresh enemy troops on their eastern flank when a Marine patrol ambushed an advance party of 34 of the newcomers, killing 31. Noting these troops were clean shaven and wore fresh uniforms, and carried maps that outlined the American positions, the Marines firmed up their defenses along a waterway they dubbed Alligator Creek.[7]

On August 20 the first flight of Marine aircraft arrived. Lloyd notes that they were launched off the *Long Island*. Originally the *Mormacmai*—a cargo ship launched on January 11, 1940, from the Sun Shipbuilding and Dry Dock Company of Chester, Pennsylvania—she was the first ship to be converted into what became known as an escort carrier. Major General Vandegrift welcomed the arrival of 19 F4F Wildcats and a dozen SBD Dauntlesses piloted by Leathernecks with tears welling in his eyes.[8] While the Marine airplanes touched down, offshore the *Colhoun*, *Gregory*, and *McKean* reappeared to drop off another 120 tons of rations.

Before the Americans would have an opportunity to ingest the new supplies, the Japanese force to the east attacked after midnight. Charging across a sandbar at the mouth of Alligator Creek, some 200 determined enemy warriors were cut down with machine guns, rifles, and canister fire. Marines killed those who made it across the sandbar in fierce hand-to-hand combat. Those Japanese soldiers who did not engage in the initial assault were now exposed to a flanking maneuver that was deliberately executed the next day with the assistance of tanks and Wildcats flying out of Henderson Field. By nightfall, another 600 Japanese lay dead. After fierce fighting, the Japanese threat to the east had been eliminated. In addition to decimating a veteran Japanese Army unit, the Marines captured an impressive cache of pistols, rifles, machine guns, flamethrowers, and highly desired shovels.[9]

Lloyd also noted the Makin Island raid that occurred on the night of August 17–18. Some 220 men from the 2nd Marine Raider Battalion were transported to the Central Pacific Japanese outpost located in the Gilbert Islands by the submarines *Nautilus* and *Argonaut*. Led by Lt. Col. Evan F. Carlson and the President's son,

Recently opened Henderson Field as seen from the northwest on August 22, 1942. Planes on field are F4F Wildcats. (Archives Branch, Naval History and Heritage Command, Washington, D.C.; 80-G-12216)

Maj. James Roosevelt, "Carlson's Raiders" rowed ashore in the rough sea in inflatable rafts and launched an assault on the small Japanese garrison. The Marines succeeded in decimating the defending force, destroyed the facilities, and fought off two Japanese floatplanes that flew in to assist the doomed garrison. With most of the Marines back onboard the two submarines, a heavy column of black smoke could be seen rising on the island. Excepting the loss of some of the raiders, the mission was a success. However, hopes that the raid could divert Japanese forces away from Guadalcanal proved a bit optimistic.[10]

With Henderson Field becoming operational, the Japanese became increasingly concerned. On the day the Marines mopped up the initial Japanese assault along the Tenaru River, they also scored a victory in the air as a Marine Wildcat shot down a Japanese Zero. With the arrival of an Army fighter squadron the next day and Navy aircraft on August 24, the Americans could better defend themselves and strike out at Japanese naval forces lingering in the vicinity during daylight hours. Appreciating the threat, the Japanese pushed additional forces into the region. As Lloyd noted, the *Atlanta* had yet to fire a shot in anger. That would soon change.

CHAPTER 18

Battle of the Eastern Solomons

23 August

4 transports, with 2 CA's, 4 DD's, reported 180 miles N of Tulagi headed S at 17 kts. AP's that can make 17 kts, to my mind, are a fat target in themselves, not to mention the CA's & DD's which we could overwhelm. This is the sort of thing that has gone on daily since we came in here—a couple a day, loading troops into all the coves and bays of Florida, Guadalcanal, Malaita, etc. What do we do about it? Head south east!!!! God damn this pusillanimous bastard to hell anyway. We run SE half the night, because those CA's and DD's might attack our puny force of only six CA's, three CL's, 19 DD's, 1 BB, and three carriers. In the morning we'll be about back where we started—200 miles from Tulagi, about 100 mi. NE of the center of San Cristobal.

24 August '42

Just after midnight the Tulagi garrison reported our friends of yesterday standing in from the N. and some others from the West. But us reluctant dragons are safe from harm, by Jesus Christ. Why in God's name this sap doesn't operate a detached cruiser & DD wing to mop up these soft touches at leisure, I'll certainly never know. That is of course, until enemy carriers arrive, at least, certainly. They have been accounted for up north until recently, but are expected soon.

   * An engagement today—our first. About 1330 GQ went; arrived on deck to see smoke from a reported 2 Eng. L.P. bomber acting as shadower, shot down by F4F's about 25 miles from our formation. Assume we were spotted. At same time, contact report in on small enemy CV 260 miles bearing 350° from us. Apparently fueling forced into action as a defensive measure, inasmuch as we'd been sighted. *Saratoga* air attack was launched about 1400 to go for this CV, and the CA & 2 DD's with it. PBY patrol kept info coming from time to time. About 1630 an accumulation of

contact reports indicated about 2 CA's, 3 CL's, some DD's, about 80 miles east of the CV, headed S. at 24 kts (Evidently their surface forces still aren't scared to bore in on us.) (No wonder!!) *Wasp* group complete, by the way, is off fueling today. TF 61 tells CTF 16 (*Enterprise*): "If you think these last reports are good, launch your attack group" (Weasel words). CTF 16 ("Frank" on voice radio) must have thought so, because he called "Bill" back to ask for prospective navigation data. He got it. While we were running 25 kts on 310°, indicating we'd hold that till 1830, then turn to 130°, and said he was going to launch. But then "Bill" comes crawling back to announce that "After further consideration," he did not think he could hold 130° till 1830, "because of the danger of night torpedo attack." I'd thought I'd jump overboard then and there—clear as a bell, full moon due, 2 CV's, 2 CL's, 3 CA's, 1 BB, 13 DD's running like rabbits from a couple of Japs because they might attack us (the nasty mans.) So we couldn't launch the attack because for some reason "Frank" figured he needed 310° till 1630 to do it; these Jap ships, therefore, which we are so valiantly to "gun, bomb, and torpedo to destruction," in the words of CinCPac's dispatch, are to run us out of their ocean again with a quarter of our force!!!

Well, indecision, incompetence, inaction and trembling super-caution are their own rewards. The Jap, low and behold, comes after us. He must not have read the same primer that our fart-heads learned to fight out of. Here he comes, picked up by radar at 100 mi. or so, and coming at us. The usual buggered-up carrier tactics had, as always, gotten us some 20 mi. ahead of the *Sara* group, so first "Bill" says "Close me immediately," then turns to 130° degrees and goes to 25 knots. We do the best we can at 28, which is about all, or just a shade more, than the *N.C.* [*North Carolina*] can do. But it is evident the Japs will get in a couple of licks. Fighters being vectored out on 300°, 310°, 320, to intercept, trying all altitudes. Reports come in on fighter-director circuit "Tally-ho," "36 of 'em," "Some low, watch out for torpedoes," "I got the son-of-a-bitch," etc., etc.

In the face of the imminent attack, the decision on the *Enterprise* air group attacking is again changed, and at about 1700 planes started taking off.

Though the sky was nearly cloudless, there was a bright high haze in the glittering sun that made high planes almost impossible to see, and we did not spot the Japs until they were in their dive. Aichi 99's, about 18 of them. We opened director-controlled barrage fire, to intercept their dive path above the carrier; fired 264 rds. 5", 2,000+ of 1".1, and about 1,100 20mm. The planes evidently came on in from about 310°, passed across the carrier, pulled off in succession beyond her, and dove in on

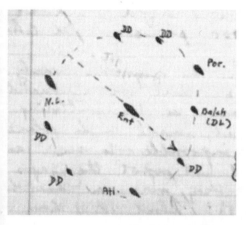
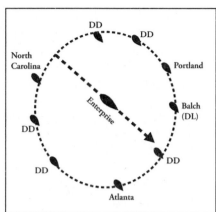

Lloyd Mustin's illustration, re-drawn for clarity.

about the reverse of their approach course. Formation was the "Repel air attack" standard, all screen ships on 2,000 yd circle, about equally spaced, about as below: (spacing of heavy ships on bearings which remained from our stations in the cruising disposition axis 100°) degrees.

First ones spotted were just on our port bow, diving in, at about 45° angle, from about 12,000 feet to 1,000–1,200 ft. release point, pulling out and retiring low. Everybody opened up, and the sky was just a solid sheet of tracers and shell bursts—impossible to tell your own. First plane missed and flew off (don't know how many the fighters got going out—or how many coming in, for that matter). Second & third missed and crashed. Some came apart in mid-air, some just fell wildly out of control, some came down burning, and some just flew on into the water in various stages of pullout. Majority of all that attacked was shot down.

Enterprise went hard left, and was in her turn when first bomb fell. She changed left about 90°, during which time I saw 1st 8–10 attacks, with no hits. Then she reversed rudder, while I was searching to starboard for reported torpedo planes, coming right 180°, by which time attack was over. I looked back in time to see the last couple, by which time she had been hit twice aft and was on fire. I think she got hit while she straightened out during the reversal of her turn. George & Pete had said they figured to stay in the turn throughout a given attack, and I think it's best.

She had 75 killed, 100 wounded, after 2 starboard 5"/ 38's out of commission, and underwater damage from near misses that listed her 5° starboard and gave her steering-gear trouble. List soon off, but steering damage seems more permanent. Meanwhile *Sara* attack group was returning (not having even found their target), and kept getting reported as "bogies." As darkness fell, we joined up with *Sara*, & both started recovery. Two *Ent.* planes landed in water (crews saved by DD's); two crashed on flight deck, causing many to have to land on *Sara*. *Ent*'s rudder jammed hard right once during operation, which didn't help. All hands then started S. at 25 kts, with *Enterprise* attack group dribbling in all night up to nearly midnight, they not having found target either. It must have been dark (sunset about 1830) before they even reached the target area. Some, apparently, were lost altogether. All in all we inflicted a total loss on the Japs of a few planes, at the cost of some ourselves, plus damage to the *Enterprise* which will reduce her effectiveness at the time when the strategic situation is coming to climax. *Sara* group to S. of us, not touched.

Score another one for the Japs.

25 August

Late reports last night said Army B-17's spotted two *Shokaku* class CV's to north, in addition to the *Ryujo*; claimed bomb hits on two of them. As usual when the photos were developed these claims of damage were not substantiated.

This AM we rendezvoused with tankers, about due West of Espiritu Santo, for fuel. *Gwin, Monssen, Grayson, N.C.* and ourselves are detached from TF 16 to TF 11. Looks as though *Enterprise* is going to be kept out of action, either in rear area or actually to leave, for repair. *Wasp* group (TF 18) is fueled and somewhere around; we now have *Sara* & *Wasp* against whatever the Japs bring, including, of course, all those CA's and DD's that we could and should have knocked off in detail. We do have a respectable surface force, it's true.

26 August

Here we are in TF11, course and axis 000°, headed for trouble I hope. Actually I think we now have a total of 9 DD's.

Being on the Northern side of the circle, we should have a crack at anyone who comes along. (Provided there's no other carrier nearer, for them to work over.) No dope on *Wasp* outfit; also, nothing more on the Japs. Looks like those carriers have flown the coop.

Later—attached dispatch came out. Summarizes from better sources than I could follow, naturally—but sounds a touch optimistic. Look at the AA score! Jesus—no wonder every plane that came in seemed to wither. Also, thank God the *Sara* air group apparently did find something after all. Funny we didn't hear about it. But where the hell are all the

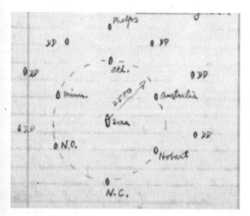
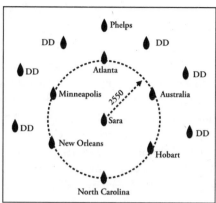

Lloyd Mustin's illustration, re-drawn for clarity.

"damaged" ships now? Thanks to our running like hell all night the 24th, and fueling the 25th, they must be about to Truk by now.

MESSAGE

FROM: COMTASKFOR 61
TO: TASKFOR 16 & 18

ESTIMATED RESULTS OF ACTION TWENTY FOURTH X ENEMY CONSISTED OF TWO CARRIER TASK FORCES ONE OF SMALL CV AND ONE OF TWO LARGE CV PLUS OTHER STRONG BATTLESHIP CRUISER AND TRANSPORT TASK FORCES X SARATOGA AIR GROUP ATTACKED THE SMALL CV OBTAINING HITS AND LEAVING HER SMOKING SHE WAS LATER SIGHTED DEAD IN WATER X ON SAME ATTACK SANK ONE DD AND ONE CRUISER HIT BY TORPEDO X IN ANOTHER ATTACK OBTAINED ONE TORPEDO HIT ON CRUISER AND ONE THOUSAND LB BOMB HIT ON A BB X INFORMATION LOCATION OF TWO LARGE CV NOT OBTAINED IN TIME FOR ATTACK X ENEMY ATTACK GROUP CONSISTED OF EIGHTY PLANES X ENEMY LOSSES SHOT DOWN BY OUR AIRCRAFT FORTY SEVEN BY AA TWENTY FOUR X ENTERPRISE HIT BY THREE BOMBS X OWN LOSSES EIGHT PILOTS MISSING X EARLIER IN DAY VF SHOT DOWN ONE TWIN ENGINED LAND PLANE TWO FOUR ENGINED PATROL PLANES AND ONE SINGLE ENGINE TWIN FLOAT SEAPLANE X MARINES AT CACTUS SHOT DOWN ELEVEN ZEROS AND TEN BOMBERS SAME DAY X FOLLOWING DAY GRAYSON PROBABLY SANK ONE SS AND ENTERPRISE SBD OBTAINED DIRECT HIT WITH ONE THOUSAND LB BOMB ON ANOTHER X

END MESSAGE

***

With the establishment of the airfield at Henderson Field and the stunning defeat of a Japanese assault force at Alligator Creek, the Japanese commanders acted urgently to move naval forces into the region. Vice Admiral Ghormley's staff pieced together submarine and aircraft sightings of enemy ship movements portending a thrust at Guadalcanal from August 24–26. Awaiting the arrival of the Combined Fleet that included Vice Admiral Nagumo's carriers, Rear Adm. Raizo Tanaka embarked to lead another resupply mission down the slot on August 23. A Catalina patrol plane caught sight of Tanaka's convoy at 0950 and the report subsequently was entered into Lloyd's diary. However, rather than close on Tanaka's ships, *Atlanta*'s war diary indicated that the task force changed at 1135 from a departing course of 135 degrees true at 10 knots, to 180 true degrees at 15 knots. While Lieutenant Commander Mustin takes Vice Admiral Fletcher to task for running away from Tanaka's convoy, Fletcher did receive reports from *Enterprise* aircraft that afternoon of three Japanese submarines heading southwards toward him. Those familiar with Japanese tactics surmised they could be advance scouts for the anticipated combined fleet.[1]

Fletcher, receiving additional reports from the Catalina shadowing Tanaka's convoy, finally acted that afternoon, and at 1510, *Saratoga* launched 31 Dauntlesses and six Avenger torpedo planes in an attempt to intercept Tanaka's ships. From the bridge of *Atlanta*, Lloyd, who was standing the 1200–1600 watch as OOD, kept one eye on the flight operations and the other for enemy periscopes. Tanaka, having been taunted by the sight of the Catalina for most of the day, won permission to reverse course. The course change, combined with some murky weather conditions, enabled him to successfully evade not only the *Saratoga* air strike, but also nine dive-bombers and 12 fighters launched from Henderson Field. Both air groups landed at Guadalcanal that evening.[2]

Meanwhile, another scout plane spotted Vice Adm. Nobutake Kondo's advance force of cruisers and destroyers that served as the vanguard of Admiral Yamamoto's Japanese Combined Fleet that included Vice Adm. Chuichi Nagumo's carriers *Shokaku* and *Zuikaku*. To keep Allied aircraft from spotting his carriers, Vice Admiral Nagumo swung the main body on a northerly heading at 1825. Kondo's advance force also reversed course.

The sighting of the Japanese cruisers sans carriers combined with an intelligence report sent from Pearl Harbor placing Japanese carriers at Truk led Fletcher to believe a carrier battle was not imminent. Lloyd's diary entry early on August 24 reflects this intelligence and ponders why surface forces were not being sent forward to meet Tanaka's convoy (which had reversed course just before midnight and was again en route to Guadalcanal) or to take on Kondo's cruisers. With orders from Ghormley to refuel a carrier, Fletcher released *Wasp* and her escorts to meet up with the oilers.

As Lloyd projected at the end of his entry of August 23, Task Force 61 (Vice Admiral Fletcher) consisting of Task Force 11 centered on *Saratoga* and Task Force 16 around *Enterprise*, was steaming on a westerly heading east of Tulagi and northeast of San Cristobal, the next island in the Solomons chain located some 40 miles southeast of Guadalcanal as the sun rose on the morning of the 24th. At

0230, *Atlanta*'s war diary noted the task force came to a course of 270 degrees true with slight adjustment to 280 degrees true at 0705, as Fletcher wanted to close the distance to Henderson Field to recover his aircraft.

Scout planes launched at daylight from the opposing fleets probed in each other's direction with no sighting success. It was a Catalina that spotted the Japanese light carrier *Ryujo* at 0935, which was steaming ahead of the main body escorted by a cruiser and two destroyers. The placement of the light carrier served two purposes. Assuming American carriers were not located, *Ryujo*'s aircraft could attack Henderson Field and provide cover for Tanaka's convoy. However, the light carrier served a tactical purpose to draw Fletcher to launch an air attack, exposing the Americans to a stronger counterpunch from the two Japanese heavy carriers. Fletcher learned of the sighting 12 minutes later and hesitated to take the bait, in part because he looked down at an empty flight deck as his dive-bombers and torpedo planes were returning to *Saratoga* from their overnight at Guadalcanal.[3]

With the *Saratoga*'s planes recovered during the late morning, at 1212 *Atlanta*, steaming in company with *Enterprise*, recorded a course change to 000 degrees true. At about the same time, Wildcats off *Saratoga* spotted a Japanese flying boat over the horizon and quickly dispatched the lumbering four-engine patrol plane. Rather than immediately attack *Ryujo*, Fletcher ordered *Enterprise* to launch 23 aircraft to search an arc from 290 to 90 degrees true. As the *Big E* added turns to her screws to obtain more wind over deck, *Atlanta*'s log recorded: "Increased speed to 18 knots and maneuvered with ENTERPRISE launching planes."[4]

The next entry read: "Japanese plane sighted to northwest, went to general quarters. Plane shot down by own fighters." As Lloyd recorded, as he arrived on deck en route to his station aft by Battle II, he could see the smoke from what proved to be a land-based Betty bomber. Lloyd surmised that the Japanese aircraft must have transmitted a contact report. Fletcher assumed likewise. In reality, the task force combat air patrol had splashed the Emily and the Betty before either could send a sighting message to their fleet. Remaining unaware of the presence of the American carriers, Capt. Tadao Kato turned *Ryujo* into the wind to launch 15 Zeros and 6 Kates to attack Henderson Field, only to be met by Marine and recently arrived Army aviators who put up a spirited defense.[5]

Saratoga's air search radar detected the attacking aircraft 100 miles distant. Plotters quickly discerned that they were heading toward Guadalcanal and vectored out the direction whence they came. As Lloyd notes in his diary, at about 1400, *Saratoga* launched 30 Dauntlesses and eight Avengers (two aircraft had to immediately return due to mechanical issues) against the *Ryujo* and her escorts. Fletcher had taken the bait.[6]

At 1431 *Atlanta*'s war diary recorded: "Observed another plane shot down to westward." This proved to be a floatplane launched by the cruiser *Chikuma*. Surmising that this scout was lost to enemy carrier aviation, Vice Admiral Nagumo now had a vector to direct strike groups from his two big deck carriers. At approximately 1500 and then 1600, two attack groups flew off *Zuikaku* and *Shokaku*, totaling 73 aircraft.

Meanwhile, the scouts dispatched by *Enterprise* began to report back, affirming the location of the *Ryujo* for *Saratoga*'s attacking air group. However, more troubling for Fletcher was the news from a pair of *Enterprise* SBDs that had dived on *Shokaku*, which scored some near misses, killing six Japanese sailors. With news of the sighting of the two big Japanese flattops, radio attempts to divert the *Saratoga*'s strike against *Ryujo* further north failed.

Eventually, *Saratoga*'s strike group, led by Lt. Cdr. Harry D. Felt, did come upon the light Japanese carrier, and Captain Kato ordered a hard-right rudder that saved his ship from at least 10 falling bombs. However, other Dauntlesses apparently found their mark, claiming four bomb hits, a number Captain Kato would later refute. What would assure *Ryujo*'s demise was one, possible three, torpedo hits from *Saratoga*'s Avengers which had approached the small flattop from two sides. Turning parallel to one torpedo spread simply exposed the hull to a broadside from another spread.[7]

As *Ryujo* maneuvered to evade attack, Task Force 61 prepared for the anticipated onslaught of enemy aircraft. A 1530 entry into *Atlanta*'s war diary read: "Set course 335° (T) at 20 knots to close reported enemy carrier group." Sitting up in the aft gun director patched into the radio net, Lloyd grimaced at the discussion about when to reverse course. As at Midway, he pined for a surface engagement, especially with the battleship *North Carolina* in the task force order of battle.

At 1602, *Enterprise*'s radarmen momentarily detected a flight of aircraft bearing 320 degrees true at 88 miles. The *Atlanta* war diary entry for 1637 read: "Unidentified planes reported bearing 300° (T). Changed course to 100° (T) and increased speed to 25 knots." By this time the Japanese were closing to within 25 miles of *Enterprise*. During the 35 minutes between the *Enterprise* radar sighting and the *Atlanta* war diary entry, *Saratoga* and *Enterprise* launched 53 Wildcats to intercept the first enemy strike group. In addition, the carrier launched a strike group to go after Nagumo's carriers.[8]

The American intercepting aircraft took a heavy toll on the oncoming Japanese that were closing on *Enterprise*. By mid-afternoon, the independent maneuvers of *Enterprise* and *Saratoga* had caused a 10-mile separation between the two carriers, with *Enterprise* positioned northwest of Fletcher's flagship. To protect *Enterprise* the screen commander, Rear Adm. Marion Tisdale, placed *North Carolina* astern of the carrier and placed his remaining two cruisers and six destroyers in a circular formation. With *Portland* off *Big E*'s port bow and *Atlanta* off the starboard bow, unfortunately placing Lloyd's ship on the opposite side from where the enemy's attack was emanating from, but from his perch aft near Battle II, Lloyd had a panoramic view of the combat.[9]

Enterprise's radar plotters had tracked the incoming attackers and at 1642 reported: "The enemy planes are directly overhead now."[10] With that, the

Japanese Val dive-bombers that had survived the gauntlet of Wildcats intentionally overshot *Enterprise* as well as *Atlanta* and turned around to make their dives, descending in seven-second intervals. Because of a high haze in the late afternoon sun, the lookouts did not spot the Vals until they were well into their steep dives. On *Enterprise*, Capt. Arthur C. Davis executed an S-turn, turning hard left. Lloyd later recalled all of the ships in the formation followed suit. As the formation turned, the relative position of *Enterprise* shifted from the port quarter to the port beam, enabling both the three forward gun 5-inch dual mounts controlled by Bill Nickelson and the aft three mounts operated by Lloyd Mustin, as well as the portside 20mm and 1.1-inch guns, to engage the diving Vals.[11] With concentrated fire from *Enterprise*, *Atlanta*, and other ships in the formation, the determined Japanese pilots pressed on to what was becoming a suicide mission. Davis's maneuver thwarted the first bomb-dropper, who evaded the gunfire. Lloyd observed that the second and third planes crashed near the carrier. Others came apart in pieces, with burning aviation gasoline following the descent. Davis then reversed his rudder, a fateful decision. Having listened in on the conversation between his stepfather and Pete Mitscher over in *Hornet* at Pearl Harbor three months earlier, Lloyd opined that continuing the hard-left rudder could have been more evasive. Years later Lloyd recalled: "Unfortunately the *Enterprise*, having made a sharp evasive turn to her left, then undertook to reverse course and swing around to the right and right in that interval when her center of gravity was moving in a straight line she took a couple of quick hits."[12]

Two near misses, their concussive effects, and the geysers of water shot into the air, slackened the gunfire pouring up from both sides of *Big E*'s flight deck. Then *Atlanta*'s war diary recorded: "Observed bomb hit on flight deck aft. There are several near misses and at least five enemy planes shot down." From around the defensive screen, hundreds of sailors could see smoke billowing out from two bomb hits that landed blows in a span of 15 seconds. The first bomb pierced the wooden flight deck on the forward right corner of the number three elevator, slicing through several decks before exploding in the petty officer's mess, killing 35. Then a second projectile landed just 15 feet outboard of the first, hitting a 5-inch gun tub, claiming the lives of another 33 sailors. Two minutes later, a third bomb hit forward near the number two elevator, creating a 10-foot hole in the flight deck, but caused no fatalities.[13]

Despite the damage on deck, *Enterprise* was able to turn into the light breeze and land her fighters and other aircraft that were low on fuel. Not all of the aircraft were successfully recovered. *Atlanta*'s war diary noted: "Two F4Fs made forced landings close aboard during evolution, one plane crashed on deck, another into side of carrier." Meanwhile, *Enterprise*'s radarmen tracked the second Japanese strike group. Fortunately for the Americans, these aircraft flew toward a point 50 miles astern of the *Enterprise* group and then proceeded to close to a point just beyond the horizon before they turned away. Had they continued they would have found

This bomb hit aft of the island was captured on film by Photographer's Mate 3rd Class Robert F. Read and reportedly the blast claimed his life. (Archives Branch, Naval History and Heritage Command, Washington, D.C.; 80-G-17489)

Enterprise vulnerable due to steering gear failure that jammed her rudder hard to starboard. After 38 minutes of slowly circling at 10 knots, the problem was resolved and control was restored to the helm.[14]

Of the smattering of American bomber and torpedo aircraft that lifted off from the two carriers in the moments before the Japanese attack, seven planes off *Saratoga* were able to locate the cruisers of Vice Admiral Kondo's advance force. Five Avengers made torpedo runs against the Japanese warships and failed to register hits. Two Dauntlesses set upon the seaplane carrier *Chitose*, and near misses cracked hull plates that caused flooding of machinery spaces and the detachment of the ship to head to Truk for repairs.[15]

As darkness fell, the two opposing carrier forces disengaged and recovered returning aircraft. The Japanese turned on their searchlights to aid the return of the second strike group, but four of the Vals never made it. Another ditched and its crew was recovered. The Americans also had aircraft recovery issues in the dark. *Atlanta's* war diary recorded: "Six ENTERPRISE planes approached. Maneuvered to recover but second plane crashed on deck and it was necessary to send remaining four to SARATOGA."[16]

Throughout the night Task Force 61—which consisted of Task Force 11 under Vice Admiral Fletcher in *Saratoga* and Task Force 16 under Rear Adm. Thomas C. Kinkaid in *Enterprise*—continued on a southerly heading, and in the early morning light shifted to a course of 245 degrees true. Within an hour *Atlanta's* lookouts spotted on the forward horizon the oilers *Platte* and *Cimarron* and their escorting destroyers *Clark* and *Gwinn*. During the rest of the day the ships of Task Force 16 based around *Enterprise* refueled from the two floating gas stations. *Atlanta* spent an hour and 10 minutes alongside *Cimarron*, which proved to be a most challenging piece of seamanship for Captain Jenkins and his bridge team, as during the refueling the heading of the task force changed from 180 degrees true to 030 degrees true. To complete the maneuver the two ships made course adjustments to the left in small increments, with the guide ship maintaining speed and the other adjusting speeds to maintain position abeam.[17]

That evening *Atlanta* received orders to report to Task Force 11 along with *North Carolina*, and the destroyers *Monssen* and *Grayson*. As the oilers and their escorts departed to the southwest, *Enterprise* and her remaining escorts continued to the northeast en route to Pearl Harbor to undergo repairs. As Lloyd's diary indicated, just after midnight on August 26, *Atlanta* had joined up with Fletcher's task force and was steaming back north.[18]

At the conclusion of his entry of August 26, Lloyd taped in a copy of Vice Admiral Fletcher's assessment of the action of August 24. Mustin, who wrote "score one for the Japs" at the conclusion of his lengthy entry of August 24, was correct that the report was "a touch optimistic." While the devastation wrought on *Ryujo's* air assault was spot on, the only other Japanese warship that the Americans were able to severely damage was a seaplane carrier. The success of the Marine aviators defending Guadalcanal from *Ryujo* was also exaggerated, as the enemy lost three Zeros and three Kates in the airspace around the island. However, those pilots that returned to *Ryujo* found there was no flight deck left to land on and they had to ditch their aircraft to be picked up by her escorts. As for the tally on Japanese aircraft that attacked Task Force 16, Nagumo launched two waves totaling 73 aircraft, of which the second wave never reached its objective. Thus Fletcher's claims that the Americans shot down 71 of the 37 planes that actually attacked were beyond far-fetched. In reality the Americans knocked down 17 Vals and 3 Zeros over the skies around *Enterprise*, and 4 additional Japanese aircraft would not make it back to their home flightdecks. Fletcher was not the only one guilty of exaggeration. The Japanese pilots from *Shokaku* and *Zuikaku* who survived the raid on *Enterprise* reported they had disabled two American carriers. The pilots from *Ryujo* who conducted the raid on Henderson Field claimed that of the 15 American fighters they engaged, all were shot down. This would have implications for the next day.[19]

What Lloyd missed in his diary on August 25 and 26 was actions up in the slot that determined the true outcome of this phase of the campaign in favor of the United States. The Japanese strategic objective was to reinforce the Japanese garrison at Guadalcanal to facilitate the removal of the U.S. Marines and operate the now completed airfield under the flag of the rising sun. In deploying the Combined Fleet southwards towards the Eastern Solomons, Admiral Yamamoto intended to provide air support to cover Tanaka's passage from Rabaul and hopefully draw out American carrier forces for the long-awaited decisive battle that would be set on Japanese terms. On midday on August 24 Tanaka again retired his ships to the west to evade Allied aircraft, again turned course back toward Guadalcanal once darkness arrived, only to be instructed to reverse to Rabaul. However, receiving the news that two American carriers had been placed out of action and Guadalcanal's air forces denuded, Vice Admiral Mikawa directed Tanaka to steam to his assigned objective. As the calendar shifted to August 25, Tanaka, embarked in the light cruiser *Jintsu*, steamed southeast with five destroyers to escort the transports *Kinryu Maru, Boston Maru*, and *Daifuku Maru* carrying vital supplies and 1,500 troops.

As Tanaka's ships firmly plowed forward on their new heading, a moonlit sky exposed them to overhead observation by a Catalina, and by 0500, Henderson Field had been alerted, and ground crews feverishly prepared eight dive-bombers and an equal number of fighters to intercept the convoy located 180 miles up the slot and closing. With Tanaka's ships bathed in the morning light, five Marine-piloted dive-bombers descended on *Jintsu* with 2nd Lt. Lawrence Baldinus scoring a hit between the cruiser's two forward turrets, killing numerous sailors and knocking Tanaka unconscious. Three Navy-piloted Dauntlesses from *Enterprise* that had taken refuge at Henderson Field the previous evening went after the *Kinryu Maru*, and Ens. Christian Fink scored a hit, setting off a massive blaze.[20]

Revived, Tanaka switched his flag to the destroyer *Kagero* to oversee the extraction of his ships out of danger. The destroyer *Mutsuki* closed on the *Kinryu Maru* to assist the billowing ship that served as a smoke flare to three high-flying B-17 bombers that *Mutsuki's* commander chose to ignore. At last, one of the bombs dropped found its way into *Mutsuki's* engine room, a fatal blow that killed 40 and sent the warship toward a collision with the ocean bottom in just over an hour. *Kinryu Maru* preceded her, having been scuttled with a torpedo fired from the *Mochizuki*.[21]

With the withdrawal of the relief convoy, the Japanese failed in their strategic objective; thus, the battle of the eastern Solomons was a greater American success than Lloyd Mustin recognized at the time.

CHAPTER 19

Attack on USS *Saratoga*

29 August 1942

Task Force 17 joined up this morning. *Hornet,* with *Northampton, Pensacola, San Diego,* and 5 DD of the *Sims* class. George in command—we got word last month that he'd hoisted his flag. I knew he'd make Admiral when he was a Lt. Comdr., Exec of the *Wright,* and have thought so all the more ever since. Not only that, but I know I will too—if I survive this war. Also, if I don't tramp on too many toes in the meantime with my bitter criticisms.

We now have a tidy little group of three carriers, 1 BB, 3 *New Orleans* class CA's, one *Northampton* class CA, the 2 *Pensacolas,* 3 of the four *Atlanta* class CL's, a *British County* class CA (HMAS *Australia*), HMAS *Hobart* (CL), and about 20 DD's. In the hands of a fighter with plain horse sense, the ability to think on his feet, and (maybe most important of all) a competent staff, what hell we could raise with the Japs in the whole East Indies area. I think that the staffs out here are not only incompetent, but based on an impossible system that can never give full efficiency to any task force until their basic way of functioning is changed. In other words, these units are called "Task Forces," and the commander a "Task Force Commander," but he certainly isn't such in the way a German task force commander, for example, is. Nor are these real task forces—they are just assemblages of ships, with the peacetime "Type organization" perpetrated to its last ridiculous extreme within the assemblage. "Commander Cruiser Task Force 18"!!! Christ Almighty.

30 August

New task force reorganizations went in today. We have *Sara.* [*Saratoga*], *N.C.* [*North Carolina,*] *Minn.* [*Minneapolis*] & *N.O.* [*New Orleans*], with *Phelps, Farragut, Dewey, Monaghan, Worden, Monssen, Grayson.* The two Australians went to Task Force 18, which lost *San Juan,* who went off to join the remnants of 16 (enroute Pearl Harbor, I guess, for repairs). The *Phoenix* arrived this morning, giving them; *Wasp, San Francisco, Phoenix, Australia, Hobart,* and seven DD's that I don't know. *Salt Lake City* went from 18 to 17, as did *Bagley* and *Patterson* from us, so Task Force 17 is now *Hornet, Northampton, Pensacola, Salt Lake City, San Diego,* those 2 DD's and 5 of the *Sims* class including the *Mustin* (DD 413).

As far as we are concerned the shift was the usual comedy of mismanagement and bumbling. Changes were to be effective at 0800, but nothing happened. Finally *Australia* requested permission to shove. New station assignments had not been forthcoming, so we started for the nearest new one to us. Then the *Minneapolis* ("ComCru TF 11") decided he'd go there, so we hauled ass to the next nearest. When we got there, he got out his station assignments (finally), putting all the heavy ships on stations that didn't exist according to "Cruising Instructions." After some further fumbling, and after everyone had completed the resultant shift, he got the word and shifted us back where we'd been. This all taking place during turns into the wind by the carrier, for air operations (us trying to follow her as guide), zigzagging, and a rotation of the axis. Truly a ducky exhibition.

Meanwhile we continue to steam in endless circles, waiting for something to come S.E. of the Solomons. I suppose; the war moves on to lower and lower depths for the Allies; the majority of the Pacific Fleet lets its guns accumulate rust; and the Jap comes and goes as he damn well pleases throughout the Solomon area—and everywhere else.

My little Henry's going to be nine tomorrow (or is it today??) Wonder when (and if) I'll ever see them all again. How I miss my little family.

31 August

This morning we got something we've been asking for—a torpedo into the *Saratoga*. Leisurely steaming along at 13 knots, in this same area we've been in since the start of the month, where we couldn't help having been sighted by some of the subs which are known to have been gathering steadily in the area. Last night we had DF reports on locations of many. But "it can't happen here" prevailed, as usual. 0745, on base course 140°, zigzagging by Plan Eight (very casual—five to ten minutes on the straightaway of each leg)—a report on voice radio (TBS): "Torpedo approaching *Saratoga*, starboard bow," by one of the DD's. About 0747 it hit—she'd had plenty of warning but hadn't been able to do much about it—thanks to her general lack of maneuverability which is certainly not helped any by a 13 knot speed. Probably also a lot of mental un-maneuverability on the bridge.

Our lookouts reported a miss astern, making a surface run, and one ahead; the hit almost amidships, starboard side. We bore 115° from her, and she turned to starboard, so it was all on the off side from us, but the misses came our way. The hit (or hits?) stopped her. I don't know why. Quite spectacular, apparently—the blast rose to twice her stack height, some said—that would be a tidy 300 feet. She came to dead in the water; listed 5 degrees starboard, down by the stern somewhat, much fuel oil on water. By the zigzag plan, we'd all been on course 180° since 0741—4 minutes for Tojo to get set to groove his fish.

About 0850 underway again on course 150° at 8 knots, still streaming much oil. *N.C.* had been sent to TF 17 (17 & 18 vanished), the 3 cruisers on a division are seesawing back & forth across her wake and feverish activity by the DD's ahead. Mad rushing and circling while she was dead in the water; much concern, no doubt about further attack. Several DD's dropped D.C.s [depth charges] a few times, apparently with no great success. 2, with a plane, have been left in the attack area.

Christ Almighty—now we have another CV out of action. And what in God's name have we done to the Jap fleet, in the month and a half of exposure that has led to this almost inevitable damage, to balance it? Not one goddamn thing worth recording, most particularly when compared to what we could have done. Two carriers left in the Pacific in operation—to about nine for the Jap.

Later—the old lady got underway at 8 kts, own power, and started the long trip home. Boy, will it be long. Flew off some planes for Guadalcanal, I suppose. She seems to have been hit about ¼ of her length from the stern. Must have flooded a motor room, perhaps with considerable resultant electrical damage elsewhere, and perhaps also with some shaft misalignment. By 1058, she stopped again. *Minneapolis* passed towline and got her underway, but then she started again. Got up to 13 knots, then started to run more slowly. List all off, but down by the stern, and trailing a wake of oil, operating her planes for search, etc. Seems she is going to land remaining planes and equipment at Tongatabu.

Hear that the *Calhoun* (APD) was sunk at Tulagi by one of the Jap daily raids; that the Marines lose 26% of their VF [fighters] and about 16% of their VSB [scout bombers] weekly, and that six Jap carriers are now in the Solomon area. New CarDiv1, of the *Shokaku*, *Zuikaku*, and *Ryujo*, who were there in our 24 August brush and new CarDiv2, of the

Hitaka, *Hayataka* and *Zuiho*. Old CarDivs 1 and 2 were wiped out at Midway. Things are now shaping up just as I've said: that is, the Nips, at their leisure and in their own good time, have assembled a force that can make it plenty sad for us around here.

We are heading through between Santa Cruz & Espiritu Santo tonight.

31 August '42 [New Entry]

The old lady is wallowing along at 10 kts—not even zigzagging, I suppose because she can't spare the distance. Makes me sick at heart to see her struggling along. Still flies off her patrols. *Navajo*, salvage tug, joined up tonight. This is *Sara*'s 2nd torpedoing, and 3rd torpedo, this war.

2 September '42

We have run South just E. of the New Hebrides and met the *Guadalupe* today about 120 miles E of Efate. All but the *Sara* are to fuel. We didn't get to today before dark, however. But mail was expected to leave in her, so the Wardroom gathered, as normal, to censor the outgoing. My god—one man had written 32 letters! What a session these censorings sometimes are.

3 September '42

0800 L.18–23 S., λ172–02 E. Fueled from *Guadalupe*—130,000 gals. She had 31 bags of mail for us—pleasant windfall. She got it in Pearl Harbor with no real information that she would ever see us here. Mine runs from 24 July to 7 August; the last previous batch came up to 8 July. So 16 days are blank—probably some of it around these various island bases. We didn't transfer mail to her, because we are designated to escort *Sara* all the way to Pearl Harbor, so will get there as soon as the tanker. To our surprise we got a new officer—Lee Gratton, Ens., D-V(S)—in her. What a tour he's had, on his way to us. We expect to lose Bud Newhall and Joe Wallace in Pearl, to go back for aviation—they are long overdue, on orders mailed out in June and received here August 18th, just before that engagement. Christ—BuPers [Bureau of Personnel] is certainly red hot with its orders.

Much depth charging today, of a reported sub contact. No word on how the DD's came out. At any rate, it now appears that it's likely they got the one the other day that got the *Sara*, because evidently her damage is not known to the enemy yet.

6 September 1942

Arrived at Nukualofa Anchorage, Tongatabu this morning. This small way station on the road to Australia (as the Japs have made the road lie, of course) is where we were last in harbor, July 24th. That is, if our 6 hour stop for fuel and a few stores can be counted. Actually the intervening 45 days have not been so bad—we've certainly gotten grooved in our sea routine.

The experts are to have a look at *Sara* here, apparently to see what's next. May be a few days. Meanwhile all hands provision up, but the brilliant staff work seems to have made a slight oversight in the small matter of fuel. There isn't any.

We gave half our depth changes to the *Monssen*—it was she who perhaps got the sub that got the *Sara*. Plenty of depth charging on the way here, some every day. At first people would go up on the topside to see the fun upon feeling the characteristic shudder through the ship. But it finally got so that few bothered. Our DD's were all low on ash cans on our arrival.

South Dakota & *Juneau* our Kearny sister are here. Headed back where we came from, I suppose. Came here direct from Panama. Got underway about 1300 to be on their way, after a hurried visit to us by *Juneau* officers to get the dope—then about 1600 came in again! Something had been changed.

Much mail here. Seems to be a collection of all that we have been missing all along, dating way into early July. All the 4th of July magazines with the flag on the cover.

7 Sept '42

One story on why *South Dakota* came back in is that she ran onto a coral head on the way out. Opened up her bottom some, salted her feed bottoms. Anyway, the *Juneau* has gone on again. I can't see why the *South Dakota* had to pick this way of taking herself off the credit side on our war-resources ledger, because it's no longer new. The *Boise* evaded Makassar Straits & Java this way—also, we lost the *Truxton* and a cargo ship at Argentia, on the rocks. There must still be a few original ways for us to throw away our ships, that she might have tried. I admit there are damn few ways left, though.

HMS *Achilles* came in today. Also, there are lots of transports here, whether loaded or not I don't know.

Sara is careened way over—looks like repairs to her hole are being made.

9 Sept '42

S.D. [*South Dakota*] apparently is pretty much busted up. The coral head was one that was supposed to have been blasted out, but wasn't quite. The ship was well over it before she touched, because of having an appreciable drag, so the damaged areas are back in the engineering spaces. She drove right on over and into deep water, which is lucky because otherwise she'd have hung up tighter'n hell. At any rate, the damage seems pretty serious and her fighting strength is definitely lost to us. She'll have to go to Pearl, or, if that's too crowded with cripples, to the states. She at least can escort the *Sara*, so we now are rushing to fuel up and get provisions and get back where we came from. With the *Yamato*, two of the *Haruna* class, and seven (count 'em) carriers of the little bastards gatherings down here, it looks like we're going to need everything we can get.

Anyway, the *Washington* is expected soon. God dammit, it's those babies that we need—something that can fight like <u>hell</u>, instead of dropping near misses and then running. Of course our wasted opportunities of last month are not only water of the dam, but water which after getting over the dam has started eroding the frail foundations of our bridges in this area. So that now when at last we get cornered and forced into a fight in this remote corner, far from the support of adequate bases, we can be sure that it will be under the most unfavorable conditions and against the worst kind of odds. However, I (perhaps foolishly) cling to the fond hope that some one of our admirals, some day, will force the fight—will go after these bastards at a time of our choosing, and with forces arrayed to our satisfaction, and will blow the bloody bastards clean to hell. And the *North Carolina* and *Washington* are some of what it takes to do that job.

Add stories on the *Sara*'s torpedoing: the sub fired from outside the DD screen, just ahead of the *Monaghan* (*MacDonough*—I forget which it was that was with us?). The DD saw her periscope immediately afterwards, still headed in. It came on in as the DD forged ahead, got in to very close to her outboard side, and according to our version, actually collided with and scraped along the side. The DD dropped DCs as she passed on over. But Christ—the Goddamn fools had them set on "Safe", and that's where they were when dropped! What any screening DD is doing with her ash-cans set on safe, I'll have to have explained in words of one syllable by some marvel at argument—but it seems that our fund of blunders is totally inexhaustible.

Plenty of shuffling in the commands, both high and low, is going to have to be done before this war gets in hand.

Have heard many stories of Tulagi action, by various of the people who were in there. There is no other way of describing the affair of the night of 8 August, other than to say that for the Japs, it was a brilliant and daring offensive strike, beautifully executed in the teeth of overpowering odds, taking perfect advantage of every bit of fumbling that our situation in there was sure to produce. For us, it was a humiliating and fearfully costly illustration of exactly what our whole course of action in that area couldn't help but do. The wolves got into the sheepfold in the dark, and the utter confusion, lack of action, total ineffectiveness and inefficiency, and of course the slaughter, were terrific.

***

At 0645 on August 29, *Atlanta*'s war diary noted, "Sighted Task Force 17 to eastward." Lloyd Mustin, having the deck as OOD when the sighting was made, had the pleasure of seeing the return of his recently promoted stepfather George Murray to sea duty as Commander Task Force 17 centered around the carrier *Hornet*. The carrier had been notably absent from the front lines over the previous two months. Following the battle of Midway, she returned to Pearl Harbor to receive new electronics, additional antiaircraft weapons, and additional provisions. In addition, Admiral Nimitz felt it prudent to maintain the carrier at Pearl as a strategic reserve.[1]

Perhaps Lloyd came off as cocky in his assertion that he was destined for flag rank so long as he survived the war and didn't offend too many people. However, as a mid-grade officer who had grown up in a Navy family, who had a flag officer stepfather as a "sea daddy," and had punched the right tickets regarding assignments at sea, Lloyd appreciated his standing with his peers. That the Navy had invested funds to educate him at MIT and support follow-on orientation at the Washington Navy Yard and Dahlgren added to his confidence. Indeed, Lloyd will make flag and someday serve as a mentor to his "little Henry" who would be later be known as "Hammering Hank."

Lloyd questions the efficiency and effectiveness of the Navy's Task Force Command structure. For administrative efficiency, the Navy had a "Type" commander where a junior flag officer or senior captain and a small staff would oversee ships of a similar type, such as destroyers or oilers, to assure they were logistically supported and to evaluate the capabilities of each of the ships and crews under his purview to rank the commanding officers for future promotion opportunities. To suddenly "dual hat" these type commanders and their staffs to perform combatant duties within the task force struck Lloyd as a folly and resulted in incompetent staff work.

At 0800 on August 30, *Atlanta*'s war diary reflected the shuffling of the ships. "Task Force 61 Op. Order 4-42 became effective and ATLANTA became a unit of Task Group 61.1 consisting of Vice Admiral Fletcher in SARATOGA,

NORTH CAROLINA, MINNEAPOLIS, NEW ORLEANS, PHELPS, DEWEY, FARRAGUT, MACDONOUGH, WORDEN, MONSSEN, and GRAYSON. HMAS AUSTRALIA, and HOBART plus PATTERSON and BAGLEY left disposition for new assignment." As Lloyd elaborated, the two Australian warships were reassigned to Task Force 18 built around the *Wasp*, and the two American destroyers departed to reinforce Rear Admiral Murray's screen around *Hornet*.

Subsequent war diary entries that day reflected *Atlanta* changed its station off *Saratoga* four times over the next nine hours as the carrier conducted flight operations.[2]

The next morning at 0655 with the task force located some 260 miles southeast of Guadalcanal, *Atlanta's* war diary noted a change of course and axis to 140 degrees true. "Took Station 2.5/315." The formation also slowed to 13 knots, a speed thought to give the escorting destroyers the best opportunity to attain underwater contacts on their respective sonar gear. Thus *Atlanta* was positioned nearly directly east of *Saratoga* at a range of 2,500 yards. Lloyd recalled heading up to the bridge that morning and hearing a torpedo alarm on the TBS voice radio. "I just about had enough time to look up and see an enormous pillar of spray rise into the air alongside *Saratoga*." *Atlanta's* war diary duly noted at 0747: "Observed torpedo hit on *Saratoga's* starboard quarter."[3]

As Lloyd noted, *Saratoga* and her group were steaming on a base course of 140 degrees true and were executing a zigzag plan along that course to disrupt a potential target solution, but Cdr. Minuru Yokota of *I-26* had enough time, following the most recent formation pivot to a course of 180 degrees true, to fire a spread. Though the torpedoes were spotted, the 13-knot speed of advance limited the ship that was built on a battle cruiser hull to take evasive action in time. The resultant puncture flooded a boiler room which was not operational at that moment and unmanned. Three decades later, Lloyd recalled: "... the terrific shock of this torpedo hit had damaged the electrical controls in her." With her turboelectric machinery jarred, *Saratoga* slowed and was soon "Dead In Water" (DIW). No Americans were killed—just 12 injured. Among the injured was Vice Admiral Fletcher who had been jolted up to bang his forehead on the bridge ceiling.

With the Japanese submarine launching her spread from the opposite side of the *Saratoga*, the next ship in line of the trajectories of the remaining two underwater missiles was *Atlanta*. As the General Quarters alarm sounded, lookouts spotted one torpedo pass astern and another ahead. *Atlanta* increased speed to 20 knots and steered various courses to guard the wounded flattop. As for the destroyer that failed to sink the Japanese submarine, Lloyd confuses the *Monaghan* and *MacDonough*. In subsequent narratives, *MacDonough* and *Monssen* pursued the elusive *I-26*. Subsequently, Lloyd writes of later transferring half of their depth charges to *Monssen*. Though he places the *Monaghan* with the group in his August 30 entry, the war diary lists the *MacDonough* as part of the task force. *I-26* apparently scraped the hull of *MacDonough* with her periscope during the attack. Years later, Lloyd recalled that the submarine "momentarily lost its depth control with the discharge of the salvo of some number of torpedoes that he had fired and broached underfoot of one of the destroyers over there on that side of the screen."[4]

Crippled, *Saratoga* with its unscathed flight deck, with a fair breeze, could still conduct flight operations while under tow and then at slow speed under her own power. Though the ship would be lost from the front lines for the next three months, her air wing would be distributed to Espiritu Santo, the carrier *Wasp*, and finally Guadalcanal, where the aircrews would join with those who had recently arrived from *Enterprise*.[5]

Lloyd Mustin's narrative from late August 31 through September 6 reflects what is reported in *Atlanta's* war diary, which noted the arrival of the salvage tug *Navajo* and destroyer *Laffey* late on September 1, the arrival of the oiler *Guadalupe* and destroyer *Dale* the next day, and notes on fueling from 0700 to 0847 the following morning. Later that day, on September 3, the war diary stated that the destroyers *MacDonough* and *Worden* dropped depth charges on a sonar contact with no results. Again the following morning, *MacDonough* rolled ash cans over the side with no success.[6]

At 0735 on September 6, *Atlanta's* war diary recorded, "Sighted Tongatabu bearing 115° (T) distant 15 miles." Nearly four hours later, *Atlanta* had anchored in berth 31 off Nukualofa, Tonga, and proceeded to receive provisions. In addition to supply boats, a launch from *Atlanta's* Kearny sister ship arrived with a contingent from her wardroom to meet with their counterparts to gain an appreciation to operating in the Southwest Pacific. That *Juneau* arrived with *South Dakota* provided an extra morale boost for Lloyd, who had longed for the inclusion of more 16-inch guns in the front-line arsenal. Lloyd was equally encouraged with news that the battleship *Washington* would soon be arriving.[7]

Lloyd anticipated that *Atlanta* would be assigned to escort *Saratoga* back to Pearl Harbor, but unfortunately *South Dakota* left that afternoon only to return a short while later having sustained an 18-inch-wide gash down the aft section of her underside thanks to running over a coral reef. *South Dakota* and *Saratoga* would remain at Tonga for another six days undergoing nominal repairs and evaluation in preparation for drydocking in Hawaii. Instead of *Atlanta*, the damaged *South Dakota* along with the cruiser *New Orleans* and five destroyers headed with *Saratoga* to Pearl Harbor.

Vice Admiral Fletcher also headed back to Pearl Harbor with the flotilla, eventually receiving orders for duty ashore. The frustration that American naval forces in the Southwest Pacific seemed reluctant to engage the Japanese extended beyond Lloyd's repeated diary entries. On August 19 Admiral Nimitz sent a message to

USS *Saratoga* (CV 3) receiving temporary repairs at Tongatabu, Tonga Islands, in September 1942 after being torpedoed by a Japanese submarine on August 31. Because the carrier had been hit on the starboard side amidships, it is assumed the list to port was deliberately caused to bring the damaged part of the carrier's hull out of the water. (Archives Branch, Naval History and Heritage Command, Washington, D.C.; 80-G-12967)

the Pacific that concluded: "We cannot expect to inflict heavy losses on the enemy without accepting the risk of punishment. To win this war we must come to grips with the enemy. Courage, determination and action will see us through."[8]

The diversion of Task Force 11 centered on *Saratoga* apparently stressed an already challenged fuel distribution chain. To keep her boilers fired, on September 9 *Atlanta* took black oil from the cruiser *New Orleans*.[9] During *Atlanta*'s one-week stay at Nukualofa, Tonga, the crew had the opportunity to go ashore for some well-earned liberty.

CHAPTER 20

Noumea

13 September

Sunday, as usual. Underway for Samoa (or at least, probably, a rendezvous off Samoa), where we are to join the escort of a convoy to Noumea. Fifteen kts, with no DD's! Seems just like asking for it, to me.

Saratoga left yesterday, with Newhall and Wallace aboard. In their places we have two reserves, Craighill (who has been aboard all along), and Grattan, our new arrival. We now have 5 regulars and 8 reserves in Gunnery—but that's O.K. with our Exec.

Sara may go to Bremerton for 2½ months work there! Add that to the time there and back, and the 12 days already thrown away on this business, and the real cost to us of that torpedo hit to which she was so callously exposed, begins to show up.

South Dakota went with her. Her loss to us may be considerable too—of course the fat-head skipper of the *Sumner* who reported we had blasted out the channel where she grounded, and had wire-dragged it to 40 feet, got a Navy Cross out of his supposed job, this tidy little contribution.

15 Sept

Picked up our rendezvous this morning—about 8 ships, including the *Matsonia* and *Lurline*, with just the *Detroit* as escort. Why in Christ's name the Japs don't make a killing on one of these I'll never know—some ships in the group only had 16–18 kts, and not a DD in sight. Met about 30 mi. S. of Pago Pago. The rest went on in to Pago; *Lassen* and *Hammondsport* are our sheep enroute for Noumea. With the *Lassen* (same as the *Rainier*) being presumably full of 4–5,000 tons of ammo, and the *Hammondsport* with her usual load of a hundred planes or so, we have a pretty valuable convoy.

More of this goddamn zigzagging by British convoy zigzag plans, and using their Merchant Signal Book (mersigs). Cumbersome damn stuff—why three U.S. Navy commissioned ships do this beats me—it was the same with *Rainier* & *Kaskaskia* when we brought them down this way from Pearl in May.

At dark tonight passed the *Kitty Hawk* (the other "aircraft transport" (APV), ex-Caribbean train ferry), headed the other way—going back for another load no doubt.

19 Sept '42

Arrived at Noumea; anchored in Dumbea Bay. No mail, no leave or liberty on account of an epidemic ashore. A pretty harbor though—many reefs around outside, then well inside their line the hilly promontories and island that make the harbors.

Our two U.S.N.A. '43 officers, Underwood and Colleran, came aboard. They've had quite a trek catching us—were in one of the transports that went into Tulagi 7 August, and later were in the *Enterprise* on 24 August. One to the Engineers, and one to Gunnery. Also a Lt. (jg) Hereford, U.S.N.R. whose total naval experience is zero—he just started in as a junior grade, expecting to go into the Supply Corps on account of his previous experience as a banker. Of course the Exec thinks it's all wonderful—we'll make a gunnery officer out of him—just any old officer can be a gunner. The goddamn stupid fool.

Hell of a lot of ships in here. There's going to be a killing made in here by the Japs before this war is over, and I just hope it doesn't happen until after we get the hell outa here.

***

Marmaduke Gresham Bayne, a graduate of the University of Tennessee, entered the Navy through the V-7 program, and after receiving his naval reserve commission, commanded a patrol boat on anti-submarine duty off the East Coast. Bayne then applied and was accepted to attend submarine school, eventually receiving orders to the submarine *Becuna* for a successful war patrol in the Pacific. At the end of the war, Bayne declined an acceptance to graduate school at Harvard to apply instead for a regular commission in the Navy. Appearing before an Augmentation Board consisting of three senior officers—all graduates of the Naval Academy—Bayne was given a hypothetical scenario of 10 years down the line where he and two Naval Academy graduates would be recommended for a very fine assignment and asked: "Who do you think would be the third choice for that good assignment?"

Bayne responded: "If in ten years the people who made decisions about those jobs were only Naval Academy graduates, I would have made a bad decision making the Navy a career, but I suspect by then people like me who had fought in the war and then augmented into the regular Navy would be having a say about such assignments." Bayne would retire as a vice admiral.[1]

If Lloyd Mustin had a bias against naval reserve officers he would have likely confessed "guilty as charged." However, the reality of the war and the rapid expansion of the Navy dictated that the Navy commission officers from sources other than the Naval Academy or NROTC. It should also be noted that even officers from those traditional sources were not as polished. Ensigns Underwood and Colleran of the Naval Academy's Class of 1943 graduated a year early. Colleran still had a month to go before he turned 21. In contrast, though lacking the experience of Annapolis, the V-7 program attracted many young men with at least two years of college education and experience in the civilian sector, which offered the Navy a more mature individual that could better relate to many of the sailors from similar backgrounds whom they were assigned to lead.

As the war progressed, the quality of stateside training combined with combat experience blurred the difference between Annapolis graduates and officers commissioned through the naval reserve. Toward the end of the war Admiral Halsey stated: "I do not know which of my officers are reserves." Illustrating why this was so, the percentage of department heads having USNR commissions on major combatants ranged from 41 to 50 percent.[2]

However, in the summer of 1942, these future department heads were serving as junior officers in *Atlanta* and other fleet units and would have to prove themselves to their more senior Annapolis brethren. Robert Graff reflected, "There really was a line between those people who graduated from Annapolis and those people who were civilians in uniform and the line was in all kinds of ways, but it was there and you knew you were there on sufferance, if you like, because this was their ship and their navy, and you were coming over the transom." Having said that, Graff acknowledged that many of the better senior officers would take "a shine" to the V-7 90-day wonders and take it upon themselves to make the new officers "their ensigns." This also extended off-ship where Annapolis wives embraced the spouses of the naval reserve ensigns to indoctrinate them on social norms and expectations.[3]

Atlanta's war diary and dog log echoed Lloyd's summary of the voyage to Noumea, faithfully recording all course changes that were dictated by the Merchant Signals Book. What Lloyd's narrative and the war diary both overlooked was a transformation of the situation regarding Guadalcanal that further challenged the Americans.

After the failed effort to resupply Guadalcanal as an outcome of the battle of the eastern Solomons, Rear Adm. Shintaro Hashimoto relieved Rear Admiral Tanaka of command of the Japanese reinforcement effort and changed tactics. Rather than using freighters or towed barges that would be exposed during daylight hours, Hashimoto employed speedy destroyers to carry soldiers down the slot, minimizing daytime exposure. On the last hour of the last day of August, Gen. Kiyotaki Kawaguchi disembarked off the destroyer *Umikaze*, joined by nearly 1,200 soldiers who had ridden with him and on seven other Japanese tin cans.

So began what became known as the "Tokyo Express," an almost nightly arrival of Japanese destroyers loaded with solders and supplies. Having discharged their human and materiel cargoes, the Japanese warships would serenade the Marines ashore with an early morning bombardment. In addition, to suppress the American air threat, the Japanese also ran almost daily bombing raids against Henderson Field. Fortunately, the daylight flight requirements for the squadrons of Betty bombers that were used dictated a predictable midday arrival that was forewarned by coast watchers stationed along the flightpath and an SCR 270 air search radar. Thus the bombers often arrived over an airfield devoid of flyable aircraft, having been forced to fend off attacks from many of the conglomeration of what was known as the Cactus Air Force.

As *Atlanta* got underway at 0700 on the morning of September 13 for the approximately 1,200-mile westward trek to the port of Noumea located on the southeastern end of New Caledonia, Marine defenders under the command of Lt. Col. Merritt Edson were assessing the outcome of what had been an aborted Japanese assault. On the previous day, General Kawaguchi committed his fresh troops for a thrust up the center of the island to occupy the northern plain and take Henderson Field. Edson's Marine defenders used the terrain south of the airfield to tactical advantage. However, what thwarted Kawaguchi's initial assault on the evening of September 12 had more to do with the Japanese general's loss of command and control of his advancing battalions who found themselves lost in the jungle, though American artillery gutted one Japanese advance that had split the American line. On September 13 Edson positioned his Marines further up the ridge line and dug in. That evening, well-coordinated use of artillery, mortars, machine-gun fire, and marksmanship combined to thwart the brunt of Kawaguchi's well-coordinated assault. Tenacious Japanese soldiers made some advances, briefly overrunning a secondary airstrip under construction with some infiltrators gunned down within 20 yards of General Vandegrift's tent. The action, which became known as the battle of Edson's Ridge, only served to reinforce a belief within the Imperial General Headquarters that control of Guadalcanal was a numbers games that ultimately would be decided by which belligerent was quicker to land overwhelming ground forces.[4]

The Americans made the same assessment. As *Atlanta* met up with the convoy it was to escort on the morning of September 15, another flotilla of escorted transport ships were steaming toward Guadalcanal from a previous day's departure from Espiritu Santo with the reinforced 7th Marine Regiment.[5]

Loss of USS *Wasp*

20 Sept

Ah me! I've exhausted my vocabulary of terms to express the lowness of my opinion for the conduct of the war in the South Pacific. Damned discouraging, because another new low has been reached!

The *Wasp* has been sunk!

It all happened at dear old "Torpedo Junction"—our beloved area South of the Solomons where our carriers have been under orders to steam back and forth endlessly, waiting for the Japs to get all ready to take a crack at them, and assembling everything, air, surface, and sub-surface, that they've got to do it with. In other words, right where the *Saratoga* got it on 31 August.

But the *Wasp* got 3 fish, and now is no more. The beach here is crowded with her survivors. The *Saratoga* showed signs that the torpedo that hit her must have been one of the babies with 800 pounds of Lexomite in the warhead, and I think three of those would finish the *Wasp* with ease.

Somewhere along the line the *North Carolina* apparently got one too, because she's on her way home for repairs.

If anyone in the Atlantic were to be told the story of what measures have been standard in this outfit for giving anti-sub protection, I don't think they'd believe it. The sheer bumbling stupidity is just too much for comprehension. And boy—how it has now paid off.

Frank Jack Fletcher can't add these latest to his toll, which no doubt already exceeds in tonnage all losses in previous wars through the history of the U.S. Navy, and of course easily tops Kimmel's Pearl Harbor exhibition. Leigh Noyes, a communicator who succeeded as No. 1 now that Fletcher has been recalled to Pearl, must take the credit. But boy, between them they have certainly fixed up the Pacific Fleet. Christ, we haven't got one any more—a few old BB's that they're scared to take the wraps off of, some scattered cruisers here and there, and the *Hornet*.

One CV here now, to the Japs seven-plus; no BB's to their three-odd—the position of our naval forces in the Solomon Island area would now appear to me to have been rendered truly untenable. The beautiful result of another long series of unmitigated bungles.

Just incidentally, the *O'Brien* (DD 415), in the *Hornet* outfit, has also apparently soaked up a fish which raised hell with her. Jesus H. Christ—we are making a wonderful effort to give away this war.

At any rate, we managed to turn in our star shells here to the *Rainier*, in exchange for some we hope will work. We certainly would have been in a wonderful fix if we'd attempted any night star-shell illumination. Of the 45 or so of our service stars that we've fired, only two have functioned properly.

***

When Vice Admiral Fletcher departed the scene with *Saratoga*, Rear Adm. Leigh Noyes assumed command of Task Force 61, becoming the ranking carrier commander in overall command of the carrier support forces in the Southwest Pacific. A graduate of the Naval Academy Class of 1906, Noyes was a latecomer to naval aviation, earning his wings of gold in 1937 following his command of a cruiser. With his aviator's ticket punched, he received orders to command *Lexington*. During the attack on Pearl Harbor he served as Director of Naval Communications in Washington. Arriving at Pearl Harbor, Noyes was assigned to Vice Admiral Halsey's staff and could have been a logical choice to succeed Halsey as Task Force 16 commander at Midway; however, Halsey recommended Spruance. Eventually, with the arrival of *Wasp* from the Atlantic Fleet, Noyes took charge of Task Force 18 centered on *Wasp*. With Fletcher's departure Noyes flew his Task Force 61 flag from *Wasp*.[1]

As previously noted, a convoy of five ships carrying the reinforced 7th Marines—protected by the carriers *Wasp* and *Hornet* and escorts including battleship *North Carolina*—had departed Espiritu Santo early on September 14, and rather than steam the direct 600-plus-mile route to the northwest to Guadalcanal, elected to steam to the northeast to evade Japanese scout planes and then turn west to dash toward their objective. However, having been spotted by a large Japanese floatplane late morning of September 15, the logistics force commander, Rear Admiral Turner, considered a course reversal to protect his precious cargoes of Leatherneck livestock from Japanese air attack. At the time his transports were on their westward leg, steaming on behind the two carriers *Wasp* and *Hornet*, each operating independently within their separate screening circles of screening combatants. The two carriers proceeded on parallel courses 7–10 miles apart when at 1420 both carriers turned to the southeast to catch the prevailing oncoming winds needed to assist with flight operations.[2]

Unfortunately for the Americans, the Japanese also deployed submarines to intercept reinforcement efforts as well as locate and destroy American combatants. An hour and a half before the carriers changed course to launch and land aircraft, Cdr. Takatchi Kinashi in *I-19* received reports of propeller noise and popped his periscope up into choppy seas that masked its presence to lookouts on *Wasp* and her escorts.

After 12 minutes in which *Wasp* launched 26 aircraft and then recovered 11, Capt. Forrest Sherman came to starboard to resume a westerly heading. In doing so he steered his carrier into an easy firing solution for *I-19*. Kinashi prepared to launch a spread of six Type 95 torpedoes. A close cousin to the famed Type 93 Long Lance torpedoes that exacted a toll at Savo Island, the Type 95 had a smaller diameter to fit in a 21-inch tube. Dependent on the variant, the torpedo was the fastest in the world, with speeds ranging from 45 to 51 knots, and as Lloyd noted, a powerful warhead. However, the feature that literally outdistanced it from the competition was its range, which varied between 4½ and 6 nautical miles—triple that of its "Made in the USA" Mark 14 counterpart.

To dispose of *Wasp* Kinashi did not need that range, as upon the completion of flight operations at 1442, the carrier turned toward him and closed to 1,000 yards when he fired his six fish. Watch standers on the flag bridge helplessly watched the incoming torpedo wakes. Forewarned, Rear Admiral Noyes braced for the shock. Contrary to Lloyd's narrative, only two torpedoes struck *Wasp* on the starboard side forward, landing punches into gasoline stowage tanks and abreast of the forward bomb magazine. Two proved to be more than enough though, as topside aircraft flipped up like hotcakes, and planes stowed in the hangar overhead came crashing down on aircraft being serviced on the hangar deck. Volatile aviation gasoline pouring out cracked tanks mixed with more high-octane fuel gushing from ruptured fueling stations, creating a combustible vapor that quickly ignited as the below waterline inferno caused by the two torpedoes shot up through the forward part of the ship.[3]

From the bridge wing of the *Hornet*, where Lloyd's stepdad stood as Commander Task Force 17, it appeared a volcano had erupted on the horizon as a billowing blackish plume soared into the cloudy sky. Unfortunately, the *Hornet* formation was steaming into the path of the remaining speeding Type 95s. Five minutes after the first two torpedoes achieved their objective, a lookout in *O'Brien* spotted the wake of one of the fish, and a hard-right rudder only dodged fate for a few seconds as another underwater missile caught the destroyer's port bow. The resultant explosion, throwing up smoke and sea spray, temporarily masked the small combatant from the rest of the formation, but the physical damage seemed limited on the unoccupied anchor chain locker. However, the shock wave that shot back to the stern, merely wounding two bluejackets, caused structural stresses within the hull that ultimately proved fatal. After steaming nearly another 3,000 miles some 35 days later, while en route for permanent repairs in San Francisco, *O'Brien*'s bottom gave out. All hands were saved.[4]

USS *Wasp* (CV 7) ablaze and sinking after being torpedoed by a Japanese submarine as seen from USS *San Francisco* (CA 38). (Archives Branch, Naval History and Heritage Command, Washington, D.C.; 80-G-391481)

More profound in the short term, a minute after *O'Brien* sustained what would be a fatal nick on her fo'c'sle, *North Carolina* took a port-side blow abreast of her forward turret housing a forward battery of three 16-inch guns. Again, George Murray on *Hornet* must have felt a sense of increasing horror as he viewed a plume of water mixed with black oil shoot up past the height of the new battlewagon's funnels. The powerful warhead ripped a gaping hole below the waterline large enough to drive a truck into. As a precaution, the forward magazine loaded with shells and powder bags was flooded. To counterbalance the 5.6-degree list, starboard compartments were flooded. Despite the blow that claimed six sailors, the ship that had earned the nickname "Show Boat" was able to continue steaming at 26 knots but would need to divert to Pearl Harbor for repairs.[5]

Back on *Wasp*, the situation transitioned from grim to desperate. Captain Sherman turned the carrier and ordered backing bells to allow the prevalent winds to blow the flames and smoke away from the unscathed aft section. However, at 1505, another vapor-explosion enveloped three sides of the island, and five minutes later another blast blew out the number two elevator. The ship continued to quake as

Rear Adm. Richmond Kelly Turner, USN (left), working on the flag bridge of USS *McCawley* (AP 10), with Major Gen. Alexander A. Vandegrift looking over his shoulder. (Archives Branch, Naval History and Heritage Command, Washington, D.C.; 80-CF-112-4-63)

bombs in the forward magazines cooked off, causing further eruptions. With a half hour passing since the torpedo hits, Captain Sherman consulted with his executive officer Cdr. Fred C. Dickey and then consulted Rear Admiral Noyes of his intent to abandon ship.

With the order given at 1520, 40 minutes transpired as 1,946 of a crew of 2,247 were able to leave off the stern section before Captain Sherman lowered himself into the Pacific. Mindful of the Japanese submarine threat, the crews of the destroyers *Laffey*, *Lansdowne*, and cruiser *Helena* skillfully picked up the survivors and tended to the wounded.

That evening *Lansdowne* attempted to scuttle the blazing ship, hitting *Wasp* with three torpedoes. However, the carrier continued to burn on in defiance, until finally at 2100 she began to settle by the bow.[6]

Having suffered crippling blows on September 15, the remaining carrier in the Southwest Pacific, *Hornet*, her escorts, and the screening ships that had picked up the carrier's survivors now headed to Noumea where Lloyd learned of the fiasco.

Rear Admiral Turner, with his transports, took a calculated risk to continue on without the escort. On the evening that *Wasp* went under, the Japanese offloaded another 1,000 soldiers from seven destroyers which subsequently harassed the American garrison with gunfire. Knowing of this, Turner correctly guessed that he could arrive at Cactus early on September 18, and by 0700, fresh Marines were going ashore. Eleven hours later, 4,157 Marines, 137 vehicles, 4,323 barrels of fuel, rations, tents, and other supplies were ashore and wounded evacuees embarked for departure. That night, Japanese destroyers returned to drop another 170 soldiers and then patrolled in vain to catch Turner's long-departed vessels, only to greet the newcomers with a harassing bombardment.[7]

CHAPTER 22

TF 17 and Tongatabu

21 Sept '42

Underway to join TF 17 (George still in command) at a rendezvous East of the New Hebrides. We are in TF 66.4, with *Helena* and *Salt Lake City* and *Lansdowne* (486), *Benham* (397), and *Walke* (416).

23 Sept

Joined TF 17 this morning. Quite an aggregation, with DD's fueling from the heavy ships. Rendezvous at 0900 was about 200 mi. E. of Efate. 1800 tonight *San Francisco, Salt Lake City, Helena,* and four DD's shoved off for parts unknown, on course about 300. I hoped they were to be a detached cruiser striking force to work 100 mi. or so toward the enemy from us and raise a little hell, but that seems too good to be true. As long as this war is run by Admirals at desks somewhere out of the operating areas we can be sure no dash or drive will ever be allowed to be shown.

Anyway, there remains the *Hornet, Washington, Northampton, Pensacola, Atlanta, Juneau, San Diego* and about ten DD's, including the *Mustin* and also including some brand new babies—haven't got them all straight yet.

George has out a batch of new orders amplifying instructions for various situations. Most important & valuable, this class is treated separately in AA defense and stationed to take advantage of our special characteristics. With 3 of us here, an air attack should certainly be met with a startling display—the *Washington* adding no small two cents worth. Unfortunately we are still on the alleged "defensive" mission of protecting a line of communications, which means no advantage can be taken of the power of the force, and it all just comes back to a question of time before the next torpedo hit.

24 Sept

Got a message this morning from George saying he was glad to have two Mustins (meaning me and the destroyer) in his outfit. And about that time, in accordance with what orders we have no idea. *Washington* (CombatDiv 6) shoves off for Tongatabu at 19 knots, telling *Benham*, *Walke*, and ourselves to follow.

26 Sept

Back in Tongatabu; arrived 1000 today. Nothing much here—the *Vestal* and the *Barnett*. No clues as to why we're here but lots of guesses. I wouldn't be surprised if a carrier were due, with which we'd form a task force. Either that or some special mission—the assignment of the *Atlanta* and the *Washington* to a job certainly indicates that something special is up.

29 Sept

Morgan Wesson and some of the junior officers had a couple of Army nurses from the hospital, ashore, out to dinner tonight. First females, white, black, or indifferent, that I've seen since some indeterminate time in July, when a couple were in sight at the Officer's Club at Pearl.

They seem to have quite a hospital here, with 50-some nurses. All tents now, but when the buildings are completed there'll be about 40 of them.

30 Sept

This A.M. the press carried, under a Pearl Harbor dateline, a quotation by "Vice Admiral Halsey, Senior PacFlt TF Commander." Best shot in the arm we've had in a long time, to think maybe he's back to duty. Speculation: maybe he'll come down in the *Enterprise* when she's repaired and join with us to make old Task Force Sixteen again. If so, stand clear, Tojo.

6 October

Got our first mail today since that that was here for us when we came in on Sept. 6. This mail comes up to 12 Sept., but there was only a very little bit, and at least 3 weeks worth in August are missing. The mail situation down here is really a monument to the total ineffectiveness of Ghormley's staff work.

A dispatch in last night's traffic from Com Gen. Guadalcanal ("Cactus") is illuminating. This one reports the landing of 1,300 Japs from 5 DD's, apparently a larger force than their usual almost daily landings. He now says he is unable to handle the situation; they are coming faster than he can get hold of them; his most intense aerial activity cannot prevent their coming. In other words, just once again are we having the usual lesson on one of the limitations of air power that has been forgotten in the blind swing of the pendulum. Also, in other words too, the situation is now rapidly shaping up just as I said it would, and the almost totally free coming & going of the Japs is making itself felt. ComGen urgently recommends that a surface striking force support him by taking action against these bastards. What dough-head will do about it remains to be seen—no doubt there will be much trembling at the thought of letting a surface force operate within 500 miles of Rabaul. They probably think it's done with mirrors or something. When the Japs come right in to the same damn island we have our air base on, with surface forces, and get away with landing troops. Or, more likely, they just don't think about it—or anything else.

7 October

Underway for points west, with *Washington*, *Benham* (397), and *Walke* (416). We are Task Group 17.8. May rendezvous with TF 17, or, maybe, we will operate independently—the two-months overdue surface striking force that this area has needed. God knows we can be a honey of one—give us a couple more cans and we are almost invincible. Too fast for much danger from air attack, too powerful in AA for those that try anything, to get in except at prohibitive cost, and just plain poison for the surface outfits we meet. Of course this is all wishful thinking—Ghormley couldn't produce such an obviously potent plan of activity. God no! There would be "risk" in it! Much better to keep all the ships "safe"—have them steam slowly back and forth at Torpedo Junction there, South of the Solomons, doing nothing venturesome like picking on inferior Jap groups, but instead staying clear away from everything but a few paltry subs, which have only, so far, in that area, wrecked the *North Carolina* and *Saratoga* and sunk the *Wasp*. (Jesus Christ, what end does he think he gained, to compensate for that?)

Twelve days in Tongatabu! Whew.

9 October 1942

Went through between Efate and Eromanga during my watch, the first dog, and into the Coral Sea again. We had a false (so it proved) sub contact as we went through just to liven things up and remind us all where we were.

Combatdiv 6 got his "further orders" today in a code we don't have, so we're still in the dark. Course 290, tonight then fuel the DD's in the morning, out of the *Washington*. Maybe, but only maybe we are going up toward Bougainville to raise a little hell. The situation in Cactus seems to be getting bad fast now—Jap landings continue unchecked. Something has got to be done. TF 17 raided Buin and Faisi the other day by air. Full carrier attack group (air) got one hit, on a reported CA (probably a DD). The continuous contact reports on Jap forces moving all over the area show that they haven't been scared off, not by a damn mile. Guadalcanal is going to be another Wake Island if fathead Ghormley doesn't get off his lard and make a move.

✳✳✳

Elsewhere in the world, Gen. Erwin Rommel's famed Afrika Korps was pushing the British 8th Army back into Egypt where its new commander, Field Marshal Bernard Montgomery, assembled a numerically superior force that would be employed in a successful counter-offensive at the end of October at El Alamein. To support the eventual ouster of Axis forces from North Africa, the United States made preparations along the eastern seaboard for a cross-Atlantic thrust at Morocco. In Eurasia, the German 6th Army continued operations aimed at the conquest of Stalingrad and the destruction of Red Army forces defending the city. In Asia, Chinese and British forces continued to defend against further Japanese army forays deeper into the mainland and in Burma.

As climactic turning points in the war loomed on the horizon in the struggle against the Third Reich, a consensus was reached by Japanese military leaders that Guadalcanal represented such a turning point that called for all-out victory. Imperial Japanese Army units were reassigned. With the German thrust into the Caucasus drawing Red Army reserves stationed in the Siberia, even Japanese troops stationed in Manchuria could be redirected to the Southwest Pacific.[1]

However, for a few weeks the greater struggle for Guadalcanal would be placed on hold, leaving the ground forces of the two belligerents to continue to battle for acres of jungle. For the United States, now down to one aircraft carrier, the prudent strategy was to remain out of harm's way. Thus, on September 21, *Atlanta* got underway and joined with *Helena* and *Salt Lake City* to rendezvous with Task Force 17 centered on *Hornet*. After a day of steaming where the three cruisers conducted gunnery exercises, on the morning of September 23 Lloyd found himself in company with two of *Atlanta*'s AA gun-laden sister ships as well as the battleship *Washington*, which had recently arrived from the East Coast, guarding the carrier from air attack while a screen of destroyers that included the *Mustin* sought to engage Japanese submarines before their torpedoes could score another crippling blow. Rear Adm. George Murray acknowledged his stepson's presence, with the message early on September 24; however, that message proved to be more of a farewell, as at 0724, *Washington, Atlanta, Walke,* and *Benham* received orders to proceed to Nukualofa, Tonga. For the *Washington,* this represented a return trip, as the newly arrived battleship had briefly stopped at Nukualofa to pick up Rear Adm. Willis A. "Ching" Lee.[2]

Meanwhile, extraterrestrial factors slowed Japanese reinforcement activity. An approaching full moon glimmered light off the ocean waters, making nighttime interdiction flights from Henderson Field a threat to Tokyo Express operations. On the evening of September 20, four barge-towing Japanese destroyers were attacked by 10 Henderson-based Dauntlesses, slightly damaging *Shikinami.* The next night four more Japanese tin cans came under fire from above, with strafing causing flooding in *Kagero.* On September 24, the Japanese attempted one more supply run down the slot. Bomb splinters damaged two Japanese destroyers, killing or wounding over a dozen sailors.[3]

Given the danger of Henderson's night fliers, the Japanese chose to wait for the dimming of the nocturnal lightbulb in October before attempting further reinforcement operations. Meanwhile, both sides continued to reinforce their air strength in the region, and the Japanese pressed ahead with bombing and strafing attacks on Henderson Field. The long flight from Rabaul meant the Japanese would meet American resistance well before arrival over Henderson. In addition, the Japanese airfields were not immune to harassing attacks from B-17s assigned to General MacArthur's Army Air Forces. An important factor that would assist the Japanese in the forthcoming reinforcement effort was the completion of an airstrip at Buin on the southeastern tip of Bougainville Island. Located along the slot and nearly halving the distance to Guadalcanal, the new airfield would allow the Japanese to employ the Model 32 short-range Zero that simply lacked the range to fly from Rabaul. In addition, longer-range Type 21 Zeros could fly from Buin and loiter over Guadalcanal, providing support to Japanese troops ashore.[4]

As these preparations proceeded for what would become the next climactic point in the struggle for Guadalcanal, Lloyd found himself parked with the Navy's only fast battleship in the region at Tonga, for 11 days, apparently for fuel-conservation purposes.

For Lloyd, the voyage to Nukualofa provided an opportunity to conduct target practice and witness the broadsides of *Washington,* as *Atlanta* served as the target ship for the battleship's gunnery exercises. Early on September 25, *Washington* and *Walke* broke away to a position 35,000 yards distant, a distance that placed the battleship beyond the horizon with the exception of the top of her mast. Lloyd recalled he stationed himself on the fantail of the light cruiser with a measuring device to report back where "these projectiles landed relative to where they were supposed to land."

Lloyd recalled it was one of those "typically bright sunny South Pacific days," and when the *Washington* fired, he described what he saw:

... this enormous blast of familiar yellowish brown muzzle smoke from the guns. After a predictable lapse of time, crash would be the salvo landing in our wake. The first sound you would hear would come after that ... the familiar crack of the projectiles in the air at supersonic speed, and then finally the last thing you'd hear would be the sound of the guns firing over the horizon.[5]

As the sister ship of the *North Carolina* continued to fire salvos, Lloyd could only stand back in awe. "These salvo patterns would be very tight and very small ... the second thing was they came right down on the wake—they didn't come over or short ... meaning that the *Washington*'s battery was beautifully aligned and beautifully calibrated."[6]

No doubt the feedback from *Atlanta* must have pleased Rear Admiral Lee, who took keen pride in marksmanship, having honed his skills on the Naval Academy's rifle team. Subsequently participating at the 1920 Summer Olympic Games at Antwerp, Lee earned five gold medals, plus a silver and a bronze. Lloyd admired Lee, who was open to the potential advantages of new technologies such as radar.[7]

Arriving at Tongatabu (or Tonga) on the morning of September 26, the light cruiser anchored at berth 22 at 1000 and Captain Jenkins allowed half of the crew to go ashore on liberty. Those who did not get ashore on September 26 had the opportunity the next day, a peaceful Sunday. The following day *Atlanta* got underway in the late afternoon to pull alongside *Sabine* to refuel. Taking on black oil from the fleet oiler's other side was the battleship *Washington*. The next morning at 0600 the light cruiser broke off from the oiler and shifted to berth 23, and a portion of the crew was again allowed to go ashore on liberty. Meeting Army nurses ashore, Ensign Wesson invited the caregivers for dinner on the light cruiser—an invitation gladly accepted.[8]

Though Lloyd noted the embarkation of Army nurses for dinner in *Atlanta*'s wardroom, he chose not to write about his trip over to *Washington* during his time in Tonga that likely occurred when the two warships refueled together from *Sabine*. New ships in theater always sought "the dope" and *Washington* was no different. One of the gunnery officers in *Washington*, Lt. Cdr. Ed Hooper, one of Lloyd's colleagues at MIT, recommended to his XO, Commander O'Brien, that Lloyd be sent over. Summoned by his XO, Commander Emory, Lloyd complied with the invitation. That Emory did not hesitate to send Lloyd Mustin instead of the more senior gun boss, Lt. Cdr. Bill Nickelson, probably had much to do with *Atlanta*'s Gunnery Department head being "one of the most inarticulate people you could ever know." In addition, Lloyd Mustin noted that Bill Nickelson, who graduated Annapolis with the Class of '27, had gunnery experience in World War I vintage "four-piper" flush deck destroyers, ancient in comparison to the 5-inch 38-caliber mounts that *Atlanta* carried as a main battery and *Washington* as a secondary.[9]

For Lloyd, it was his first time on the battleship that had spent the earlier part of the year over in Great Britain to reinforce the Royal Navy to prevent the *Tirpitz* from attacking Allied shipping. He had visited the sister ship many times while *Atlanta* and *North Carolina* were berthed in Brooklyn, to share many a cup of coffee with another MIT graduate, Corky Ward, to discuss the systems that were being fitting on both ships.

Once aboard, Lloyd was hustled into the wardroom, where Ed Hooper had gathered the key gunnery department officers as well as some others, including the XO. He recalled his talk as quite informal, going through *Atlanta*'s past five months in the Pacific in chronological order. Ironically, during that time the light cruiser had only directly engaged enemy aviation at the battle of the eastern Solomons, yet Lloyd had insights about gun and radar performance, how to best employ ships with differing capabilities, and eventually he provided his narrative of the Guadalcanal campaign and how it came to the United States operating with just one carrier left in the South Pacific. As Lloyd spoke into his fourth hour during the ongoing give-and-take, he noted the wardroom continued to fill as he gave his candid assessment of the lack of spine shown by some of the Navy's senior leaders, with particularly harsh words about Vice Admiral Fletcher.

The battleship's XO had heard enough and called out the guest speaker for being insubordinate. Lloyd recalled: "He took considerable exception to not the facts as it happened but to my presuming to describe it as turning tail on a magnificent opportunity." Despite O'Brien's dress down, Lloyd maintained his views. When Commander O'Brien brought the topic of Lieutenant Commander Mustin's perceived insubordination to *Atlanta*'s skipper's attention, Captain Jenkins brushed him off.[10]

What ultimately proved Lloyd's salvation was that others in much higher pay grades shared his assessment of the direction of the naval operations. His mention on September 30 of the news item that described Vice Admiral Halsey as a Pacific Fleet task force commander proved prescient.

A day prior to Lloyd's September 29 entry, Admiral Nimitz arrived by seaplane to Noumea to meet with his Southwest Pacific commander and other senior leaders in Vice Admiral Ghormley's flagship, *Argonne*. Looking at Ghormley's deployment of forces, Nimitz expressed dismay. As Lloyd noted in his September 23 diary entry, the cruisers *San Francisco*, *Salt Lake City*, *Helena*, and four destroyers had been detached as a striking force to operate closer to the Japanese and perhaps "raise a little hell."[11]

This flotilla of gunships, designated as Task Force 64, was placed in command of Rear Adm. Norman Scott. A 1911 graduate of Annapolis, Scott did not shirk a fight, having earned national recognition as an intercollegiate fencing champion. As Task Force 64 struck out on its own, Scott began his own series of exercises, employing the same sort of offset firing drills that Lloyd had witnessed with *Washington*.

However, in the week following their detachment, Nimitz noted they had not been operating close enough to the contested waters off Guadalcanal to make an impact, being too far south to "do much about visiting enemy ships." Nimitz was also frustrated that his lone battleship in the region, *Washington*, was at Tonga, some 1,800 miles from the fighting, "so far removed from the critical area that she might have been in Pearl or San Francisco."[12]

While presiding over the conclave, Nimitz sized up Ghormley, who lacked a firm command of the facts and seemed to have been drained from a self-imposed confinement within *Argonne*'s flag quarters. The defeat at Savo Island had instilled a sense of defeatism that could be discerned in the discussion. Nimitz could not obtain a satisfactory response to why Ghormley had not attempted a surface ship interdiction of the Tokyo Express.[13]

The next day Nimitz flew to Guadalcanal to meet with General Vandegrift and spend the night. After presenting well-deserved medals the next morning to a number of the ground defenders and aviators who had performed brilliantly in the harshest combat conditions, the Pacific Fleet commander flew to Espiritu Santo for another overnight and then returned to Noumea and shared with Ghormley a laundry list of areas that required improvement. Among the items on the list that Lloyd had long noted as a failing was mail distribution. That Ghormley had yet to set foot on Guadalcanal nearly two months after the first landings only enforced Nimitz's lowering esteem of his commander. Then Nimitz further learned that Ghormley had been hesitant to respond to a request from Washington for preliminary plans for follow-on operations after Guadalcanal. As he prepared to depart Noumea for Pearl Harbor, Nimitz pressed Ghormley to include his assessment of who should be accountable for the Savo Island debacle.[14] As Nimitz winged his way back to Hawaii, he thought about accountability on a broader scale.

As Lloyd remained at Tonga and September turned to October, nighttime celestial conditions enabled the Japanese to resume their nighttime sojourns down the slot with stepped-up daytime air raids in support. On the evening of October 1, three destroyers delivered Major Gen. Yumio Nasu, his headquarters staff, and an infantry regiment. The next morning the Japanese shifted air tactics. Rather than use bombers escorted by fighters to attempt to attack American airpower at Henderson Field, the Japanese used bombers as a feint and swept in with Zeros to overwhelm the Cactus Air Force in a series of air duels where the Japanese enjoyed modest success. That night five more destroyers offloaded troops and supplies to further bolster Japanese forces facing Vandegrift's Marines.

On October 3, the Americans adjusted to the Japanese shift in tactics, and Marine Wildcats climbed to gain an altitude advantage on the incoming Zeros. A third of the 27 Japanese fighters that took part in the raid never returned to Rabaul. That evening a combination of Tokyo Express runs featured a seaplane tender, and nine destroyers delivered over 800 more troops, artillery pieces, and over 30 tons of supplies. A night raid by Henderson Field-based Navy dive-bombers on the offloading Japanese vessels did cause the Japanese seaplane tender to abort her mission.

No enemy air raid on October 4, but once again that evening, five Japanese destroyers added 750 troops and 24 tons of supplies to reinforce their army brethren who were strengthening their positions around the American perimeter. This conforms to the report that Lloyd cited from General Vandegrift in his October 6 diary entry, only that Vandegrift's numbers nearly doubled that of what went ashore.

To stem the flow of Japanese forces down the slot, on October 5 Lloyd's stepfather, embarked in *Hornet*, received orders from Vice Admiral Ghormley to raid Japanese shipping massed at Shortland Island. Lloyd refers to these raids in his October 9 entry. Meanwhile, Army Air Force B-17s and Henderson-based aircraft would attack other Japanese shipping hubs. Unfortunately, inclement weather nullified any chance for a productive day.

Thus the Tokyo Express continued on schedule that evening, with six destroyers sent carrying 650 men and a pair of artillery pieces. Henderson Field-based Dauntlesses caught two of the destroyers on the inbound leg, forcing one to depart with heavy damage and the other suffering a damaged bow thanks to bomb fragments. A third destroyer detached to escort the heavily damaged combatant, meaning that evening only three Japanese tin cans were able to make their deliveries.

No disruptions to the Japanese supply effort occurred on the evening of October 6, thanks to wet weather covering the delivery by six destroyers of additional artillery pieces and another 600 men.[15]

As those Japanese warships sped away in the early hours of October 7, Captain Jenkins set the Sea and Anchor detail in response to a message that Vice Admiral Ghormley sent a day earlier. *Atlanta* finally departed Tonga at 0744 on a westward heading to rejoin the war in company with the battleship *Washington* and the destroyers *Benham* and *Walke*. For Jenkins, he was heading into battle with a more senior wardroom at least on paper, as an ALNAV [All Navy] message had been received promoting seven of the light cruiser's junior officers.[16] Rear Admiral Lee, embarked in *Washington*, commanded Battleship Division Six, which would have included the *South Dakota* and *North Carolina* had those ships had not been sidelined with self- and enemy-inflicted wounds. He also was assigned as Commander Task Group 17.8, in operational command of the four-ship flotilla that included *Atlanta*.[17]

For the next three days the four ships continued westward, passing into the Coral Sea late on October 9. At this time, Lloyd now stood watch as an officer of the deck:

We were always in Condition 3 which was a watch in all of the ship control and damage control, gunnery, and everything else stations. During Condition 3 we had three Officers of the Deck. There was Paul Smith of the Class of '30 who was our Communications Officer, Jack Wulff—Class of '31, who was the Assistant Engineer, and I was the Assistant Gunnery Officer of course.[18]

As the four ships sped west, *Atlanta* and the two destroyers formed an anti-submarine screen to protect Lee's battleship; however, the speed averaging 18 knots rendered sonar equipment ineffective. However, that speed, matched with an effective zigzig plan, hopefully would frustrate any undersea attackers.

Reflecting decades later, Lloyd understood that the Japanese submarine threat meant "mortal danger stood at hand 60 minutes in an hour, 24 hours in a day … and yet that wasn't what one thought about." Tension and stress affect individuals in different ways and Lloyd professed to be strain-free. A non-smoker, Lloyd never had the urge to take up the habit, especially seeing the impact of smoking on fellow bridge watchstanders who could not light up at night. "The absence of it would upset them, but no such gnawing pangs beset me."[19]

CHAPTER 23

Battle of Cape Esperance

11 October

About 0900 we sight T. G. 62.6, AP's *Zeilin* and *McCawley*, DD's *Sterett* (407) and *Nicholas* (449), and 3 DMS's, *Hopkins*, *Trever*, and another. Rendezvous 200 mi. due N. of NW end of New Caledonia. They are taking an Army regiment in to Guadalcanal for reinforcement; we are the support force.

Meanwhile ComGen Cactus reports very heavy air raids all day, which prevent his getting off an attack group against a force of 3 Jap CA's and 6 DD's sighted coming in, presumably with more Jap troops. He says that unless they are stopped he'll be in a poor position. ComSoPac answers that Scott has orders to attack if conditions are favorable. Evidently Scott (*San Francisco*, flagship) had the group that left TF 17 on 23 September, *Pensacola*, *Helena* and 4 DD's, and is operating up there to pick up a few Japs here and there. Best sign so far, though I hate that weaseling "if conditions are favorable".

We turn North, with TG 62.6, keeping in sight of them and more or less to their N.W.

12 October

Scott found the Japs last night, and drove them off. *Boise* was with him too apparently—must have at last gotten back out from the states. She was hit & set afire, and fell out of formation, but then rejoined. DD's *Duncan* (485) and *Farenholt* (491) are missing. Five ships, possibly including 1 CA, were seen on fire as the action broke off—could have included our 2 DD's. No dope on our damage, but it must have been appreciable, as Scott is withdrawing (so are the Japs at least, with their mission defeated). Planes ordered out from Cactus to find our stragglers, and pound on any limping Japs.

By afternoon, more dope in. *Farenholt* rejoined; had been hard hit and dropped out, then got clear. *Duncan* found abandoned but afloat, taken in tow by *McCall* (DD 400). 183 survivors also found and picked up, plus some Japs—evidently at least one of their DD's went. *Duncan* sank during the afternoon. Planes have apparently located all the rest of the Jap force limping off at 15 knots, so 1 DD each looks like the night's score.

But the slowed condition of their remnants is costing them. 1 group of undamaged DD's got the works from our SBD's with, as is the sad rule in the case of air attack on fast and small surface ships, no hits. However, one of the damaged CA's was stopped by a fish and some bomb near misses, and put in bad shape, and an apparently damaged DD with her got two bombs plus some near misses, which seems to have cooked her goose. A second attack put another hit on the stopped CA, which the Japs were abandoning, and seems to have gotten another DD. No dope has reached me, at least (with our hush-hush communication policy) from which to figure what happened to the rest of the original Jap force. I get my dope second hand from a bunch of guys whose minds don't integrate successive fragments of dope very well—I put it together myself.

At sunset tonight (about 1800, zone (-)11 time) we are due E. of Guadalcanal. The transport group turns west and goes in, north of San Cristobal and S. of Malaita. We are to stick around out here, to cover them when they come out tomorrow night. They will be in before dawn tomorrow, unload all day, then move out to the E. at night. This is now the standard procedure, a small lesson our bright boys learned after sacrificing only 4 CA's in that death trap on 8 August.

***

Departing Tonga as Task Group 17.8, the transit of *Washington, Atlanta, Benham,* and *Walke* was relatively uneventful. During Lloyd's first dog watch on October 9,[1] sonar reported a contact and Lloyd sounded General Quarters and maneuvered the light cruiser toward the direction where the sound was believed to come from; however, after a few minutes, the contact was lost and Lloyd brought the cruiser back to the original heading. The next day *Atlanta* pulled alongside *Washington,* which provided Jenkins' ship gulps of black oil from her significantly larger bunkers. That day would be the last of independent streaming for the battleship, light cruiser, and two destroyers. *Atlanta's* war diary noted that in the early afternoon, *Atlanta's* machine-gun crews took the opportunity to fire on a target sleeve towed by one of *Washington's* scout planes. As Lloyd noted, on the morning of October 11, lookouts spotted Task Group 62.6 centered on the *Zeilin* and *McCawley* on the westward horizon. Having departed from Noumea, the two transports carried a regiment of 2,837 Army soldiers along with 210 ground crewmen from the 1st Marine Air Wing. Also contained within the hulls of the two vessels were jeeps, trucks, heavy guns, and 4,200 tons of cargo. For three hours the two groups of ships converged on a northerly heading until *Washington*, *Atlanta*, *Benham*, and *Walke* fell in with the convoy to provide a protective layer of firepower to assure the critically needed reinforcements arrived at Guadalcanal. For Lloyd, the convoy escort duty would prove to be the ticket that would get *Atlanta*, which hadn't fired in anger for nearly six weeks, back into the fight.[2]

Instead it was another group of combatants—Task Force 64, under Rear Admiral Scott—that would plunge the U.S. Navy into the first significant surface engagement with the Imperial Japanese Navy since Savo Island. On both October 9 and 10, Scott steamed during daylight hours outside the arc of enemy scout planes and then steamed northwards to interdict the Tokyo Express. However, with no sightings of Japanese ship movements, Scott withdrew back beyond range of enemy aircraft. On October 11, Scott received news that the Tokyo Express was back in business.

However, this would be no ordinary express. Rear Adm. Aritomo Goto's force of three cruisers and two destroyers would follow a reinforcement convoy centered on seaplane carriers *Nisshin* and *Chitose* and six escorting destroyers. As the eight Tokyo Express ships offloaded guns, supplies, and additional troops, Goto's guns would fire shells armed with fuses designed to detonate before impact, scattering fragments to render parked aircraft unserviceable.[3]

As with previous runs down the slot, the prior daylight hours featured air attacks against what had become known as the Cactus Air Force. This time the Japanese initiated a two-stage attack, with phase one aimed to draw the defenders into an air-to-air dogfight against Japanese Zeros, and phase two hitting the American aircraft on the ground at Henderson with a bomber and fighter attack after they landed to refuel. Weather and coordination issues nullified the ability of the Japanese to achieve their desired objective to cripple American airpower; however, the air combat in the vicinity of Guadalcanal kept the Americans from flying out to attempt to strike at their incoming surface forces which were shielded by rotations of shorter range Zeros operating from the new airbase at Buin.[4]

American scout planes did sight the reinforcement group centered on the two seaplane tenders that were incorrectly reported as cruisers. No sightings were made of Goto's following bombardment group centered on the actual cruisers *Aoba*, *Furutaka*, and *Kinugasa*. With the reinforcement group sighting relayed to Scott, the American rear admiral ordered his nine-ship flotilla to intercept. In contrast to the Savo Island fiasco of two months earlier, it was the Japanese who failed to capitalize on sightings that could have warned Goto of a forthcoming reception. In the case of *I-26*, the Japanese submarine commander, upon seeing an American cruiser speeding north, chose to dive and attempt an attack before radioing a sighting report. Scott also tipped his presence by launching his scout planes to Tulagi, ostensibly to clear his ships of these highly flammable liabilities but also to scout ahead for the incoming Tokyo Express run. However, the Tokyo Express had already arrived off Guadalcanal at Tassafaronga and had started to offload. Had reports of Scott's overhead scout planes been forwarded to Goto, the Japanese admiral could have been forewarned.[5]

With the moon having set, Scott's column of the destroyers *Farenholt, Duncan, Laffey*; cruisers *San Francisco, Boise, Salt Lake City, Helena*; and destroyers *Buchanan* and *McCalla* steamed toward the vicinity of Savo Island, still unaware that there were two Japanese flotillas in the area with one having arrived off Guadalcanal. The ambiguity was enhanced by a scout plane sighting of the Tokyo Express group off Guadalcanal, yet Scott still suspected more ships would be arriving from the northwest.[6]

To keep his column between the ships sighted off Guadalcanal and present a broadside to the ships he still anticipated coming down the slot, Scott had his column steam on a heading of 050 degrees true until 2333, when Scott ordered his column to reverse course to 230 degrees true. It was the type of maneuver that fleet commanders loved to perform at pre-war naval reviews before shorelines crowded with awed spectators and could have been ordered as a "column," meaning the column follows the wake of the guiding lead ship or as a "turn," meaning all of the ships would turn simultaneously and the rear ship would now take the lead and become the guide. Scott ordered a column to port, meaning the *Farenholt* would swing around to the left, and *Duncan* and the remaining ships would follow. Unfortunately, the bridge watch team on Scott's own flagship misunderstood the radio signal that had been sent out from the flag bridge one deck below and executed an immediate turn to port. Confused, *Boise* followed *San Francisco*'s wake as did the remaining ships, effectively cutting the first three destroyers out of the column formation. *Farenholt* and *Laffey* eventually would catch up and steam off the starboard beam of Scott's re-formed column, placing themselves between the American cruisers and the anticipated Japanese surface force. *Duncan* would go rogue.[7]

Unbeknownst to Scott, in the moments before the turn, *Helena* and *Salt Lake City*'s radarmen had detected Rear Admiral Goto's bombardment group nearly 14 miles distant. As *Boise* turned, her radar beams also started picking up echoes of the oncoming steel.[8] Also detecting the rapidly closing enemy were the operators of the fire-control radar for *Duncan*, a ship that Lloyd would have witnessed taking form at Federal Shipbuilding a year earlier. On her bridge the Commanding Officer, Lt. Cdr. Edmund B. Taylor, determined that Scott's turning column was vulnerable to the oncoming Japanese and independently chose to order flank speed to charge Goto's ships to launch a torpedo spread.[9]

Reflecting years later, Lloyd Mustin criticized Scott for his decision to reverse his column by ordering a column turn. "Tactically that is a terribly poor thing to do because the last ship doesn't complete the turn until it has run all the way down to where the leading ship was at the time this thing was executed." Lloyd pointed out the time entailed in completing the maneuver introduced an element of vulnerability. "Half of the ships' fire is masked by the other half as they pass in essentially the reversed course."[10]

Having spent the previous two hours burrowing through driving rain squalls at high speed, at 2343 Goto slowed his five-ship formation to 26 knots, approaching Guadalcanal in a "T" formation with the cruisers *Aobe*, *Furutaka*, and *Kinugasa* in column, and the destroyers *Fubuki* and *Hatsuyuki* positioned off *Aobe*'s starboard and port beams. As the formation slowed, lookouts on *Aobe* began to notice warship silhouettes over 5 miles distant. Goto assumed it was the reinforcement group and ordered recognition signals to be sent. As the range closed further to less than 3 miles, the lookouts could clearly discern that the hulls they were staring at were not Japanese. Goto remained unconvinced, ordering the recognition signals to continue.

In response, the Americans finally opened, with *Helena* firing the first broadside at 2346. The shells that ripped through *Aobe*'s flag bridge likely came from *Boise*. Though they failed to detonate, the projectiles still killed many watch standers and mortally wounded Goto. Other American salvos ripped into the Japanese flagship's forward turrets and gun director. Within five minutes *Aobe*'s engine room received orders to make black smoke to attempt to cloak the blazing vessel. The second cruiser in the Japanese column, *Furutaka*, took on several shells, with a hit on a torpedo tube causing a flare-up that provided a further aim point. The third Japanese cruiser prudently turned away to avoid the American broadsides as did the destroyer *Hatsuyuki*, which suffered two hits.

Unfortunately, Goto's bombardment group were not the only warships to suffer the wrath of American 6- and 8-inch shells. Scott feared that due to the botched course reversal, friendly fire posed a horrific possibility, and he called for a ceasefire only a minute into the battle. Though the *San Francisco*'s 8-inchers went silent, other ships in the column either didn't receive the radio directive or ignored it. Bursting shell fragments killed several of *Farenholt*'s topside bluejackets, and an American-made 6-inch shell pierced a fuel bunker just above the waterline. A fragment from this shell and another forced the abandonment of the forward boiler room. The wounded destroyer managed to pass through Scott's battle line to safety.

Meanwhile, *Duncan* attempted to launch a torpedo attack from her flank position, managing to get two fish off, but also took on shellfire from both Goto's and Scott's ships. Ablaze with loss of steering control, *Duncan* began to steam in a counterclockwise circle away from the fighting.

As the midnight hour approached, the cruisers *Aobe*, *Furutaka*, and destroyer *Fubuki* continued to draw fire. However, as the calendar switched to a new day, the unscathed *Kinugasa* launched a spread of torpedoes. Spotting the wakes of two of the Long Lances, *Boise* turned hard right into their paths, allowing the two fish to streak by to port and starboard. Though *Boise* was able to dodge *Kinugasa*'s torpedoes, she could not avoid salvos of accurate gunfire from the last intact Japanese cruiser. After one Japanese 7.9-inch shell pierced *Boise*'s forward barbette, placing the turret out of commission, the dreaded magazine hit occurred under the first two of the three forward turrets that were a unique feature of cruisers of the *Brooklyn* class. The exploding shell set off gunpowder and stowed ammunition, and rapidly expanding flaming gasses enveloped the forward section of the ship, snuffing out or incinerating 107 sailors. However, buckled hull plating allowed Pacific water to reach the incandescent flames before they could reach the forward black powder storage hold. *Boise*'s commanding officer, Capt. Edward Moran, broke the formation and increased speed, barely avoiding being hit by the next salvo. Now steaming away from the fight, *Boise*'s aft two turrets continued to fire at the Japanese.[11]

In *Boise*'s wake *Salt Lake City* took on the duel with *Kinugasa*, with each ship scoring light blows. At 16 minutes past midnight Scott turned *San Francisco* toward the Japanese to press the attack but after a few moments halted, concerned that his flagship could accidently draw friendly bullets. With his formation semi-scattered, Scott elected to regroup, anticipating further combat. For the next two hours *Boise*'s damage control teams continued to battle the blazes emanating from the two forward turrets, finally extinguishing the flames and patching leaks at 0220. By 0305, *Boise* had rejoined the remaining ships of Scott's task force, minus *McCalla* and *Duncan*, now en route to Noumea to get beyond the range of Japanese aviation.[12]

Peppered with some 40 hits, *Aoba* retired with *Kinugasa* and eventually would make it back to the home islands for repairs. *Furutaka*, having absorbed over twice as much punishment including a possible torpedo hit, would sink before sunrise. The heavily damaged destroyer *Fubuki* also succumbed to the sea. Unfortunately for the Americans, the crew of *Duncan* could not stem the flames that were fed by cooking off shells that contributed to a dangerous pyrotechnic display. With no way of escape but over the side, the bridge watch jumped overboard at about 0130. Though the stern section of the ship had been spared during the battle, exploding ammunition in the forward magazines rained debris down, forcing the remainder of the crew to abandon ship over the next half hour.[13]

Scott initially left *McCalla* (DD 488) behind to tend to *Boise* and *Farenholt*. In his narrative Lloyd identifies the Kearny-built destroyer—a recent addition to the fleet—as the older *McCall* (DD 400), which at the time was at Pearl Harbor. Given the name similarities, Lloyd's error is understandable. As noted, *Boise* was able to rejoin Scott's flotilla. *Farenholt* would make her way to Noumea separately, escorted by the just-arrived destroyer *Aaron Ward*. Seeing a blazing hulk in the distance, *McCalla* chose to investigate and sent a party to board the sister Jersey-built destroyer that was quickly pulled with the realization that the flames were approaching the aft magazines. At daylight the charred destroyer, having nearly burnt herself out, was visited by another *McCalla* boarding party intent on salvaging the hulk who raced to douse the remaining forward fire and patch holes. However, as the salvagers paused for midday rations, a major bulkhead failure rumbled the vessel, and the onrush of sea water led to the conclusion that *Duncan* could not be saved. She went under later that afternoon 6 miles north of Savo Island. Fortunately, *McCalla*, in company with small craft sent from the Coast Guard-managed Naval Operating Base at Guadalcanal, eventually recovered 195 of *Duncan's* crew from the shark-infested waters. *McCalla* also came upon *Fubuki* survivors, pulling three Japanese aboard against their will.[14]

As Lloyd Mustin's narrative details, the combat element of the story also continues into the next day. Like Mikawa just over two months earlier, Scott missed an opportunity to strike at that evening's express shipment and thus the Japanese achieved one of their objectives. However, by blocking Goto's bombardment group, Scott spared Henderson Field and its parked aircraft from damage that night, and that would prove costly to the Japanese when the skies began to brighten in the east.

As the Japanese reinforcement group escaped back up the slot in the early morning hours, the destroyers *Shirayuki* and *Murakumo* detached to investigate if the crippled *Furutaka* could be saved or at least recover survivors. In addition, *Asagumo* and *Natsugumo* sped ahead to meet up with the lightly damaged *Kinugasa*, which would double back to assist in covering the withdrawal of the remaining ships from the reinforcement group.

At 0700, five Henderson Field-based planes attacked *Kinugasa*, failing to score hits but deterring the cruiser from coming any further down the slot. An hour 20 minutes later, 11 American dive-bombers also challenged their skills in dropping bombs on *Shirayuki* and *Murakumo* and also flew away hitless. A follow-on strike involving dive-bombers, torpedo planes, and fighters proved more lethal, with a torpedo hit broaching *Murakumo's* engine room, stopping the warship in what had become dangerous waters. *Asagumo* and *Natsugumo* joined *Shirayuki* to assist the damaged destroyer, and that afternoon all four ships came under attack from Henderson-based aircraft. A bomb hit amidships and two near misses proved fatal to *Natsugumo*. Unable to maneuver, *Murakumo* received further bomb damage and had to be scuttled.[15]

Scott initially indicated that Japan lost three cruisers and four destroyers, and that assessment must have filtered down to Lloyd. In reality, Japan's loss of a cruiser and three destroyers plus substantial damage to another cruiser was a significant setback but by no means a turning point in the struggle for Guadalcanal.

Though acclaimed as an American victory, the battle of Cape Esperance could have been a much greater triumph for the U.S. Navy in Lloyd's estimation: "The requirement to be ready to execute simple tactics in the dark while engaging the enemy is one of the things that you'd expect naval officers would be taught from the time they became midshipmen. The heart and soul of a tactic which we practiced from time to time in peacetime should have a lesson fairly well engraved." Regarding observations that Scott's force never had the opportunity to train together:

> Well that's just so much balderdash. Of course, they didn't have much time together and of course it is essential that they be working together as a team. But they should be able to work together as a team on no advance notice whatsoever by virtue of working to a single uniform common U.S. Navy doctrine.[16]

CHAPTER 24

Desperate Times

13 October

Some tension today. Heavy Jap forces sighted by various planes, etc., moving toward Cactus. Jap carrier plane crashed South of Guadalcanal, raising a strong prospect they have a carrier force in the Coral Sea. We are on our beat E of Guad., when an as yet still unidentified plane heaves in view—suspected a Jap. We are wandering around, TG 62.6 not sighted—sort of in strategical support.

Scott's outfit sighted by recon plane enroute Button (Espiritu Santo). Some damage evident. Our AP's go there next—maybe we'll all go too, then join him for another go at Tojo.

We have orders to transfer a JG or Ens, "experienced in communications," to ComSoWestPac for duty, probably as liaison, communication aide, or what have you, for British or Anzac [Australia New Zealand] forces operating under our communication procedures around here. Many other ships have similar orders, providing an interesting speculation as to why so many are needed, all of a sudden.

Also interesting is the communication outfits' scramble to not lose one of their officers. Boy how the required "experience" is going to be interpreted if they have their way. Hereford, who they helped the Exec decide should be in Gunnery, on account of his broad naval experience and training of nothing, and who has now been on board since 19 Sept. is the candidate. The Comm Officer only has 4 J.O.'s [junior officers] under him, plus the 2 paymasters for Code watches, so he figures he's overworked and short-handed as hell.

14 October

Picked up 62.6 this morning and started S.E. Sub contact by *Benham* in the morning, which she and *Sterett* (from 62.6) worked on a long time. Haven't heard results.

Jap reconnaissance plane sighted us about 1330. Didn't get a crack at it—about ten miles was as close as he came, with us watching him all the way in from 20. By 2100 we had a message from CinCPac saying there were indications we'd been sighted. At least that end of our organization is in the groove.

Heavy Jap concentration now close in on Cactus. 6 AP's, many DD & CL, 1 BB. And we continue South.

15 October

Off to "Button" (Espiritu Santo, New Hebrides Island) this morning, at dawn. Changed to 125° at 2300 last night, then to 108 at 22 kts this morning. Scott, with three cruisers and six DD's is coming out of there, back to the Solomons, to try to help stop the Jap avalanche. Trust we will fuel up and get the hell going ourselves.

The Japs shelled Cactus one and one half-hours last night, with 14", 8" & 5", and today are still landing troops. The big push seems to be on. Cactus, meanwhile, reports out of aviation gasoline! Boy, such masterful planning as this campaign has produced. I can't see how the Marines there can but be outnumbered, by now; their planes are grounded; the Japs come down daily from Rabaul by air; and they control the sea! Call it what you will, their navy is exercising every function of control of the sea and every single resultant advantage is accruing to them.

Tonight they have carriers (plural) between here and Cactus! The thought of each of our successive steps in building this situation up for ourselves just kills me—if we had only failed in just one place to do the wrong thing, it would at least be a little better. But the usual indecision, fear of a surface fight trying once more to do it all by plane in the teeth of steadily repeated proofs that it couldn't be done that way, has now brought us to this.

So now we have one carrier, the *Hornet*, with TF 17, where I don't know, a field full of grounded planes at Cactus, and at last we are forced into a surface fight. Only now the Jap has at his leisure completed all his preparations for that and we are going out into Lord knows what superiority on the surface, backed by several carriers, and, even for all that, his landing operations may have reached such a stage that anything we could do would be too late anyway! We have dodged surface actions time after time, under circumstances where every advantage would have been overwhelmingly with us, and when, cumulatively, we might have eliminated the Jap's striking power, only to find ourselves at last forced into action with all those favorable factors balanced on the other side!

We leave tonight, our same units, to join Scott with the *San Francisco*, *Chester* & *Helena*, plus 6 DD to form TF 64, with Admiral Lee, our boss in command. We are to operate SW of Guadalcanal to attempt to intercept Jap surface units. No doubt we will find plenty of them, particularly after we have tangled with plenty of their air units—I just hope to Christ those poor Marines can hold out.

Irony: after the *McCawley* and *Zeilin* finished getting that Army regiment in the other day, the air was blue with congratulatory messages, for all hands and the ship's cook who had been anywhere within a couple of hundred miles of the operation. That was the same day the Japs started in with the 6 AP's, with possibly several full regiments, on what was their umpteenth perfectly successful landing of troops on this little island, supposedly so firmly defended by "our aircraft," based right on the god damned thing.

16 October 1942

Sighted Scott's group during the morning watch, and joined up. We left Button last night after fueling, formed up outside at about 2200, and started NW at 22 knots.

Jap shadower in sight all forenoon—Kawanishi 97 four-engine FB. Trouble cannot help but ensue. G. Q. to be at 1215; probably stay there all day, and maybe all night.

Hope—belay the word. Visibility down to 8,000 yds by 1400 from a low haze, and .7 cloud ceiling at 2,900 feet. Shadowers lost us. Two came within radar range at 1400, but passed on without ever seeing us, or us them. So chance of air attack seems negligible.

Afternoon estimates of forces in the area:

Japs	CV	BB	CA	CL	DD
Buin Area	2	3	3	5	15
Savo Island	-	1	1	1	5
Faisi	-	-	1	-	-
At sea	1	1	2	-	5
(North of Button)	3	5	7	6	25

Our forces, this group and TF 17, total 1 CV, 1 BB, 4 CA, 3 CL, 15 DD. The current Jap landing on Guadalcanal immediately supported by the Savo Island force is about <u>10,000 men</u>, with much <u>heavy artillery</u>. No wonder we have got to do something, and that damn soon. The Savo group is our present objective, plus bombardment of the Japs' Guadalcanal beachhead. It was the group N. of Button that caused everything in there to get the hell out, just as we pulled in to fuel—carrier air attack expected. All the above are within 300 mi. of Cactus.

More change: 1800 we reverse course to 145. Word received that Savo group has shoved off, its job completed; we are, as expected, too late. Nothing to do now but keep out of touch with Jap recco, and wait for their next group to come down for further landings. They know we're in the area, though, and I feel that either (a) they'll send down overwhelming support next time, or (b) more likely, because of its perfect success so far, resume their infiltration-type of reinforcement, producing large numbers of small fast groups of ships which we, before, so stupidly failed to act upon. Fortunately, I hope, Admiral Lee is not the boy to be hoodwinked by such hoary tactics—I feel he'll handle the bastards.

Not only that, but, unless expressly forbidden by the stupe in Noumea, I think he'll handle whatever covering force the Japs send in, if they use their other alternative. And not run away after round one, leaving the field to the enemy undisturbed, as Scott's force did the other day.

That whole business was just one more bit of boobery on the part of Ghormley. To begin, of course, we were in the area, and once our AP's were out, should have joined Scott then and there, to do the job we are now too late for, thanks to the round-trip to Button by all concerned. Secondly, we were directed (we found out the afternoon we reached Button) to rendezvous with Scott on his way out of there back to the scene of activity. But TF 17 had been ordered to fuel by Ghormley, who had made a slight oversight in forgetting that his organization still included us as a part of 17! So we were in Button for totally unnecessary fuel at the time we were supposed to be meeting Scott some hundred miles or so to the West. Might not have been too late if this bit of staff butchery hadn't cost us 200 miles.

Two DD are detached about 1830 to go up and bombard the Jap's beachhead—hope there was some suitable target still not moved off into the jungle when they got there. The rest of us turn south from our closest approach, a point about 200 mi. south of Rennell Island, and start the old circling.

Saw the *Boise* in Button. One turret seems out; heard she had 100 killed. Most holes patched; suppose she is now enroute to the States.

Wonder when we are going to move our own urgently needed supplies and reinforcements into Cactus—if the utter jug-heads in Noumea have been able to plan any such operation. I can hardly believe, on the record, that they can have completed any plans, worthy of the name, at least, for any such perfectly obvious move. It would have been too easy.

***

On October 12, as American aircraft attacked remnants of Goto's bombardment group and the reinforcement group, *Atlanta* continued on a northerly heading as an escort to the troopships *Zeilin* and *McCawley*. Having maneuvered to a position eastward of Guadalcanal by midday, the formation of ships turned to a westerly heading at 1438 and increased speed to 18 knots. Two hours and 12 minutes later, the *Atlanta* along with *Washington*, *Benham*, and *Walke* broke off and turned to a southwesterly and then a southeasterly heading as the troop transports made their final run into Cactus.[1]

Arriving on the morning of October 13, the two transports feverishly worked to offload the Army troops, composed of a National Guard unit from the northern plains, while fighter aircraft roared off from Henderson Field to intercept two waves of attacking Japanese aircraft. Surprisingly, when presented with the opportunity to attack the offloading transports and strike a blow to the American logistical effort, the incoming Betty bombers stayed with their assigned target and dropped their payloads on Henderson Field, buckling stretches of steel runway matting and torching some 5,000 gallons of aviation fuel.[2]

That afternoon, American scout planes detected some 200 miles distant a convoy centered on six "*Marus*"—cargo ships that could bring substantial numbers of troops and tonnage to more than match what *Zeilin* and *McCawley* had just delivered. Eight destroyers escorted the small convoy. The convoy represented a break from the Tokyo Express delivery system that had been delivering troops and supplies piecemeal over the past month. However, almost as fast as the warships assigned to express duties could add to the numbers ashore, those numbers were depleted by combat and sickness. Malaria affected the Japanese as much as the mosquito-borne parasites immobilized Americans. To bring a victory to the Emperor, the Japanese recognized that a onetime thrust of overwhelming force onto the island was needed to end the stalemate.[3]

However, as learned from the battle of the eastern Solomons, the slower cargo ships would be vulnerable to Henderson Field's growing air armada for many daylight hours preceding their arrival. By bringing elements of the Combined Fleet to include battleships and aircraft carriers, Admiral Yamamoto felt confident that the *Maru* convoy could get through.

Back on Guadalcanal that evening, dirt geysers erupted on the west end of Henderson Field, indicating that a heavy artillery piece that had been offloaded from the Japanese seaplane tenders on the evening of October 11 had been positioned to lob steel down on the American airfield, restricting air operations to the eastern portion of the field. However, that gun—later to earn the nickname "Pistol Pete"—proved to be the opening act for a very long program that evening. Steaming down directly from the north undetected, Rear Adm. Takeo Kurita brought with him the battleships *Kongo* and *Haruna* escorted by a light cruiser and nine destroyers. With the pre-World War I British-built *Kongo* and Japanese-constructed sister ship *Haruna*, the Japanese committed two warships that had undergone significant upgrades over their three decades with the Imperial Fleet. From the magazines deep within their hulls, special ammunition designed to burst over the target and spread sub-munitions were loaded onto the hoists that fed the main batteries of 14-inch guns.[4]

The Japanese thoroughly planned the massive shore bombardment mission, placing a gunnery officer from the battleship *Yamato* ashore on an overlooking perch to assist with the spotting, as well as launching four aircraft to provide additional spotting and illumination services. Just after 0130 *Kongo* fired her first salvo, shortly followed by *Haruna*. The sister battleships methodically placed their rounds across the airstrips, adjacent tarmac, and into the aircraft maintenance support areas. After 40 minutes, the 14-inch guns went silent to allow the two battleships to reverse course and resume fire. Having expended their special fragment rounds, the Japanese fired armor-piercing shells at Henderson.[5]

Five-inch shore batteries tried to answer the heavy barrage, but the Japanese were well out of range. Instead it was left to four PT boats to carry the fight to the enemy. The small wooden speedy torpedo boats valiantly approached the two behemoths, successfully launched torpedoes, and claimed hits. Though the Japanese sustained no damage, the harassment caused Kurita to cease the bombardment five minutes ahead of schedule. Having expended 973 shells, Kurita's ships departed. As dawn approached, the Japanese resumed firing their heavy artillery piece, but with a limited supply of shells, the firing would be annoyingly sporadic.[6]

The morning light unveiled the devastation. Cratered Henderson Field was unusable. Had it been usable, only seven of 39 Dauntless were still flyable and no fuel remained to fly them. Fortunately, the satellite fighter strip fared better, with 30 planes remaining available for combat. The other silver lining that emerged in the wake of the overnight bludgeoning was that there were only 41 fatalities among the 20,000 Americans ashore that memorable evening.

Though the Japanese believed they had ceased American air operations, the Cactus Air Force still was able to send out scouts to confirm that the Japanese convoy remained on schedule to arrive that evening. A noontime raid by 26 Betty bombers went unchallenged as aircrews on the ground hurriedly siphoned aviation gas from the damaged planes to fuel the unscathed fighters. These planes were able to rise to and fend off a second raid. Later in the afternoon and in the early evening, the Cactus Air Force was able to launch attacks on the oncoming convoy but registered only a light hit on one of the escorting destroyers.

Lloyd Mustin's frustrated diary entries reflected the reality of the situation. There was little the United States Navy could do to intercept the reinforcement convoy. Scott's surface force had retired to seek fuel. Lloyd's stepfather, embarked in *Hornet*, also could not act, as the bunkers of that ship were being refilled with black oil at a location northwest of New Caledonia. Peering out and seeing *Washington* steaming nearby, Lloyd must have wondered what may have been the outcome had they taken the two transports to Guadalcanal and remained to take on the two Japanese battleships. Instead, early on October 14, *Atlanta*'s lookouts spotted *Zeilin* and *McCawley* coming west where they had departed Guadalcanal the previous evening. Upon meeting up, the *Washington*, *Atlanta*, *Walke*, and *Benham* provided escort services till midday, when the battleship, light cruiser, and two destroyers parted company from the transports to head south to meet up with Scott's ships at Button—the code word for Espiritu Santo. As the two groups of ships parted, at 1235, lookouts spotted enemy aircraft in the distance and Captain Jenkins called his crew to General Quarters. No attack ensued.[7]

As Lloyd made his diary entry that day, he apparently had not heard of the overnight battleship bombardment on Cactus. His entry the next day reflected news of another overnight barrage on Henderson, this time by the cruisers *Chokai* and *Kinugasa*. No 14-inch shells that night, but during a 30-minute bombardment in the early morning, the two cruisers bracketed the American runways with 752 8-inch shells.[8]

As the two cruisers fired away, Japanese reinforcements came ashore from not only the transports that had arrived that evening but also from another Tokyo Express delivery from the light cruisers *Sendai* and *Yuri*, seaplane tender *Nisshin*, and four destroyers that landed not only 1,100 additional soldiers but also the advance elements of a planned midget submarine facility. However, while the Express warships could discharge their cargoes and speed off back up the slot under the cover of darkness, the *Marus*, having arrived at midnight, needed more time to empty their hulls of some 4,500 ground troops, heavy artillery pieces, tanks, ammunition, and provisions. As daylight broke, Marines and the newly arrived soldiers could actually see the superstructures of the Japanese cargo ships. That morning light also revealed the early morning bombardment had effectively negated efforts by the Cactus Air Force ground crews to reassemble a credible bomber threat. Overhead, Zeros from the Japanese carriers *Hiyo* and *Junyo* vigilantly guarded the vulnerable former Japanese merchantmen that had been pressed into military service, and they were quickly challenged by six Wildcats that lifted off and were able to strafe the offloading vessels. With only three Dauntlesses left unscathed from the early morning bombardment, the exhausted ground crews again took on the task of reassembling airplanes, and with fuel found from some hidden caches, the Cactus Air Force launched a mid-morning strike that not only featured a dozen SBDs and a dozen fighters, but a PBY-5A that had two torpedoes rigged under its large wing. With the dive-bombers coming in upon the transports from one direction, the lumbering Catalina evaded gunfire from the defending destroyer screen to plant one of the torpedoes into the *Sasako Maru*. The blow proved fatal, but the ship successfully had offloaded her troops and cargo. A similar fate fell on the *Azumasan Maru* thanks to a noontime bomb that fell from a raid of 11 B-17s that had lifted off earlier from Espiritu Santo. Another American air attack in the early afternoon claimed the *Kyushu Maru*. In both cases, the cargo ships had offloaded their troops, artillery, and tanks, but the ammunition and fuel to operate those tracked vehicles went up in flames.[9]

Of the three *Marus* left, one had completed its troop and cargo offload just before the B-17 attack and had cleared the area with a destroyer escort. The other two were pulled away for a few hours with the intent to return at sunset for one final offload attempt. However, another SBD attack and the prospect of a moonlit sky led the Japanese commander to order the two remaining cargo ships and their escorts to return to Rabaul.

Overall though, the Japanese succeeded in landing over 5,000 troops between the cargo convoy and their Tokyo Express run and offloaded an impressive quantity of armaments and provisions, but not without cost—three burned-out cargo ship hulls would become rusting fixtures on the Guadalcanal shoreline for years to come.

Lloyd's entry of October 15, that contained the disturbing report of the presence of Japanese carriers between *Atlanta*'s position off Espiritu Santo and Cactus, was inaccurate only in that the carriers were in waters east of the Stewart Islands in hopes of locating *Hornet*. Though they were operating north of the direct path between Button and Cactus, that direct path was well within range of their aircraft.

Given the desperate fuel situation at Cactus, the Americans attempted to mount their own over-water supply run, with worse results. Having departed Espiritu Santo on October 12, the destroyers *Nicholas* and *Meredith* escorted the cargo ships *Alchiba* and *Bellatrix*, the PT boat tender *Jamestown*, and the fleet tug *Vireo*. In tow were three barges carrying barrels of fuel and 500-pound bombs. However, reports of Japanese aircraft carriers led Vice Admiral Ghormley to abort the mission on the morning of October 14, and the cargo ships and *Nicholas* reversed course. *Meredith* and *Vireo*, with one barge in tow, pressed on. On the morning of October 15, as the Japanese were fending off American air attacks at Guadalcanal, two Japanese aircraft swooped down on the two American naval vessels which evaded the attack. Upon receiving a report that two Japanese warships were in the vicinity and that a follow-on air strike was a certainty, the captain of *Meredith* decided to offload the crew of the fleet tug and sink the slow World War I-vintage auxiliary to facilitate a speedy dash out of the area. Before *Meredith* could sink *Vireo*, Japanese carrier aircraft arrived and plastered the American destroyer with multiple bombs and three torpedoes. Ironically, six of the survivors made it back to the drifting *Vireo*. When rescuing destroyers arrived three days later, only 88 men from a combined crew of 325 remained.[10] *Vireo* would be placed back in service and survive the war.

Yet aware of the fate that befell *Meredith*, in the late afternoon *Atlanta* steamed through straits leading to Luganville on the southeast side of Espiritu Santo and nudged alongside *Kankakee* for what Lloyd contended was an unnecessary fueling. As the light cruiser took on black oil, Lloyd could see *Boise* nearby and the damage to her forward two turrets. At 1800 that evening Vice Admiral Ghormley's directive to form Task Force 64 built around Rear Admiral Lee in *Washington* took effect. *Atlanta* departed Luganville harbor with the battleship *Washington* and destroyers *Walke* and *Benham* shortly afterwards to join up the next day with the cruisers *Chester*, *San Francisco*, and *Helena*, and the destroyers *Aaron Ward*, *Lansdowne*, *Lardner*, *Laffey*, *Buchanan*, and *McCalla*.[11]

Reflecting years later, Lloyd appreciated the opportunity to steam in company with *Washington* and the Task Force 64 commander Rear Admiral Lee. "With Admiral Lee we never felt the lack of knowing what he expected us to do or wanted us to do. He was the perfect example of an officer who could and did do these little bits of deciding what he wanted done and making sure everyone knew what he wanted done."[12]

As the American surface combatants proceeded to their next day rendezvous, at Guadalcanal the newly arrived Japanese troops began to settle down for their first night's stay on the contested island. That night they could hear the reassuring thunder of naval gunfire as the heavy cruisers *Myoko* and *Maya*, accompanied by destroyers, fired 926 8-inch shells and 253 5-inch rounds into the American defensive perimeter.[13]

Yet despite the additional damage wrought on the American air facilities on Guadalcanal, the flights resumed the next day, October 16, targeting the new arrivals and their stores before they could move inland. There were 58 combat sorties launched from Henderson that day. They were joined by sorties launched from the *Hornet*, which had surged forward from waters off New Caledonia to not only attack Japanese positions on Cactus, but also go after Japanese facilities that supported seaplane operations at Rekata Bay located on the northern end of Santa Isabel, the next large island in the Solomons up the slot.

Besides launching combat missions that day, Henderson's airstrips welcomed a steady stream of cargo planes that brought barrels of fuel. Unfortunately, some 40,000 gallons of fuel and ammunition that had been offloaded onto a barge from *McFarland*—a World War I era flush-deck destroyer that had been converted to a seaplane tender—exploded into a massive fireball thanks to an evening attack from Japanese Vals flying from Buin. The dive-bomber attack also landed a bomb, clipping *McFarland*'s stern, forcing the aging warship to seek refuge at Tulagi.

USS *Atlanta* photographed coming alongside USS *San Francisco* (CA 38) to refuel on October 16, 1942. (Archives Branch, Naval History and Heritage Command, Washington, D.C. NH 97807)

As the Japanese made their attack, 19 Marine Wildcats arrived to restock the Cactus Air Force. Despite flying in on fumes, the squadron leader Lt. Col. Harold F. Bauser saw the attack and shot down three of the departing Vals.[14]

As this activity swirled around the skies and ground at Guadalcanal, Task Force 64 formed up that morning after *Atlanta*'s lookouts sighted Scott's ships to the west at a point nearly halfway between Button and Cactus. As noted in Lloyd's diary and in *Atlanta*'s war diary, the task force came under surveillance at 0958 from a Kawanishi 97 four-engine floatplane. Since the shadower was not a threat, Captain Jenkins remained in Condition 3 through the morning. At 1215, in expectation that Japanese reconnaissance plane set an attack in motion, *Atlanta* sounded General Quarters. However, with low visibility, Jenkins decided to stand down at 1239, though he kept the gun mounts manned. As Lloyd noted, the destroyers *Aaron Ward* and *Lardner* detached that evening to head up to Guadalcanal to shell Japanese troop concentrations on the northeast end of the island.[15]

CHAPTER 25

Halsey Arrives

19 October 1942

This morning comes word that a couple of Jap cruisers and DD's are on their way to Guadalcanal. We happen to be on 335°, so we start up to 20 kts, apparently to get up there and do something about it. It looks, though, as if after figuring it over the Admiral decided we couldn't make it, because we slowed again. Our aimless circling had brought us to a spot some 350 miles away, down abreast of Button! And Ghormley had had the craw to tell ComGen Cactus that he'd support him to the limit of the forces at his disposal! That, of course, was in reply to ComGen's message that he had to have naval support or else. What Ghormley's idea of "support" is, I can't fathom—but he knows how to support himself, anyway, by getting a cover up message on the record. Of course, this Jap force may be only a feeler, preliminary to the arrival of bigger game, such as what brought in the 10,000 troops right after Scott's engagement of the night of 11–12 October. In that action he got the *Furutaka* and, I believe, the *Kinugasa* was the one that was damaged and gotten later by planes; also three of their DD's, total seem to be checked off. Fair enough, in exchange for damage to the *Boise* and the *Duncan* lost. But why in hell: (1) couldn't the remaining ships have stayed on the scene, and joined us, to go after the next bunch, already reported enroute, and (2) don't we figure on doing the same thing now? No reason why he couldn't have kept the sea, and no reason why we couldn't now, in case we had a go at this present outfit and then heard of another following them up. Only god damn thing to do, as I see it—this bunch may be only another small infiltration outfit, all too many of which have been stupidly left unmolested because we couldn't see our way clear to wipe out the small fry while awaiting the big stuff. Enough of the small fry wiped out, over the period we've been in Tulagi, would have hamstrung the big stuff long since. Worse than that, it looks to me like only a couple more infiltrations, plus bombardments of our own positions, will provide the straws to break the camel's back.

The *McFarland* (ex 4-stacker, AVD-14) got in to Cactus with some gas the other day and was congratulated by CinCPac. Hell of a fine base we have when a destroyer is to be congratulated for running in to it. Now the *Amberjack* is down here, a sub fitted with gas tanks. A fine thing, when we have to sneak our gas in by submarine! All because the Japs are conceded, without dispute, every prerogative of control of the sea in this area! They damn near have it, too. The other day while we were over in Button, the *Meredith* (434) was escorting the *Vireo*, towing an aviation barge to Cactus. 9 Jap dive-bombers caught them and the *Meredith* hasn't been seen since. Recco planes saw the *Vireo*, dead in the water and damaged, the barge adrift four miles away, and no sign or word from *Meredith*. Another incident in the handling of this Tulagi campaign also adds to my perpetual burn—the sacrifice of three APD's in there, early in September. *Gregory*, *Colhoun*, and *Little* (ex 4-stackers) were sent in there, in the face of the usual unopposed Jap DD bombardments, and got caught. Needless to say, they were totally outclassed, out-gunned, out-sped, out-protected, out-equipped, what have you, and were simply shot to pieces. All just a stone in this vast mosaic picture of the results of perfectly incompetent, unqualified, stupid and pusillanimous leadership that has characterized this campaign from start right on down to now, when a bitter, costly, and disgraceful finish is only just around the corner.

20 October 1942

This morning in our wanderings some 200 mi. S of San Cristobal, we fell in with *Gwin* (433) and *Grayson* (435), maneuvering around a drifting lighter full of Avgas. Turned out to be a second one, besides the *Vireo*'s, which had been in tow of the *Aldebaran*. They had picked up *Vireo* and gotten it to Cactus, and were to take this to Button. About then *Benham* had a sub contact, close under our quarter, as a matter of fact, which she and *Laffey* (459), from 64.2, worked on a long time—no positive results. Later we saw what appeared to be *Gwin* & *Grayson* heading on in—looks as if they must have sunk the lighter, instead of towing it in.

67 survivors, not including the Capt., have been picked up from the *Meredith*—she's gone, alright. Japs hit her with three aerial fish and three dive-bombs—what in hell kind of evasive maneuvers she executed to let them get that many hits I'd like to know. *Vireo* crew was all aboard *Meredith*, *Vireo* having been simply abandoned when the air attack came

along. Jesus, what kind of a Navy have we anyway? Same enemy operation (carrier based) damaged *Aldebaran* and caused her to drop her tow.

The *Nicholas* (449—2100 tonner) came out from Button and joined us today, along with *Aaron Ward* and *Lardner*. They were the two detached on the 16th, after we found we were too late to get the Japs at Savo, to go up and bombard their landing area, under direction of ComGen Cactus. Then they went in to Button to fuel and reload with ammo—no dope on their results, but CinCPac seems pleased. Question: if the results amounted to anything, why haven't we done this before during these three months, and why aren't we doing it some more? Also, why aren't similar DD's, new and powerful, in that area most of the time in general, to gobble Japs for one thing, and to prevent such futile sacrifices as those of the 3 APD's. Two of their three captains, incidentally, were lost. Anyway, the answer: Utter incompetence in Noumea cannot visualize even the most obvious means of reaping the advantage of superiority through timely use of force.

Best news today since the raid on Tokyo: Halsey, Wild Bill, the man who shook the Japs to the marrow with old TF 16, and who carried the 14 B-25's that made that Tokyo raid, is back to duty. And, to double the gain, Ghormley is out. Halsey replaces him. There'll be some changes made in the Solomons, Mr. Moto—this is the greatest shot in the arm we've had this war.

Maybe it means something, maybe not—but we have been working back to the North since noon today.

Finishing touch for the day: 2130 *Chester* torpedoed. Might as well have been midnight, as far as those off-watch were concerned, because 10 minutes after we secure from the usual dusk G.Q., everyone who can has caulked off. Certainly did bring all hands up with a run—the flash was thought to be gunfire (she and the rest of 64.2 had drawn off to one side from us) and General Quarters went. Brilliant ¾ moon, perfect visibility—beautiful submarine weather. Utter confusion seemed to reign on the voice radio (T.B.S.)—everyone going in all directions, DD's whipping around, etc., etc., and all telling each other about it. *Chester* was hit amidships and our watch reported several flashes—perhaps more than one fish. It stopped her for almost an hour—then finally underway at 5 knots. No doubt the sub escaped, on the surface after getting a little clear. The word will get out, and they'll be back trying to finish her.

21 October '42

This morning we are in *Chester's* general area, covering her withdrawal. Sighted her at about 0900, speed 6 knots. *Washington* and ourselves have been TG 64.1 of TF 64 all along, with 2 DD—our old *Walke* and *Benham*. Today *Walke* is away and *Lansdowne* is here instead—happened in the shuffle last night. Don't know where 64.2, the other cruisers & DD's, is.

Jap reconnaissance, another Kawanishi 97, has been with us all morning. No doubt the subs will be converging on the poor old *Chester*, and perhaps even carrier air attack. Button is about 200 mi., 110° away—not an especially dangerous, but nevertheless possible, spot for air attack. Fortunately the weather is bad for that and worsening—but it lets the subs surface and move around, and may also let a fast raiding force sneak down. They certainly must know her whereabouts closely.

Sighted her about 1700. She is in bad shape. One shaft broken, and likely to pull out if she speeds up. Oil in her feed bottoms makes further use of her boilers for generators and pumps as well as propulsion, look like not much of a certainty. And needless to say the Japs will make every effort to finish her off.

64.2, I find, has gone in to Button to fuel. When they are out again in position to support the *Chester*, I suppose will go in.

Learned that the *O'Brien* (DD 415) is no more—she broke in two and sank last night, enroute Noumea to Pearl. She'd taken a torpedo around here somewhere, and her skipper reported her as unfit for the trip without strengthening, etc. But the complete and utter boobs in Noumea started her off anyway, so now we have still another less destroyer. And they have one more feather for their bonnet—it looks like a chief's war bonnet already.

23 October

Went in to Button at dawn today, passing through Bougainville Straits with the *Chester* & her DD's. She got in just after us. We have a couple of leaky tubes in the water wall of the superheater side of #3 boiler. They have been plugged and now the inevitable result of the heat, the burning of the dry tubes, with their collapse followed by that of the furnace wall behind them, has started. There's nothing we can do without new replacement tubes, but this boiler is now good for only a few more hours of steaming. One of the cruising turbine bearings is throwing oil, too, so that cruiser can't be used.

We fueled from the *Willamette*, about 200,000 gals, got 4 hours for repair work on the above, picked up a scattering of the weeks and weeks of mail we've not yet received, and shoved off after a total of 8 hours in. Through the straits, then course 310°, 20 knots.

24 October

Rendezvoused with 64.2—*San Francisco* and *Helena*. We brought 5 DD with us and they have 4, including *Fletcher* (445), another of the 2,100-tonners.

Jap Kawanishi 97 F.B. shadowed us a long while today. Then just after he left we got report from PBY which encountered one in about the proper position to be ours, and shot it down. A battle of elephants. We continue west and north.

***

Pusillanimous: lacking courage and resolution—marked by contemptible timidity … as defined by the Merriam-Webster Dictionary—just one of a cascade of denigrative words used by Lloyd Mustin in his critique of the leadership in the South Pacific.

On October 16, Admiral Nimitz transmitted the following to Admiral King in Washington:

> For Admiral King only. Ultra from CINCPAC. Halsey his Chief of Staff and Intelligence Officer will be with Ghormley sixteenth our date. In view Ghormley's 160440 and other indications including some noted during my visit I have under consideration his relief by Halsey at earliest practicable time. Request your comment. If Halsey becomes Comsopac would expect him utilize Ghormley as long as needed.

King responded:

> For Admiral Nimitz only personal and secret. Most secret. Your 160937 approved.[1]

Given the situation confronting the Marines at Guadalcanal with unchallenged nightly bombardments, daily bombing raids, nightly troop reinforcements, and the quantitative edge in sea power in the region, Vice Admiral Ghormley had sent a plea stating: "My forces totally inadequate to meet situation."

Vice Admiral Halsey had recently been cleared to return to duty and embarkation with Task Force 16 centered around the repaired *Enterprise*. As the newly repaired *Big E* and escorts departed Pearl Harbor for the Southwest Pacific on October 16, Halsey had flown ahead, arriving at Noumea, New Caledonia on October 18. There a sealed envelope awaited and when Halsey opened it, he read instructions to relieve Ghormley and assume the duties as the theater commander.

For Lloyd Mustin the change could not have happened soon enough. On the evening of October 23, Halsey gathered the senior leaders in the area to confer at Noumea. Major General Vandegrift, having flown in from Guadalcanal, provided the bushy browed admiral a history of the campaign to date and his assessment of the current Japanese order of battle on the island. Halsey pressed Vandegrift on whether he could hold. Vandegrift responded: "Yes, I can hold," but caveated that he needed more active support. Halsey promised the two-star Marine "to give you everything I have."[2]

As Vandegrift confidently assured Halsey that his forces would hold, the Japanese proceeded to employ their recent arrivals in an offensive campaign to finally overwhelm the American defenders and destroy any naval forces sent to evacuate the desperate remnants. Recognizing that a thrust along the northern coast at Henderson Field would confront well-entrenched Marine positions, Lt. Gen. Masao Maruyama planned a flanking movement through the dense jungles south of Henderson with an anticipated thrust at the lightly defended American perimeter on the evening of October 22. A feint attack supported by tanks and recently arrived artillery along the direct northern coast axis aimed to draw a concentration of American defenders.

The Japanese offensive plan had two major flaws. First, in contrast to the information that trickled down, the Japanese convoy operation had landed half of the 10,000 number of fresh troops that Lloyd inked into his diary. Still, with the Japanese ground force now tallying over 14,000 soldiers, Maruyama felt he had a numerical advantage over an American garrison that he understood numbered 10,000. In reality, Maruyama's soldiers were attempting to overcome a ground force of over 20,000 Marines and National Guardsmen. The terrain proved to be the second flaw. The plan anticipated that it would take the Imperial Army's 2nd Sendai Division four days to hack through over 30 miles of jungle and organize into attack formations along the American southern and eastern perimeters on the evening of October 22. However, the harshness of the terrain drenched in constant rain exhausted the Japanese infantrymen who were loaded down with weapons, ammunition, and rations. It was not until evening of October 24 that Maruyama's fatigued troops were in position to attack Marine companies under the command of Lt. Col. Lewis B. "Chesty" Puller.[3]

Puller, with the help of the National Guardsmen and artillery, fought off the onslaught of Japanese troops that night. The next morning a reconnaissance plane from Rabaul winged in low over Henderson, looking out for waving Imperial soldiers. It was shot down. Japanese Navy surface ships also charged toward Guadalcanal, anticipating that its guns would subdue remnants of American resistance. The warships also carried airfield operations personnel that would immediately place Henderson Field in service for the Emperor. Arriving mid-morning, several destroyers attacked two World War I-vintage destroyers converted to minesweepers *Zane* and *Trevor*, other small craft, and Marine positions ashore. Marine shore batteries damaged one Japanese destroyer and a Marine Wildcat strafed another. In the early afternoon, Henderson-based SBDs hit the Japanese light cruiser *Yura* and damaged another enemy destroyer. Hit again later that day, the light cruiser had to be scuttled.[4]

Adding to the threat from the sea, overhead bombers and fighters sporting the red meatball appeared throughout the day, and the Cactus Air Force engaged and exacted a toll on the intruders.

Having suffered heavy casualties the first night, Maruyama attempted one more breakthrough the night of October 25. Canisters of steel balls, fired from Marine 37mm guns pummeled many contemporary samurai. Others fell to machine-gun fire and effective artillery barrages. Japanese losses over the two days of offensive ground operations numbered well over 2,000.[5]

Amid all of this action at Cactus, *Atlanta* steamed to the south as part of Task Force 64 which was split into two groups of surface combatants. Task Group 64.1 centered on *Washington*, *Atlanta*, and *San Francisco*, with the latter serving as the guide. The cruisers *Helena* and *Chester* served as the centerpieces of Task Group 64.2. Throughout October 19, the two groups remained within visual range.[6]

On October 20, *San Francisco* detached to join with *Helena*, *Chester*, and six destroyers to shell Japanese positions in the vicinity of Cape Esperance on the northeastern tip of Guadalcanal. That evening the three cruisers were heading back toward Espiritu Santo to the south of Task Group 64.2, which also steamed on a southeasterly heading. At 2120, *Atlanta*'s war diary recorded: "Sighted explosion and gunfire to southward in the direction of Task Group 64.2 ..." As Lloyd noted, many of his shipmates had just secured from General Quarters and had retired to their racks when the General Quarters alarm again sounded.[7]

Atlanta followed the movements of *Washington* as the bridge watch attempted to reconstruct what had happened through the constant radio chatter. At 2158, a war diary entry noted that *Chester* had been hit and that the destroyers *Walke* and *Aaron Ward* had been sent to add to the protective destroyer screen around the crippled warship. Another product of the Garden State, *Chester* suffered a hit amidships on the starboard side. *I-176* had caught the silhouettes of the three cruisers and had fired a spread of torpedoes. As they came toward the end of their runs, one exploded off *Helena*'s starboard quarter; a second detonated between *Helena* and *San Francisco*; and the third self-destructed about 1,200 yards off *San Francisco*'s port beam.[8]

As damage control crews contained the flooding, the cruiser began to slowly make way toward the safety of Espiritu Santo. The next morning, *Washington* and *Atlanta* caught up with *Chester*. With both ships' extensive antiaircraft capacities, they were ideally suited to serve as a covering force along with a screen of destroyers for the maimed ship, as the Japanese floatplane observed the withdrawal from the distance. The other cruisers and a small vanguard of additional tin cans forged ahead to Espiritu Santo.

On the morning of October 23, *Atlanta* once again returned to the southeastern side of Espiritu Santo where she anchored in Segond Channel. As Lloyd noted, some 200,000 gallons of black oil poured into her bunkers from *Willamette*, and repairs were made to band aid some problems with one of the boilers and a cruising turbine. Most welcome was the weeks' backlog of letters from home. After eight hours at anchor, *Atlanta* raised her hook for a late afternoon departure and headed west around the southern tip of the island. *Atlanta*'s 1548 war diary entry read: "Underway in company Task Group 64.1 and stood out to sea. When clear of minefields formed circular screen on WASHINGTON. ATLANTA in station 4000. LANSDOWNE, LARDNER, McCALLA, AARON WARD and BENHAM on circle 4 also base course 270 degrees true at 18 knots."[9]

By the next day the formation was operating well to the west of Espiritu Santo with Task Group 64.2 centered on *San Francisco* and *Helena* and their destroyer screen steaming within visual range. Once again Japanese scouting planes reported back to Admiral Yamamoto the position of the two surface groups. What Yamamoto was even more interested in was the location of the American carrier forces.[10]

CHAPTER 26

Battle of Santa Cruz

25 October

Sunday—what a day of rest! Dispatches indicate Jap push on Guadalcanal. 2 CV, 2 BB, 2 CA, 3 CL, some DD moving down in support of 6 AP's. Halsey's orders to us and to TF 62 (*Enterprise*, now back in the area, plus *Hornet*): "Strike."

The *Nicholas* (449) has joined giving us 10 DD. We are fairly far out, but push off at the *Washington's* near top [speed], a shade over 26. At 1400 we go to G.Q. just as we start past the N. side of Rennell Is. Visibility not too good; ceiling low; no shadowers—but shore observers on Rennell, plus previous shadowers plus our position, make air attack likely. Plan is to enter the inland waters of the Solomons West of Guadalcanal, make a sweep through the area the Japs have used for landings, bombardments, etc., and smash anything we find. Frequent rain squalls, maybe a close-range, shot-guns-across-the-dinner-table, sort of affair.

At sunset we take battle disposition, 6 DD in van; *Atlanta* supporting van DD's; *San Francisco, Helena, Washington* as main body, next in column; 4 DD's rear. Weather now clearing, Guadalcanal in sight to N 50 miles or so; prospects are now for good visibility, which with the full moon make surprise unlikely.

At 2200 we turned North, passing West of Russell Island, into the expected enemy area. Went North, then NorthEast, then East, then Southeast, headed directly for Savo. Meanwhile *San Francisco* had catapulted three planes to search the area, moonlight now being very bright and visibility phenomenal. Their reports showed no Japs present, and off Savo we turned to 220° and stood out. Secured from G.Q. at 0230, and then I had the 4–8 watch! So it goes.

26 October

Headed S. at 25 kt, expecting air attack. Shadowed all morning by a Nakajima 97 twin-float seaplane, probably from Buin, and then by a Kawanishi 97. No immediate developments, but we spent some hours at G.Q. during time of expected attack.

Got the news of what the carrier group found the 25th—the night of our foray that found us arriving to see the bird flown. Theirs hadn't. *Hornet* lost, also *Porter* (356) in an engagement off the Stewart Island to East of Solomon area, with a strong Jap force. *Hornet* got several bomb and aerial torpedo hits and had to be taken in tow by *Northampton*. A second attack then got to her, as a result of which it was decided to torpedo her—which I suppose has been done; haven't heard. *Enterprise* was there, as were our 3 sister ships and the *South Dakota*—must have been a heavy air attack to get through that effectively. Although its success is of course enhanced by our phony carrier tactics, which I have long decried. What corresponding damage we were able to do I dunno, but am afraid it falls far short of being worth it. So now we are back to one carrier, again.

27 Oct

Sub took a shot at *Washington* this morning, no doubt put on the trail by yesterday's shad. Missed. One detonated at end of run, between her and us, another ran right up our wake, porpoising, and sank about 800 yds away. Evidently, her spread was fired from extreme range, outside our screen. They have about 20 subs known to be in this area, so can afford long shot at such of our remaining effective units as they find. Needless to say, we got the hell outa there, continuing on Southeast, to fuel.

***

By midday on October 24, Task Force 64 was positioned equidistant from Cactus and Button and steamed on a variety of courses in waters that had been dubbed "Torpedo Junction," awaiting an opportunity to steam north to engage Japanese naval forces. That opportunity appeared the next day as Imperial Japanese naval forces closed on Guadalcanal in anticipation of a breakthrough by Lieutenant General Maruyama's Sendai Division. As Japanese destroyers appeared off Lunga Roads mid-morning, the contact report reached Lee before noon, and the powerful American surface flotilla surged on the northwesterly heading at 22 knots. At the time of the sighting, Lee's ships were to the southeast of Rennell Island, a large coral island located some 100 miles directly south of Guadalcanal.[1]

By 2000, Task Force 64 was positioned off the southwestern quadrant of Cactus, and an hour later, *Washington*, *San Francisco*, and *Helena* each launched scout planes. At 2154 *Atlanta*'s war diary recorded "Changed Course to 000°(T)," and six minutes later Lee's ships slowed to 22 knots as they inserted themselves into the slot.

With the Japanese surface forces having extracted themselves before sunset, Lee's scout planes searched in vain over the moonlit waters northwest of Cactus for any sign of a Tokyo Express column or a flotilla of Japanese heavy warships charging down for yet another bombardment mission of Henderson Field and environs in support of Maruyama's last gasp attacks that evening. Satisfied that no surface engagement would occur that evening, at 0215 early on October 26, *Atlanta* stood down from General Quarters and Condition 3 watches were set. At 0315, now heading due south, Task Force 64 formed a cruising disposition, with the major combatants following *Atlanta* in column while the destroyers steamed parallel to Jenkins' light cruiser in a line abreast. At 0535 Task Force 64 once again split. Task Group 64.1, centered on *Washington* and *Atlanta*, continued to steam south. At 0605 lookouts in *Atlanta* spotted a Japanese seaplane to the south, "well beyond gun range." By 0800, Task Group 64.1, now well clear of Cactus, steamed in waters west of Rennell Island.[2]

That afternoon, as Lee's ships continued deeper into the Coral Sea, the screening destroyers took an opportunity to refuel with black oil that could be spared from *Washington*'s bunkers. As the destroyers took turns at the battleship fuel trough, *Atlanta* steamed astern in a lifeguard position. That night, Lee's formation steamed well south of Rennell Island to stay out of range of Japanese carrier aircraft. However, as Lloyd recorded, submarines also posed a threat. At 0329, early on October 27, *Lansdowne* reported a torpedo approaching *Washington*. Having evaded the underwater missile, Lee's force cleared the area only to find themselves facing another spread of torpedoes just over two hours later. Lloyd recalled that with dawn breaking, the ship had been called to General Quarters per standard operating procedures. He went on to describe what happened next:

> … lo and behold, we had a submarine contact. The submarine fired torpedoes and everyone turned successfully to evade them including *Washington*. They had been firing at the *Washington* from the other side from where the *Atlanta* was so when they missed her they came on past us too. We just watched them run down each side as we threaded between them.[3]

The torpedo avoidance incident represented the closest Lloyd came to actual combat with the Japanese over the span of these three significant days in the Southwest Pacific. For his stepfather, the narrative would prove much different.

For several weeks since the loss of *Wasp*, *Hornet*—the centerpiece of Task Force 17—remained the U.S. Navy's remaining carrier in the region, and Vice Admiral Ghormley used it sparingly, given the Japanese land-based air threat and reports of Japanese carriers. Fortunately, with the arrival of *Hornet*'s older sister *Enterprise* and Task Force 16 on October 24, the balance of naval power evened, though still favoring the Japanese. Not only did American carrier strength double, but with the return of the patched *South Dakota*, the American Navy now fielded 18 16-inch guns to take on a surface duel with Japanese heavies. Under the command of Rear Adm. Thomas Kinkaid, Task Force 16 brought an additional heavy cruiser *Portland*, the light cruiser *San Juan*, and eight additional destroyers. The return of *San Juan* meant that all four *Atlanta*-class light cruisers were serving in the region, with *Juneau* and *San Diego* assigned to Rear Admiral Murray's Task Force 17.[4]

As the two task forces rendezvoused at 1400 on October 24, the more senior Turner took command of the overall American formation as Commander Task Force 61. Turner's immediate superior, Vice Admiral Halsey, remained ashore at Noumea, having moved his staff off the cramped quarters that had been provided by *Argonne*. Halsey and his boss, Admiral Nimitz at Pearl, matched wits with their Japanese counterpart, Admiral Yamamoto, who maintained his flag on the super battleship *Yamato* at Truk. That this behemoth of a battlewagon remained well away from the action illustrated that the Japanese faced the same problem that confronted the Americans and their battleships in the earlier months of the war—fuel consumption.

That fuel was needed to sustain the Tokyo Express and maintain Vice Adm. Nobutake Kondo's support force. Kondo steamed with the advance force, having Carrier Division 2 with the carriers *Hiyo* and *Junyo* backed with two battleships, five cruisers, and 10 destroyers. Fortunately for the Americans, the Japanese numeric flattop superiority dropped as an engineering space fire forced *Hiyo* to depart the area on October 21. Meanwhile, the bulk of Japanese striking power lay with the main body centered on Vice Admiral Nagumo's Carrier Division 1, having Pearl Harbor veterans *Zuikaku* and *Shokaku* and the light carrier *Zuiho*. These carriers were lightly protected by a screen that included a cruiser and eight destroyers. Rounding out Kondo's command, a vanguard force commanded by Rear Adm. Hiroaki Abe boasted serious surface firepower from two battleships, four cruisers, and seven destroyers.[5]

Despite the Japanese advantages not only in carriers but in surface combatants, Halsey intended to ease enemy naval pressure on Cactus. While Lee and Task Force 64 swung up from the Coral Sea to interdict Japanese forces coming down the slot, Halsey directed Kinkaid to take Task Force 61 to well northeast of Guadalcanal north of the Santa Cruz islands and sweep from east to west.

Though the Japanese held numeric advantages, the side with carriers that launched "firstest with the mostest" had the best chance of prevailing, so reconnaissance proved critical. On October 25, the Americans gained the supposed upper hand due to multiple sightings of Japanese forces by PBYs and B-17s, leading to a launch of torpedo planes and dive-bombers off *Enterprise*. However, Vice Admiral Nagumo, appreciating the consequences of being sighted, prudently reversed course and took his carriers beyond the range of *Enterprise*'s fliers who had to return to their carrier after sunset.[6]

Night-flying Catalinas with airborne radar not only continued to give the Americans a spotting leg up on the Japanese, but also an offensive capability. Having again reversed his course and wondering if the Americans were aware of his presence in the pre-dawn hours of August 26, Vice Admiral Nagumo found out when four bombs dropped from one of the American PBYs exploded a mere 300 yards off

Zuikaku at 0250. Nagumo, fearing that the rising sun could obscure swarms of American carrier aircraft, again changed Carrier Division 1's course to a northern heading. Unfortunately for the Americans, Rear Admiral Kinkaid embarked in *Enterprise* could not discern a clear picture of the Japanese forces from the nocturnal reports of the PBYs, so prior to sunrise the *Big E* launched a combat air patrol of Wildcats and eight pairs of Dauntlesses to obtain a positive fix on the enemy carriers.[7]

One pair of the SBDs came across Abe's Vanguard Force at 0630 bearing west of *Enterprise* at a distance of 170 miles. Twenty minutes later, a second pair observed Nagumo's main force to the northwest at a distance of 200 miles. Nagumo's own combat air patrol chased away this and another pair of U.S. Navy dive-bombers that responded to the contact report, but a third pair found gaps in the Japanese fighter defense and pressed an attack on *Zuiho* at 0740, scoring a hit aft. Though Japanese damage control teams quickly extinguished the flames, *Zuiho* no longer could conduct flight operations and factor in the evolving battle.[8]

At the time the Americans had placed *Zuiho* out of action, that light carrier, along with the two heavy carriers, had already launched a potent strike of 62 aircraft in a southeasterly heading in response to a Japanese scout plane sighting of Task Force 16. Nagumo, confident his aviators would knock out the sighted American flattop, ordered Abe to steam east to close for a decisive surface action. If the first wave of Japanese dive-bombers and torpedo planes did complete the job, the follow-on smaller waves of Val and Kate aircraft would mop up what was left.[9]

As a total of 110 Japanese aircraft headed toward Task Force 16 as well as Task Force 17, a smaller cadre of American planes lifted off *Hornet* and *Enterprise*. *Hornet* provided the bulk of the American initial strike force with 15 dive-bombers and 6 torpedo planes escorted by 8 fighters. Whereas the Japanese used aircraft catapulted from battleships and cruisers for scouting purposes, the American practice of deploying scout planes from carriers limited the number of airframes available for a strike. That morning's dispersing of 16 SBDs from *Enterprise* cut that carrier's contribution to a mere 20 aircraft. A half hour after *Hornet*'s first launch, Lloyd's stepfather watched another 25 aircraft lift off and turn to the northwest.[10]

With two groups of warplanes heading to opposing objectives, not surprisingly they met along the way. As the Japanese were first in the air, their initial strike group had gained higher altitude. Somehow *Hornet*'s planes passed in the vicinity unnoticed, but their Zero escorts spotted the smaller *Enterprise* group and dove on the Americans. The ensuing dogfight cost the Americans four Avenger torpedo planes and four Wildcats, while the Japanese lost four Zeros and suffered damage to a fifth.[11]

Forewarned by radio and then radar, *Hornet* scrambled more fighters to meet the onslaught of Japanese aircraft that had George Murray's task force in sight as Task Force 16 had slipped into a rainsquall 10 miles to the northeast. As Wildcats from both *Enterprise* and *Hornet* struggled to gain height to meet the oncoming attackers, Capt. Charles P. Mason brought *Hornet* up to 31 knots on a northeasterly heading, and her escort of four cruisers pinched in to increase the number of gun barrels aimed skyward. Off her bow, sailors on the heavy cruisers *Northampton* and *Pensacola* scanned the skies as did sailors on *Atlanta*'s two sisters, *San Diego* and *Juneau* astride her stern.[12]

Though those sailors could see some evidence of the Wildcats challenging the Japanese on the western horizon, the combat air patrol had been poorly directed and there simply were too many attackers. At 0910, nearly 20 Vals started to descend on *Hornet* one by one. Captain Mason's evasive action plus voluminous gunfire caused the first two dropped bombs and bomb-dropping aircraft to fall to starboard of the bridge; however, three Vals scored bomb hits on the flight deck adjacent to the bridge, and between the midship and aft elevators. Another Val crashed against *Hornet*'s stack, spraying the signal bridge area with burning aviation gas. The remnants of the plane and its undetonated bomb reached the crew's galley, setting off an intense fire.[13]

The skill exhibited by the Val pilots was matched by Japan's torpedo plane crews as they divided into two formations that approached the burning carrier from two directions, assuring that a turn to straddle one spread of fish would simply expose *Hornet*'s broadside to a second set. Two torpedoes pierced the carrier's hull. One on the port side punched a hole into the forward engineering space, and the other hit on the starboard quarter into compartmentalized spaces. In one final blow, another Val flying from astern flew over the bridge and plunged itself on the port side of the flight deck, eliminating a number of gun mounts and their crews.[14]

Only minutes after *Hornet* withstood what would prove to be fatal punishment, her aviators exacted some revenge on *Shokaku*. Dauntlesses scored hits, tearing up her flight deck aft of the bridge. Near misses also damaged the big carrier as well as a screening destroyer. *Hornet*'s torpedo planes, the following *Enterprise* planes, and the second *Hornet* strike, failed to locate Carrier Division 1 and attacked Japanese surface combatants if they could be found. The second group from *Hornet*, which included bomb-laden Avengers, located and delivered a savage attack on the cruiser *Chikuma*.[15]

Meanwhile, the Vals from Carrier Division 1's second strike arrived in the vicinity of the two American task forces past 1000 and passed over the billowing *Hornet* to search further for the other American carrier. Having met nominal American fighter resistance, the Japanese dive-bombers located Kinkaid's flagship and positioned themselves for their steep descent. Though guarded by fewer cruisers, with the heavy cruiser *Portland* close to her port bow and *Atlanta* sister ship *San Juan* to starboard, there was the battleship *South Dakota* astern. With the carrier's and battleship's recent repair visit to Pearl Harbor, both ships were each fitted with 16 Bofors rapid-fire 40mm antiaircraft guns.

As with the attack on the *Hornet*, the Japanese aviators scored hits at great cost. One bomb passed through the forward port flight deck only to travel into and out of the forecastle to clear the ship's interior before detonating, and then a second hit the flight deck aft of the forward elevator, causing damage and death on both the hangar and third deck below. One near miss sent a shock wave through the ship that bounced a plane over the side.[16]

Unlike the attack on *Hornet*, the torpedo plane attack on *Big E* was slow to develop, and the combat air patrol and gunners would have ample time to test their marksmanship. Attempting to run the gamut of American ordnance, one Kate crashed into the forward 5-inch mount of the destroyer *Smith*. With a blazing forecastle driving the bridge team out of the pilothouse, *Smith*'s commanding officer calmly regained control of the ship from the after-steering station and maneuvered the light tin can under the churning wake of *South Dakota*, which served to dampen the flames. Those planes that survived the hot metal fired in their direction failed to score hits with their fish. Of the 44 aircraft used in Nagumo's second wave, 24 would fail to return.

With still an hour before noon, the situation for the Americans grew more unfavorable. *Hornet* crippled, sought a tow from *Northampton* to clear the area as her engineers evaluated the damage, and contemplated getting steam up to get one shaft turning. Though still able to land and launch aircraft despite having its number two midships elevator locked in a down position, *Enterprise* was incapable of unleashing another strike at the Japanese. Though the Americans had forced *Zuiho* and *Shokaku* from the scene, the remaining heavy carrier *Zuikaku* and light carrier *Junyo* of Kondo's advance force, along with an impressive array of surface forces, now provided the Japanese a lopsided advantage that they intended to press.

Junyo's first strike of Vals passed over *Hornet* and arrived over *Enterprise* at 1121 as Task Force 16 ducked under the low cloud cover of a heavy rain squall, forcing the Japanese to glide in on their target. Though the defending gunners could only pick out the incoming attackers on their final approach, they splashed a number of enemy aircraft. Unfortunately, one bomb detonated 8 feet off the starboard side had the carrier heeled over to port, shuddering the ship and causing below-waterline damage comparable to that of a torpedo.

Junyo's fliers also went after some of the other ships in the task force. *San Juan* became the first ship of the *Atlanta*-class to be bloodied when a bomb passed through her thinly plated stern section to explode beneath the ship, jamming the rudder in a full right position. With *South Dakota*'s AA batteries dispatching broadside attackers, one Val pilot took a head-on approach and successfully lobbed a bomb onto the battleship's forward turret. Shielded under heavy steel, the turret survived unscathed but the exploding bomb fragments wounded over 50, killing two.[17]

As surviving *Junyo* pilots turned their aircraft homeward bound, *Hornet* and *Enterprise* aircraft returning from the raid on Nagumo's carriers could finally be landed. *Big E*'s landing signal officer successfully trapped 57 aircraft. Tragically, one Avenger damaged in the attack on *Zuiho* ditched ahead of the destroyer *Porter*, jarring its torpedo loose to commence an underwater voyage that, despite desperate strafing by overhead Wildcats, would end up hitting *Porter* between her boiler rooms, killing 15 of her crew. Rather than spare a warship to tow *Porter* out of harm, Rear Admiral Kinkaid elected to order Lt. Cdr. Wilbur G. Jones in *Shaw* to recover the surviving crew and sink *Porter* with gunfire—the first ship that day on either side to be sunk.

No longer fearing American naval airpower, Vice Admiral Kondo detached *Junyo* to join Nagumo's main body and surged forward with his advance and vanguard forces to bring the Americans within range of his 14-inch guns. To delay any potential departure of the American forces from the scene, both *Junyo* and *Zuikaku* launched early afternoon strikes.[18]

Appreciating that the numbers now heavily favored the Japanese and having no interest in engaging in a gun duel, Rear Admiral Kinkaid ordered Task Force 16 to withdraw to the southeast. Kinkaid's departure with *Enterprise* meant no air cover for a struggling *Hornet* that *Northampton* attempted to take under tow. Lloyd's stepfather had transferred his flag to that cruiser just before noon. Meanwhile, destroyers pulled close by the crippled carrier to take off the seriously injured and hundreds of others who no longer were needed. Other sailors remained aboard to flesh out gun crews or work below to place at least one shaft back in operation.[19]

At around 1500 the Japanese aircraft arrived in the vicinity. Without air cover, *Northampton* released the towing line and presented a stern aspect to the slow descending Kate torpedo planes off of *Junyo*. Though *Hornet*'s gunners dropped several of the attackers, a torpedo struck on the starboard side at 1523 aft and above

USS *Hornet* (CV 8) dead in the water with a destroyer alongside taking off crew following the decision to abandon ship. (Archives Branch, Naval History and Heritage Command, Washington, D.C.; 80-G-34110) (Archives Branch, Naval History and Heritage Command, Washington, D.C.; 80-G-304514)

an earlier hit. It was a crushing blow that erased any hope of recovery as the ship listed close to 15 degrees. As *Junyo*'s torpedo planes departed, Vals from *Zuikaku* arrived and scored near misses by *Hornet* and *San Diego*. Bomb-carrying Kates made a level bombing run, dropping a pattern of projectiles of which one penetrated the stern of the doomed carrier. By this time Captain Mason had ordered the remaining crew to abandon the carrier that had once carried Doolittle's raiders on their famous strike on the Japanese homeland. Mason was last to step off at 1627.[20]

Just after 1700, more Vals from *Junyo* appeared and made a run on the now-empty listing hulk that was *Hornet*, scoring yet another hit on the hangar deck. With Admiral Nimitz relaying to Rear Admiral Murray that radio intelligence indicated that heavy Japanese surface forces were converging on his position, Murray detailed the destroyer named for his wife's first husband and Lloyd's father to assure *Hornet* would not fall into enemy hands. Of the spread of eight torpedoes *Mustin* fired, three exploded against *Hornet*'s hull. However, the workers of Newport News Shipbuilding Company built one solid warship, and *Mustin* failed to observe any progress toward expediting *Hornet*'s plunge into the Pacific. Soon *Mustin* was joined by *Anderson*, which doubled *Mustin*'s score with her spread of eight fish. However, the six additional blows to *Hornet*'s hull still failed to flip her over. As the day receded, Japanese scout planes flew over to observe the odd scene of two American destroyers peppering one of their most prized ships with 5-inch rounds. Alerted of the potential of capturing an afloat albeit crippled American carrier, Vice Admiral Kondo's forces accelerated, and he sent destroyers ahead to engage and chase off the two American surface ships that were attempting to foil their attempt at capture. At 2015, *Mustin*'s radarmen reported contacts to the west, and soon numerous contacts could be discerned. Having expended hundreds of rounds of ammunition into the dying carrier's blazing hull, the two American tin cans exited the area at flank speed, chased by Japanese floatplanes. Twenty minutes after *Mustin* and *Anderson* departed, the burning pyre drew the Japanese destroyers *Akigumo* and *Makikumo* to close quarters. As the Japanese capital ships came over the horizon with their commanders, hopes for towing home an American carrier to impress the Emperor faded as the list on *Hornet* increased to 45 degrees. Concluding that the carrier was beyond salvage, Vice Admiral Kondo gave the two destroyers permission to finish her off with two Long Lance torpedoes apiece. Early on October 27, a day that had been celebrated in the United States for two decades as Navy Day, *Hornet* finally began her plunge to the ocean floor.[21]

Lloyd recalled his stepfather was a quiet person who privately remained bitter on how *Hornet* was abandoned as his long-time friend, Thomas Kinkaid, departed, leaving Task Force 17 with no air cover. "I think what had been a friendship for many years between those two officers was never the same thereafter."[22]

Scott Embarks

28 October

***

This date and just this date marked the last entry into Lieutenant Commander Mustin's diary. During October a directive was issued forbidding the keeping of personal diaries. Either Lloyd decided to obey this directive or the uptick in tempo over the next two weeks leading to the naval battle of Guadalcanal kept Lloyd away from putting his thoughts down on paper.

That morning just before 0800 in waters between New Caledonia and Espiritu Santo *Atlanta* steamed alongside the heavy cruiser *San Francisco* to take aboard Rear Admiral Scott. With the arrival of Scott and his staff to *Atlanta*, ComSoPac dispatch 271108 came into effect, reorganizing Task Force 64 to establish Task Group 64.2 under Scott's command. Led by *Atlanta*, serving as Scott's flagship, Task Group 64.2 also included the destroyers *Aaron Ward*, *Benham*, *Fletcher*, and *Lardner*.[1]

The reassignment sort of represented a demotion for Scott, the recent victor at the battle of Cape Esperance. However, Vice Admiral Halsey, as the

Prior to promotion to flag rank, Norman Scott served as the commanding officer of USS *Pensacola* (CA 24). (Archives Branch, Naval History and Heritage Command, Washington, D.C.; 80-G-20823)

new area commander, took his prerogative to bring in his own staff. Consequently, Ghormley's chief of staff, Daniel Callaghan, himself recently promoted to flag rank, was now without work. Relieved of this exhausting duty, Halsey decided to send Callaghan back to his old cruiser to take command of the cruiser surface action group.[2]

Though a demotion for Scott, his arrival and the mission he was being assigned to carry on excited Lloyd. Though the battle of Cape Esperance had flaws in execution, Scott's leadership impressed Lloyd: "He knew exactly what his little force was and what he intended to do with it." In Lloyd's mind, Scott had "brought off a thundering victory" and provided the whole South Pacific Navy "a great shot in the arm." *Atlanta*'s assistant gun boss later reflected: "In that remote part of the world aggressive leadership was a scarce commodity. It seemed to me that in his quiet way Norman Scott was one of those who had it."[3]

The arrival of Scott and his staff placed a small burden on a warship not designed to serve as a flagship; however, Lloyd remembered those two-plus weeks with the admiral embarked really seemed "like a long and a very pleasant and interesting interlude."[4] Lloyd observed that Scott seemed most comfortable on board, despite *Atlanta*'s lackluster accommodations. Scott was familiar with the class, having hoisted his flag earlier that summer in *San Juan*. Part of the reason for Scott's comfort is he enjoyed spending most of his awake hours on the bridge. Whereas Captain Jenkins occupied the chair on the starboard corner of the pilothouse, Rear Admiral Scott made himself at home in the chair that occupied the port corner.

Since Lloyd Mustin now stood officer-of-the-deck duties along with Communications Officer Paul Smith and Assistant Engineering Officer Jack Wulff, he had ample opportunity to engage with Scott, "who was very friendly and conversational, discussed anything and everything, and relied primarily on we three officers of the deck to serve the purpose that in more elaborate organizations is served by a senior watch officer."[5]

The next day proved uneventful as the five-ship flotilla closed in on Cactus. Having circled around the eastern side of the island after dark, the small flotilla arrived off Lunga Point in the early morning hours of October 30. Each ship took on a couple of map-carrying officers who had pinpointed Japanese troop concentrations, artillery positions, and supply depots for annihilation. Once embarked, the five warships proceeded westward with *Atlanta* in the van to bombard Japanese positions ashore. Lloyd recalled this was a hurried "Hit-and-run" concept: "We were supposed to get in there, do the job, and get the hell out before counteraction by Rabaul air reached us."[6]

With Captain Jenkins at the conn, the firing commenced at 0629. Lloyd recalled that *Atlanta* "fired 4,093 rounds of 5 inch in something like an hour fifty minutes." The destroyers, having smaller magazines and single-mount 5-inch guns, added to

SCOTT EMBARKS • 231

the carnage ashore. "It was quite a sight because there were no holds barred … it was just a sort of have at them fellows—the sons of bitches are right over that way."[7]

As Scott's flotilla worked their way along the northwestern coast from the Matanikau River delta to Tassafaronga Point, *Atlanta's* gunners fired whatever the ammunition handling crews would send up. Lloyd observed the 5-inch common projectiles with a solid nose and base delayed fuse penetrated through the jungle canopy to "blow in bunkers and foxholes." Some antiaircraft rounds, in contrast, detonated upon hitting the trees or ground, while others were set to explode over the tress to rain metal fragments down on exposed Japanese troops.[8]

Later asked if such a volume of gunfire wore down the bores, Lloyd noted that the expenditure of just over four grand in ammunition on a ship carrying eight twin mounts amounted to a mere 250 rounds fired per gun. What amazed Lloyd in the aftermath was the mountains of cartridge tanks commonly called shell casings that piled up behind each gun mount, as for each round fired a casing was kicked out the back of the mount.[9]

By 0920, Scott's small task group was again underway, arriving at Espiritu Santo the next afternoon to take on fuel and ammunition.[10]

As Scott's task group replenished, Major General Vandegrift took advantage of the raking that had just been completed of the Japanese positions to take the offensive, ordering two battalions of the 5th Marines to push across the Matanikau River delta. The Japanese defenders put up a token resistance and avoided being routed only because Vandegrift couldn't spare any further Marines or soldiers from his perimeter defenses. Halsey, having delegated overall command of the naval forces in the Guadalcanal vicinity to Turner, remained committed to giving Vandegrift the type of support that was demonstrated by Scott's group on October 30. Turner, in turn, ordered Callaghan to take his ships up to Cactus for a repeat performance. Thus, on the morning of November 4, the Japanese were peppered by a combination of 5-, 6-, and 8-inch shells from the destroyer *Sterett*, light cruiser *Helena*, and Callaghan's flagship *San Francisco*.[11]

Despite these offensive actions, the Japanese still had an overall advantage in the region. At the battle of Santa Cruz, the Japanese had scored a tactical victory by sinking *Hornet* and damaging *Enterprise*. True, the Japanese had a light and a heavy carrier temporarily removed from their order of battle for immediate operations; however, *Zuikaku* and *Junyo* remained as well as an impressive array of battleships, cruisers, destroyers, and submarines. Still the Japanese could not exploit this advantage. Though Japanese naval forces steamed over waters that hours earlier had hosted two American task forces, the overnight harassment by American Catalinas proved to be one of several factors to lead Vice Admiral Kondo to cease pursuit operations and withdraw. More significantly, fuel levels had declined, and though two carriers remained, the number of available aircrews available for further flight operations had been cut down by the increasingly effective antiaircraft gunfire from

American combatants as well as from defending Wildcats. Such was the loss that the unscathed *Zuikaku* would also need to be recalled to Japanese home waters to provide a training flight deck for aircrews coming up through the pipeline.[12]

This temporary withdrawal gave Halsey's and Vandegrift's forces at sea and on the ground some temporary breathing room, though the Tokyo Express kept making runs down the slot to deliver reinforcements. A day and a half after Rear Admiral Callaghan's bombardment run, a light cruiser and 15 Japanese destroyers dropped off yet another regiment of Japanese soldiers to confront the American Marines. Still, this piecemeal deployment of forces onto the island would only serve to preserve a stalemate. Admiral Yamamoto recognized the only way to achieve victory was to place overwhelming ground forces onto the island, and in early November American intelligence confirmed that the Japanese were marshalling forces to do just that.[13]

On November 6, a coastwatcher counted 33 Japanese vessels near Shortland Island less than 300 miles northwest up the slot from Cactus. Two days later, on November 8, another coastwatcher caught a glimpse of a dozen transports further distant at the northern tip of Bougainville. That evening Halsey, having feasted on a banquet of Spam, dehydrated potatoes, and beans with Vandegrift at Guadalcanal for an overnight visit, gained a better appreciation for the situation on the ground by experiencing a nighttime bombardment by a Japanese destroyer.[14]

The following morning, having been provisioned with fuel, food, and ammunition, Scott's light cruiser and four-destroyer task group departed from Espiritu Santo with the destroyer *McCalla* substituting for *Benham*. This journey would take longer due to the assigned escort mission to assure the Navy cargo ships *Betelgeuse*, *Libra*, and *Zeilin* would make it to Cactus unscathed. Besides vitally needed supplies and ammunition, the three escorted ships carried a Marine aviation engineer battalion and other replacements to support Henderson Field's operation. Following Scott a day later, Callaghan's more potent task group left Espiritu Santo with his three cruisers and six destroyers. Scott and Callahan's immediate operational commander, Turner, was also en route to Guadalcanal from Noumea. Embarked on his flagship, the transport *McCawley*, Turner oversaw a surface movement that included three other transports, the cruiser *Portland* and *Atlanta*'s Federal twin *Juneau*, and four additional destroyers. Turner's four transports carried the bulk of the 6,000 Americans who would join the fight on the ground, including most of an Army regiment, a Marine replacement battalion, and a sorely needed 155mm howitzer artillery unit.[15]

Unfortunately, Scott's slower passage did not go undetected, as lookouts spotted a Japanese seaplane on November 10, with Guadalcanal still beyond the horizon. His force retraced their path taken at the end of October and arrived off Lunga Point at 0530 on November 11. With calm seas and a slight breeze, the three cargo ships immediately began offloading operations before the anticipated air attack by nine Val dive-bombers escorted by Zero fighters arrived. Lloyd would later lament that *Atlanta*'s radar failed to pick them up and the first sighting was visual. Offloading ceased and the ships got underway, with *Atlanta* leading *Betelgeuse*, *Libra*, and *Zeitlin* in a column, and the four destroyers taking flanking positions 1,500 yards off the column's port and starboard sides. Lloyd recalled: "They came in at a characteristic dive bomber altitude of 15,000." Lloyd remembered the Japanese dive-bombers approached the formation in a line abreast: "Evidently the leader was on his right-hand end of the line. He started his dive first. The others all turned to their right and flew roughly to the same point in the sky where the leader had started his dive and then they pushed over into their dive."

With *Atlanta* positioned ahead of the cargo ships that proved to be the focal point of the Japanese, Lloyd's aft batteries would carry the brunt of the light cruiser's response. Focusing on the three cargo ships, the Japanese dive-bombers were met by a gauntlet of gunfire thrown up by *Atlanta*, the four destroyers, as well as sailors stationed on the three cargo ships looking up at the airplanes that were diving directly on them. Lloyd recollected:

> So here we were in a familiar situation gunnery wise. Regardless of how much information we had earlier, we had to shift very speedily to a new target whose movements were quite different from anything that we had generated into our computers and do something about opening effective fire on them. That's just what we did with this technique of sluing the director to the dive bomber in its dive following him down on his dive path while using the best estimate for what the computer operator would crank in for range and speed and so on. We were careful to know what the typical speeds were of various planes in various altitudes. Rate controlling while following with a sluing sight to get a hitting solution. We did that with the after battery which I was controlling and which was nearest to the Jap's target.[16]

Lloyd claimed they fired at as many as six different aircraft by following one down, ceasing fire, and sluing back up to another one. He lamented that background interference from the mountains of Guadalcanal and other airplanes rendered the range-finding radar as less than optimal so there was a great reliance on the optical range finder. Another lament was fuses on the shells had to be set mechanically, and several factors contributed to incorrect settings being locked in. That said, Lloyd did note that misses could and did contribute to hindering the enemy aircraft's descent.

Gunfire claimed about half of the attackers. Three near hits on *Zeitlin* caused a hold to flood, and the other two cargo ships sustained minor damage. Marine Wildcats caught up and shot down the remaining Vals and tangled and shot down some of the escorting Japanese fighters. Asked if his guns accounted for some of the Japanese losses, Lloyd simply could not recall because he was constantly sluing the director up to the next diving plane and lost focus on the aircraft he had been firing on.[17]

At midday a larger Japanese air strike arrived using twin-engine bombers to drop ordnance on Guadalcanal. Lloyd recalled, "I don't remember the time very strongly because not only did hours blend into one another but so did the days in those days having been awake for 36 hours or so and living at the air defense station topside." With clear visibility, Lloyd could see the formation of three Vs of Japanese Bettys approaching. Again, Scott had the cargo ships and their escorts weigh anchor and steam northward in using a defensive screen around the cargo ships. Because they approached at an altitude of 28,000 feet, Lloyd was not surprised that they could not be challenged by Henderson Field-based Wildcats, as he understood those planes had difficulty operating at that height. Though not directly attacked, Scott's ships contributed to an antiaircraft barrage that reached up at the Japanese aviators. Lloyd recalled:

> As the *Atlanta* displaced herself toward the north and as they came in, the captain just kept the ship turning to port so that our full broadside bore on this formation. Jim Shaw in Plot kept telling me, 'They are out of range ... They are out of Range.' We had the Mark 1 computer, of course. It has a dial on its face that reads target altitude although that's not really a component of the solution to hit. The upper limit of the reading was 25,000 feet. These planes were at 28 as I mentioned. So this was the source of his comment that 'They were out of range.' I couldn't believe it from looking at them so I kept asking him what the range was and the range in yards was closing. The maximum setting on our time fuses at that time was 45 seconds so I just kept asking him what the fuse calculation was. As soon as it got down to 45 seconds I ordered commence firing.

In retrospect, Lloyd marveled that he could give this order despite having a chain of more senior officers embarked, including a rear admiral. "It was a situation that had been made fully clear as a standing bit of doctrine," he reflected, in contrast to the pre-war era, "where you had to get permission from almost God Almighty before you could presume to pull the trigger on shot number one."

Lloyd believed *Atlanta*'s guns accounted for two Bettys falling out of their formations. Whereas Samuel Elliot Morison dismissed the attack as yet another attempt to disable Henderson Field, Lloyd observed the bomb-drop zone to be the area where they had just offloaded cargo. Later Lloyd Mustin learned that the impact of the Japanese bombs on the stored goods had been nominal. Ironically, the fragments of over 300 bursting shells rained down on Henderson Field, limiting flight operations as ground crews swept over the runways to clear shards of steel.[18]

Offloading operations continued through the afternoon. With *Zeitlin* damaged with a flooded hold, Scott ordered her to depart that evening and assigned *Lardner* as her escort. Scott then took *Atlanta* and his three remaining destroyers into the Indispensable Strait north of Lunga Point that night where they were met by Callaghan's force that arrived at 2200. Leaving three destroyers to guard the two remaining cargo ships, Callaghan pushed ahead, taking Scott in *Atlanta* along for two thorough sweeps to the east and west of Savo Island to interdict any Tokyo Express deliveries scheduled for that evening. There were none.[19]

For Lloyd, the sortie to the western end of Guadalcanal meant two back-to-back nights up in the gun director. Lloyd recalled there was no great strain and much good humor. Runners brought up food and good water from the galley, and sailors were allowed to quickly break away from their battle station to use the head and clean up as needed. "Least of all, Captain Jenkins was perfectly calm as far as the ship's company was able to observe." Lloyd continued: "He was a thoroughly practical leader and commander and wonderful one."[20]

Having returned from their westward sweep, Callaghan and Scott waited for the arrival of Turner's transports and escorts from Noumea, which arrived at 0530. As the morning brightened, six vessels now stood off the American beachhead. *Betelgeuse* and *Libra* remained anchored a mile east of Lunga Point, while Turner's four transports including his flagship dropped their hooks off Kukum Beach. With the assistance of the small craft of the Cactus Navy, offloading operations proceeded. Not surprisingly, the arrival of the additional transports and escorts drew Japanese attention, and at 0718, "Pistol Pete" began to lob shells down upon the *Betelgeuse* and *Libra*. Lloyd observed:

> It wasn't a very big gun ... but it had enough range to reach out and plop single shells upon those transports. I could judge by the size of the splash that it was not a very big caliber projectile, but nonetheless a hit by such a projectile on a crowded transport full of troops, ammunition, and supplies was something not to be taken lightly.

The Japanese artillery piece immediately drew counterbattery fire from American artillery ashore as well as from gun barrels afloat on the destroyers *Barton*, *Shaw*, and the cruiser *Helena*. Unfortunately, the ships that were assigned to provide counterbattery fire were simply guessing at where the Japanese gun was located, as from their positions the gun was well hidden by the jungle canopy. In contrast, Lloyd could clearly see the opening and the muzzle flashes: "Our director officers were able to put the directors directly on, measure the range to it with the optical range finders, and were prepared to shoot effectively." Lloyd informed the bridge of this but could not get permission to engage. "Somewhere between Captain Jenkins and Admiral Callaghan the proposition of going in there and engaging this thing with the *Atlanta* died and was forgotten."[21]

This last statement from Lloyd reflected a recent change in the command structure that had occurred thanks to the arrival of Callaghan's and Turner's forces. Turner, as the overall on-scene naval commander, decided to consolidate the command of the screening cruisers and destroyers to the slightly more senior Callaghan, leaving Scott and his small staff to be relegated as guests of Captain Jenkins and his crew. Turner had urgent reasons for the decision. Earlier that morning he learned that patrol planes had spotted either two Japanese battleships or heavy cruisers, a cruiser, and six destroyers heading down the slot with a speed of advance that would place them off Lunga Point late that evening. To meet the threat Turner have could formed his ships in a defensive alignment around his transports. Instead he formulated a plan to send Callaghan out to meet the incoming Japanese strike force, hoping an engagement would deter a crippling bombardment of Henderson Field.[22]

With a clash pending for that evening, the Americans would still need to get through the day. Knowing that the calm waters off Lunga Point offered a target-rich environment for torpedo-armed bombers, the Japanese launched an air strike of 21 Bettys, escorted by Zeros, that arrived just after 1400.

As the attack unfolded Lloyd observed: "In they came and a fairly awesome sight it was." Lloyd noted that the screening combatants on the side from which they were approached "did a very fine job on them." As the enemy planes came within 5,000 yards, the main batteries of the cruisers *Helena* and *San Francisco* unleased salvos aimed to confront the attackers with tall geysers of sea spray. More effective was the 5-inch and smaller caliber fire thrown up which unnerved many of the Japanese pilots who chose to pull up rather than press on, but in doing lost airspeed and exposed their undersides to the American gunners.[23]

As the attack came close to its conclusion, *Atlanta* finally got to shoot at Japanese planes that were on the left side of their line abreast. From Lloyd's perspective, they

This photograph, taken from USS *President Adams* (AP 38), depicts USS *President Jackson* (AP 37) maneuvering amid a Japanese air attack off Guadalcanal, November 12, 1942. In the center background is smoke from an enemy plane that had just crashed into the after superstructure of USS *San Francisco* (CA 38). (Archives Branch, Naval History and Heritage Command, Washington, D.C.; 80-G-32366)

came in from the right side. "That's where we were and we had a chance to shoot with the after group because they just flew down and flew across our stern ... we had a chance to fire at about two, perhaps more, but at least two that we fired on we saw go down in the water between us and Guadalcanal."[24]

The pilot of a crippled Japanese plane, having aimed his dropped torpedo at *San Francisco*, apparently elected to add devastation by flying at the heavy cruiser. Though the torpedo missed, the Betty did not, smashing into the structure aft of the stacks that housed the control station for the aft triple 8-inch gun turret. Besides taking out the control station, the after antiaircraft director and radar were damaged, and three 20mm mounts were destroyed, killing their gun crews. Spilled aviation gas from the plane caused a fireball and additional casualties. Though Rear Admiral Callaghan stationed on the forward flag bridge was spared, the ship's executive officer received severe burns on his legs. Many of *San Francisco*'s wounded were transferred to the transport *President Jackson*, which hosted more extensive medical facilities.

No enemy torpedoes found their mark, a stunning testament to the ferocity of the anti-air barrage put out by the defending ships and heroism of the Cactus Air Force. In addition to the damage sustained by *San Francisco*, *Buchanan*'s aft stack was hit by a friendly 5-inch round which killed five sailors, wounded seven more, and damaged the torpedo tubes. With the skies cleared of the Japanese, Turner turned the formation back to Lunga Point to enable the transports and cargo ships to continue offloading men and materiel. Lloyd recalled steaming past the floating fuselages and pieces of the fallen aircraft. "We must have been no more than 100 yards from one of these Bettys ... it passed down our starboard side and we looked at it."[25]

CHAPTER 28

Friday the 13th

Years later, thinking about the remnants of those Japanese aircraft that had been blown out of the sky over the waters off Guadalcanal, Lloyd Mustin reflected:

> It was a small event in the history of the war, no doubt, but it was large in the struggle for Guadalcanal in that in three air attacks over a period of two days the Japanese had substantially depleted their immediate available air resources and had been unable to interfere with what had turned out to be for that time and place in the world a pretty important reinforcement operation by the U.S.

Thanks to reports from coast watchers and scout planes, Lloyd had an appreciation for what lay ahead that evening. "Really big Japanese forces were converging from the north as they usually did from Truk and from the northwest, the Rabaul and Shortlands complex."[1]

As evening approached, the transports and cargo ships completed offloading as much materials as feasibly possibly, and by 1815 all of Turner's ships were heading eastward, led by Callaghan's screening cruisers and destroyers through Sealark Channel. Once through the channel into the Indispensable Strait, Turner proceeded onward to Espiritu Santo, with *McCawley* along with the five other transports and cargo ships. They would be escorted by the destroyers *Buchanan*, *McCalla*, *Shaw* and two World War I-vintage destroyers, *Hovey* and *Southard*, which had been converted to high-speed minesweepers to clear the area and return. Callaghan in *San Francisco* took the remaining combatants back through the more southerly Lengo Channel in a column formation. It was a tactical move that Lloyd approved of. "It was undoubtedly wise to have taken the whole force out to the east as darkness fell in order to contribute to deceiving the Japanese as to whether we had left or not."[2]

Lloyd Mustin remembered the 13-ship column having the five cruisers bracketed by four destroyers in the van and four more to the rear. "A column, of course, was the only way to run any of those eastern channels." *Atlanta* led the five cruisers. From his perch in the aft gun director Lloyd could see the flagship *San Francisco* steaming 700 to 800 yards astern in *Atlanta's* wake. Lloyd did the math and estimated the column was over 3 miles in length. For those who were superstitious, the idea of going into battle with 13 ships as a component of Task Force 67 seemed ominous. Then, as midnight passed, the calendar turned to Friday the 13th.[3]

In his oral history, Lloyd recalled the sequence of events and critiqued the performance of the U.S. Navy that evening:

> What was really troublesome from the very beginning of this ballgame was the fact that Admiral Callaghan had given himself a very cumbersome formation and he was handling it in an extraordinarily cumbersome manner. He had limited himself to that. He had given no statement of how he intended to use his forces. Any such a plan, even a bad one, would in all probability have been better than none at all. He hadn't given us any.

Lloyd levied additional criticism for the how the single-frequency TBS radio was employed to maneuver the formation. Assuming the Japanese could listen in on the voice transmissions, an encryption technique using a simple substitution cypher dubbed the Shackle Code was employed. Unfortunately, the shackling and unshackling of course and speed changes hindered rapid formation maneuverability. Accentuating the problem, Lloyd recalled Callaghan's tactical voice radio talker "put out these signals in this lengthy labored manor … would repeat the whole thing, and then finally execute it."[4]

Callaghan's column steamed westward, passing north of the Lunga Point beachheads. As the island coastline curved in a northwesterly direction, adjustments were made to the column's heading to keep the formation parallel to the coast. Reflecting later, Lloyd meted out harsher criticism for not having a cruiser carrying an SG surface search radar further up the column. The fourth ship in the column ahead of *Atlanta*, the destroyer *O'Bannon*, did carry a set. *Atlanta* did not carry this equipment nor did Callaghan's flagship *San Francisco*. *Portland* did. Lloyd had learned about the capabilities of the SG before *Atlanta* had left the Brooklyn Navy Yard. Steaming behind *Portland*, the light cruiser *Helena* had an SG set as did the trailing cruiser in the column, *Atlanta*'s sister *Juneau*. Lloyd recalled, "It was on a frequency of 3,000 megacycles … this gave this radar a very narrow beam for a modest size of antenna." He noted it was the first Navy radar planned position indicator (PPI) scope that truly enhanced the operator's ability to interpret surface tactical information. *Fletcher*, the other destroyer that carried this radar, steamed in the rear.

Perhaps Lloyd's harshest words were saved for Callaghan who elected to lead the formation from his former command:

> The tactical commander should have been in a ship with that kind of equipment so that he could have it first hand if this was at all feasible. I have no doubt that if Callaghan had any understanding of things, he would have given fairly serious thought to moving over to *Helena*. He had ample opportunity to do this even before he ever arrived at Guadalcanal or during the time he was there placing *Helena* in the leading cruiser position.[5]

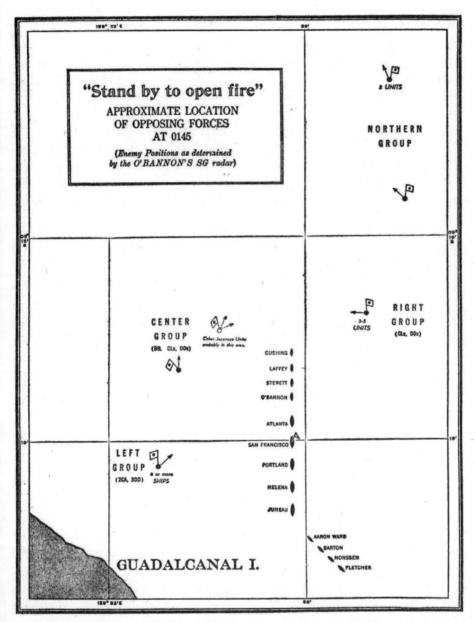

"Stand by to open fire"
APPROXIMATE LOCATION
OF OPPOSING FORCES
AT 0145
(*Enemy Positions as determined
by the O'BANNON'S SG radar*)

2 UNITS

NORTHERN
GROUP

CENTER
GROUP
(BB, CLs, DDs)

*Other Japanese Units
probably in this area.*

RIGHT
GROUP
(CLs, DDs)

3-5
UNITS

CUSHING
LAFFEY
STERETT
O'BANNON
ATLANTA
SAN FRANCISCO
PORTLAND
HELENA
JUNEAU

LEFT
GROUP
(2CA, 3DD)

6 or more
SHIPS

GUADALCANAL I.

AARON WARD
BARTON
MONSSEN
FLETCHER

Chart from the Office of Naval Intelligence *Combat Narrative of the Battle of Guadalcanal*, published in 1944. (*Solomon Islands Campaign: VI—Battle of Guadalcanal, 11–15 November 1942*, Office of Naval Intelligence, United States Navy: Publications Branch, 1944, p. 18)

The enemy force that Callaghan's force sought to engage on a dark night, featuring a partial overcast sky with flashes of lightning arcing over Guadalcanal and Florida Island, had consolidated earlier that afternoon, when Vice Admiral Abe's bombardment force—centered around the battleships *Hiei* and *Kirishima*—met with Rear Adm. Tamotsu Takama's destroyer force to make the final run to Guadalcanal. Takama's destroyers were sent ahead with the objective of scouting the waters off Lunga Point before the arrival of Abe's two battleships, light cruiser, and additional destroyers.[6]

As Abe's force surged forward in a southeasterly heading in a rather disorganized formation, *Helena*'s radar operators had a clear picture of the enemy force. Even *Atlanta* with its air search radar was tracking surface contacts to the northwest at 11 miles. "These were big targets and they showed up on our radar." Lloyd recalled that *Helena* used TBS to radio the contact reports to *San Francisco* so as to apprise Rear Admiral Callaghan of the situation. As the reports were transmitted, the column was in the midst of its final course change, with the four lead destroyers now leading the column heading due north.

As *Atlanta* pivoted to follow in the wake of *O'Bannon*, her two gun directors turned to track targets off the port bow. Lloyd called down to Jim Shaw on his sound-powered phone to look at the faces of the two Mark 1 computers to confirm the directors were tracking two separate targets. Shaw affirmed that they were on two separate targets closing fast. That the American ships held back their fire on the oncoming unsuspecting enemy formation was due to the fact that Callaghan had put out the order "Stand by to commence firing." That inhibited every ship from engaging, because as Lloyd later explained that order implied, "I the issuer of the order intend to issue the other one," which is to commence firing.[7]

For the gunnery team embarked in *Atlanta*, the situation became similar to engaging enemy aircraft where computer solutions were superfluous. Lloyd recalled:

> If the range is very short and you are shooting at a target the size of a ship, you really don't need a solution in a computer. All you need is a point of aim, and the minute your director is on target you can and should start shooting then and there ... We had insisted the gun mounts be in automatic control following the directors signals ... in other words that the gun mounts would experience these rapid sluings.[8]

Just over a mile ahead of *Atlanta* at 0142, the *Cushing*'s commanding officer spotted Japanese destroyers crossing ahead from port to starboard, turned to port to unmask both her torpedo tubes and aft gun mounts, and requested permission to launch her fish. According to Lloyd's recollection, collision avoidance also factored into *Cushing*'s turn to port. Indeed, though Callaghan ordered *Cushing* to resume her due north heading, the destroyer's commanding officer had no choice but to turn further to port to avoid hitting the Japanese destroyers *Yudachi* and *Harusame*. The threat of collision also forced the following destroyers to take evasive action. *Laffey*, then *Sterett*, and then *O'Bannon* made a sharp hard left rudder to avoid collision. By now lookouts in the two Japanese destroyers spotted *Cushing* and the following American column emerging from the shadows of Guadalcanal. The American tactical advantage of being able to see in the dark thanks to radar had been fretted away.[9]

Lloyd, noting the crossing of the Japanese destroyers, focused his attention on a larger oncoming target: "I saw the target that I believe that the after director had been following because I was standing at the foot of it and kept searching my binoculars in the direction it was pointed. Here came into view the very familiar silhouette of the Japanese light cruiser, fairly old design."[10]

Lloyd had spotted the *Nagara*. Built in 1922, it was the lead of a class of six light 5,000-ton warships that would be fitted with Long Lance torpedo tubes. *Nagara*'s main gun armament consisted of seven barrels 14 cm in diameter, or roughly 5.51 inches. As Lloyd took in the three-stack silhouette of the light cruiser, the report up from main plot placed her only 6,000 yards away. "6,000 yards is nearly point blank for modern gunnery."[11]

While looking at *Nagara*, Lloyd was alarmed that *O'Bannon*'s turn to port had slowed that destroyer's speed of advance and she was falling back toward the advancing column. He recalled, "We had a collision situation facing us in the eye." Captain Jenkins, seeing *O'Bannon* now falling back on him, also turned his ship to hard port. Up in the aft gun director, Lloyd hung on as the light cruiser heeled hard to starboard. Lloyd's aft group of 5-inch 38 twin mounts remained fixed on *Nagara* off the starboard bow, awaiting Callaghan's order to commence fire.[12]

Suddenly *Atlanta* was illuminated by a powerful searchlight from abaft her port beam likely from the Japanese destroyer *Akatsuki*. Lloyd recalled, "This searchlight seemed so powerful and high up in the air as seen from my position in the after air defense station that I thought it was a big ship with a huge searchlight located way up in the superstructure of a cruiser or battleship." Lloyd reacted:

> I ordered 'action port' … Here we were, gun batteries trained out by now on the starboard bow on this Japanese light cruiser, suddenly slue around roughly to the port beam with the searchlight source as our target. While I was swinging I gave the Plotting Room an estimated range 2,000 yards. As soon as the directors said 'on target.' I ordered 'commence firing' and we did.

In theory, the Japanese destroyer, having made the decision to use her searchlight to illuminate *Atlanta*, should have immediately followed up with gunfire from all her unmasked batteries. Captain Jenkins and his crew had been, in effect, ambushed. Yet Lloyd recalled:

> I remember quite vividly that although this ship had illuminated us, no shots had been fired at us visible or audible to me or anybody else until *Atlanta* commenced firing on that searchlight … our capabilities were preoccupied to the north and this fellow was south. We were able to shoot first. We got out from the after group something like ten or twelve rounds per gun on that target.[13]

Lloyd saw some of his shells hit the water short of the destroyer, but a good number passed above. "Both Director Officers saw the same thing completely independently ... both had the same reaction ... both of them used their elevation spot to bring their tracers down into the hull of the destroyer which was passing." As the Japanese destroyer came within 600 yards, Lloyd could see the effects of the common round shells that featured a much thicker wall than the AA rounds and a slight delay in the fusing to enable deeper penetration. "Shooting into a destroyer size hull at 600 yards you just don't miss ... you just don't miss." By this time the searchlight had been extinguished. The *Atlanta* may have put it out," Lloyd surmised.[14]

Lloyd could also see that other ships had taken the offending destroyer under fire. Some 2 miles to the south of *Atlanta*, *Helena* had been impatiently waiting for Callaghan's order to open fire. With the sudden illumination coming from the near distant horizon, *Helena*'s gunnery officer asked Capt. Gilbert Hoover for permission to open fire. "Open Fire!" Hoover responded. Lloyd "saw this very recognizable stream of tracers from *Helena*."[15] Adding to the incoming 6-inch shells from *Helena* came 8-inch shells from *San Francisco*.

Unfortunately for the Americans, the massed fire on one ship enabled other oncoming Japanese ships to take a calculated aim with guns and torpedoes at their unexpected foe. Alert to this hazard, Callaghan ordered, "Odd ships commence fire to starboard, even to port."[16] Lloyd never recalled hearing the order, attributing that to the loud claps of gunfire emanating from his after batteries. In retrospect, Lloyd saw the order as "a display of futility."[17]

Atlanta's rapid volleys along with star shells that were fired by Abe's battleships silhouetted the light cruiser for two Japanese destroyers that had been trailing *Akatsuki* and had just emerged from the cover of a rain squall. The Japanese destroyer *Inazuma* launched a spread of six torpedoes.[18]

Atlanta had already sustained some close-range gunfire damage from her encounter with *Akatsuki*. Then the torpedo hit, actually two torpedoes, but fortunately the second one did not detonate, presumably because it had been fired at such close range that the detonator had not had time to set. However, the detonator on the first torpedo, which penetrated *Atlanta*'s hull in the forward engine room, close to the bulkhead separating that space with the forward fire room, just had enough time to set. "It was a shattering blow. It just staggered the ship," Lloyd vividly remembered:

> A monstrous column of water and oil rose on our port side and cascaded all over the ship, drenching all of the topside. The people were thrown to their knees, including me, by the shock of the explosion ... The explosive force flew up through the armored deck over the machinery spaces into the compartment above, which was the messing compartment. There was such an explosive overpressure in that compartment that all door fore and aft accesses into it were jammed.[19]

Ironically, the light armor plating that covered her hull and main deck contributed to the light cruiser's demise, as the explosive force contained by the thicker steel in the overhead and port and starboard sides of the ship wound up venting fore and aft against the weaker interior bulkheads. Lloyd recounted:

> So, in addition to putting the Forward Fire Room out instantly, probably with the immediate loss of every man in the space, it bilged and ruptured slightly the forward bulkhead of the Forward Fire Room and immediately forward of that was the Plotting Room. Worse, as we were concerned, it also ruptured the after bulkhead of the Forward Engine Room. This was the division between that Engine Room and the After Fire Room so sea water started coming into the After Fire Room as well as the Forward Fire Room.[20]

With water rapidly rising in the after fire room, the boiler technicians who kept the large boilers fired with a steady flow of black oil had little choice but to cut off the fuel to the boilers and, as a final step during the abandonment of the space, lift the safety valves to enable built-up steam to escape to the atmosphere through the aft stack.[21] Of course, located just aft of the number two stack was Lloyd in the after control station. He recalled: "It was absolutely deafening … it was impossible to communicate by voice, even by putting your mouth to someone's ear and shouting."[22]

The loss of both boiler rooms cost *Atlanta* her source for propulsive power, and the stricken light cruiser slowly drifted to a halt. As steam served as a primary source for electrical power which was needed for the 5-inch 38 twin mounts, the fire control radars, etc., *Atlanta* had effectively been defanged and was defenseless as incoming rounds continued to hit the ship.

Looking aft, Lloyd noted there were two clusters of four chemical smoke tanks on the stern:

> As we lay there dead in the water headed west, the wind was from our stern and there were assorted strangers shooting at us that I didn't think was too admirable. I wanted to make smoke … One of my immediate thoughts was 'well let's get those smoke tanks to work and cover us in a cloud so that every Tom, Dick, and Harry won't see those fires and take a few shots at us.'[23]

Unfortunately, when Lloyd opened the valves from the after control station to send compressed air back to the tanks to force the chemical compound into the atmosphere where it would form a cloud, nothing happened. "Somewhere down below the lines were out and we had no air." At that moment, the aft director officer, Lt. (jg) Al Newhall, had climbed down from his perch and stood aside Lloyd. With the steam still roaring out the aft stack, Lloyd Mustin grabbed Newhall and stepped into the base of the aft director, slammed the hatch shut behind him, and cupped his hands on his ear to yell instructions to grab a pistol to run back aft to shoot into the tanks. "He never did get the message."

Though the torpedo hit caused flooding in the engineering spaces that knocked the ship out of the battle, the blast had not caused any fires. However, shellfire hits did. In his first night action facing the Japanese, Lloyd was impressed with the Japanese use of flashless powder. Essentially, at night the Japanese used a traditional gunpower formulation that produced a lot of smoke which masked the muzzle flash. "All you could see would be just a wink of light—a dot of light." Because the Japanese had been set to bombard Henderson Field, the Incoming rounds were not armor-piercing.[24]

All three forward 5-inch 38 mounts were knocked out of commission. Two or three of the barrels were rendered inoperable thanks to being dinged by flying ordnance. Lloyd recalled:

> Two of them had taken hits on their shield structure in addition to hits on their gun barrels. As I recall it, two, I think at least two of them had been hit in the bulkheads of their upper handling rooms which were about an inch and a quarter armor. This had either detonated or broken up these bombardment projectiles. There was unconsumed explosive visible on the outside impact point but men killed on the inside. We lost a lot of men in those three forward mounts.[25]

With the crippled light cruiser now drifting on a westerly heading, she suddenly came under fire from *San Francisco*, which lay a mere 2,000 yards abaft *Atlanta*'s port beam. A salvo from the heavy cruiser's 8-inch main battery, again thanks to smokeless gunpowder, lit the ship up. "It was as easy to recognize *San Francisco* in the flash of her own guns as it would have been at high noon in San Francisco harbor."[26]

Lloyd recalled the friendly warship fired two or maybe three salvos. Rear Admiral Callaghan, recognizing what was happening, reportedly ordered "Cease Firing, Friendly ship."

However, tragic damage had been done. With *San Francisco* firing armor-piercing shells, Lloyd later counted seven neat 8-inch holes that were punched into and exited out the opposite side of the aluminum forward superstructure just beneath the pilothouse where Rear Admiral Scott, Captain Jenkins, and the rest of the bridge watch team had stood at their GQ stations. However, one round apparently came in higher and pierced the modest 4-inch steel armor of the pilothouse aft on the port side and was slightly directed forward, exiting out the starboard side with catastrophic effect. Lloyd recounted:

> Captain Jenkins commented later that he and Admiral Scott had been standing outside of the pilothouse on the starboard bridge wing looking north, which was where the battle seemed to have gone, when there was some alarm on the port side. Jenkins went around the catwalk to the port side to see what was going on. When he came back there was no starboard bridge wing. This *San Francisco* salvo going through there had just removed it. I am afraid that, as everyone knows, Admiral Scott died in the *Atlanta* in that battle and I have a feeling that was the salvo that did it. A couple of his staff officers were standing behind him and they simply vanished. There was no burial at sea—there was nothing to bury. They were just gone.[27]

Another grouping of armor-piercing shells passed through the aft superstructure at the main deck level below where Lloyd was standing, which took out the port and starboard 5-inch 38 mounts. As the mount on the port side had been trained forward, it received two 8-inch rounds that entered on its left side. With one of the shells hitting the breech mechanism, the resultant explosion blew out the back of the gun mount with fatal effect for those inside. Other rounds simply punched through the aluminum superstructure to damage the corresponding starboard 5-inch

38 mount. As if there was any doubt as to the culprit in this regrettable friendly fire incident, Lloyd noted that the after group of shells left ample forensic evidence, as armor-piercing rounds at the time were loaded with a very fine dye powder at the tip of a collapsible nose cone that would disperse upon water entry and color the subsequent splash. Ships were assigned different color dyes.

> *San Francisco*'s were green. We knew that. We had been with her. There was green dye scattered all throughout where these eight inch had gone through, green dye all over the place. In addition, a number of fragments from these eight-inch shells were recovered around the ship picked up by me. It didn't take anything like my experience at Dahlgren or my eight-inch experience in *Augusta* to recognize very clearly a U.S. eight-inch shell by every characteristic, including lot numbers and whatnot stamped on some of these base fragments.[28]

Mercifully for *Atlanta,* the northerly direction of the American column and the decision of the Japanese forces to also turn northward took the light cruiser that was illuminated by blazes on the forward section of the ship out of the battle.

With no water pressure to the fire mains piping throughout the forward section of the ship, crewmembers rallied to battle the fires, forming bucket brigades. "Things like long battle telephone lines served admirably as long lanyards to bend on to the handles of buckets that you could drop over the side and bring up full of seawater," Lloyd recalled. In addition, the damage control teams were able to use some portable gasoline-powered pumps that sucked up water using a hose dropped over the side to dampen down some of the blazes.

Throughout the remainder of the night, *Atlanta* would be hit with some sporadic machine-gun fire. Later, as dawn approached, Lloyd saw something in the darkness passing on occasion. Positioning himself at the starboard torpedo tubes that still were available for action, Lloyd was tempted to fire at the mysterious target: "I was sort of standing on my toes ready to do it before it shot at us, but fortunately common sense prevailed ... when daylight dawned what we had seen was *Portland.*" As with *Atlanta*, the heavy cruiser had been hit by a Long Lance torpedo. Having lost a section of her stern and the ability to steer, *Portland* still had propulsion and elected to stay in motion, steaming in a circle.[29]

Many shells that penetrated the forward superstructure entered living and workspaces. Two examples cited by Lloyd included the gunnery office and first lieutenant's office, where small-caliber shells "detonated inside and did astonishing amounts of damage."[30] Joiner bulkheads were blown down, eliminating the thin partitions that divided offices, passageways, and staterooms. Burning mattresses tended to smolder, creating a thick acrid smoke.

With *Atlanta* adrift, as a precaution to prevent grounding up against the Japanese-held side of the island, Lieutenant Commander Nickelson led a working party that arduously struggled to pay out the starboard anchor chain 100 fathoms, with the thought that the anchor would catch on the bottom, holding the ship from beaching too close to the shore. Lloyd had doubts, knowing the depth drop into Ironbottom Sound was fairly steep.

CHAPTER 29

Giving Up the Ship

With first light, Lloyd Mustin was better able to survey the ship to gain a better appreciation of the ferocity of the first moments of the action of Friday the 13th. Looking up at the mainmast just forward of his after control station, Lloyd could see the 10-inch-diameter pole had been holed in three spots. Looking over the port side, he noted the unexploded Long Lance that had its warhead firmly planted into the hull.[1]

Not all of the Japanese ships that fought in the engagement had made their way back up into the slot. Thanks in part to salvos from *Atlanta*, the Japanese destroyer *Akatsuki* rested on the floor of Ironbottom Sound. Afloat between Cape Esperance and Savo Island, the crippled destroyer *Yudachi* drifted with no power. *Portland* still had power to her forward 8-inch triple turrets and took aim on the wounded enemy warship that floated on the near horizon some 6½ miles distant. A salvo hit the enemy tin can midships, detonating a magazine. "There was a fantastic mushroom cloud that rose above that ship in the rays of the just risen sun," Lloyd recounted.[2]

With the light cruiser's relative position to the Japanese-held section of Guadalcanal and the currents pushing the ship toward the shore some 3 miles distant, Lloyd feared the ship could come within range of small-arms fire. Finding the remains of the gunner's mate who kept the key to the armory, Lloyd removed the key and went down to the armory located near the uptakes from the forward fire room. He found it difficult to get at due to distorted bulkheads and bent doorframes, but he succeeded in opening the locker and issuing out all of the Springfield rifles and ammunition, taking care to keep a rifle for himself.

Lloyd would regret issuing the rifles, as some of the crew, seeing Japanese survivors adrift in the water, began firing on them. Word was quickly relayed with orders to cease. In the meantime, small craft from Guadalcanal began to appear to take off *Atlanta*'s wounded and to search for survivors in the water and take off wounded sailors. These boats were joined by a motor whale boat that *Atlanta* managed to place in the water. As the boats approached Japanese survivors, most would inevitably swim away to avoid capture. There were exceptions. Lloyd recalled a big landing craft, a Mike boat, came alongside having picked up survivors en route from Lunga. He peered down:

> Here stood up in the boat a Japanese boatswain mate. He had his white uniform jumper on and his boatswain insignia unmistakably on it. He was gesturing he wanted some rags. He showed us he had about six or eight men there who were wounded in various ways and all covered in oil. He was taking care of all of them. A couple of them American, a couple of them Japanese. They were all immobile. They were perhaps unconscious. This one Japanese boatswain mate had taken it upon himself to take care of all of these sailors.[3]

Throughout the morning water continued to seep into voids below, settling the ship slowly into the sound with a discernable list to port. In addition to the two port and starboard mounts that had been taken out of action thanks to *San Francisco*'s salvos, Japanese gunfire had damaged the mount immediately behind the aft gun director, leaving the cruiser just two unscathed twin mounts on the stern section of the ship. The operating aft generator provided nominal power for an emergency radio so Captain Jenkins could keep abreast of the tactical situation. Over the net came the report of incoming enemy aircraft. If only the aft diesel generator could power the aft mounts. With some perseverance, the electricians rigged a cable between the diesel generator and an electrical switchboard in the upper level of the partially flooded after engine room that fed power to the aft mounts.[4] On the horizon came a Betty bomber which came in toward *Atlanta*. Lloyd recalled: "We were prepared. We were able to put the director on him so that they could see him in their sights. Then the Director Officer called down over the phone circuits sight settings and fuse settings to the mount, and we opened fire on this plane coming in."[5]

The rounds expended proved to be *Atlanta*'s last shots in anger. The Betty veered off, leaving Lloyd to speculate it had been merely on a reconnaissance mission.

Of the senior leadership, besides the CO and XO, remained the assistant engineering officer, Lt. Cdr. Jack Wulff, the gunnery officer, Lt. Cdr. Bill Nickelson, and Lloyd Mustin.

Surveying the superstructure and the hull, Lloyd tallied 53 different shell hits.

At this point Lloyd could discern that the ship was still taking water as the freeboard on both sides of the ship decreased. Wulff and Mustin felt that if the ship could be moved to a shelter anchorage such as Tulagi Harbor or just off Lunga, it might be possible to salvage the ship. Nickelson and the XO felt otherwise and recommended to Captain Jenkins the ship be scuttled. Jenkins concurred.[6]

With the decision to scuttle the ship, additional boats were sent from Guadalcanal to offload the crew. As Higgins boats arrived to offload the remaining crew, those who had access to their belongings packed bags and pillowcases of personal belongings—letters, pictures, toiletries, skivvies, and other uniform items. Lloyd packed his diary. He would not witness the scuttling.[7]

With Lloyd and the surviving crew having departed, at about 1730 Captain Jenkins set off the explosives placed in the stern and scampered down a cargo net into an awaiting motor whaleboat. *Atlanta* remained afloat with heavy smoke billowing for the next two hours and 45 minutes. Finally, at 2015, the flames apparently reached the aft magazine, resulting in a massive explosion. Lloyd's ship began her descent to the floor of Ironbottom Sound where she remains today.[8]

CHAPTER 30

Epilogue

As Lloyd Mustin waded ashore with one of the last contingents of the crew to be evacuated by small boat, a voice from the distant past greeted him: "Hello Mustin, glad to see you." Lloyd looked up at Capt. Bill Greenman, the former captain of the cruiser *Astoria* that had been lost in the battle of Savo Island. Lloyd knew Greenman back from his midshipman days a decade earlier when Greenman had been assigned there, and following the early morning debacle of August 9, Greenman requested and received orders to command naval operations at Guadalcanal and Tulagi, giving him the formal title of Commander Naval Bases CACTUS RINGBOLT.[1]

Pointed in the direction of a coconut grove, Lloyd and his shipmates came upon a designated camping site, and a few Marines showed them nearby foxholes where emergency rations had been placed. The Marines also provided tents. It was left up to the sailors to erect them. Lloyd, who had camped with his mother and stepfather on the eastern shore of Maryland, had a clue, and soon a little tent village emerged.[2]

The exhausted *Atlanta* bluejackets would have their sleep disturbed that night as the Japanese heavy cruisers *Suzuya* and *Maya* and several Japanese destroyers appeared offshore 90 minutes after midnight, and as the sky was illuminated by flares dropped by a Japanese floatplane, the enemy warships opened up for a bombardment of Henderson Field.[3]

After initial shock and terror that had everyone scrambling for foxholes, it dawned on *Atlanta*'s survivors that the shells were aimed at the airfield. Lloyd observed many left the safety of their foxholes to get a better view.[4] With the departure of the Japanese, the rattled *Atlanta* shipmates retired to their tents for a few more hours of rest.

As light arrived the next morning, the damage wrought became apparent. Most of the Japanese shells fell around the auxiliary airfield Fighter One, destroying two Wildcats and an SBD, and damaging another fifteen fighters. Henderson Field remained relatively unscathed. The departing Japanese warships returning up the slot would not. Five dive-bombers and three torpedo planes escorted by ten fighters rose to chase after the Japanese, pressing an attack at about 0830. In the meantime, emerging 200 miles southwest of Guadalcanal, *Enterprise* launched scout bombers followed by a strike. One scout planted a bomb forward the bridge of the cruiser *Kinugasa*, killing the CO and XO. Another SBD, hit by antiaircraft fire, crashed into the *Maya*, causing considerable damage. The main strike of 17 Dauntlesses finished off *Kinugasa* and damaged the cruisers *Chokai* and *Izuzu*.[5]

At this point Lloyd and his shipmates were now on the sidelines as the epic ongoing struggle for Guadalcanal was about to reach its climax. That status would soon change. The sacrifice made by Callaghan's 13-ship flotilla to stop the overnight bombardment of Henderson Field by *Hiei* and *Kirishima* merely disrupted Yamamoto's timetable to convoy transports full of Imperial Army troops and supplies down the slot by 24 hours. With the cruiser bombardment of the morning of November 14 designed to suppress the Cactus Air Force, a 23-ship convoy centered around 11 transports departed from Shortland Island the previous evening under the command of Rear Adm. Raizo Tanaka.[6]

Making good progress toward an arrival at Guadalcanal late that evening, Tanaka's convoy steamed under open skies that morning. That abruptly changed at 1250, with the arrival of 18 SBDs and 7 TBFs from Henderson Field. The Navy and Marine airmen ripped into one of three transport formations Tanaka had set up, sinking two *Marus* and sending a third scurrying back to Shortland. Follow-on air attacks from Henderson and *Enterprise* claimed four more *Marus*. With his destroyers taking on surviving soldiers off the sinking transports, Tanaka chose to plod on with his remaining four transports guarded by five destroyers, with four additional destroyers following with the recovered soldiers. As darkness approached, Tanaka received warning of an American surface force of two cruisers and four destroyers approaching Guadalcanal. Though a threat, overcoming the American surface force would not be insurmountable, given that Vice Admiral Kondo was returning to waters off Lunga Point with *Kirishima* and two cruisers to complete the mission that had been disrupted by Callaghan two nights earlier. Kondo's bombardment force would be screened by the light cruiser *Nagara* and six destroyers. Ahead of this potent surface force, the light cruiser *Sendai* and three destroyers scouted for the reported American surface force.[7]

Late that evening, Lloyd recalled, "we could see the flashes of gunfire clearly from the beach … much of it took place only ten to fifteen miles from where we were and we stood there in a great deal of ignorance as to what was going on."[8] Unbeknownst to the Japanese, the two reported American cruisers were actually the battleships *South Dakota* and *Washington* under the command of Rear Admiral Lee embarked on the latter. Lloyd was just as surprised as Kondo and Tanaka: "We didn't know he was coming in … apparently he was unsure that the forces on the island had been made aware he was coming in as he had expressed some concern lest our PT boats attack him."[9]

Lloyd recalled that Lee had entered the area by passing to the west of Guadalcanal and Savo Island, and then he turned his column right around Savo and steered southward into Iron Bottom Sound. Lloyd noted that while Lee had the advantage of an SG radar on his flagship, the radar was mounted ahead of the large forward steel mast that had become a fixture in World War II American battleship design, blinding him to the Japanese forces coming from the northwest. However, once Lee turned his column of the destroyers *Walke*, *Benham*, *Preston*, and *Gwin*, followed by *Washington* and *South Dakota*, on a westerly course off the northwestern shores of Guadalcanal, the radar operators could discern three enemy ships of Kondo's scout force.[10]

The opening 16-inch salvos from the two American battleships failed to score hits on the light cruiser *Sendai* and destroyers *Shikinami* and *Unanami*, which changed course and laid smoke to evade the incoming fire. As the battleships ceased firing at 2322, the four destroyers in the van, using an FD fire control radar and good night vision, picked up warships from Kondo's screening force that the Japanese vice admiral had sent to reinforce the scout force against what he still believed were two enemy cruisers and four destroyers. Kondo, intending his bombardment group of a battleship and two cruisers to avoid the fray, steamed north of Savo Island so as to complete the mission of savaging Henderson Field.[11]

As the large rifles of *Washington* and *South Dakota* went silent, the 5-inch batteries on *Walke* and then *Benham* opened on the destroyer *Ayanami*. Five minutes later *Preston* engaged the light cruiser *Nagara* and her accompanying destroyers, and *Gwin* and *Walke* followed suit. The Japanese countered with gunfire and torpedoes and scored blows on all four American tin cans. *Walke* suffered a fatal Long Lance hit forward of her bridge, setting off a magazine that lifted the ship up and snapped the bow off. *Preston* suffered multiple shell hits, with fatal blows penetrating the engineering spaces. on the Japanese side, *Ayanami*'s counterbattery fire gave her position away to *Washington*'s gunners, who put that destroyer out of action. Before dawn that ship would join with others on the bottom of Ironbottom Sound.[12]

With his two remaining destroyers damaged, Lee ordered them to retire 12 minutes before midnight and pressed on with his two battleships. Though departing the scene, only *Gwin* would live to fight another day. *Benham* slowly succumbed the next day thanks to a torpedo hit near the bow.[13] Meanwhile, the Japanese warships that had charged to the south of Savo Island began to report the presence of American battleships. Kondo, intent on driving his bombardment group toward their objective, altered his course to close on Lunga Point. Lee altered his course to close on Kondo.

Unfortunately for Lee, *South Dakota* had been having difficulties with electrical distribution that evening, losing power for six minutes during the initial engagement and again just before midnight. For Lloyd, learning of these problems later, it simply reinforced a negative view he had of the ship and her commanding officer that had been formed earlier at Tongatabu:

> Tommy Gatch, who was the captain, didn't care for spit and polish and his Sailors never shaved or got their hair cut and they wore dirty clothes and so on. All he cared about was their fighting ability. Well this was all a bunch of specious nonsense. If he cared about perfecting their fighting abilities, he didn't care enough and he didn't perfect enough, because she [*South Dakota*] really did cause her own difficulties there.[14]

When electricity allowed *South Dakota* to see again, Kondo's force of a battleship, two cruisers, and two destroyers were a mere 3 miles off the battleship's starboard beam, close enough to allow the Japanese to spot her. The Japanese fired torpedoes, and then at midnight the cruiser *Atago* illuminated the American battlewagon with a spotlight to confirm that Kondo's force actually was confronting a battleship. Searchlights from Kondo's other ships provided all with a focal point to aim and fire their guns. Luckily for Gatch and his crew, several of the usually dependable Long Lance torpedoes exploded prematurely, giving the Japanese the illusion of devastating blows. However, shells of varying caliber scored hits around *South Dakota*'s forward mast structure, knocking out radio antennae, gun directors, and radar housings. Without sensor inputs, the battleship's three main 16-inch batteries fired only a few salvos. In contrast, the secondary starboard 5-inch 38 twin mounts countered with continuous counterbattery fire.[15]

Beyond *South Dakota*, *Washington* remained hidden in the darkness. With searchlights and gunfire focused on *South Dakota*, Lee and *Washington*'s commander Capt. Glenn Davis had a clear assessment of the tactical situation and assigned one starboard 5-inch twin mount to fire at *Atago*, another to fire star shells, and the remaining two 5-inch mounts and three 16-inch turrets to zero in on *Kirishima*. The salvos against the World War I-vintage modernized battleship disabled two 14-inch turrets, penetrated the hull below the waterline, and jammed the rudder. Besides scoring at least nine hits with her 16-inch rifles, an estimated over forty 5-inch shells caused additional damage to the Japanese capital ship. *Atago*, with Kondo embarked, suffered nominal damage, turned off her searchlight—as did the other undamaged Japanese warships—and turned on to a course of 270 degrees true to escape *Washington*'s guns and hopefully reposition for a torpedo attack.[16]

As the Japanese bombardment group, minus a circling crippled *Kirishima*, turned west at nine minutes past midnight, *South Dakota* maneuvered to clear the area harboring some 23 major fires that the battleship's damage control teams struggled to extinguish. Again Lloyd, who would later spend time embarked on the battleship during the final stages of the war, opined from what he had learned from his contemporaries, "her damage control problems were very poorly handled, discipline was lax, and efficiency low." Prejudicial to his reflections was the loss of one of his classmates who perished in fires that consumed the foremast.[17]

This left *Washington* alone against a still potent force of Japanese cruisers and destroyers scattered in the vicinity heavily armed with Long Lance torpedoes. Kondo's remaining two cruisers from the bombardment group swung to launch torpedoes at 0013 and attempted to engage with his guns to little effect. At 0025, Kondo sent a plea to the combatants of the sweeping and screening forces as well as Tanaka's inbound transport convoy to redirect to a point 6 miles to the north of Cape Esperance. Tanaka dispatched two of his destroyers to join the hunt for what proved to be an evasive American battleship. Evading multiple Japanese torpedo attacks, Lee and Davis managed to retire to the south. Though Lee understood that Tanaka's remaining convoy would reach Guadalcanal, he correctly calculated that by delaying the Japanese timetable and preventing the bombardment of Henderson Field, the Japanese reinforcement mission would fail.[18]

At dawn, *Atlanta*'s survivors looked up the coast where four remaining Japanese transports from Tanaka's convoy had beached themselves. By that time swarms of aircraft had risen from Henderson Field to attack the stationary targets. Lloyd recalled: "We wound up with our planes literally shuttling off the field loaded with whatever could be found to load them, dropping it and coming back for more."[19] Japanese soldiers embarked on these vessels jumped into the water, hoping to either be picked up with small boats or swim ashore. Lloyd remembered: "The troops were there in the water, and of course, that was a substantial concern." To address the threat of enemy soldiers making their way ashore to eventually confront the Marine defenders, Lloyd recalled that bombs were loaded with fuses that would go off on water impact.[20]

Marine Corps and Army artillery joined in. Some of the Marine Corps guns were part of a defense battalion that had been deployed to the island to set up coastal defense positions. Due to attrition, two Navy 5-inch 51-caliber guns of World War I vintages had no gun crews. The Marines turned to the *Atlanta* refugees for some help and found willing volunteers, as some of the senior petty officers who had served as turret captains had trained on those guns, as had Mustin during a midshipman cruise. Lloyd recalled:

> Lo and behold, the nearest one of these transports on the beach was within range ... around 20,000 yards. Here was a Japanese transport on the beach and a rather fine looking one, not just some old 'Rust Bucket Maru' as we used to call them, but one of their more modern ships with a flaring clipper bow and she was wedged up on the beach. They were getting cargo out of her and the men and she was in range ... they just opened fire on her and, of course, began hitting very quickly. Not much adjustment is required when the target is plainly in sight and is not moving and they just shot it to pieces—just shot it to pieces. They set it on fire ... the wind, as usual, was from the east and it was to the west so the smoke from its own fires drifted the other way and didn't conceal it. They were able to continue shooting until they figured there wasn't really anything left to shoot at and literally the ship sank. Its stern sank under water. Its bow remained out of water at a very steep angle.[21]

The charred hull of the *Yamazuki Maru*, one of the four beached Japanese transports.

Only around 2,000 Japanese troops made it ashore, with nominal supplies and subsistence to reinforce their countrymen, a fraction of what was needed to drive the Americans off the island.[22] To the relief of all, no attack materialized that night, and the next morning aircraft began taking *Atlanta*'s wounded off the island.[23]

After a few days rumors began to spread that the survivors from *Atlanta* and the other sunken destroyers would finally be evacuated. Expecting the arrival of the *Libra* and the *Betelgeuse* on November 20, the crew, minus a few who volunteered to stay at Cactus, gathered on the shoreline. Lloyd recalled it was "a beautiful crystal clear morning with not a ripple in the bay." Lloyd and his shipmates embarked on a small flotilla of small craft and charged out into the calm waters of Ironbottom Sound with the hope of spotting the two cargo ships on the horizon. No joy![24]

The two ships did arrive the next day. Escorted by the destroyer *Mustin*, *Betelgeuse* departed for Espiritu Santo on November 25. *Libra* would follow a day later. Both ships carried *Atlanta* survivors. Ironically, the only Mustin leaving Guadalcanal was the destroyer named for Lloyd's father. The son remained, having received orders to serve as the operations and intelligence officer of Naval Base Ringbolt Cactus.

Perhaps no one was more disappointed when *Betelgeuse* and *Libra* failed to show on November 20 than Lloyd Mustin. Captain Greenman had informed Lloyd that he had made a request for him to be assigned to his staff. Lloyd demurred, wanting to depart with his shipmates in the hope that they would reconstitute as the core of the commissioning crew of a new combatant. Instead, in his new role as Greenman's operations officer, Lloyd tracked resupply convoy movements and coordinated the movements of rather substantial collections of small craft to offload the arriving ships. As Greenman's intelligence officer, Lloyd worked with Cdr. Daniel J. McCallum, a Japanese language specialist, who had served as an assistant naval attaché. McCallum had arrived at Cactus two months earlier as part of a radio frequency detection unit and hoped to do some cryptoanalysis work, a task he proved adept at. Radiomen from the unit copied the dots and dashes of Kana [Japanese alphabet] script which McCallum translated into English. Ironically, Japanese lookout reports from the mountains overlooking Henderson Field often served as Lloyd's first inkling that American resupply ships were about to arrive.[25]

Lloyd was not the only *Atlanta* survivor to remain at Cactus. Several enlisted sailors, having experienced the recent carnage on the morning of November 13, elected for shore duty in a combat zone rather than reassignment to sea. Quite a few would opt to join the growing PT boat flotilla operating in the Solomons. To Lloyd's delight, Jack Wulff also stayed behind. Assigned as the new beachmaster, Jack would join with Lloyd to share a tent for the next few months.[26]

Initially bitter about being left behind, Lloyd found himself "involved in a grippingly interesting course of events from day to day."[27] Late on November 30, alerted that another Tokyo Express run of Japanese destroyers aimed to land more troops and supplies, a reconstituted Task Force 67, under the command of Rear. Adm. Carlton Wright, moved to intercept. With four heavy cruisers, a light cruiser, and several destroyers in his formation, Wright had a significant firepower advantage over Rear Admiral Tanaka's oncoming squadron. At 2321, Wright's ships unleashed their fury on the lead Japanese destroyer with devastating effect. From Lloyd's vantage point at Lunga Point, the 8-inch salvos from the American cruisers lit up the sky. Lloyd thought, "Oh boy, we are certainly giving them hell!" Furthermore, Lloyd noted little return gunfire.[28]

Unfortunately, there was a reason for this observation. Several of Tanaka's following destroyers had evaded detection and resisted opening fire on the more powerful cruiser force. Instead, between 2223 and 2233, six of Tanaka's destroyers fired 44 Long Lance torpedoes at the American column. From ashore Lloyd witnessed huge flashes that differed from 8-inch muzzle blasts: "It wasn't very long before all was silence … the radio was quite silent."

Lloyd recalled finally intercepting a cyphered message from the cruiser *Minneapolis* stating she was slowly retreating to Tulagi. Lloyd also heard radio transmissions from *New Orleans*. However, nothing seemed forthcoming from the heavy cruisers *Pensacola*, *Northampton*, the light cruiser *Honolulu*, or the escorting destroyers. From Noumea, Vice Admiral Halsey wondered what happened. At Cactus, Captain Greenman summoned Lieutenant Commander Mustin and directed him to report to Henderson Field, where a Marine SBD awaited. Lloyd received a crash course on how to fire the machine guns facing aft. Once checked out on the rear seat guns, the

Dauntless lifted off in the early morning light. Heading out over Ironbottom Sound, Lloyd could see PT boats converging toward the site of the overnight battle, and as they overflew that location, it became apparent that at least one American warship had perished: "There was oil all over the water, over a large area with obviously a big source underneath." Lloyd spotted debris in the water and quickly recognized the floating items had American origins: "There were lots of Sailors in the water, lots of them and we were able to direct the PT boats to where they were." Overflying Savo Island, Lloyd noted more sailors waving up. Lloyd would soon learn they were off the *Northampton*. He also noted numerous torpedoes that remained intact, having expended their runs at some point over the previous four months on Savo's beaches.[29]

The Marine pilot banked the dive-bomber and headed to Tulagi. Lloyd later recounted:

> Lo, here we saw a terrible sight. When we got there *Minneapolis, New Orleans,* and *Pensacola* were all in the harbor and *Minneapolis* had her bow blown off back to turret one by a torpedo head. She had actually taken two torpedoes, one of which had blown off the bow and the other was somewhere in the engineering space and this had given her staggering difficulties just to keep her machinery running so as to get her in the harbor. *New Orleans* had her bow blown off back to turret two … the guns of turret two hung out over the water, but apparently that had been her only hit. *Pensacola* had taken a hit back aft of her mainmast and this was about the after engine room and this had started a tremendous fire. The Japanese were using, apparently, very shallow settings on their torpedoes, or at least on that torpedo, perhaps to be effective against destroyers. In any case, when the torpedo warhead would detonate there was enough flash to actually ignite inflammables.[30]

After viewing the damage inflicted on the three heavy cruisers, the Dauntless vectored over Florida Island for a sweep to the northwest of Savo and then to waters off the southwestern shores of Guadalcanal for any signs of the light cruiser *Honolulu* and escorting destroyers, only to later learn they had cleared the area before sunrise.

However, despite the loss at what became known as the battle of Tassafaronga, the Americans retained the initiative at Guadalcanal as fresh Army units arrived to reinforce and relieve the Marines who had repelled repeated Japanese thrusts to eliminate the Henderson Field foothold. Lloyd spent the remainder of 1942 on Cactus, confident of the ultimate outcome and looking for any opportunity to get transferred back to the fleet.

Finally, early in the new year, Lloyd reported to the light cruiser *San Diego*, where he assumed his old job as assistant gunnery officer. In a letter written on February 12, 1943, to his mother and stepfather, Lloyd explained the chain of events that led him to one of *Atlanta*'s remaining sister ships.

> Dearest Momee & George:
>   I got here on Jan. 2nd, having hopped a DC-3 out of Cactus as soon as I could safely turn things over to my relief. One advantage of being operations officer there—I could arrange that myself even though orders didn't call for air transportation.

I hadn't been ordered there very long when this ship asked for me, but Cactus said I had to have a relief before I could be spared. That took quite awhile and I sorta began to think it would fall through—but the orders came along. One of my good friends an Ordnance P.G. [post-grad] on Halsey's staff was up at Cactus on an inspection trip of some sort while I was biting my finger nails he said he'd stir things along. Maybe that did it or maybe my frantic cries to George turned the trick. Anyway, I'm back where I can feel I'm doing something nobody can do better than I can, so I am very pleased.

My Cactus morale took a lower dip than any I ever expressed by mail when I found out what happened to the rest of the *Atlanta* officers—they all went back to the states! Of course that's the only proper thing in such a case—to give them a chance to get some uniforms, etc. and sort of rest up a bit, then put a new ship in commission and get back on the job. But god-dammit, old Greenman never thought of anything but his own wants in grabbing someone for his purposes—he got evacuated, sick, very soon after I reported by the way.

Naturally I wanted to get home very very much. But there's no hope for that or anything else down in this God-forsaken part of the world no more than when George was here. And least of all, you are lost in one of these pest-hole shore backwaters. At least in a ship you can hope to see home or Australia or something some time. When I had all hope of getting home snatched away by Greenman's whim, then naturally a ship was what I thought of without even thinking of efforts to get back home.[31]

Lloyd Mustin would eventually detach from *San Diego* in May and make his way back to Annapolis to surprise his wife and three children. The youngest, Tom, did not recognize him, as he had been an infant when his father departed, but the toddler connected the dots when his brother Henry and sister Doug screamed "Daddy, Daddy!" As previously noted, he would receive orders to the pre-commissioning crew of the light cruiser *Miami* to join with his good friend Jack Wulff.[32]

Once commissioned, *Miami* eventually joined the Pacific Fleet in time for the Marianas campaign of the summer of 1944. On June 19, *Miami*'s guns contributed to the spirited defense of Task Force 58 as the Japanese sent four waves of aircraft against Vice Adm. Pete Mitscher's Fifth Fleet. Later that month, Lloyd's guns took aim at Japanese positions ashore at Guam and Rota. As the summer progressed, *Miami* supported fleet operations against Tinian, Palau, and Yap, and would be assigned to Task Force 34 at the battle of Leyte Gulf, which was decoyed away from the landing beaches by Admiral Ozawa's northern carrier force. After Vice Admiral Kurita's central force failed to press an attack against a weak force of American escort carriers, destroyers, and destroyer escorts off the island of Samar, Kurita managed to escape back through San Bernardino Strait except for one trailing destroyer. The *Nowaki* would fall victim to salvos from *Miami*, *Biloxi*, and *Vincennes*. Following Leyte Gulf, Lloyd met his former academy roommate, who served as the gunnery officer on Vice Adm. Willis Lee's staff. Needing to journey home to care for an ill wife, the ex-roomie asked Lloyd if he could relieve him, and as the calendar turned to 1945, Lloyd joined the staff of Commander, Battleship Squadron Two. For Lloyd, long an admirer of "Ching" Lee, the assignment proved to be challenging, as the American surface ships bombarded targets on Iwo Jima, Okinawa, and the

Japanese mainland and defended the fleet against kamikaze attacks. When the war in the Pacific concluded following the dropping of atomic bombs on Hiroshima and Nagasaki, Lloyd would no longer be in theater, having returned to Washington as the flag aide to Vice Admiral Lee who commanded Task Force 69—what would become known as the Operational Development Force. From this billet he transitioned to the Bureau of Ordnance to serve as "Head, Fire Control Section, Research Division."[33]

Commander Mustin's first sea command came in October 1948, when he read his orders during a change of command ceremony to the destroyer *Keppler*. Unfortunately for the new CO, the relatively new *Gearing*-class destroyer entered Hunters Point Naval Shipyard in San Francisco to provide greater anti-submarine warfare (ASW) capabilities. Halfway through his tour, *Keppler* left the yard and proceeded to San Diego. In October, *Keppler* shifted to the East Coast, and Lloyd found himself conducting ASW exercises in the frigid waters of the North Atlantic. After a short stint in the Mediterranean, Lloyd returned to Newport, Rhode Island, where he left the ship to serve as the ASW officer on the staff of the Commander in Chief, Atlantic Fleet. Soon he was promoted to the readiness officer billet. Promoted to captain in January 1951, Lloyd left the Atlantic Fleet for duty in Washington with the Weapons System Evaluation Group, an organization that worked directly for the Secretary of Defense. For the next three years he engaged in multi-service studies evaluating the viability of strategic bombing to the advantages of nuclear submarines. Desiring to get out of the Pentagon, Lloyd applied for a second sea command and was underwhelmed when his orders to the destroyer tender *Piedmont* arrived.[34]

Captain Mustin made the most of his time on the Western Pacific-based repair ship, training the crew to be proficient with small arms and the 5-inch gun batteries. Following his tour in *Piedmont*, he received command of Destroyer Squadron Thirteen, which also operated in "WestPac." He then served as chief of staff and aide to Commander Cruiser Destroyer Force, Pacific, Rear Adm. Chester Wood. It was during this tour that Lloyd learned that he had been "deep selected" for the rank of rear admiral. Eventually promoted to the two-star rank, Rear Adm. Mustin's first flag billet was Commander, Destroyer Flotilla Two based in Newport, Rhode Island. While in this billet, he received orders to command Task Force 88, centered around the missile test ship *Norton Sound*, which cruised to the South Atlantic to fire rockets armed with lightweight nuclear warheads to detonate in the upper atmosphere, to determine if a protective shield could be created to block incoming warheads from Soviet intercontinental ballistic missiles. Known as "Project Argus," the detonations demonstrated this alone was not a viable defensive option.[35]

On June 13, 1959, Lloyd assumed command of the naval base and forces located at Key West, Florida, and a year later reported to the Pentagon where he eventually became the director of anti-submarine warfare, working for the chief of naval operations, Adm. Arleigh Burke. Due to his experience with the Argus tests, Lloyd was tapped to first serve as a deputy commander and then the commander of Joint

Task Force Eight which oversaw the Dominic series of atmospheric nuclear weapon detonations at testing facilities in the Pacific. Returning to Washington, Lloyd was promoted to vice admiral and received orders to serve for three years on the Joint Chiefs of Staff at a time when the American role in Southeast Asia was escalating. Following his Pentagon tour, he enjoyed his last afloat command as Commander Amphibious Force, U.S. Atlantic Fleet. For his final tour on active duty, he returned to Washington to serve as Director, Defense Atomic Support Agency, an organization that had been established to monitor the safety of the numerous nuclear weapons systems the nation now had in its arsenal. Sadly, a swimming accident involving a collision with another swimmer caused the loss of sight in his left eye. Lloyd Mustin retired on August 1, 1971, after serving in the Navy for 43 years.[36]

Lloyd Mustin's interest in putting bullets on target continued, and he would serve two terms as president of the National Rifle Association in the late 1970s and would serve with the U.S. Olympic Committee for shooting sports. He lived happily with Emily in Alexandria, Virginia, until brain cancer claimed her life in 1989. Eventually he moved out to Coronado, California, to live close to his daughter Doug. After a series of strokes, he passed away on January 21, 1999.[37]

Lloyd's two sons would both attend the Naval Academy, with Henry graduating in 1955 and Thomas seven years later. Both followed in their father's footsteps serving in the surface navy. Both would serve in the "Brown Water Navy" commanding riverine small craft in South Vietnam. Tom left the Navy in 1973 to pursue a law degree at Harvard. His older brother Hank would stay in and play an instrumental role in the execution of the Navy's maritime strategy against the Soviet Union in the 1980s. He retired on September 1, 1988, as a vice admiral. He would pass away on April 11, 2016.

Over a decade earlier, Hank and his brother were on hand to witness the commissioning of *Mustin* in San Diego. Named for the three generations of Mustins who ably served the nation in the Navy as well as the first destroyer *Mustin*, the *Arleigh Burke*-class missile destroyer remains on duty with the Pacific Fleet. Meanwhile, going into 2024, Mustins continue to serve on active duty, as Hank Mustin's youngest son John—a 1990 graduate of the U.S. Naval Academy—rose up the ranks of the surface navy community and Navy Reserve to assume command of the Navy Reserve with the rank of vice admiral. Also, a Lloyd Mustin continues to serve in uniform with the U.S. Navy as mid-grade surface warfare officer in the Navy Reserve. Asked about the whereabouts of the Springfield rifle that his great-grandfather once carried on Guadalcanal, "Link" Mustin proudly confessed, "I have it."

Abbreviations

ALNAV	All Navy message
AP	Personnel Transport Ship
B-17	Army Air Force Flying Fortress Bomber
B-24	Army Air Force Liberator Bomber
B-25	Army Air Force Mitchell Bomber
BuPers	Bureau of Personnel
CA	Heavy Cruiser
CinCPac	Commander in Chief Pacific
CL	Light Cruiser
ComUtWing	Commander Utility Wing
CruDiv	Cruiser Division
CV	Aircraft Carrier
D.C.	Depth charge
DD	Destroyer
DL	Destroyer Leader
E.	East
F4F-4	Wildcat Fighter
G.Q.	General Quarters
Kts.	Knots
MGs	Machine Guns
Minn.	*Minneapolis*
N.	North
N.C.	*North Carolina*
N.O.	*New Orleans*
N.E.	Northeast
N.W.	Northwest
OOD	Officer of the Deck
OTC	Officer in Tactical Command
Prop.	Propeller
PDF	Radio Direction Finder
PBY	Catalina Patrol Bomber
Rds	Rounds

S. D.	*San Juan* or *South Dakota*
S.	South
SB2U	Vindicator Dive Bomber
SBD	Dauntless Dive Bomber
Spd.	Speed
SupShips	Supervisor of Shipbuilding
TBD	Devastator Torpedo Bomber
TBF	Avenger Torpedo Bomber
TF	Task Force
TG	Task Group
W.	West
Yd.	Yard

Endnotes

Chapter 1

1   CNO Washington NAVADMIN 164/99 message dated 041653Z June 99.
2   James D. Hornfischer, *Neptune's Inferno: The U.S. Navy at Guadalcanal* (New York: Bantam Books, 2011), 244–46.
3   Samuel Eliot Morison, *History of United States Naval Operations in World War II, Volume V: The Struggle for Guadalcanal* (Boston: Little, Brown and Company,1969), 231–32; Colin G. Jameson, *The Battle of Guadalcanal: 11–15 November 1942* (Washington, D.C.: Naval Historical Center, 1994), 4–7. This monograph was a reprint of an Office of Naval Intelligence combat narrative published in 1944.
4   Samuel Eliot Morison, *The Two Ocean War: A Short History of the United States Navy in the Second World War.* (Boston: Little Brown and Company, 1963), 197.
5   Jameson, 10–11.
6   Jameson, 12–13; Morison, *Guadalcanal*, 230.
7   Morison, *Guadalcanal*, 235.
8   Morison, *Guadalcanal*, 235–36; Morison, *Two Ocean War*, 198.
9   Morison, *Two Ocean War*, 198–99.
10 Morison, *Guadalcanal*, 237–39.
11 Jameson, 16–17.
12 Jameson, 17; Morison, *Guadalcanal*, 239–40.
13 Morison, 241–42.
14 John Prados, *Combined Fleet Decoded: The Secret History of American Intelligence and the Japanese Navy in World War II* (Annapolis, MD: Naval Institute Press, 1995), 392.
15 Morison, *Guadalcanal*, 244.
16 Ibid.; *Dictionary of American Naval Fighting Ships* (DANFS): *Volume II* (Navy Department: Washington, D.C., 1963), *Cushing* entry.
17 Statement of Lt. (jg) Harlowe M. White to Commander South Pacific Force dated November 26, 1942, Ship History files, NHHC.
18 C. Raymond Calhoun, *Tin Can Sailor: Life Aboard the USS* Sterett, *1939–1945* (Annapolis, MD: Naval Institute Press, 1993), 91–92; Morison, *Guadalcanal*, 256–57.

Chapter 2

1   John Fass Morton, *Mustin: A Naval Family of the 21st Century* (Annapolis, MD: Naval Institute Press, 2003), 4–5, 139; Lloyd Mustin oral history, interview by John Mason, U.S. Naval Institute Oral History Program, 2003.
2   Lloyd Mustin Biographical Questionnaire (Mustin Questionnaire) October 29, 1946, Lloyd Mustin files, Operational Archives, NHHC.

3   Mrs. Henry C. Mustin photo *Evening Ledger* (Philadelphia) January 16, 1915, 9. Corinne is described as "one of the most popular matrons of the smart set in the city." Morton, 43; *Vandalia* I (Sloop of War), DANFS, NHHC.

4   Mustin oral history.

5   *Lucky Bag* (Glen Falls, NY: C. H. Posson, 1896), 32; Morton, 10–14.

6   Morton, 20–24; *New York* IV (Armored Cruiser), DANFS, NHHC; *Ajax* II (Collier No. 14), DANFS, NHHC; *Oregon* II (Battleship No. 3), DANFS, NHHC.

7   Morton, 29–33.

8   See Gary E. Weir, *Building American Submarines, 1914–1940* (Washington, D.C.: Naval Historical Center, 1991), 6. The Navy acquired the boat built by John P. Holland for $160,000 and commissioned it on October 12, 1900.

9   Morton, 35–37; *Kearsarge* II (Battleship No. 5), DANFS, NHHC.

10 Morton, 41; Mustin Questionnaire; *see* Edward J. Marolda, *The Washington Navy Yard: An Illustrated History* (Washington, D.C.: Naval Historical Foundation, 2013), 39–47.

11 Morton, 42–45; *Kansas* II (Battleship No. 21), DANFS, NHHC.

12 Morton, 45–46. See Thomas A. Hughes, *Admiral Bill Halsey: A Navy Life* (Cambridge, MA: Harvard University Press, 2016). Henry likely met Halsey's father who served as a division officer on *New York* in 1896.

13 Morton, 49–50.

14 Ibid., 50–51. See James Reckner's *Theodore Roosevelt's Great White Fleet* (Annapolis, MD: Naval Institute Press, 2001). Reckner provides an excellent overview of the cruise.

15 Morton, 56–65.

16 "Aviators Missing: Drowning Feared," *New York Times*, October 12, 1912; Morton, 66.

17 Mustin oral history.

18 Stephen K. Stein, *From Torpedoes to Aviation, Washington Irving Chambers and Technological Innovations in the New Navy, 1876–1913* (Tuscaloosa, AL: University of Alabama Press, 2002), 181; Morton, 74–76.

19 Mark L. Evans, Roy A. Grossnick, *United States Naval Aviation, 1910–2010 Volume I* (Washington, D.C.: Naval History and Heritage Command, 2015), 14; *Minnesota* II (Battleship No. 22), DANFS, NHHC; *Mississippi* II (Battleship No. 23), DANFS, NHHC.

20 M. L. Shettle, Jr., *United States Naval Air Stations of World War II, Volume I: Eastern States* (Bowersville, GA: Schaertel Publishing Co., 1995), 177.

21 R. D. Layman, *Before the Aircraft Carrier: The Development of Aviation Vessels, 1849–1922* (Annapolis, MD: Naval Institute Press, 1989), 111–12.

22 Morton, 97, 101; Evans and Grossnick, 16; *North Carolina* II (Armored Cruiser No. 12), DANFS, NHHC.

23 "Aero Shot From Ship," *Washington Post*, November 7, 1915, 19; Layman, 112; Evans and Grossnick, 21; Morton, 104–9.

24 Morton, 109, 112–13.

25 Ibid., 114–15; *North Dakota* I (Battleship No. 29), DANFS, NHHC.

26 Layman, 118; Evans and Grossnick, 55–56.

27 Morton, 118; Evans and Grossnick, 61–62.

28 Morton, 123–24; *Aroostook* II, DANFS, NHHC.

29 Mustin Questionnaire; Morton, 126–30.

30 Morton, 134.

31 "Pioneer in Naval Aeronautics Dead," *The Evening Star* (Washington), August 24, 1923, 2.

32 Morton, 141–42.

33 Murray Biography, Navy Library, NHHC; Morton, 143.

34 Morton, 143–44.
35 Ibid., 145; Mustin Questionnaire.
36 Morton, 148–49; *Arkansas* III (Battleship No. 33), DANFS, NHHC.
37 *Lucky Bag*, 1932, 110; Morton, 149.
38 Morton, 151–53.
39 Ibid., 153–54, 160–61; *Augusta* IV (CL 31) DANFS, NHHC.
40 Morton, 162–63; *Augusta* IV (CL 31), DANFS, NHHC.
41 Morton, 165–67. *Augusta* IV (CL 31), DANFS, NHHC. As a junior officer assigned to the Asiatic Fleet two decades earlier, Nimitz invited Togo to meet with his junior officers and was impressed with his approachability. Rear Adm. Sam Cox USN (Ret.) remarks at Fleet Admiral Seminar, Navy Museum, Washington Navy Yard, May 16, 2018.
42 Morton, 168–70; *Augusta* IV (CL 31), DANFS, NHHC.
43 Morton, 170–71.
44 Mustin Service Transcript, Operational Archives, NHHC; Morton, 174–75; *Lamson* III (DD 367), DANFS, NHHC.
45 Morton, 176.
46 Mustin Service Transcript; Morton, 176–77.
47 Morton, 177.
48 Ibid., 178–79.
49 Morton, 180–81.
50 Mustin oral history.
51 Ibid.
52 Morton, 184.

Chapter 3

1   David Palmer, *Organizing the Shipyards: Union Strategy in Three Northeast Ports, 1933–1945* (Ithaca: Cornell University Press, 1998), 106.
2   Ibid., 135.
3   Ibid., 108–20.
4   Ibid., 151–52.
5   Ship's data card, *Atlanta* file, Ships History Branch, NHHC.
6   C. L. Sulzberger, *World War II* (Boston: Houghton Mifflin Co., 1966), 32–38.
7   Ibid., 59–63.
8   Ibid., 64; Reynolds, 274–75.
9   Reynolds, 282–83.
10 Correspondence between Captain Bidwell and Mayor LeCraw from May 2 through to June 1941; Adm. C. W. Nimitz memorandum to Bureau of Ships, June 8, 1941, *Atlanta* pre-commissioning folder, Ships History Branch, NHHC.
11 "Shipyard Union calls 16,000 out on Defense Jobs," *New York Times* (August 7, 1941), 1, 12.
12 "Shipyard Seizure by U.S. Suggested at Kearny Strike," *New York Times* (August 8, 1941), 1.
13 Sulzberger, 66–67; "Navy Demands Ship Strike End," *New York Times* (August 9, 1941).
14 Ibid.
15 "Edison Asks U.S. Not to Seize Yard at Kearny; Will Try to End Strike," *New York Times* (August 15, 1941), 1, 15.
16 William H. Lawrence, "Stop Kearny Row, President Pleads," *New York Times* (August 20, 1941).
17 Vice Adm. Harold G. Bowen, USN (Ret.), *Ships, Machinery, and Mossbacks: The Autobiography of a Naval Engineer* (Princeton: Princeton University Press, 1954), 208–9.

18 Frank L. Kluckhorn, "U.S. Takes Over Kearny Shipyard, Open Tomorrow," *New York Times* (August 24, 1941), 1, 17.
19 "Vice Admiral Harold Gardiner Bowen" biography, Special Collections, Navy Department Library.
20 Ibid., 209.
21 Ibid., 210–11; "Bowen Daily Diary," Box 9, Federal Shipbuilding and Dry Dock papers, NARA New York.
22 "Knox Aide Seized Kearny Shipyard," *New York Times* (August 25, 1941), 1, 9.
23 Mustin oral history.
24 Indeed, the second batch of four cruisers of the class often referred to as the *Oakland*-class were built without the aft port and starboard mounts.
25 Mustin oral history.
26 Hornfischer, 17; Norman Friedman, *U.S. Cruisers: An Illustrated Design History* (Annapolis, MD: Naval Institute Press, 1984), 236.
27 Mustin oral history.
28 "Launching Report, September 6, 1941 from Building Way Number Eight of Federal Shipbuilding and Dry Dock Company," *Atlanta* Pre-commissioning folder, Ships History Branch, NHHC.
29 "Navy Launches Two Cruisers," *New York Times* (September 7, 1941), 1, 42.
30 Ibid.
31 Ed Corboy, *The Log of the Mighty A* (USS *Atlanta* Reunion Scrapbook, 1985), part 3.
32 Memorandum, Box 2, Folder USS *Atlanta* CL–51 Launching and Trials, Entry 157, RG 80 General Records of the Department of the Navy, NARA, New York.
33 Bowen, 166.
34 Flynn letter to Bowen of December 10, 1941, Box 9, Harold G. Bowen Papers, Seeley G. Mudd Manuscript Library, Princeton University, Princeton, NJ.
35 Ibid., 222.
36 Bowen, 203.
37 See NH 57450 USS *ATLANTA* (CL-51) posted at www.history.navy.mil.
38 Robert Graff oral history, conducted by author December 27, 2003, 8; *Atlanta* Deck Log entry of December 24, 1941, NARA II.
39 "Navy Commissions New Type Cruiser," *New York Times* (December 25, 1941).
40 Ibid.; Elizabeth R. P. Shaw, *Beside Me Still: A Memoir of Love and Loss in World War II* (Annapolis, MD: Naval Institute Press, 2002), 80–81; *Atlanta* Deck Log entry of December 24, 1941, NARA II.
41 Graff oral history, 8.

Chapter 4

1 Corboy, 5.
2 *Atlanta* Deck Log entries of January 2, 9, and 20, 1942, NARA II.
3 Mustin oral history.
4 Ibid.
5 Mustin oral history.
6 Hornfischer, 17.
7 *Atlanta* Deck Log entry of February 8, 1942, NARA II.
8 *Atlanta* Deck Log entry of February 10, 1942, NARA II.
9 *Atlanta* Deck Log entry of February 11, 1942, NARA II.
10 *Atlanta* Deck Log entry of February 12, 1942, NARA II.

11 *Atlanta* Deck Log entry of February 13, 1942, NARA II. Should there be a failure of the gyro compass, the ship would depend on the magnetic compass, and since the magnetic north pole does not coincide with the Earth's true North Pole, a difference in headings is expected.

12 *Atlanta* Deck Log entry of February 17, 1942, NARA II

13 *Atlanta* Deck Log entries of February 18–20, 1942, NARA II; William B. McKinney, *Join the Navy and See The World* (Los Angeles, CA: Military Literary Guild, 1990), 22.

14 *Atlanta* Deck Log entry of February 21, 1942, NARA II.

15 *Atlanta* Deck Log entries of February 22–23, 1942, NARA II.

16 Mustin oral history.

17 Ibid.

18 Mustin oral history.

19 Ibid.

20 Ibid.

21 Ibid.

22 Hornfischer, 18, 103.

23 *Atlanta* Deck Log entries of February 26–27, 1942, NARA II.

24 *Atlanta* Deck Log entries of February 28–March 1, 1942, NARA II; Graff oral history.

25 *Atlanta* Deck Log entries of March 2–3, 1942, NARA II; Morison, *Two Ocean War*, 88–101.

26 *Atlanta* Deck Log entries of March 4–6, 1942, NARA II.

27 USS *Atlanta* Alumni Assn. Survey—M. D. Payton.

28 *Atlanta* Deck Log entries of March 13–14, 1942, NARA II.

29 Diary of Seaman Striker John W. Harvey, Douglas St. Denis papers.

30 Mustin oral history.

31 Ibid.

32 Shaw, 82–83; McKinney, 23.

33 *Atlanta* Deck Log entries of March 24–26, 1942, NARA II; Graff oral history.

34 *Atlanta* Deck Log entries of March 28–30, April 1–3, 1942, NARA II.

Chapter 5

1 *Atlanta* Deck Log entry of April 3, 1942, NARA II; Corboy, 5. 1MC stands for 1 Main Circuit.

2 Corboy, 5.

3 *Atlanta* Deck Log entry of April 8, 1942, NARA II; Jenkins letter to Commander in Chief Pacific Fleet dated April 15, 1942, *Atlanta* file Naval Warfare Branch, NHHC.

4 Richard D. Hepburn, P. E. *A History of American Dry-Docks: A Key Ingredient to a Maritime Power* (Arlington, VA: Noesis, Inc. 2003), 95. The Navy subsequently built bigger graving docks.

5 *Atlanta* Deck Log entry April 12, 1942, NARA II.

6 Mustin oral history.

7 Ibid. Mustin quotes that follow are from Mustin oral history.

8 Ibid.; McKinney, 25; Graff oral history; *Atlanta* Deck Log entry of April 17, 1942, NARA II.

9 Morison, *Two Ocean War*, 139–40.

Chapter 6

1 Corboy, 6.

2 DANFS USS *California*, www.history.navy.mil. *California* lost 98 sailors during the attack.

3 Mustin oral history.

4   Ibid.

5   Murray File, Operation Archives, NHC.

6   Gordon Prange, *Miracle at Midway* (New York, NY: Penguin, 1983), 85.

7   *Atlanta* Deck Log entry of May 6, 1942, NARA II.

8   https://spartacus-educational.com/USAwheelerB.htm accessed November 16, 2023.

9   Speech found at http://staff.imsa.edu/socsci/jvictory/isolationism/wheeler_antiwar.htm accessed June 1, 2018.

10 John Rodgaard, Peter K. Hsu, Carrol Lucas, and Andrew Blache Jr., "Pearl Harbor—Attack from Below," *Naval History*, December 1999; Heber A. Holbrook, "The Sakamaki Submarine," *The Pacific Archives*, January 3, 2001; John C. Wiltshire, Ph.D., "The Search for the World War II Japanese Midget Submarine Sunk off Pearl Harbor, Dec. 7, 1941," at www.soest.hawaii.edu/HURL/midget/html.

11 Samuel E. Morison, *History of United States Naval Operations in World War II, Vol. IV Coral Sea, Midway and Submarine Actions* (Edison, NJ: Castle Books, 2001), 188–89, 202–03; "Thresher," *Dictionary of American Naval Fighting Ships* at www.history.navy.mil.

12 Morison, *Coral Sea*, 63; Prados, 308–12.

Chapter 7

1   Corboy, 6a; *Atlanta* Deck Log entry of May 10, 1942, NARA II.

2   DANFS, Vol. 6, 17.

3   David F. Winkler, "The UNREP Revolution," *Sea Power* (May 2001) 22; See also Thomas Wildenberg's *Gray Steel and Black Oil: Fast Tankers and Replenishment at Sea in the U.S. Navy, 1912–1992* (Annapolis, MD: Naval Institute Press, 1996); DANFS Vol. IV, 274–75.

4   DANFS, Vol. III, 600.

5   McKinney, 25–26.

6   *Atlanta* Deck Log entry of May 19, 1942, NARA II.

7   Morison, *Coral Sea*, 82–83; DANFS Vol. III, 189–90.

8   *Atlanta* Deck Log entries of May 19–20, 1942, NARA II.

9   David F. Winkler, "Destined for Glory," *Sea Power* (June 2001), 57; See also Thomas Wildenberg's *Destined for Glory: Dive Bombing, Midway, and the Evolution of Carrier Airpower* (Annapolis, MD: Naval Institute Press, 1998).

Chapter 8

1   Mustin oral history; *Atlanta* Deck Log entry of May 26, 1942, NARA II, recorded E. L. Graden as the recovered sailor.

2   https://www.thisdayinaviation.com/10-december-1941/ retrieved October 6, 2023.

3   Harvey Diary, St. Denis papers.

4   Prados, 318–19.

5   Prange, 86.

6   Mustin oral history.

7   Ibid.

8   Prange, 80–81.

9   Mustin oral history.

10 Prange, 83.

11 Ibid., 98–102.

12 Morison, *The Two Ocean War*, 145.

Chapter 9

1 Prange, 104–05; Ian Toll, *Pacific Crucible: War at Sea in the Pacific, 1941–1942* (New York: W. W. Norton & Company, 2012), 389–90.
2 Francis E. McCurtie and Antony Preston, *Jane's Warships of World War II* (New York, NY: Gramercy Books, 1989), 184.
3 Prange, 48, 54.
4 McCurtie and Preston, 183, 261.
5 Thomas B. Buell, *The Quiet Warrior: A Biography of Admiral Raymond A. Spruance* (Boston, MA: Little Brown and Company, 1974), 127–28.
6 Morison, *Coral Sea*, 90–91.
7 Mustin oral history; *Atlanta* Deck Log entries of May 29–31, 1942, NARA II.
8 War Diary USS *Atlanta*, NARA II.
9 Prange, 100–1, 110; Toll, 396–97.
10 Mustin oral history.
11 War Diary USS *Atlanta*, NARA II.
12 Prange, 162–64.
13 Prange, 174–76; Toll, 408.
14 Morison, *Coral Sea*, 82–83n.
15 Hornfischer, 22.

Chapter 10

1 War Diary USS *Atlanta*, NARA II.
2 Corboy, 7.
3 Prange, 179–84; Toll, 409.
4 Prange, 184, 187; Buell, 129.
5 Prange, 187–88, 198, 204; Toll, 410.
6 Prange, 190.
7 Toll, 410–11.
8 Prange, 225–30; Lt. Col. Robert D. Heinl, USMC, *The U.S. Marines at Midway* (Washington, D.C.: Historical Section, Headquarters Marine Corps, 1948), 35.
9 Mustin oral history.
10 Prange, 239.
11 Prange 239–40; Buell, 131.
12 War Diary USS *Atlanta*, NARA II.
13 Buell, 133; Toll, 420–21.
14 Prange 239, 241–42, 254; Toll, 421.
15 Prange, 242; Toll, 416.
16 Prange, 244–45, 256–57; Toll, 423–26. For a detailed overview of Torpedo 8, see Robert J. Mrazek, *Dawn Like Thunder: The True Story of Torpedo Squadron Eight* (Boston: Little Brown and Company, 2008).
17 Prange, 261–64, 270; Toll, 430–34. For recent profiles of two of the dive-bomber pilots, see N. Jack "Dusty" Kleiss with Timothy and Laura Orr, *Never Call Me a Hero* (New York: William Morrow, 2017) and David Rigby, *Wade McClusky and the Battle of Midway* (Oxford, UK: Osprey, 2019).
18 Prange, 279–80; Toll, 444–45; Corboy, 7.
19 Mustin oral history; Prange, 282.

20 Buell, 136–37.
21 Prange, 286–87; Toll, 451–53.
22 Prange, 290–91.
23 http://cv6.org/1942/midway/midway_4.htm, accessed October 4, 2023.
24 Buell, 139–40; Toll, 459.
25 Prange, 396.

Chapter 11

1 Morison, *Coral Sea*, 144–45; Toll, 464.
2 Prange, 325.
3 Ibid., 337, 344.
4 War Diary USS *Atlanta*, NARA II; *Atlanta* Deck Log entry of June 6, 1942, NARA II; Morison, Vol. IV, 148; Toll, 465.
5 Buell, 142–43.
6 Mustin oral history.
7 Morison, *Coral Sea*, 152; Prange, 357.
8 Mustin oral history; *Atlanta* Deck Log entry of June 6, 1942, NARA II.
9 Morison, *Coral Sea*, 155–56.
10 Ibid.

Chapter 12

1 Morison, *Coral Sea*, 156–57.
2 For an extensive critique of Yamamoto see Prange, 376–82.
3 Buell, 149.
4 Morison, *Coral Sea*, 158.
5 *Atlanta* Deck Log entry of June 8, 1942, NARA II.
6 War Diary USS *Atlanta*, NARA II; *Atlanta* Deck Log entry of June 9, 1942, NARA II; Mustin oral history.
7 War Diary USS *Atlanta*, NARA II.
8 Prange, 359–62.
9 Prange, 364–65; Buell, 148, 149.
10 War Diary USS *Atlanta*, NARA II; Mustin oral history.

Chapter 13

1 *Atlanta* Deck Log entry of June 13, 1942, NARA II.
2 *Atlanta* Deck Log entries of June 16–17, 1942, NARA II. No mention of when such a party was held is made in the records.
3 *Atlanta* Deck Log entry of June 25–26, 1942, NARA II.
4 Mustin oral history.
5 McKinney, 28.
6 DANFS Vol. VIII, 223–24; Homer N. Wallin, *Pearl Harbor: Why, How, Fleet Salvage and Final Appraisal* (Washington, D.C.: U.S. Navy, 1968), 125.
7 *Atlanta* Deck Log entry of July 2, 1942, NARA II.
8 *Atlanta* Deck Log entry of July 8, 1942, NARA II.

9 *Atlanta* Deck Log entry of July 10, 1942, NARA II.
10 *Atlanta* Deck Log entries of July 11–12, 1942, NARA II.
11 DANFS Vol. V, 108–09.

Chapter 14

1 Carl K. Hixon, *Guadalcanal: An American Story* (Annapolis, MD: Naval Institute Press, 1999), 7–8.
2 Richard B. Frank, *Guadalcanal: The Definitive Account of the Landmark Battle* (New York, NY: Penguin, 1992), 33–36; Prados, 356.
3 Hixon, 14–15; William H. Bartsch, "Operational Dovetail. Bungled Guadalcanal Rehearsal," *Journal of Military History* (April 2002), 446–47.
4 Frank, 48–49.
5 Prados, 355–56; Morison, *Guadalcanal*, 14; Hixon, 16–17; Bartsch, 450–51.
6 Bartsch, 451–52.
7 "Chock 'A' Block," Vol. I, Edition, 1. Ship History Files, NHHC.
8 Morison, *Guadalcanal*, 14–15.
9 Graff oral history, 22.
10 *Atlanta* Deck Log entry of July 24, 1942, NARA II.
11 *Atlanta* Deck Log entry of July 26, 1942, NARA II.
12 Frank, 54–55.
13 Bartsch, 464–68; Frank, 57.

Chapter 15

1 Mustin Diary.
2 DANFS online; www.history.navy.mil.
3 DANFS Vol. VII, 322–23. Roland W. Charles, *Troopships of World War II* (Washington, D.C.: Army Transportation Association, 1947), 239. *President Tyler* eventually joined the Army Transportation Service for conversion to a hospital ship but the conversion was halted at the end of the war. She wound up carrying war brides back to the United States from England.
4 *Atlanta* Deck Log entry of August 7, 1942, NARA II; War Diary USS *Atlanta*, NARA II.
5 Hornfischer, 40.
6 Frank, 60–61.
7 Hixon, 34–37; Hornfischer, 42.
8 Frank, 77–79.
9 Eric Hammel, *Guadalcanal: The Carrier Battles* (New York: Crown, 1987), 17–18. Hammel states 27 Bettys were in the first wave.
10 Frank, 68–69.
11 Hammel, 31–32; Frank, 69.
12 Hixon, 44.
13 DANFS, Vol. III, 505. Morison, *Guadalcanal*, 15–16. Hammel claims 18 Bettys and at least two Zeros were felled. Frank, 79–80, concurs.
14 Frank, 87.
15 Ibid., 88.
16 Ibid., 92.
17 Prados, 362; Frank, 92–93.

18 Jeffrey R. Cox, *Morning Star, Midnight Sun: The Early Guadalcanal-Solomons Campaign of World War II—August–October 1942* (New York, NY: Osprey, 2018), 81–83. *Kako*'s floatplane was shot down but *Aoba*'s report gave Mikawa an appreciation of what he was facing.
19 Frank, 93.
20 Morison, *Guadalcanal*, 28.
21 Frank, 95; Hornfischer, 58–59.
22 Frank, 98–101.
23 Hornfischer, 57.

Chapter 16

1   Frank, 54–55; Morison, *Two Ocean War*, 172.
2   Frank, 93, 119; Morison, *Two Ocean War*, 172; War Diary USS *Atlanta*.
3   See Commo. Richard W. Bates, USN (Ret), Cdr. Walter D. Innis, USN, *The Battle of Savo Island, August 9th, 1942, Strategical and Tactical Analysis* (U.S. Naval War College: Department of Analysis, 1950) (NAVPERS 91187).
4   Prados, 362.
5   Morison, *Guadalcanal*, 36; Hornfischer, 60, notes the gunnery officer of the *Blue* had sought permission to shoot at the aircraft but since it flew operating running lights, the commanding officer assumed it had to be friendly.
6   Frank, 102–03, states that *Yunagi* pulled out of the formation at the time of the attack either because she could not attain 30 knots or because she was assigned to target the American picket destroyers.
7   Morison, *Guadalcanal*, 37–38; Hornfisher, 61; Frank, 105.
8   Morison, *Guadalcanal*, 39; Hornfisher, 61; Frank, 108.
9   Morison, *Guadalcanal*, 41–43; Frank, 110–11.
10 Frank, 112–13.
11 Morison, *Guadalcanal*, 44–49; Frank, 116.
12 Morison, *Guadalcanal*, 51.
13 Morison, *Guadalcanal*, 46, 48, 54–55, 57–58.
14 Mustin oral history.
15 Morison, *Guadalcanal*, 61; Trent Hone, *Learning War: The Evolution of Fighting Doctrine in the U.S. Navy, 1898–1945* (Annapolis, MD: Naval Institute Press, 2018), 168–69. The Navy did not announce the ship losses until October 12, when it triumphed at the battle of Cape Esperance.
16 Morison, *Guadalcanal*, 61–62; Frank, 122.
17 Morison, *Guadalcanal*, 62–63; Prados, 365.
18 Prados, 363; Mustin oral history.
19 Bates and Innes, 369.
20 Frank, 119.
21 War Diary USS *Atlanta*, NARA II; *Atlanta* Deck Log entry of August 10–12, 1942, NARA II.

Chapter 17

1   Hornfischer, 88.
2   Unknown sailor's diary.
3   War Diary USS *Atlanta*, NARA II; *Atlanta* Deck Log entries of August 13–18, 1942, NARA II.
4   Frank, 126–27.

5   Morison, *Guadalcanal*, 67–68; Prados, 365.
6   Cox, 147–48.
7   Morison, *Guadalcanal*, 70–71.
8   Hornfischer, 107.
9   Morison, *Guadalcanal*, 71–73; Hornfischer, 111; Frank, 158.
10 Prados, 365. Unfortunately, a dozen Marines were left behind. Nine were reportedly captured and executed.

Chapter 18

1   Frank, 164.
2   War Diary USS *Atlanta*, NARA II; *Atlanta* Deck Log entry of August 23, 1942, NARA II; Frank, 165.
3   Morison, *Two Ocean War*, 179.
4   Frank, 176; War Diary USS *Atlanta*, NARA II.
5   Frank, 177.
6   Morison, *Two Ocean War*, 180.
7   War Diary USS *Atlanta*; Frank, 179. There is a 30-minute time difference between contemporary narratives, and *Atlanta*'s War Diary records the setting of Zone 11½ time on August 10 at 0623. Morison used 11½ time zone in his writings.
8   Frank, 180.
9   Cox, 175.
10 Frank, 182.
11 Mustin oral history; Corboy, 8a.
12 Mustin oral history; Frank, 182–83.
13 War Diary USS *Atlanta*; Corboy, 8a; Frank, 183.
14 Cox, 179.
15 Frank, 188.
16 Frank, 186; War Diary USS *Atlanta*.
17 War Diary USS *Atlanta*.
18 War Diary USS *Atlanta*.
19 Frank, 179.
20 Ibid., 189–90.
21 Ibid., 191.

Chapter 19

1   *Atlanta* Deck Log entry of August 29, 1942, NARA II.
2   War Diary USS *Atlanta*, NARA II.
3   Morison, *Two Ocean War*, 182; Hornfischer, 121; War Diary USS *Atlanta*; Mustin oral history.
4   Frank, 204; Hornfischer, 121; Mustin oral history.
5   Hornfischer, 122.
6   War Diary USS *Atlanta*, NARA II.
7   *Atlanta* Deck Log entry of September 6, 1942, NARA II.
8   Frank, 204.
9   War Diary USS *Atlanta*, NARA II.

Chapter 20

1   David F. Winkler, *Ready Then, Ready Now, Ready Always: More than a Century of Service by Citizen Sailors* (Washington, D.C.: Navy Reserve Centennial Book Committee, 2014), 87.
2   Ibid., 81.
3   Graff oral history, 10.
4   Hornfischer, 132; Frank, 216–46.
5   Frank, 247.

Chapter 21

1   Noyes Biography, Navy Department Library, NHHC.
2   Frank, 248.
3   Cox, 229, 231–32.
4   *O'Brien*, DANFS.
5   *North Carolina*, DANFS; Frank, 249.
6   *Wasp*; DANFS; Frank, 248–49.
7   Frank, 251–52.

Chapter 22

1   Frank, 252–55.
2   *Atlanta* Deck Log entries of September 21–23, 1942, NARA II.
3   Frank, 266.
4   Cox, 269.
5   Mustin oral history.
6   Ibid.
7   Paul Stillwell, *Battleship Commander: The Life of Willis A. Lee, Jr.* (Annapolis, MD: Naval Institute Press. 2021), 34–36.
8   *Atlanta* Deck Log entries of September 27–29, 1942, NARA II.
9   The battleship had ten 5-inch 38 twin mounts.
10 Mustin oral history.
11 Cox, 310.
12 Hornfischer, 151.
13 Hornfischer, 153; Cox, 311.
14 Hornfischer, 154–55; Frank, 276–77.
15 Frank, 279–82.
16 *Atlanta* Deck Log entries of October 3, 9, 1942, NARA II.
17 War Diary USS *Atlanta*, NARA II.
18 Mustin oral history.
19 Ibid.

Chapter 23

1   Watches typically are four hours in length. However, to enable watchstanders to enjoy the evening meal, the 1600–2000 (4–8 PM) watch is "dogged" into a pair of two-hour watches. By standing the first dog, Mustin was on the bridge between 1600 and 1800.

2   War Diary USS *Atlanta*, NARA II; *Atlanta* Deck Log entries of October 9, 10, 1942, NARA II; Hornfischer, 157.

3   Frank, 295.

4   Ibid.; Cox, 269.

5   Cox, 277.

6   Frank, 299.

7   Hornfischer, 169–72; Frank, 300–1.

8   Frank, 295. *San Francisco* and *Salt Lake City* were equipped with less capable SC models, and *Helena* and *Boise* featured SG models.

9   Frank, 301.

10   Mustin oral history.

11   Phillip T. Parkerson, *One Ship Fleet: USS* Boise *WWII Naval Legend 1938–45* (Havertown, PA: Casemate Publishers, 2023), 15–21; Frank, 305–6; Hone, 189.

12   Cox, 288–89.

13   Frank, 307.

14   Frank, 308. Two American minesweepers would rescue another 108 Japanese survivors on the following day.

15   Frank, 309.

16   Mustin oral history. For a masterful discussion defining Navy doctrine in the pre-war period, see Hone, 13.

Chapter 24

1   War Diary USS *Atlanta*, NARA II.

2   Cox, 291.

3   Hornfischer, 197.

4   Frank, 316.

5   Hornfischer, 193–95; Cox, 294–96.

6   Hornfischer, 195–96; Cox, 297.

7   War Diary USS *Atlanta*, NARA II.

8   Frank, 322.

9   Cox, 302–3.

10   Frank 324–25; Cox 303. *Meredith* was able to shoot down three of her attackers. The *Alchiba*, *Bellatrix, Jamestown*, and *Nicholas* also came under attack but evaded hits.

11   War Diary USS *Atlanta*, NARA II.

12   Mustin oral history.

13   Frank, 326.

14   Frank, 327; Cox, 306.

15   War Diary USS *Atlanta*, NARA II; *Atlanta* Deck Log entry of October 18, 1942, NARA II.

Chapter 25

1   160937 October 42 CINCPAC to COMINCH and 160245 October 42 COMINCH to CINCPAC located in Nimitz Gray Book Vol. II, NHHC.

2   Frank, 351.

3   Hornfischer, 219.

4   Cox, 321–24.

5 Frank, 365.
6 *Atlanta* Deck Log entry of October 19, 1942, NARA II.
7 War Diary, USS *Atlanta*, NARA II.
8 Cox, 314; *San Francisco*, DANFS
9 War Diary USS *Atlanta*, NARA II.
10 *Atlanta* Deck Log entry of October 24, 1942, NARA II.

Chapter 26

1 War Diary USS *Atlanta*; NARA II.
2 Ibid.
3 Mustin oral history; *Atlanta* Deck Log entry of October 27, 1942, NARA II.
4 Morison, *Two Ocean War*, 193–94.
5 Frank, 374–75.
6 Hornfischer, 223–24.
7 Cox, 335.
8 Prados, 385.
9 Frank, 382–83.
10 Frank, 383; Cox, 338–39.
11 Cox, 341.
12 Frank, 385.
13 Frank, 386; Cox, 348–49.
14 Cox, 349.
15 Hornfischer, 229–30.
16 Frank, 391–92; Morison, *Two Ocean War*, 196.
17 Frank, 392–94.
18 Cox, 382.
19 Frank, 396; Hornfischer, 232.
20 Frank, 397.
21 Frank, 399; Cox, 388–89.
22 Mustin oral history.

Chapter 28

1 War Diary USS *Atlanta*, NARA II; *Atlanta* Deck Log entry of October 28, 1942, NARA II. Mustin likely got to meet Scott during Mustin's 1200–1600 watch on the bridge.
2 Hornfischer, 238; *San Francisco* DANFS; Callaghan biography, Navy Dept. Library.
3 Mustin oral history.
4 Ibid.
5 Ibid.
6 War Diary USS *Atlanta*, NARA II; *Atlanta* Deck Log entry of October 30, 1942, NARA II; Colonel Charles H. Nees, USMC, Biography courtesy Marine Corps History Division, Quantico, VA; Mustin oral history.
7 Mustin oral history.
8 Ibid.; Hornfischer, 243.
9 Mustin oral history.

10 War Diary USS *Atlanta*, NARA II; *Atlanta* Deck Log entry of October 31, 1942, NARA II.
11 Hornfischer, 244.
12 Cox, 393–95.
13 Hornfischer, 244–45.
14 Ibid., 245–46.
15 Jameson, *The Battle of Guadalcanal*, 4–5; Frank, 431.
16 Mustin oral history.
17 Jameson, 9–10; Mustin oral history; Graff oral history, 24.
18 Mustin oral history; Graff oral history, 24.
19 Jameson, 8–9.
20 Mustin oral history.
21 Jameson, 12; Mustin oral history.
22 Hornfischer, 251.
23 Mustin oral history; Hornfisher, 252; Frank, 431.
24 Mustin oral history.
25 Frank, 431; Mustin oral history.

Chapter 29

1 Mustin oral history.
2 Jameson, 16; Mustin oral history.
3 Hornfischer, 260.
4 Mustin oral history.
5 Ibid.
6 Frank, 437.
7 Mustin oral history.
8 Mustin oral history.
9 Hornfischer, 269; Frank, 438.
10 Mustin oral history
11 Ibid.
12 Hornfischer, 269; Mustin oral history.
13 Mustin oral history.
14 Mustin oral history; Clifford Dunaway, Sr., oral history, *Atlanta* History Center Veterans History Project Oral History, YouTube, posted January 27, 2016.
15 Mustin oral history.
16 Hornfischer, 273.
17 Mustin oral history.
18 Ibid., 275–76.
19 Mustin oral history.
20 Ibid.
21 McKinney, 47; USS *Atlanta* Alumni Survey—Wayne Langton; USS *Atlanta* Alumni Survey—Kenyth Brown.
22 Mustin oral history.
23 Mustin oral history.
24 Ibid.
25 Ibid.
26 Mustin oral history.

27 Ibid.
28 Mustin oral history.
29 Ibid.; McKinney, 45.

Chapter 29

30 Mustin oral history.
1 Mustin oral history; Harvey Diary, St. Denis papers, 18.
2 Mustin oral history.
3 Mustin oral history.
4 McKinney, 51.
5 Mustin oral history; Morison, 255–56.
6 Hornfischer, 332; Mustin oral history; Harvey memoir, 19.
7 McKinney, 52.
8 Harvey diary, St. Denis papers, 20.

Chapter 30

1 Mustin oral history.
2 Ibid.
3 Hornfischer, 337–38; Frank, 464.
4 Mustin oral history; Harvey memoir, 20.
5 Frank, 464–65.
6 Ibid., 465–66.
7 Ibid., 468–69.
8 Mustin oral history.
9 Mustin oral history.
10 Ibid.; Frank, 472.
11 Frank, 475.
12 Ibid., 476–77.
13 Ibid., 484–85. *Gwin* recovered *Benham*'s crew and scuttled her with gunfire the following evening.
14 Mustin oral history.
15 Frank, 479–80.
16 Frank, 481.
17 Mustin oral history.
18 Frank, 483.
19 Mustin oral history.
20 McKinney, 57; Frank, 487–88; Mustin oral history.
21 Mustin oral history.
22 Frank, 488. In addition to the soldiers, some 1,500 bags of rice (a four-day supply) and 260 boxes of shells were landed.
23 Shaw, 111.
24 Harvey memoir; Mustin oral history; McKinney, 59.
25 Mustin oral history; Prados, 377–78. In his oral history, Mustin identifies the language officer as Arthur "Mac" McCollum. McCollum, a graduate of the Class of 1923, was assigned to General MacArthur's staff at the time. McCallum, from the Class of 1924, was assigned to Guadalcanal in late 1942.

26 Mustin oral history.
27 Mustin oral history.
28 Frank, 508–9; Mustin oral history.
29 Mustin oral history.
30 Ibid.
31 Mustin letter to mother and stepfather dated February 12, 1943.
32 Morton, 202–3.
33 Morton, 207–16; Mustin Files, Operational Archives, NHHC.
34 Morton, 229–36.
35 Ibid., 245–50; Mustin Files, Operational Archives, NHHC.
36 Mustin Files, Operational Archives, NHHC; Morton, 291.
37 Morton, 291–93.

Bibliography

Archives

Naval History and Heritage Command, Washington, D.C. (NHHC)
Ship History Files
Officer Biography Files

National Archives, New York (NARA NY)
RG 80 General Records of the Department of the Navy

National Archives, College Park (NARA II)
USS *Atlanta* Deck Logs
USS *Atlanta* War Diaries

Seeley G. Mudd Manuscript Library, Princeton University, Princeton, NJ
Harold G. Bowen Papers

Douglas St. Denis papers
Diary of Seaman Striker John W. Harvey
H. Charles Dahn, "The Death of the Mighty A," paper written December 28, 1958
USS *Atlanta* Reunion Survey

Books

Bates, Commo. Richard W. USN (Ret), Cdr. Walter D. Innis, USN, *The Battle of Savo Island, August 9th, 1942, Strategical and Tactical Analysis*. U.S. Naval War College, Department of Analysis (NAVPERS 91187), 1950.

Bowen, Harold G. *Ships, Machinery, and Mossbacks: The Autobiography of a Naval Engineer*. Princeton: Princeton University Press, 1954.

Buell, Thomas B. *The Quiet Warrior: A Biography of Admiral Raymond A. Spruance*. Boston, MA: Little Brown and Company, 1974.

Cagle, Malcolm W. and Frank A. Manson, *The Sea War in Korea*. Annapolis, MD: Naval Institute Press, 1957.

Calhoun, C. Raymond, *Tin Can Sailor: Life Aboard the USS* Sterett, *1939–1945*. Annapolis, MD: Naval Institute Press, 1993.

Charles, Roland W. *Troopships of World War II*. Washington, D.C.: Army Transportation Association, 1947.

Corboy, Ed. *The Log of the Mighty A*, USS *Atlanta* Reunion Scrapbook, 1985.

Cox, Jeffrey R. *Blazing Star, Setting Sun: The Guadalcanal–Solomons Campaign, November 1942–March 1943*. New York, NY: Osprey, 2020.

Evans, Mark L. and Grossnick, Roy A. *United States Naval Aviation, 1910–2010, Volume I*. Washington D.C.: Naval History and Heritage Command, 2015.

Frank, Richard B. *Guadalcanal: The Definitive Account of the Landmark Battle*. New York, NY: Penguin Books, 1991.

Friedman, Norman. *U.S. Cruisers: An Illustrated Design History*. Annapolis, MD: Naval Institute Press, 1984.

Hammel, Eric. *Guadalcanal: The Carrier Battles*. New York, NY: Crown, 1987.

Heinl Lt. Col. USMC, Robert D. *The U.S. Marines at Midway*. Washington, D.C.: Historical Section, Headquarters Marine Corps, 1948.

Hepburn, Richard D. *A History of American Dry-Docks: A Key Ingredient to a Maritime Power*. Arlington, VA: Noesis, Inc., 2003.

Hixon, Carl K. *Guadalcanal: An American Story*. Annapolis, MD: Naval Institute Press, 1999.

Hone, Trent. *Learning War: The Evolution of Fighting Doctrine in the U.S. Navy, 1898–1945*. Annapolis, MD: Naval Institute Press, 2018.

Hornfischer, James D. *Neptune's Inferno: The U.S. Navy at Guadalcanal*. New York, NY: Bantam Books, 2011.

Hughes, Thomas A., *Admiral Bill Halsey: A Navy Life*. Cambridge, MA: Harvard University Press, 2016.

Jameson, Colin G. *The Battle of Guadalcanal, 11–15 November 1942*. Washington, D.C.: Office of Naval Intelligence, 1944.

Jones, Jr., Wilbur D. and Carroll Robbins Jones. *Hawaii Goes to War: The Aftermath of Pearl Harbor*. Shippensburg, PA: White Mane Press, 2001.

Kleiss, N. Jack "Dusty" with Timothy and Laura Orr. *Never Call Me a Hero*. New York: William Morrow, 2017.

Layman. R. D. *Before the Aircraft Carrier: The Development of Aviation Vessels, 1849–1922*. Annapolis, MD: Naval Institute Press, 1989.

Leckie, Robert. *Delivered From Evil: The Saga of World War II*. New York: Harper and Row, 1987.

Marolda, Edward J. *The Washington Navy Yard: An Illustrated History*. Washington, D.C.: Naval Historical Foundation, 2013.

McCurtie Francis E. and Preston. *Jane's Warships of World War II*. New York, NY: Gramercy Books, 1989.

McKinney, William B. *Join the Navy and See the World*. Los Angeles, CA: Military Literary Guild, 1990.

Morison, Samuel Elliot. *History of the United States Naval Operations in World War II: Coral Sea, Midway and Submarine Actions, May 1942–August 1942 (Volume IV)*. Boston, MA: Little, Brown, and Co., 1949.

_____*History of United States Naval Operations in World War II: The Struggle for Guadalcanal (Volume V)*. Boston, MA: Little, Brown and Co., 1949.

_____*Two Ocean War: A Short History of the United States Navy in the Second War*. Boston, MA: Little, Brown, and Co., 1963.

Morton, John Fass. *Mustin: A Naval Family of the 20th Century*. Annapolis, MD: Naval Institute Press, 2003.

Mrazek, Robert J. *Dawn Like Thunder: The True Story of Torpedo Squadron Eight*. Boston, MA: Little, Brown, and Co., 2008.

Palmer, David. *Organizing the Shipyards: Union Strategy in Three Northeast Ports, 1933–1945*. Ithaca: Cornell University Press, 1998.

Parkerson, Phillip T. *One Ship Fleet: USS* Boise *WWII Naval Legend 1938–45*. Havertown, PA: Casemate Publishers, 2023.

Prados, John. *Combined Fleet Decoded: The Secret History of American Intelligence and the Japanese Navy in World War II*. Annapolis, MD: Naval Institute Press, 1995.

Prange, Gordon. *Miracle at Midway*. New York, NY: Penguin, 1983.

Reckner, James. *Theodore Roosevelt's Great White Fleet*. Annapolis, MD: Naval Institute Press, 2001.

Rigby David. *Wade McClusky and the Battle of Midway*. Oxford, UK: Osprey, 2019.

Scharf, J. Thomas. *History of the Confederate States Navy*. New York: Gramercy Books, 1996.

Shaw, Elizabeth R. P. *Beside Me Still: A Memoir of Love and Loss in World War II*. Annapolis, MD: Naval Institute Press, 2002.

Shettle, Jr., M. L. *United States Naval Air Stations of World War II, Volume I: Eastern States*. Bowersville, GA: Schaertel Publishing Co., 1995.

Stein, Stephen K. *From Torpedoes to Aviation, Washington Irving Chambers and Technological Innovations in the New Navy, 1876–1913*. Tuscaloosa, AL: University of Alabama Press, 2002.

Stillwell, Paul. *Battleship Commander: The Life of Vice Admiral Willis A. Lee Jr.* Annapolis, MD: Naval Institute Press, 2022.

Sulzberger, C. L. *World War II*. Boston: Houghton Mifflin Co., 1966.

Toll, Ian. *Pacific Crucible: War at Sea in the Pacific, 1941–1942*. New York: W.W. Norton & Company, 2012.

Wallin, Homer N. *Pearl Harbor: Why, How, Fleet Salvage and Final Appraisal*. Washington, D.C.: U.S. Navy, 1968.

Weir, Gary E. *Building American Submarines, 1914–1940*. Washington, D.C.: Naval Historical Center, 1991.

Wildenberg, Thomas. *Destined for Glory: Dive Bombing, Midway, and the Evolution of Carrier Airpower*. Annapolis, MD: Naval Institute Press, 1998.

Winkler, David F. *Ready Then, Ready Now, Ready Always: More Than a Century of Service by Citizen Sailors*. Washington, D.C.: Navy Reserve Centennial Committee, 2014.

Wright, Captain Richard L. *To Provide and Maintain a Navy, 1775–1945*. Arlington, VA: Strategic Insight, 2018.

Younger, Stephen M. *Silver State Dreadnought: The Remarkable Story of Battleship Nevada*. Annapolis, MD: Naval Institute Press, 2018.

Combat Narrative

Solomon Islands Campaign: VI: *Battle of Guadalcanal, 11–15 November 1942*. Office of Naval Intelligence—United States Navy: Publications Branch, 1944.

Dissertation

Reynolds, Charles V. Jr. *America and a Two Ocean Navy, 1933–1941* (Ph.D. diss.). Boston, MA: Boston College, 1978.

Oral Histories and Memoirs

Boutoures, Timothy. *You're in the Navy Now*, unpublished memoir. Navy Dept. Library.

Dunaway, Clifford, Sr. Oral History. *Atlanta* History Center Veterans History Project Oral History, 2016.

Graff, Robert D. Interview by author dated December 27, 2003.

Mead, Harry R. *Memoirs of a Pearl Harbor Survivor*. Washington, D.C.: Naval Historical Foundation, 2004.

Mustin, Lloyd M. Interview by John Mason, U.S. Naval Institute Oral History Program, 2003.

Reed, Franklyn LeRoy. Interview by Michael Willie of December 20, 2004, Library of Congress Veterans History Project.

Styles, Ralph. Interview by Earl Fowler, Naval Historical Foundation Oral History Program, 2001.

Diary

Diary of Lloyd Mustin.

Articles

Bartsch, William H. "Operation Dovetail. Bungled Guadalcanal Rehearsal," *Journal of Military History*, April 2002.

Holbrook, Hebert A. "The Sakamaki Submarine," *The Pacific Archives*, January 3, 2001.

Peterson, Maw C. "Naval Courts Martial," *Indiana Law Journal*, Vol. 20, Issue 2 (Winter 1945).

Rodgaard, John, Peter K. Hsu, Carrol Lucas, and Andrew Blache Jr. "Pearl Harbor—Attack from Below," *Naval History*, December 1999.

Wiltshire, John C., Ph.D. "The Search for the World War II Japanese Midget Submarine Sunk off Pearl Harbor, Dec. 7, 1941," at www.soest.hawaii.edu/HURL/midget/html.

Winkler, David F. "Destined for Glory," *Sea Power*, June 2001.

"The UNREP Revolution," *Sea Power*, May 2001.

Index